MW01623567

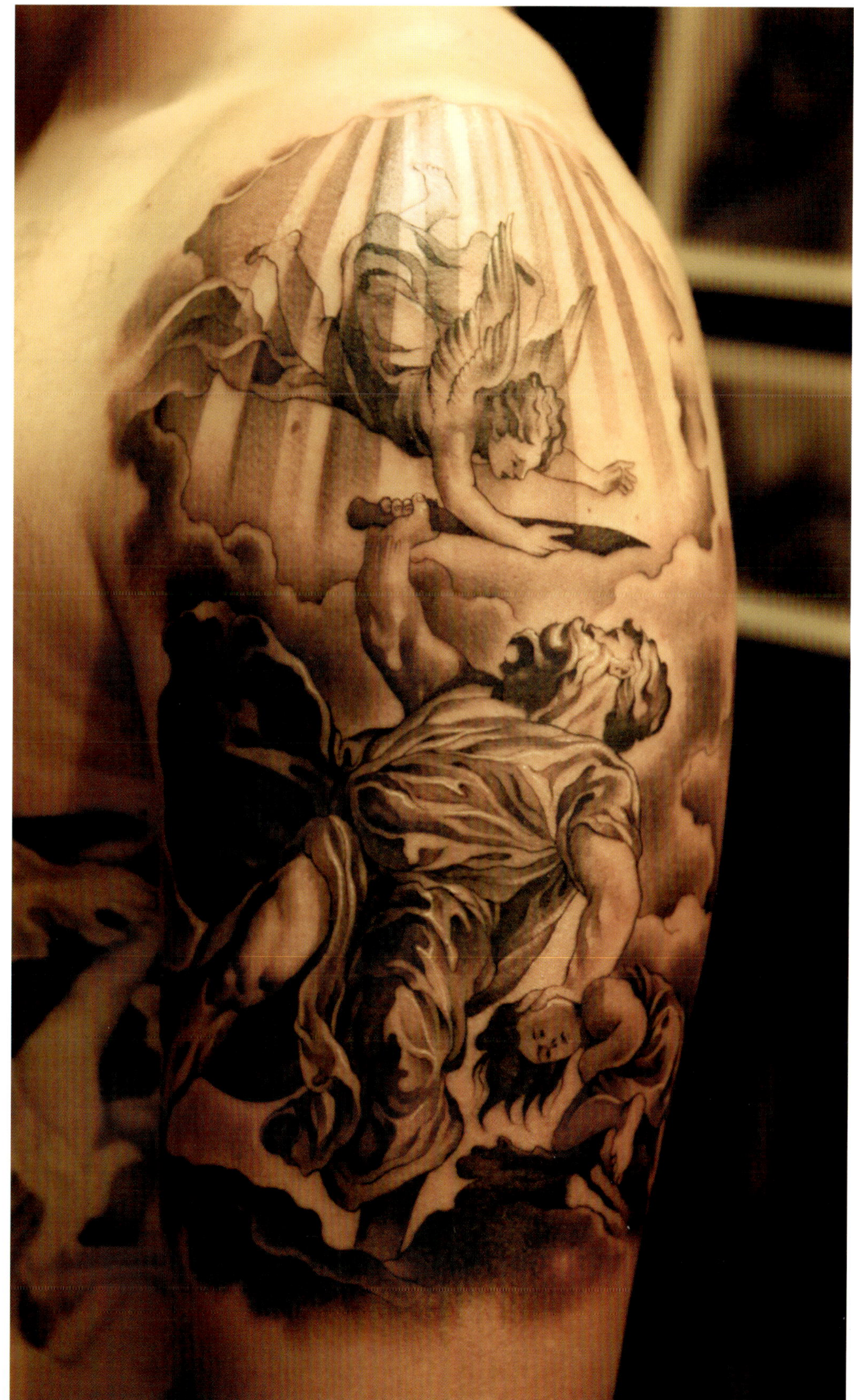

First Published in the United States of America in 2011
First edition

Gingko Press, Inc.
1321 Fifth Street
Berkeley, CA 94710, USA
Phone (510) 898-1195
Fax (510) 898-1196
email: books@gingkopress.com
www.gingkopress.com

ISBN: 978-1-58423-422-7

Printed in China

Edited by: Saelee Oh
Writer: Evan Pricco
Special Thanks: Ellen Christensen, M. Revelli, Gwynn Vitello

Previous Page Image by: Jun Cha
Opposite Page Image by: Clae Welch

Cover Image by: Jun Cha

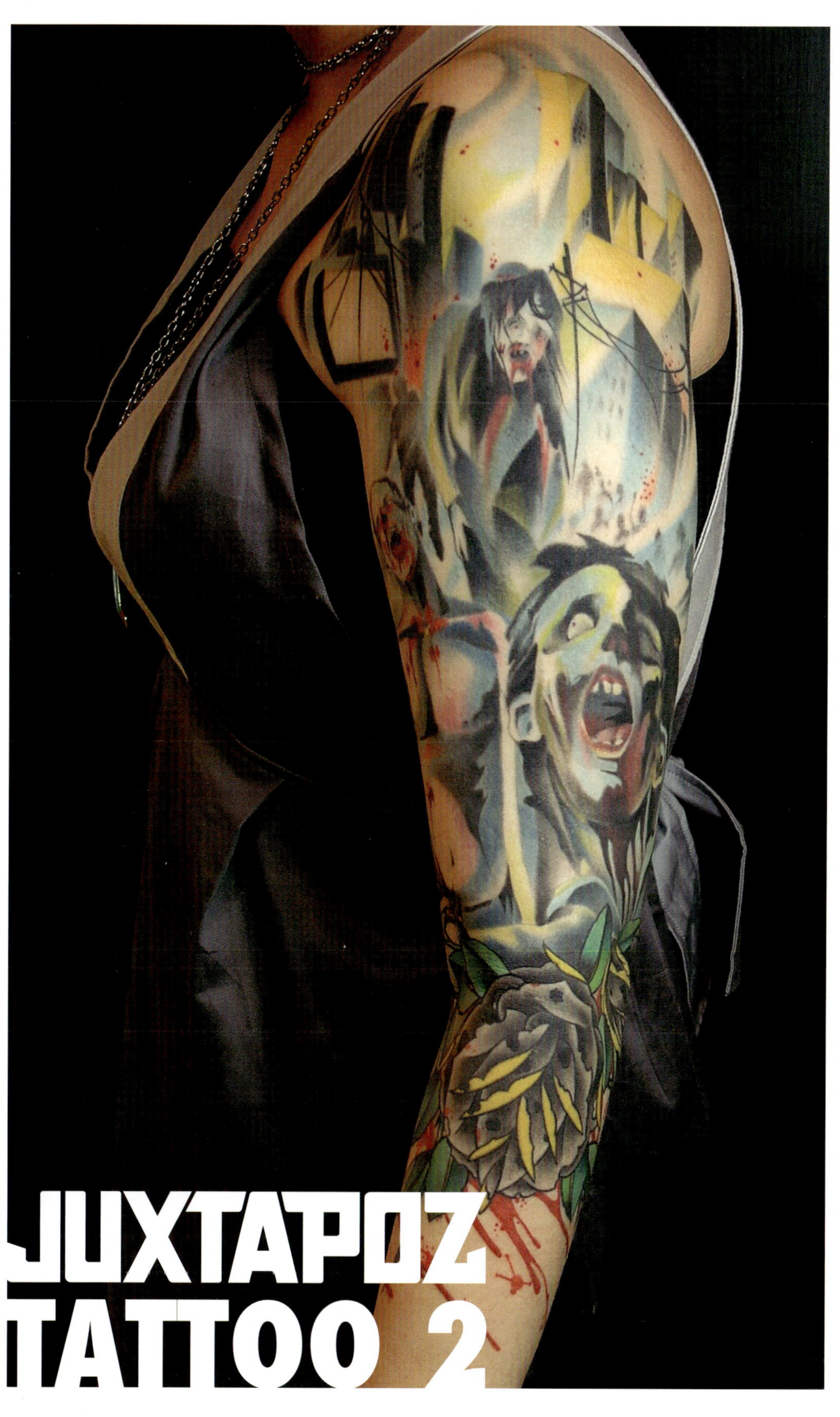

JUXTAPOZ TATTOO 2

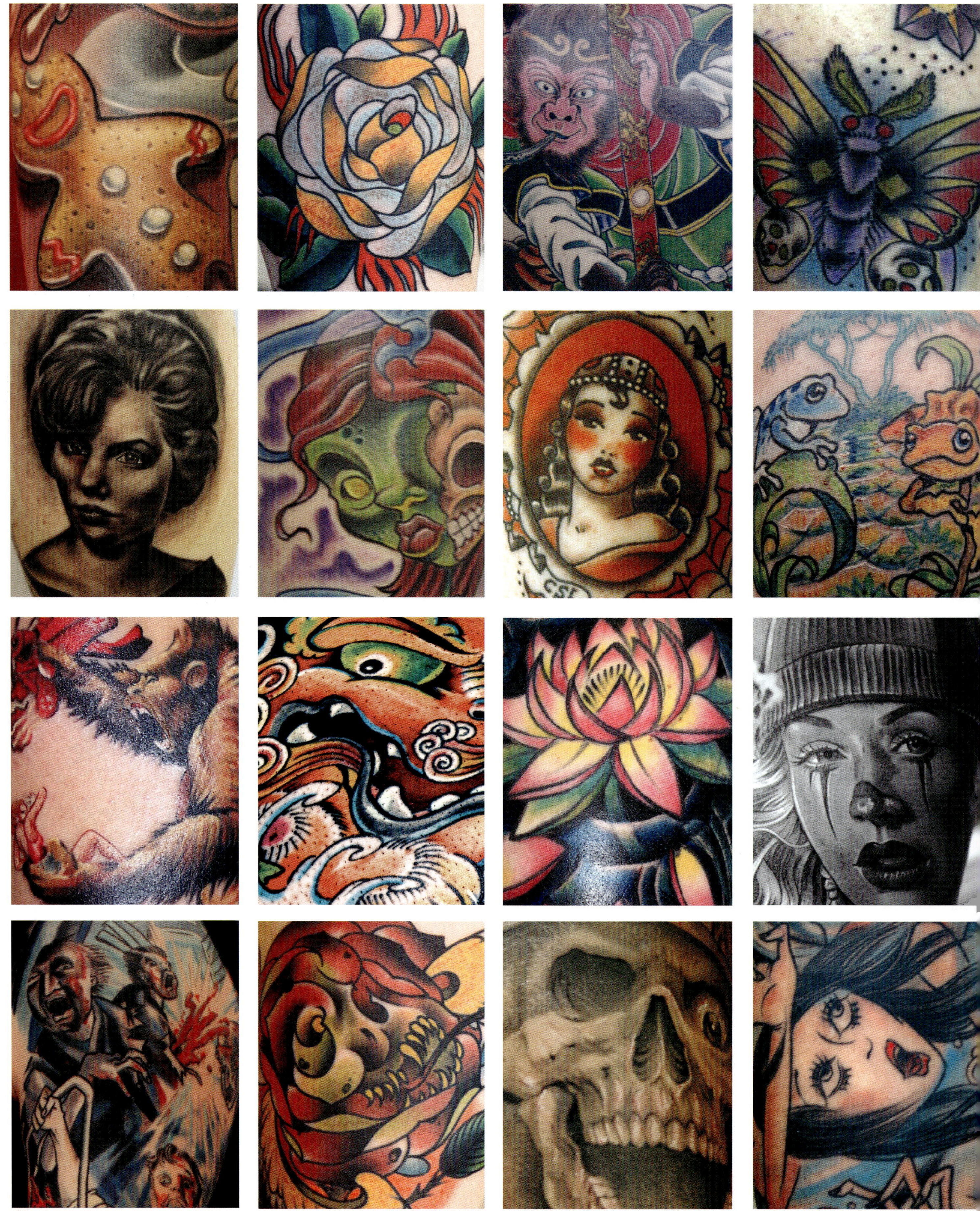
CSL

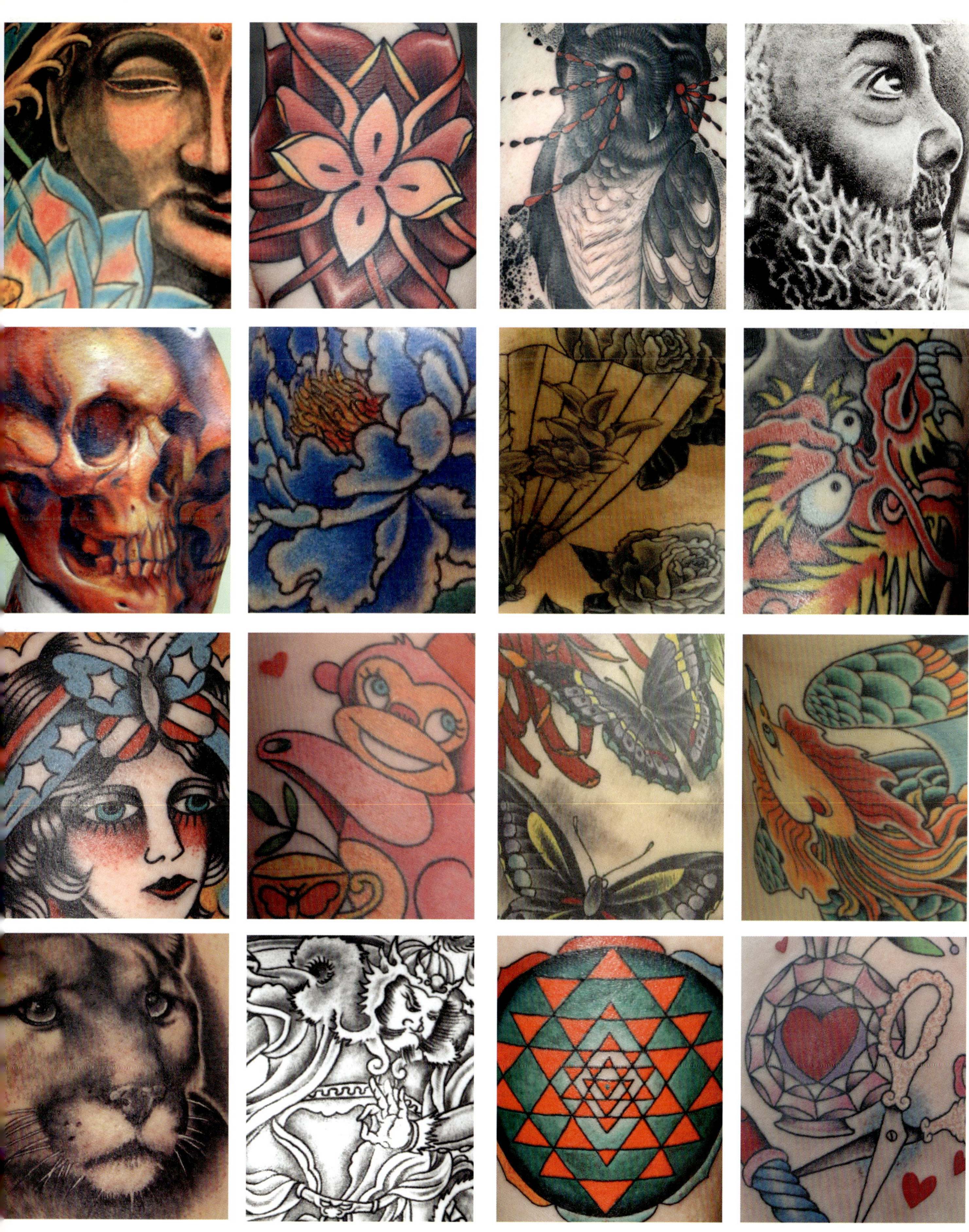

CONTENTS

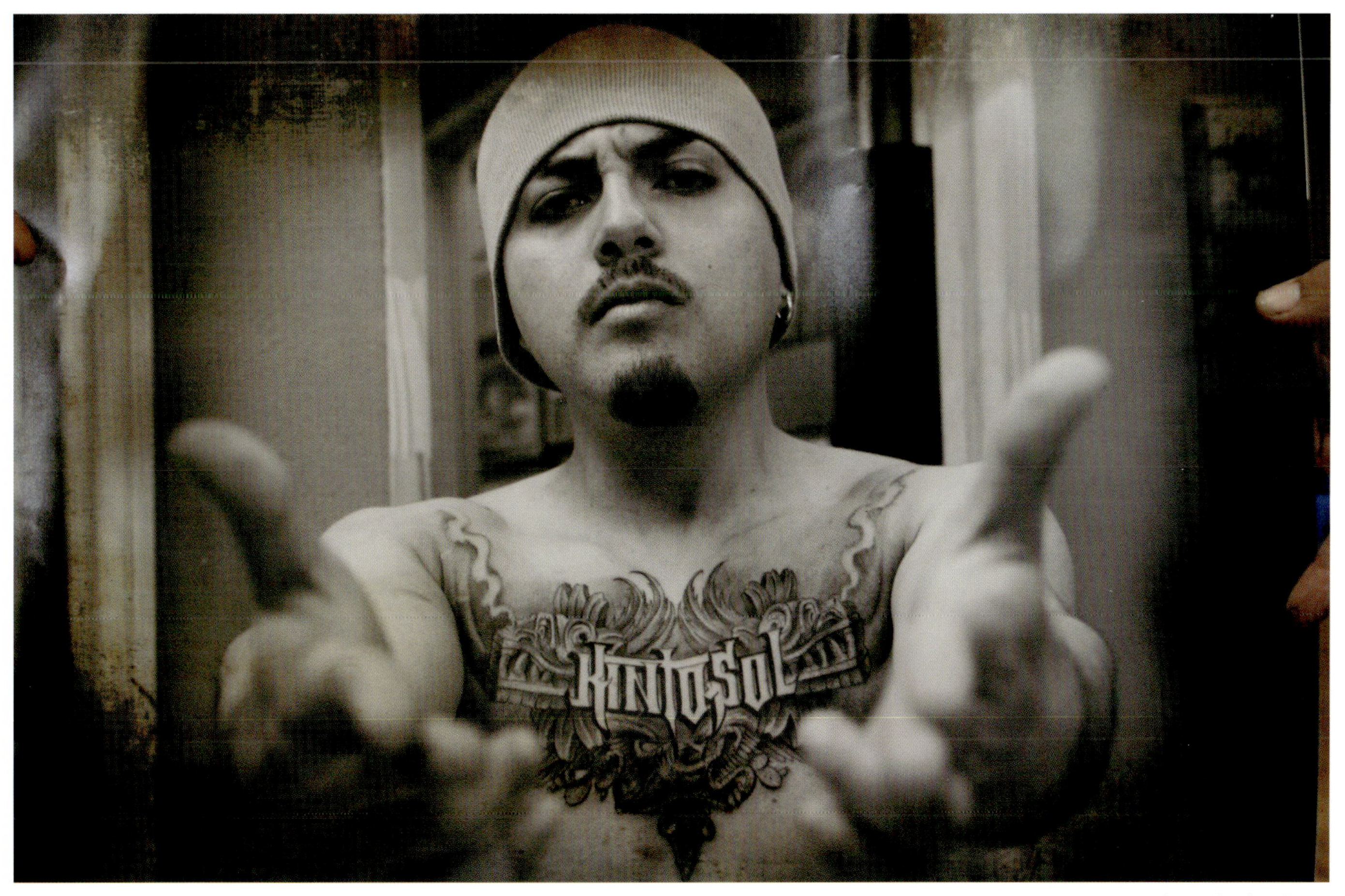

Image by: Jose Lopez

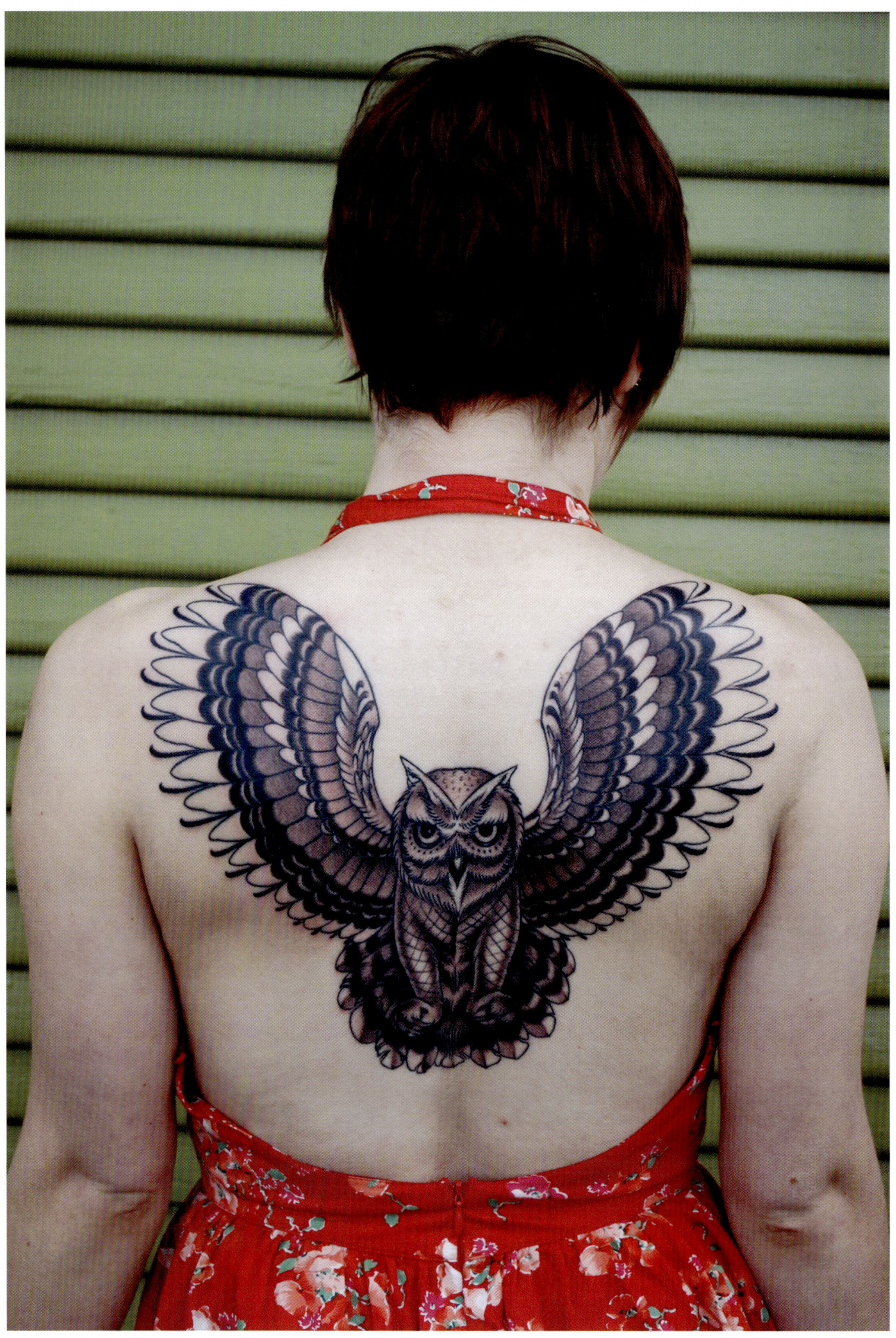

INTRODUCTION

Juxtapoz Art & Culture Magazine

When we introduced our book series over four years ago, two genres were deemed absolutely rooted in our readership and growth as a magazine and brand: tattoo art and illustration. For tattoo especially, we paid homage to the core legends of tattoo like Don Ed Hardy, Baby Ray, and Jack Rudy, and how they paved the way for a new group of influencers like Mister Cartoon, Scott Campbell, Grime, and Dr. Lakra to become the torch bearers of contemporary tattoo. And for us, the success of *Juxtapoz Tattoo* was reaffirmation that the art of tattoo will always be at the heart of the *Juxtapoz* story that is now nearly two decades in the making.

Now, in 2011, the number of people frequenting tattoo shops is greater than ever. Tattoo artists are endorsed by celebrities, as well as being celebrities themselves. Reality television series, magazine articles, art exhibits, and dedicated blogs have all contributed to the exploding international appeal of the tattoo world. And as that growth has been focused on the conceptual idea of tattoo and not solely the art, a new crop of artists has returned to the nature of tattooing as an art form and meticulous practice. More and more tattoo artists, from San Francisco to New York City, Los Angeles to Mexico City, Atlanta to Tokyo, have followed the lead of the original pioneers and become artisans in their craft. The art of tattoo is a boundless territory.

In *Juxtapoz Tattoo 2*, we spotlight some of the leading international talent working in contemporary tattoo art. Some are household names, some are longtime practitioners, and some represent the new energy that will take tattoo into the next decade. Artists such as Jose Lopez, Jun Cha, Paulie Tattoo, Mark Bode, and Sunny Buick dwell alongside Eva Huber, Liz Gruesome, Colin Stevens and Clae Welch here. Some of these artists have graced the pages of *Juxtapoz* magazine in the past, and some are new additions to the Jux family.

Documenting the dynamism of tattoo art can be problematic when one attempts to show a finished piece after the client has left the studio. But this collection captures in-depth bodies of work from each tattoo artist - some seen by readers here for the very first time.

What we have learned the second time around with Tattoo is that each year, and under the tutelage of the greats in the community, a new generation is spurred to set the standard for contemporary tattoo art, and *Juxtapoz* is proud to document that exhilaration once again.

Image by: Clae Welch

Shawn Barber

I've been a tattooed person for over 20 years and have always had an interest in the medium. When I was a teenager, I was drawing flash and designs for the local tattoo shop in trade for tattoos of superheroes and tribal lizards. At the time, the direction of becoming a tattooist was not in my immediate future. Not until after years of random jobs, going back to college, teaching art at the university level, and being a working illustrator and fine artist did I make the decision to dedicate my life to the history and craft of tattooing. I feel so fortunate to be on this path of sharing art with humanity.

To permanently mark the flesh of other individuals is a tremendous responsibility. Tattooing is not a hobbyist's game. It deserves and demands all of your energy and complete attention in the process. It's the most humbling art form known to man.

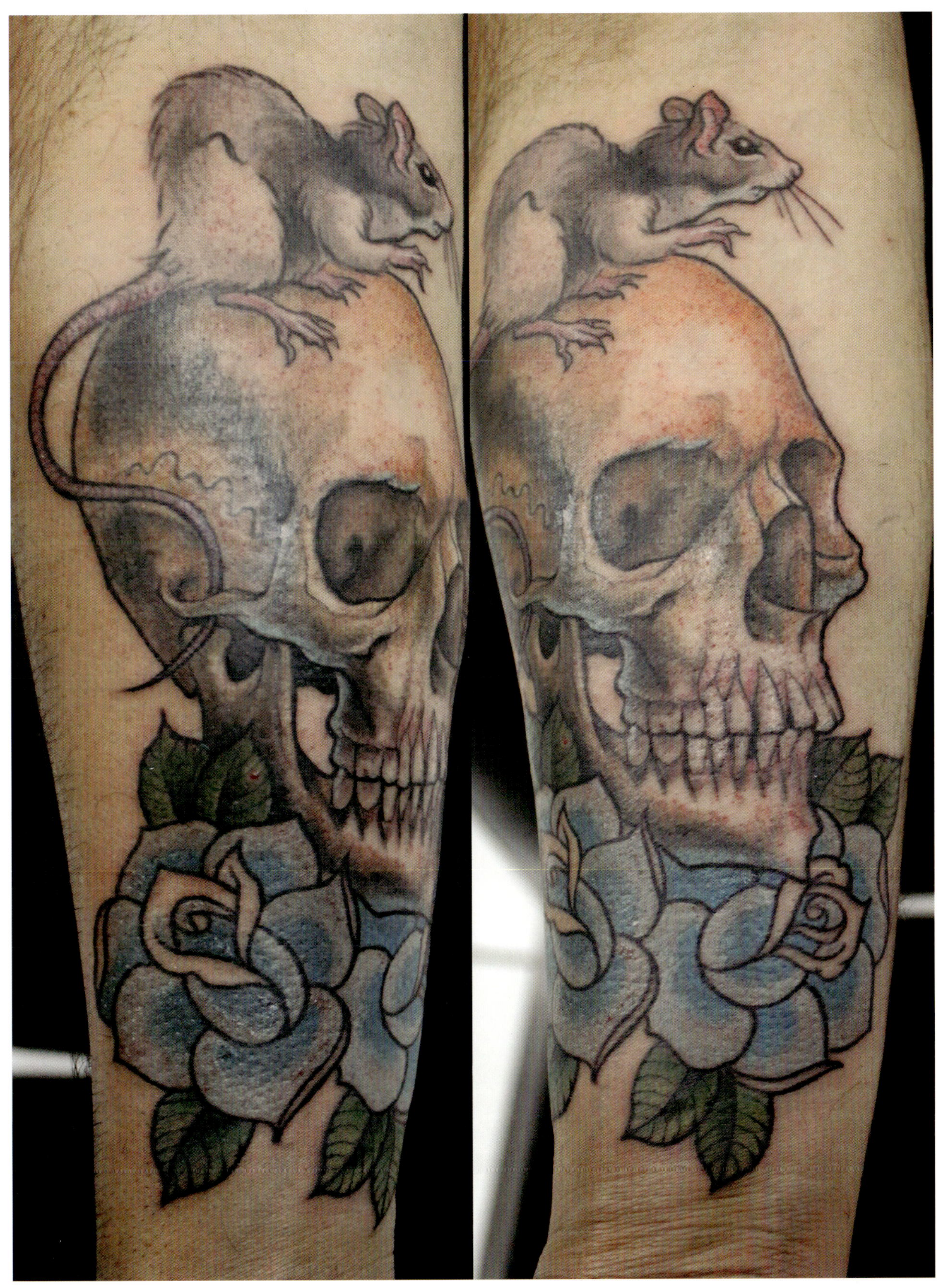

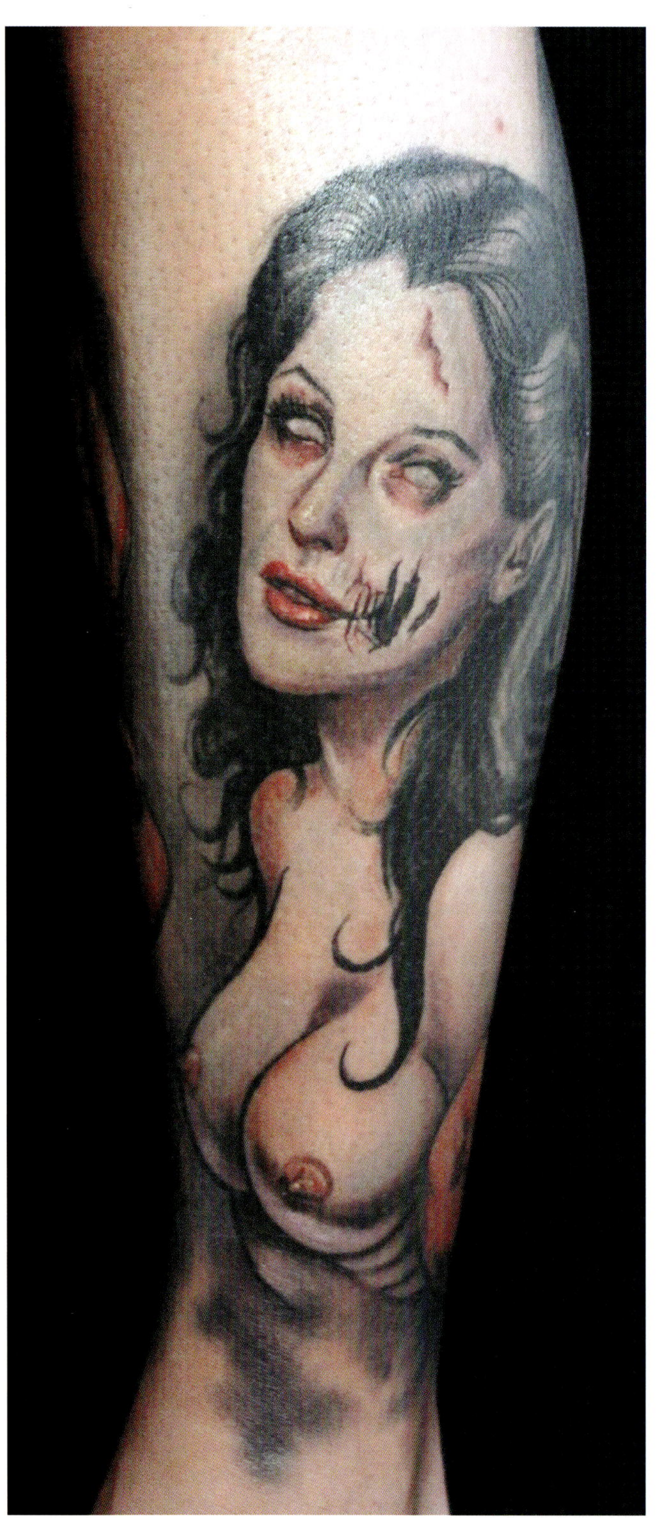

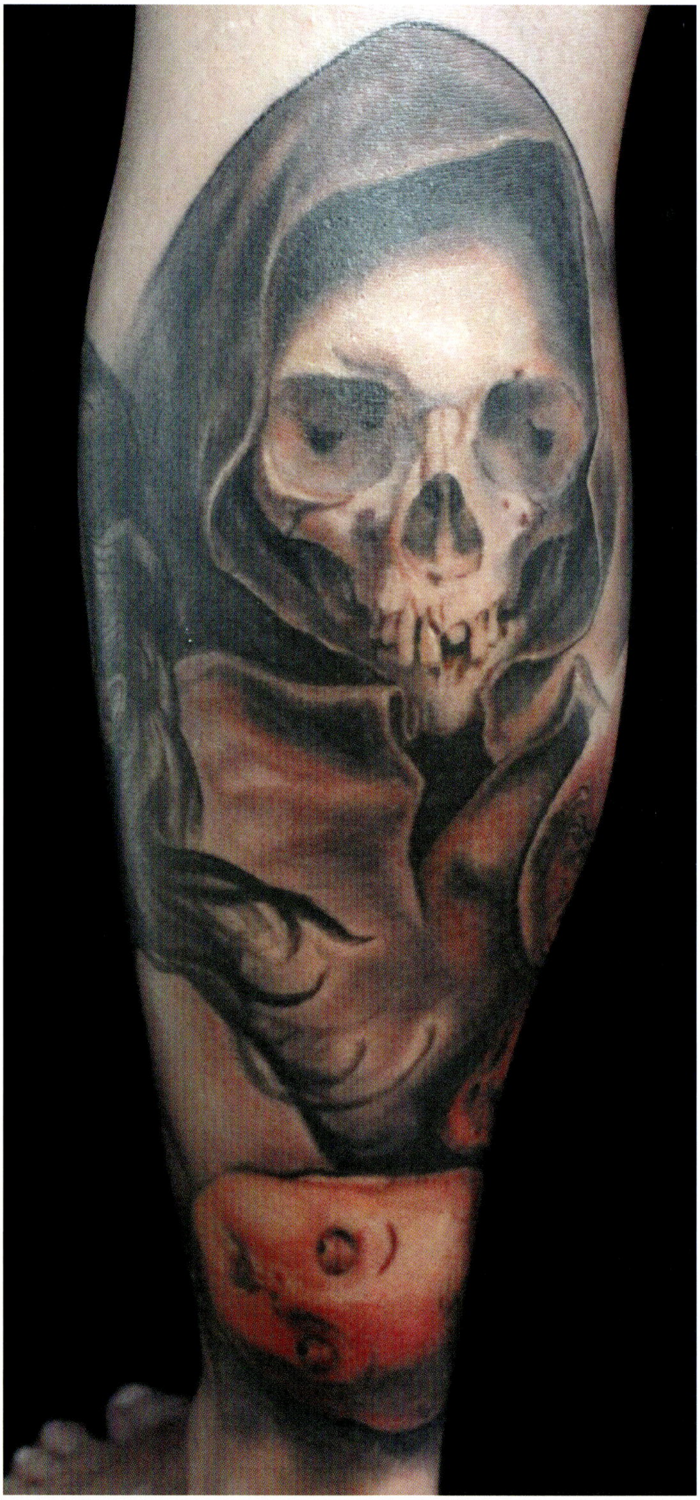

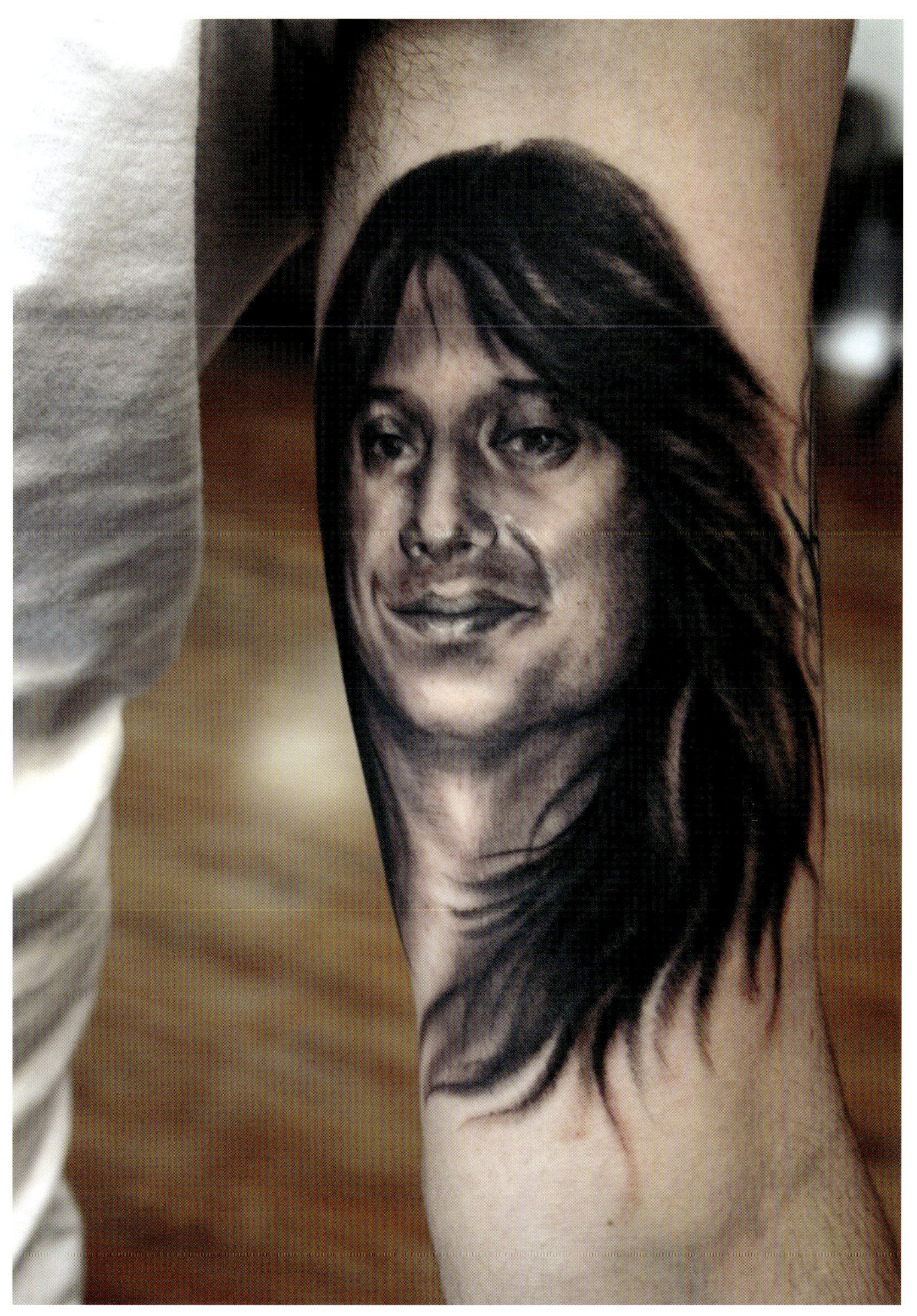

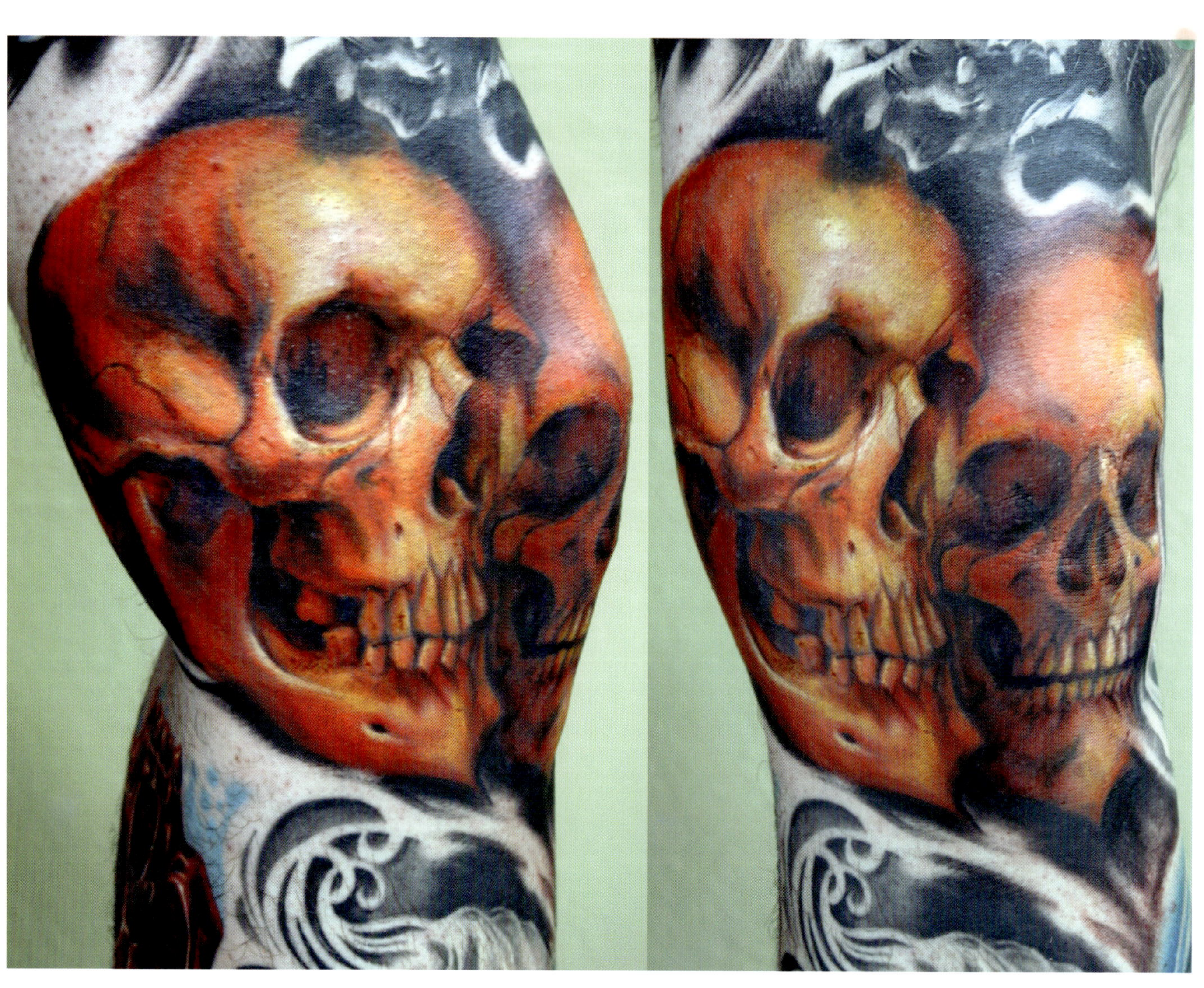

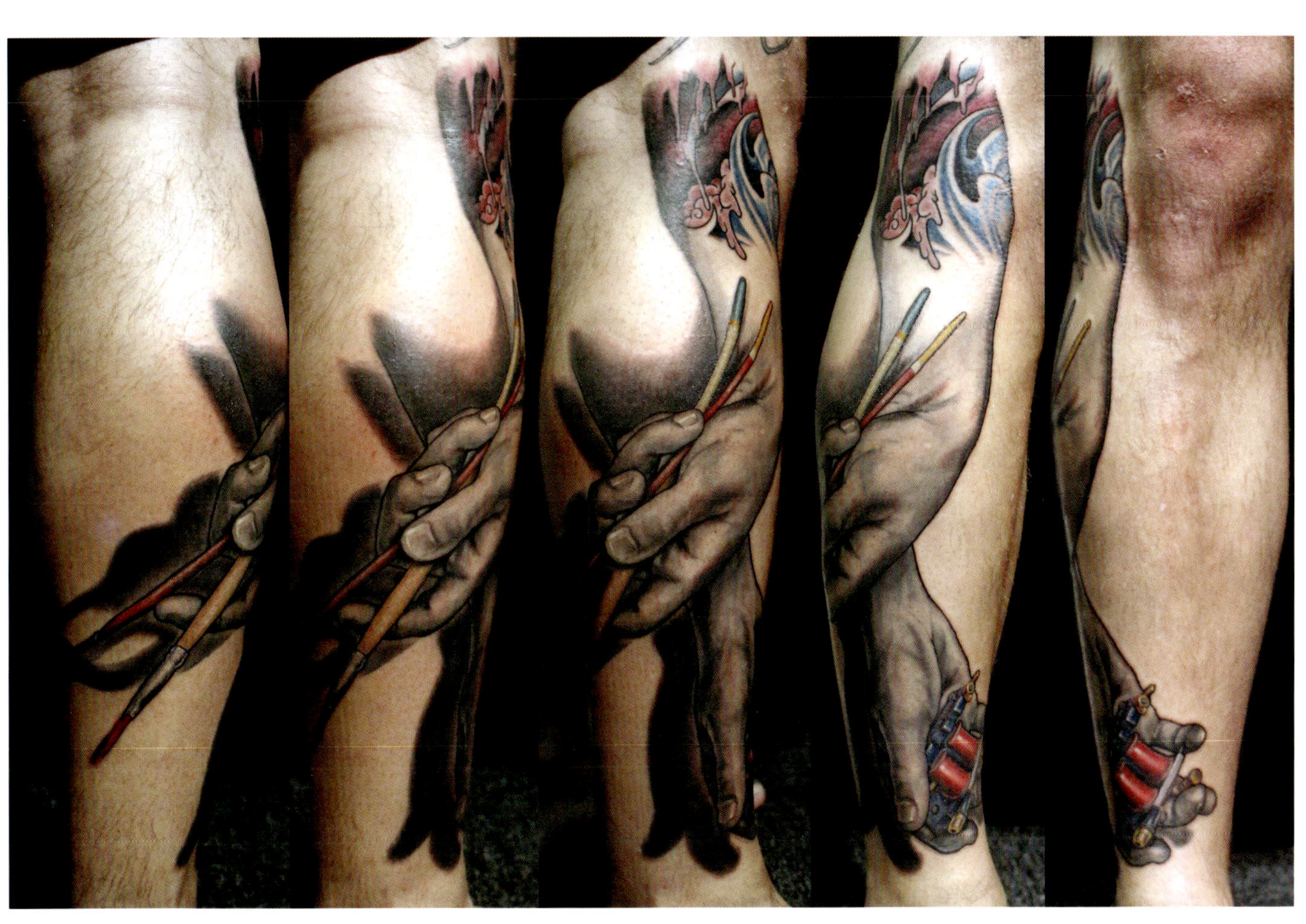

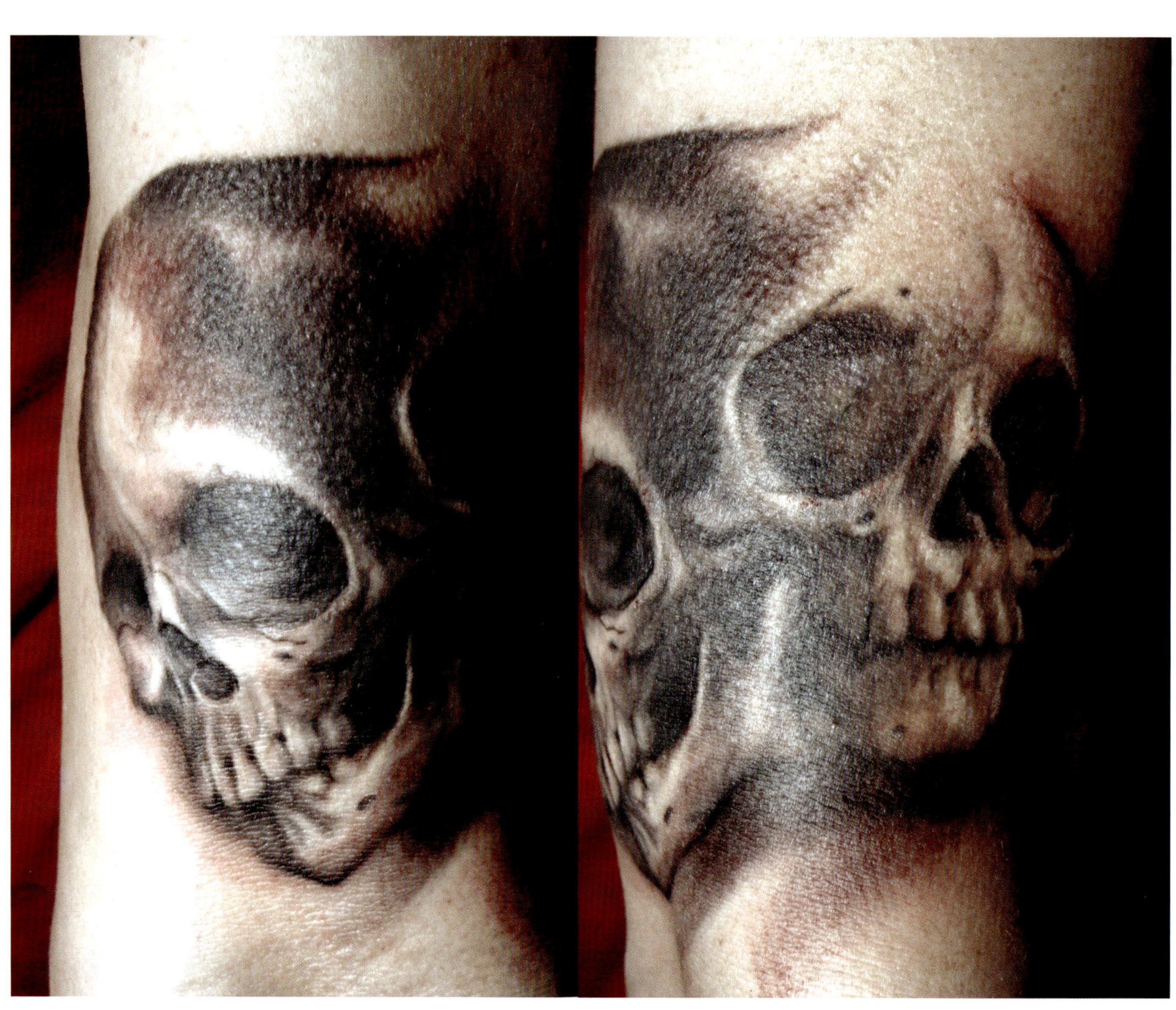

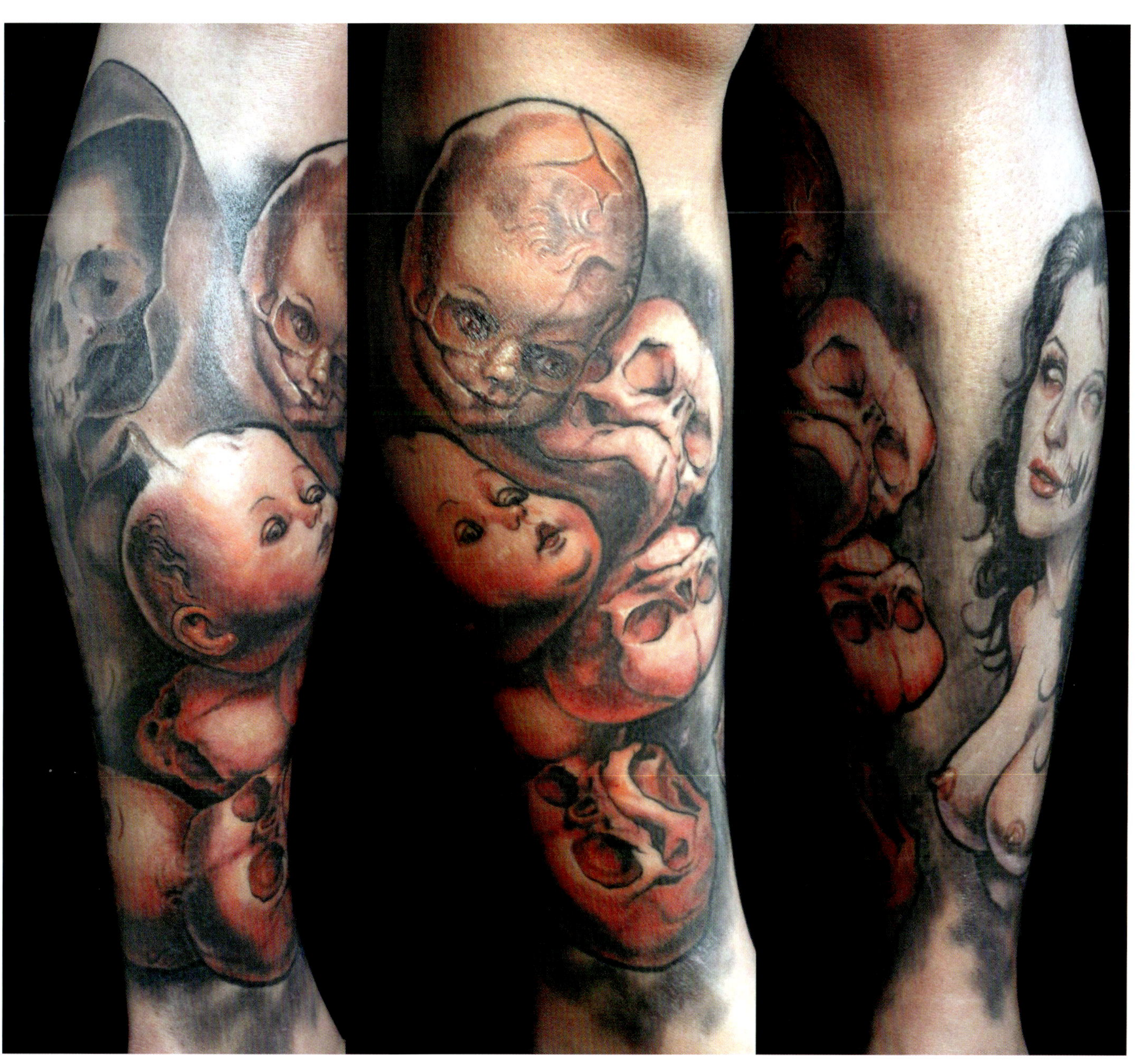

Andy Barrett

I prefer subjects that look like they could exist in the real world, but don't. Either they're just too weird, or it's a hybrid of different imagery to create something new. I generally start with my own photography, sculptures, computer models and sketches as a jumping off point. Half the time after all that prep work, I end up scrapping everything, and draw directly on the skin. As long as it's bold, dynamic and strange, then I'm happy.

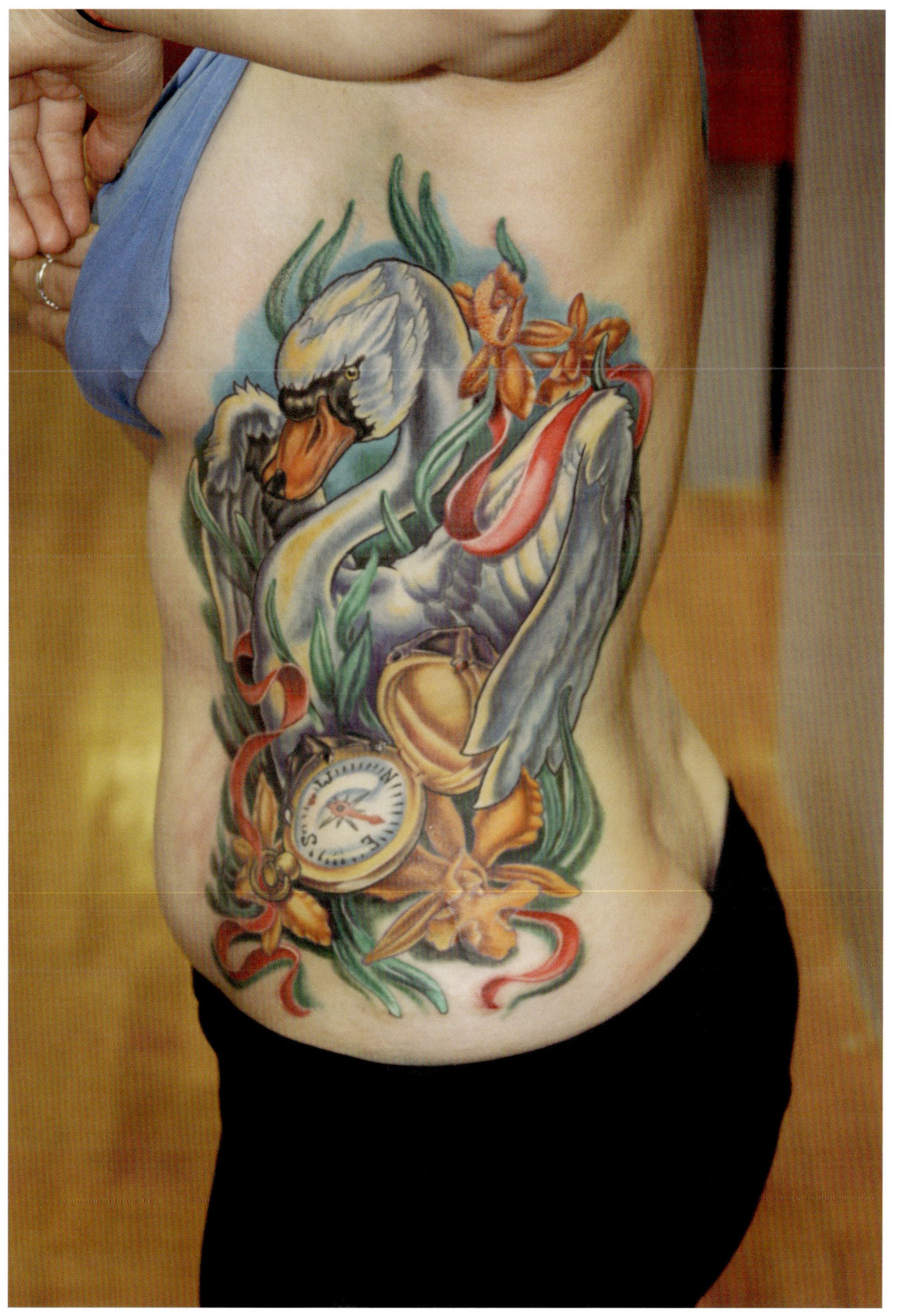

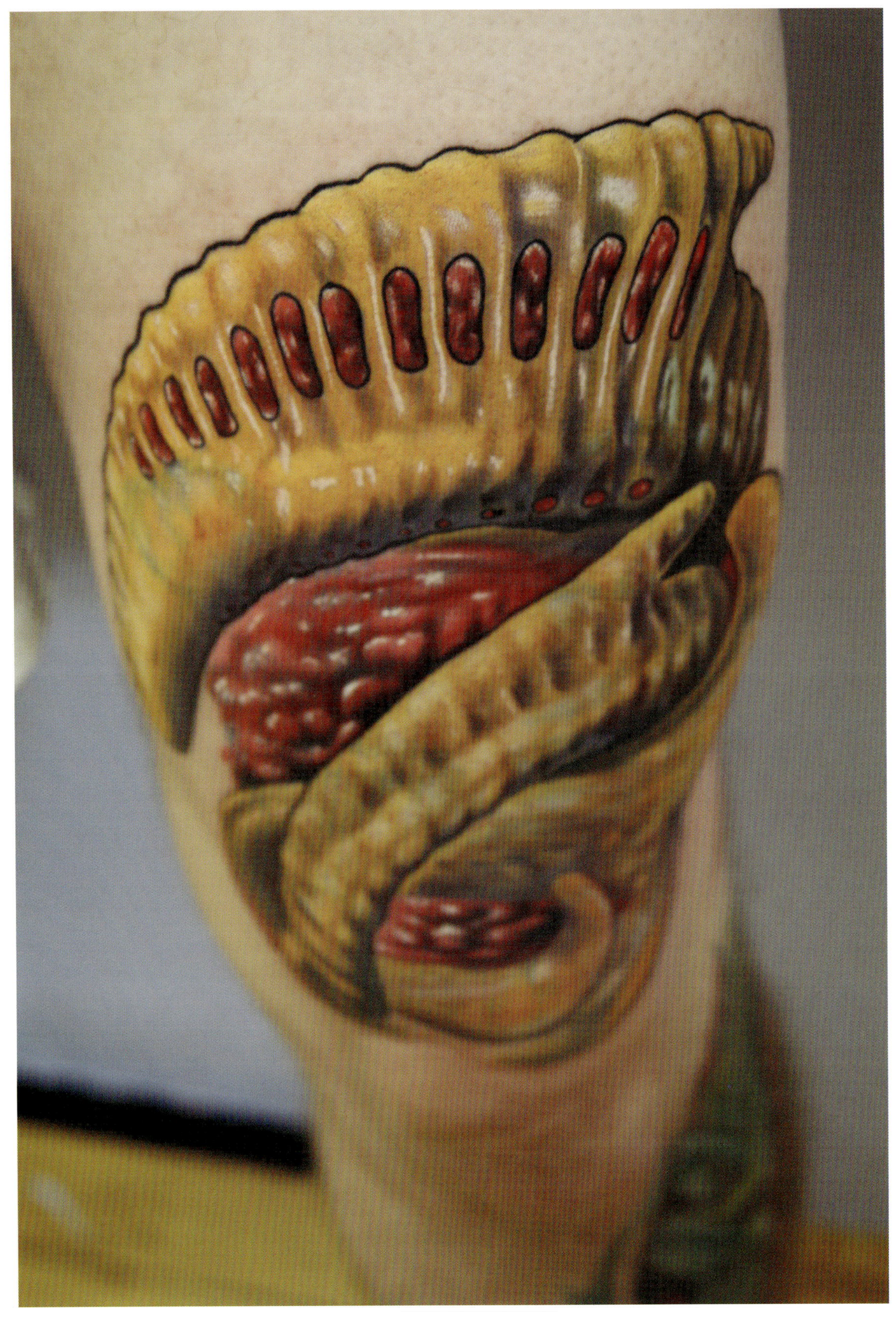

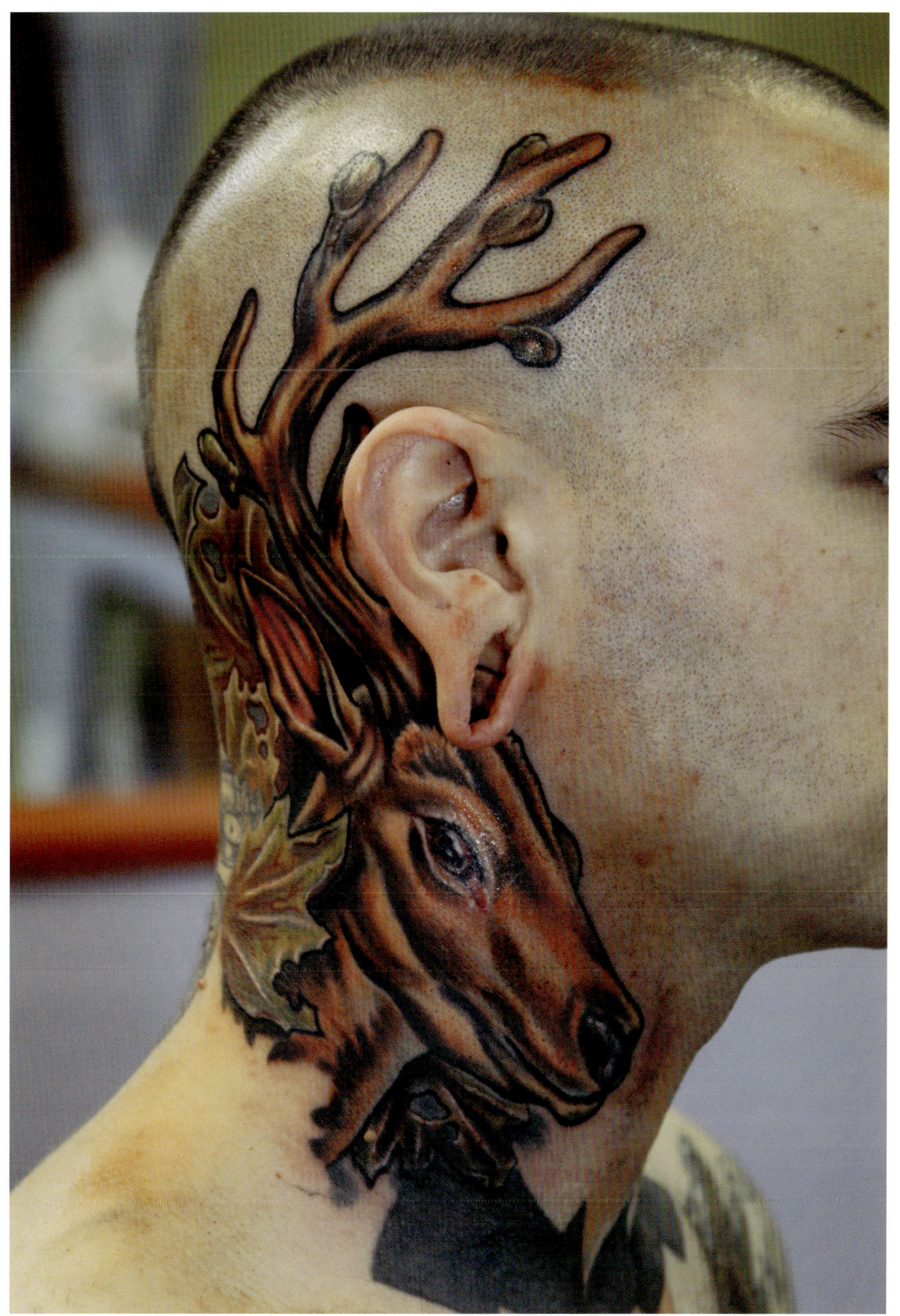

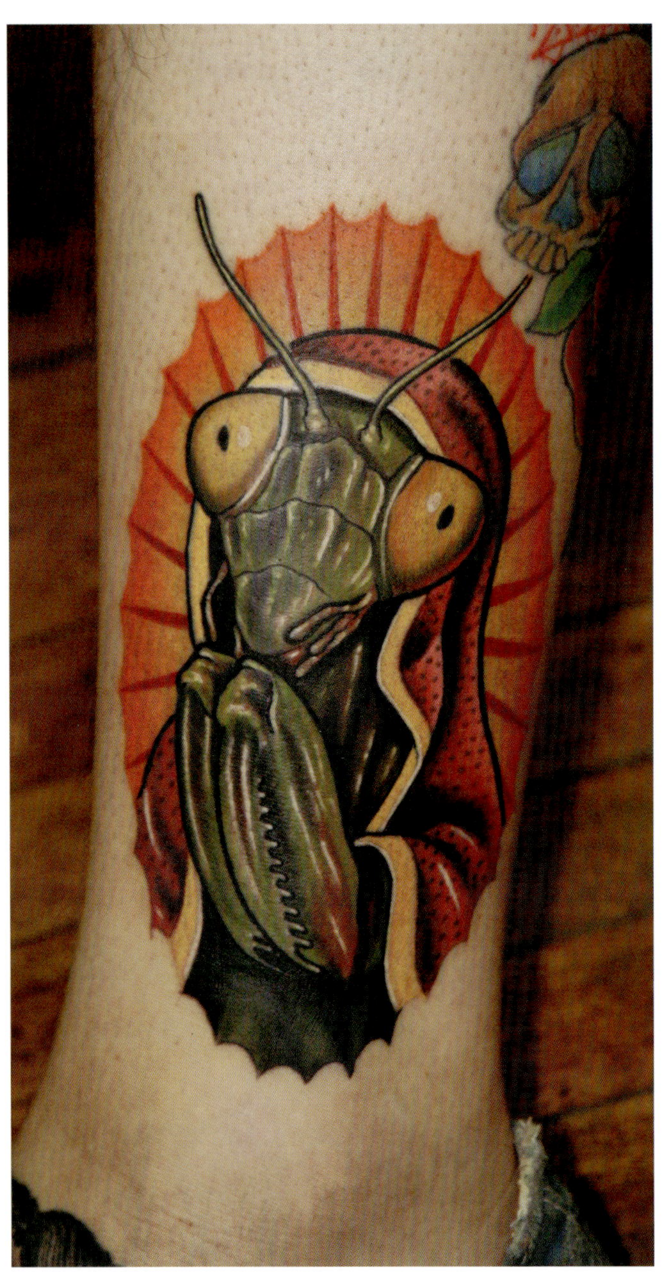

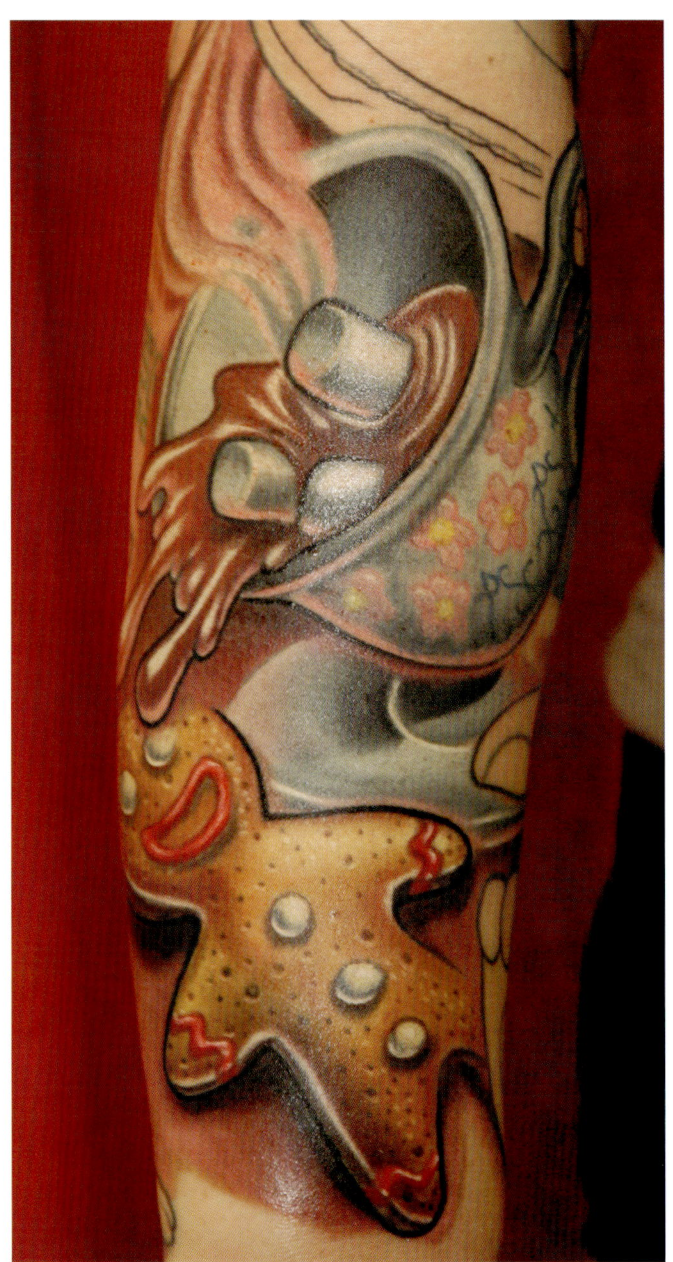

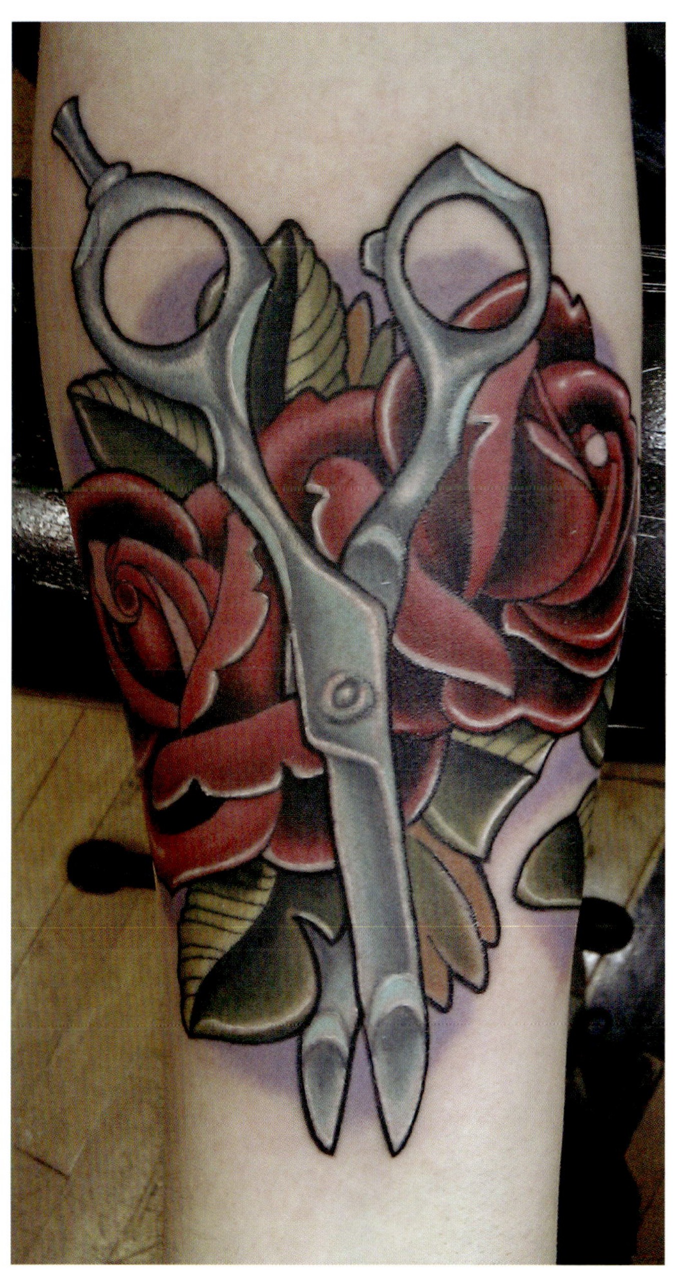

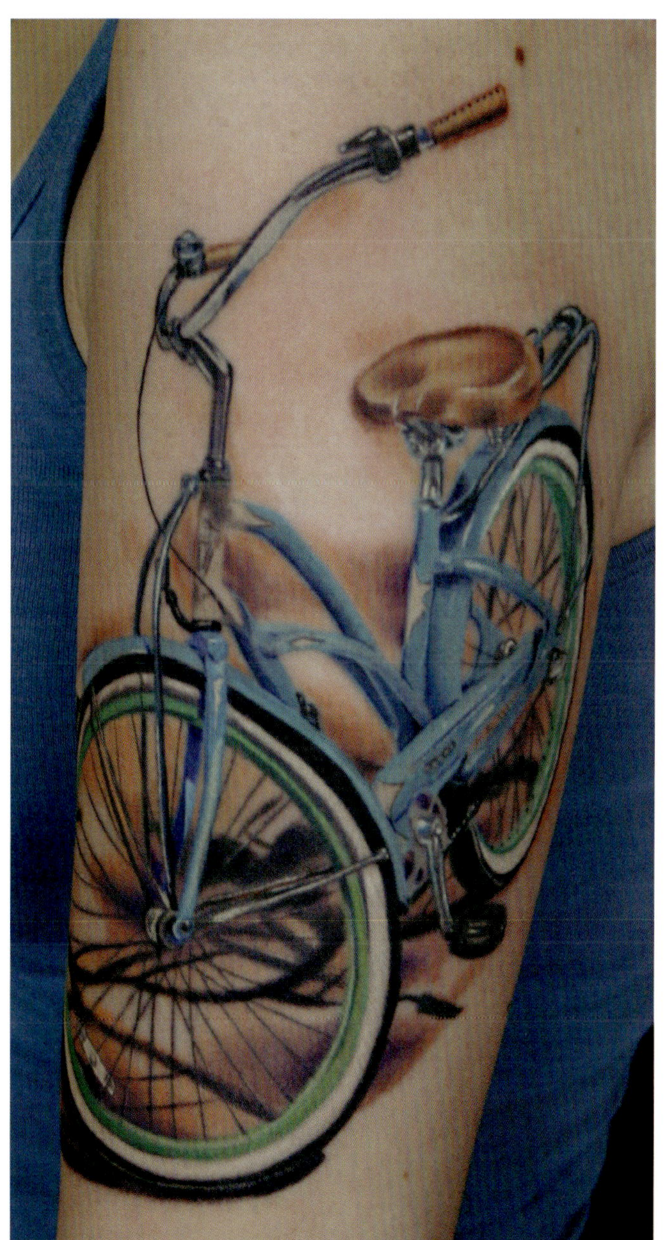

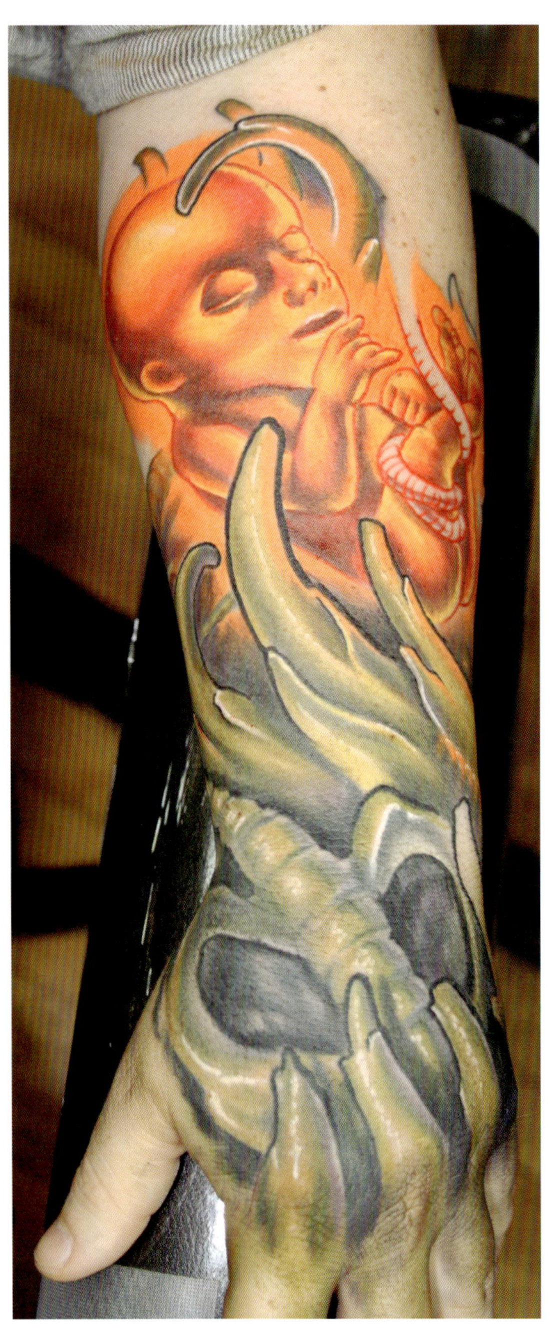

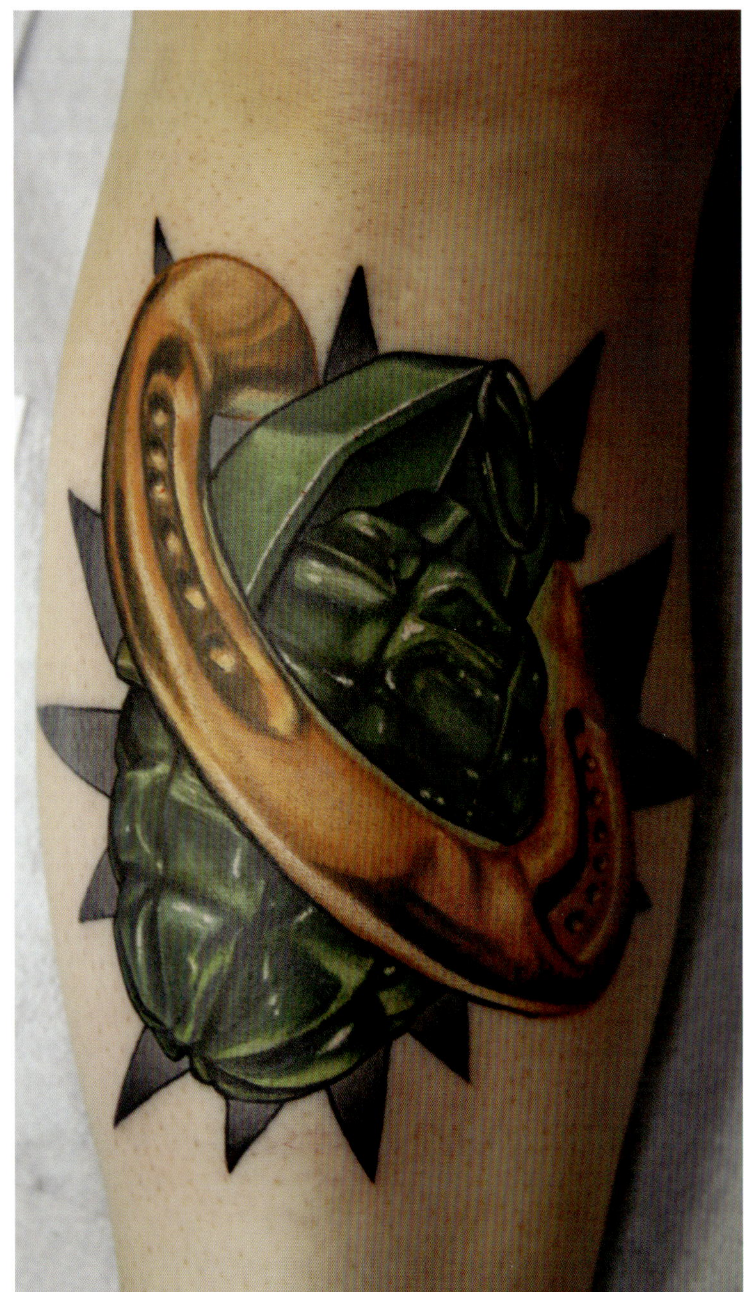

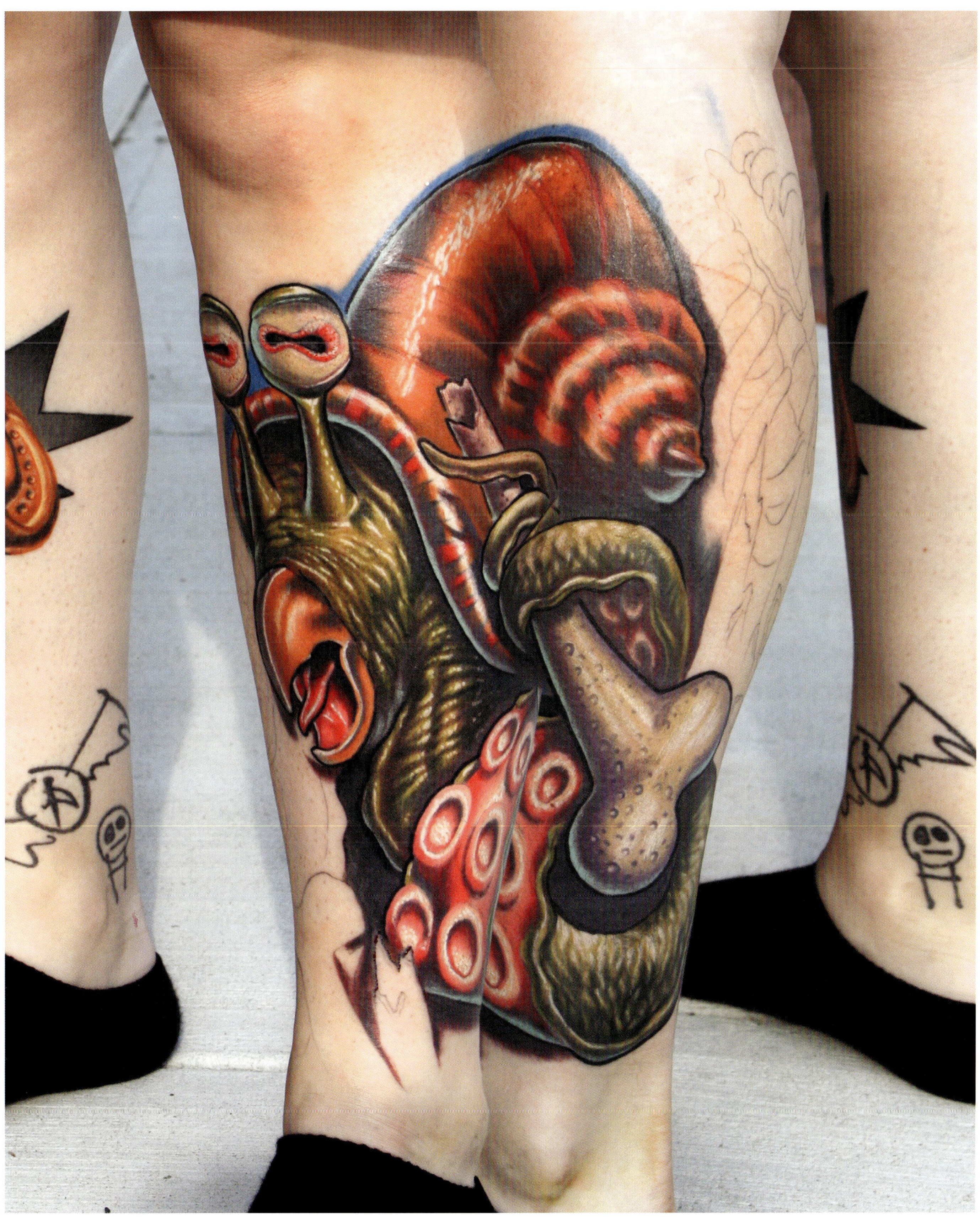

Mario Barth

I've been tattooing for over 30 years all over the world, traveling the world and meeting a lot of tattoo artists of various styles and learning from their styles. Every day my style is changing or growing, or I'm trying something new, or getting a new kind of request from a client.

I think one of my biggest strengths as a tattoo artist is that I can pull off a strong tattoo in virtually any style. There's something important about versatility as a tattoo artist where you just roll your sleeves up and get to it, whatever the task may be.

My focus has always been technique, as well as ruthless determination to give every single tattoo my best and then give it a little more. Exceeding the client's expectations EVERY time because at the end of the day, my art is on their skin forever, and they trust me to do that, and that's a really powerful thing.

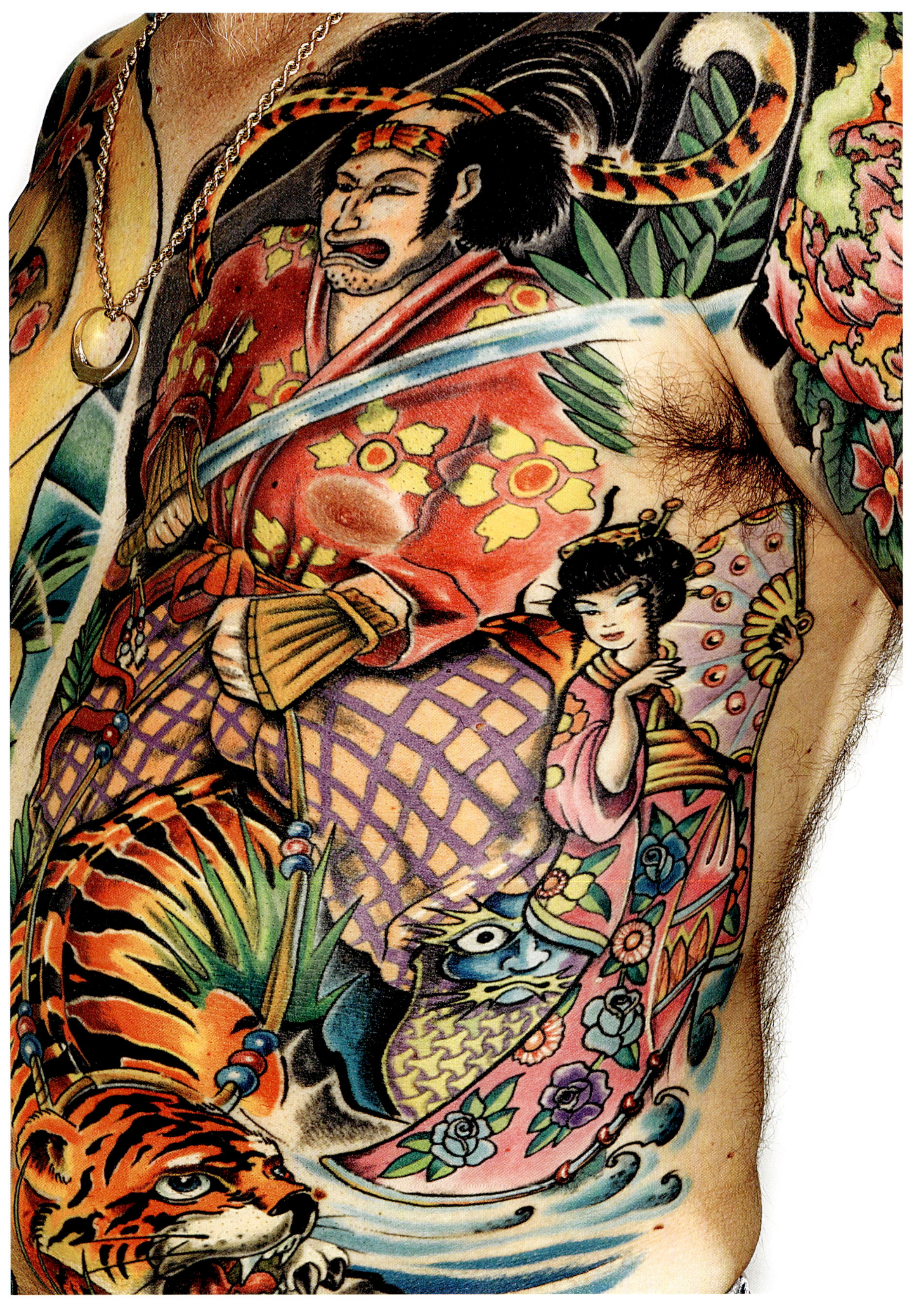

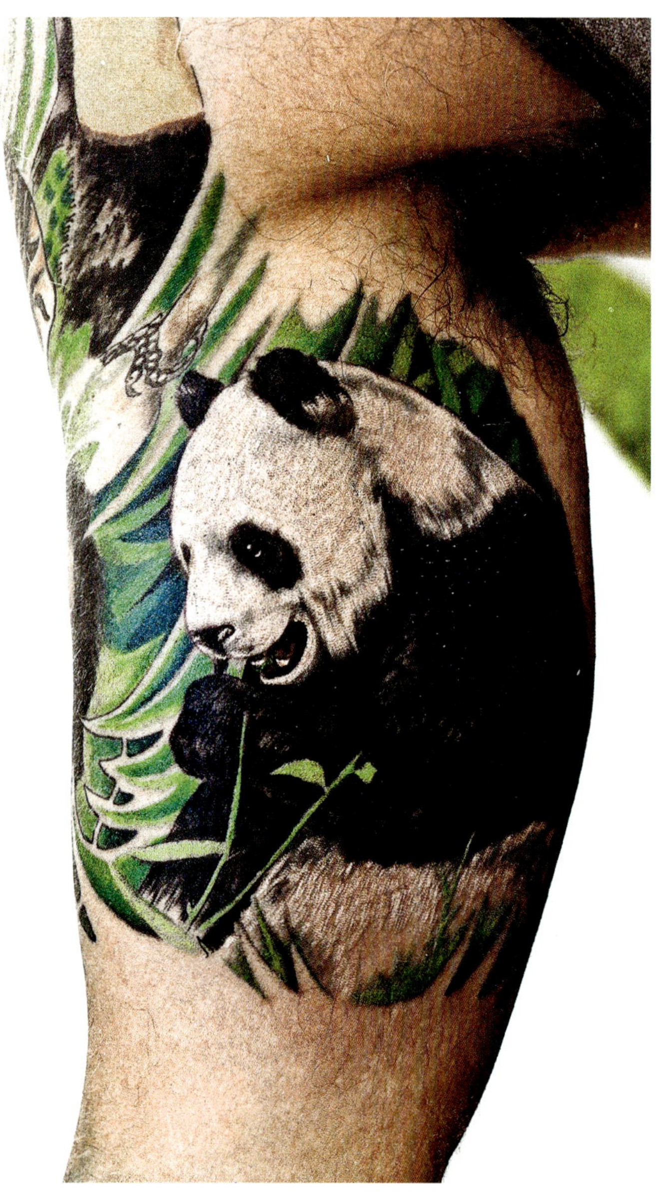

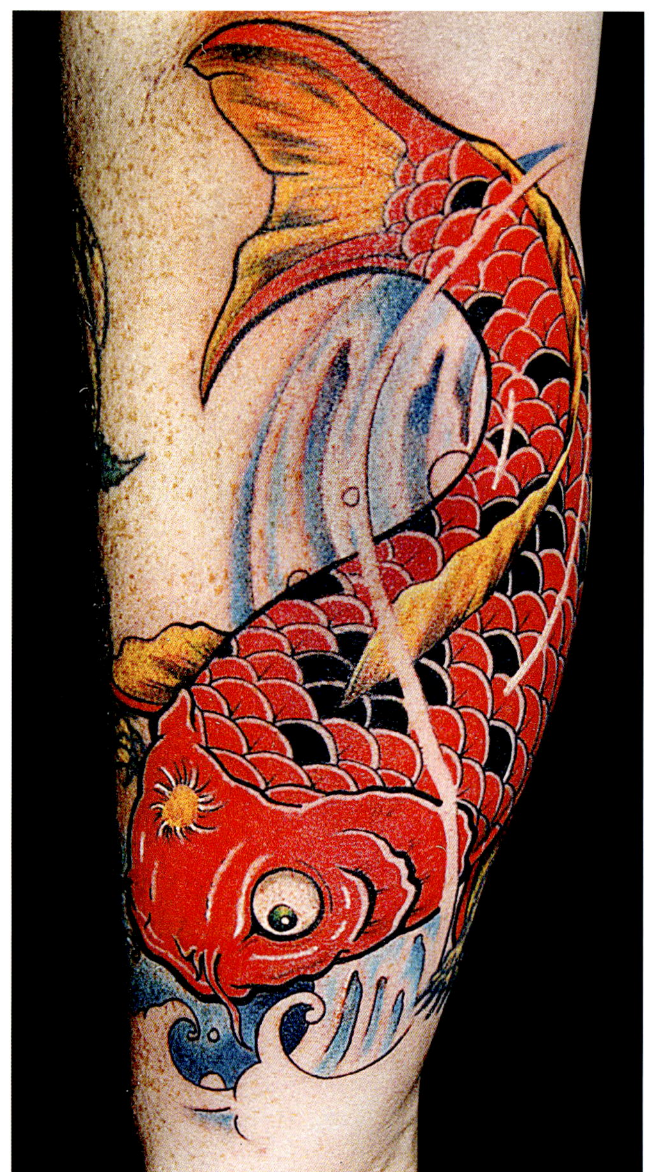

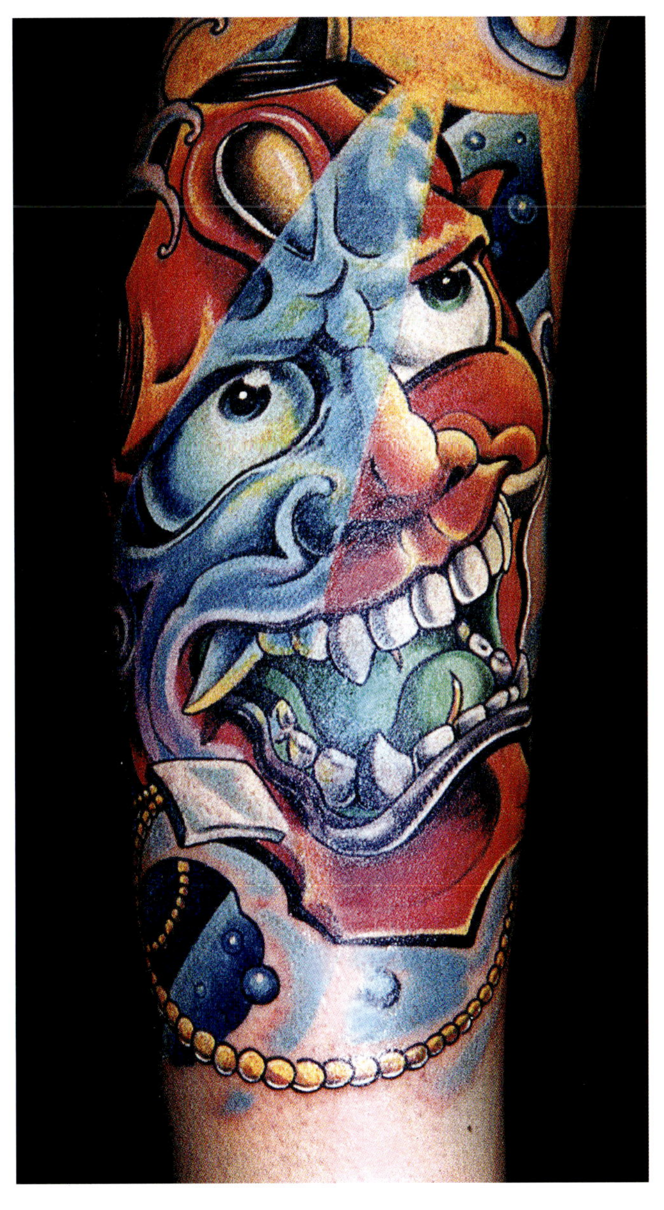

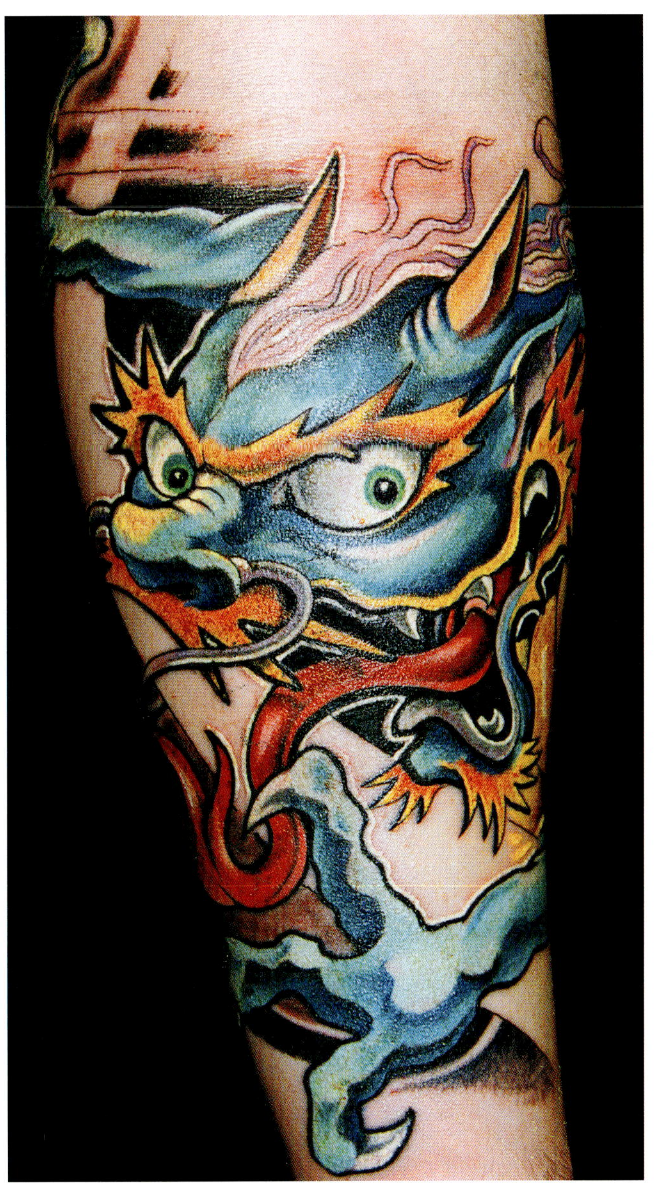

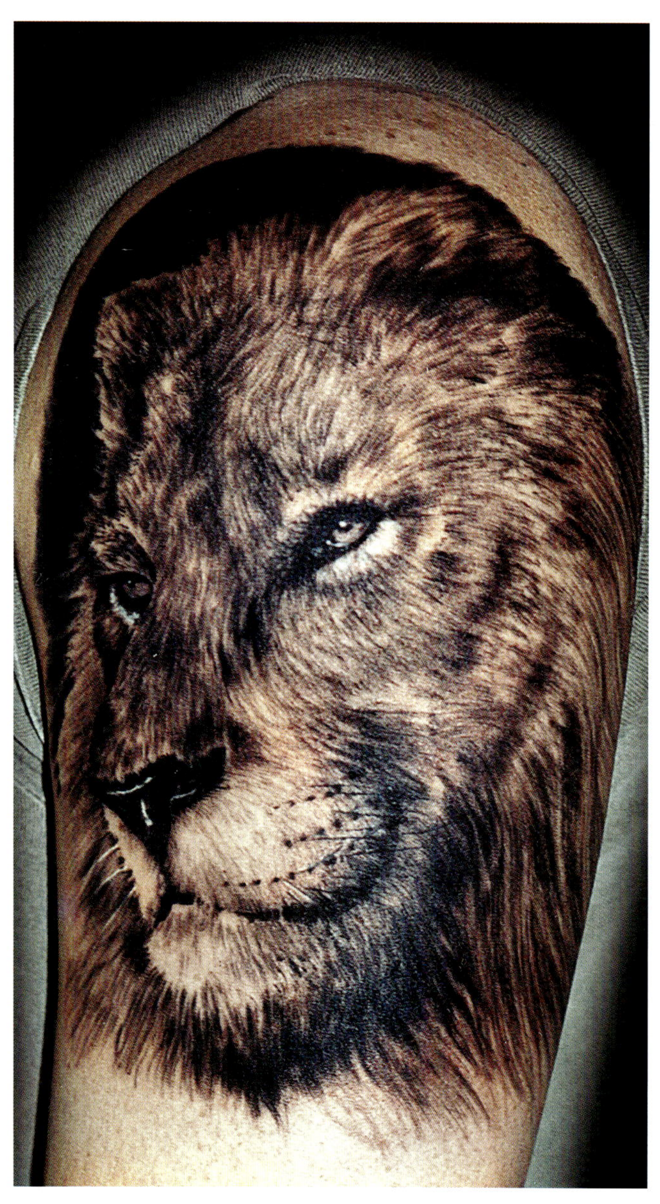

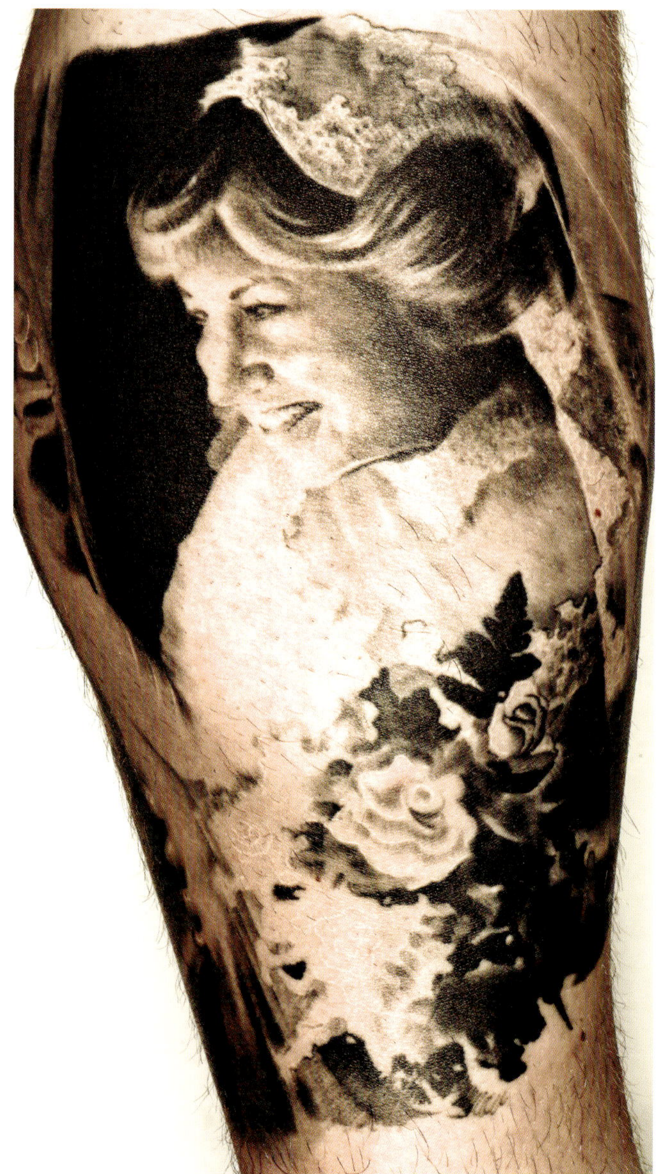

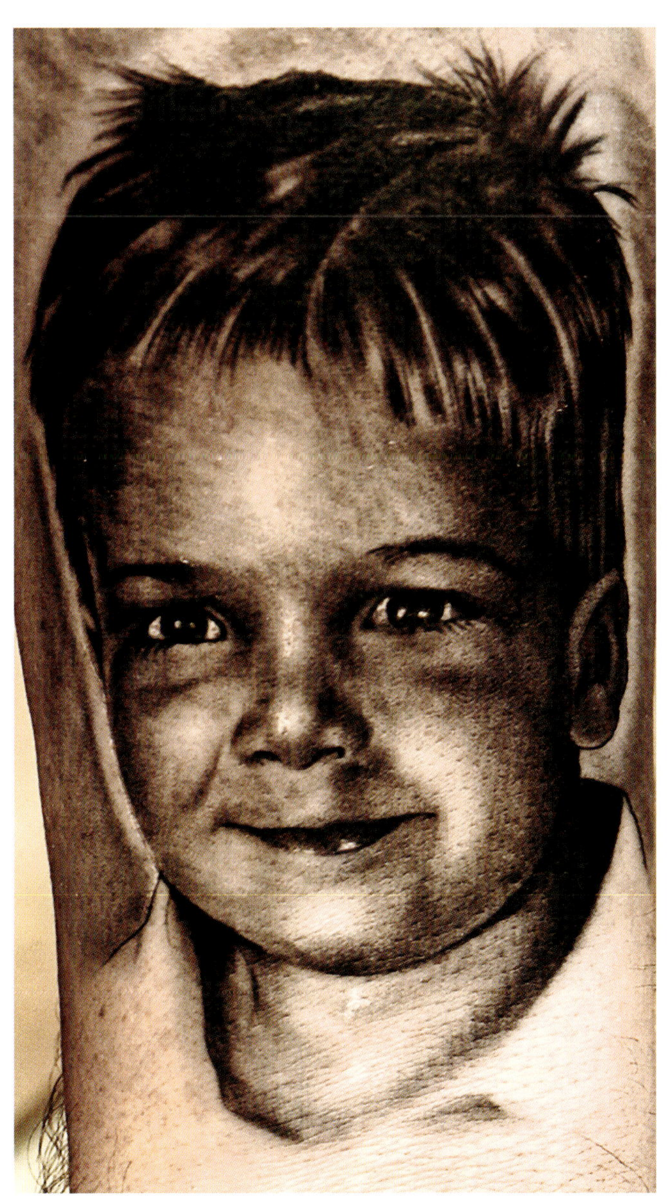

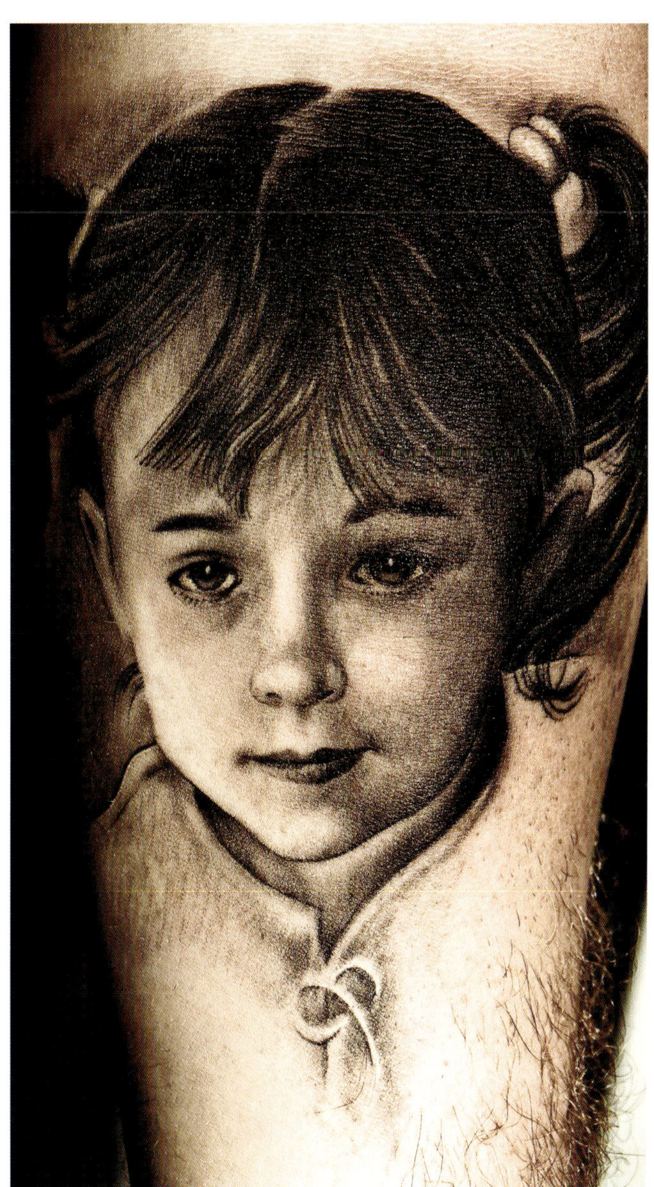

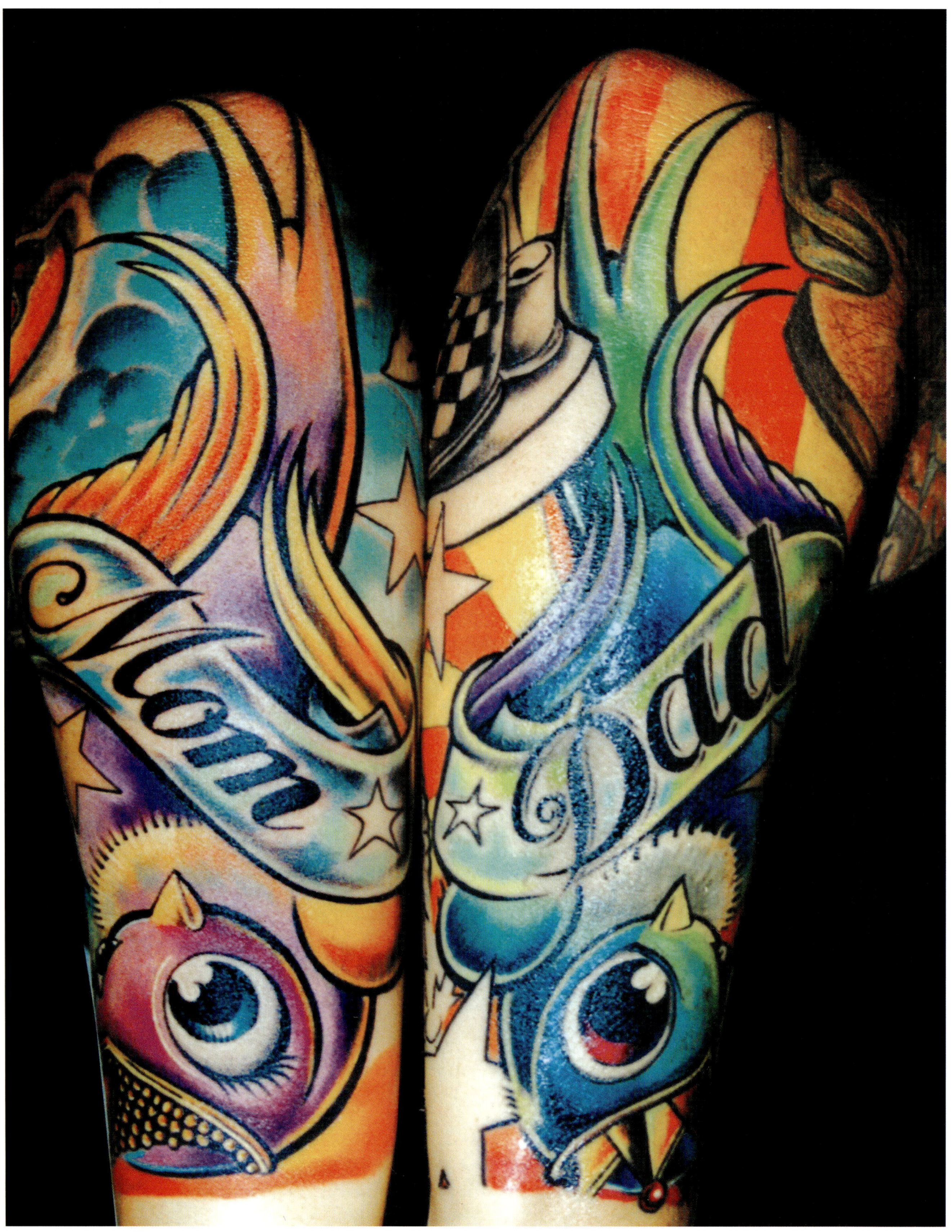
Mom
Dad

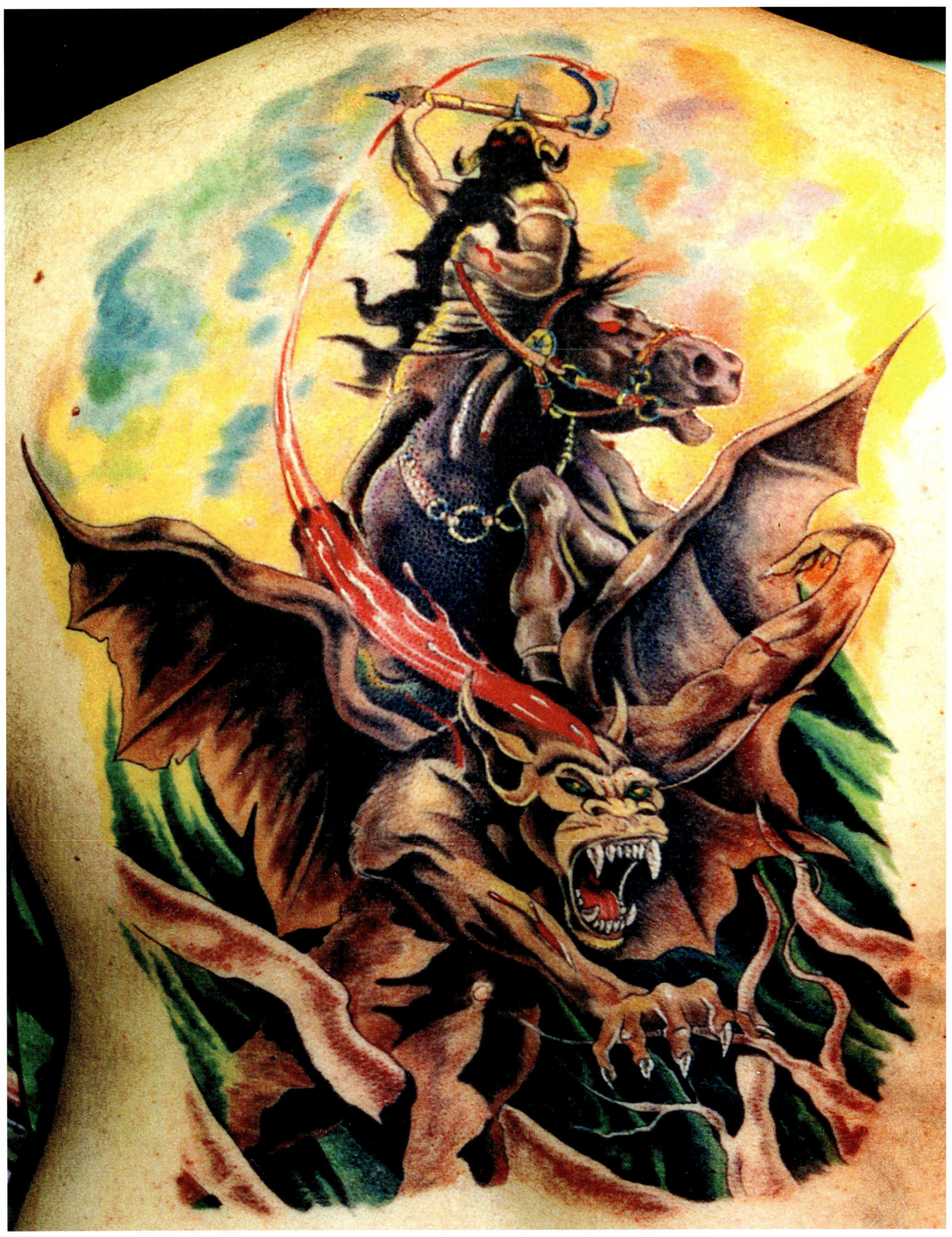

Mark Bode

I've been an artist all my life thanks to my late father Vaughn Bode. He left me an Underground trail to follow, a craggy fucked up and mystical trail, but a trail never the less. Sixteen years ago, I found comics to be a feast or famine industry and needed a more solid weekly income to feed my family. I met a Biker tattooist by the name of Al Valenta out of Northampton, Massachusetts and he said, "Everybody does your dad's characters as tattoos - why don't you quit fuckin' around and tattoo motherfuckers?" And I said, "What do I start on? Grapefruits? Chickens?" He answered, "Drunk people!" "Let's go down to the fuckin' bar!" We announced at the local watering hole, "Who wants a free tattoo by Bode?" And the hands went up! That was the start of my tattooing career. I later apprenticed properly in a shop in Connecticut since it was illegal to tattoo in Massachusetts at the time. I still do comics, and tattooing, and spray can art in the family style which my father left me to carry on with as I travel down that craggy mystical path that is the Bode Universe.

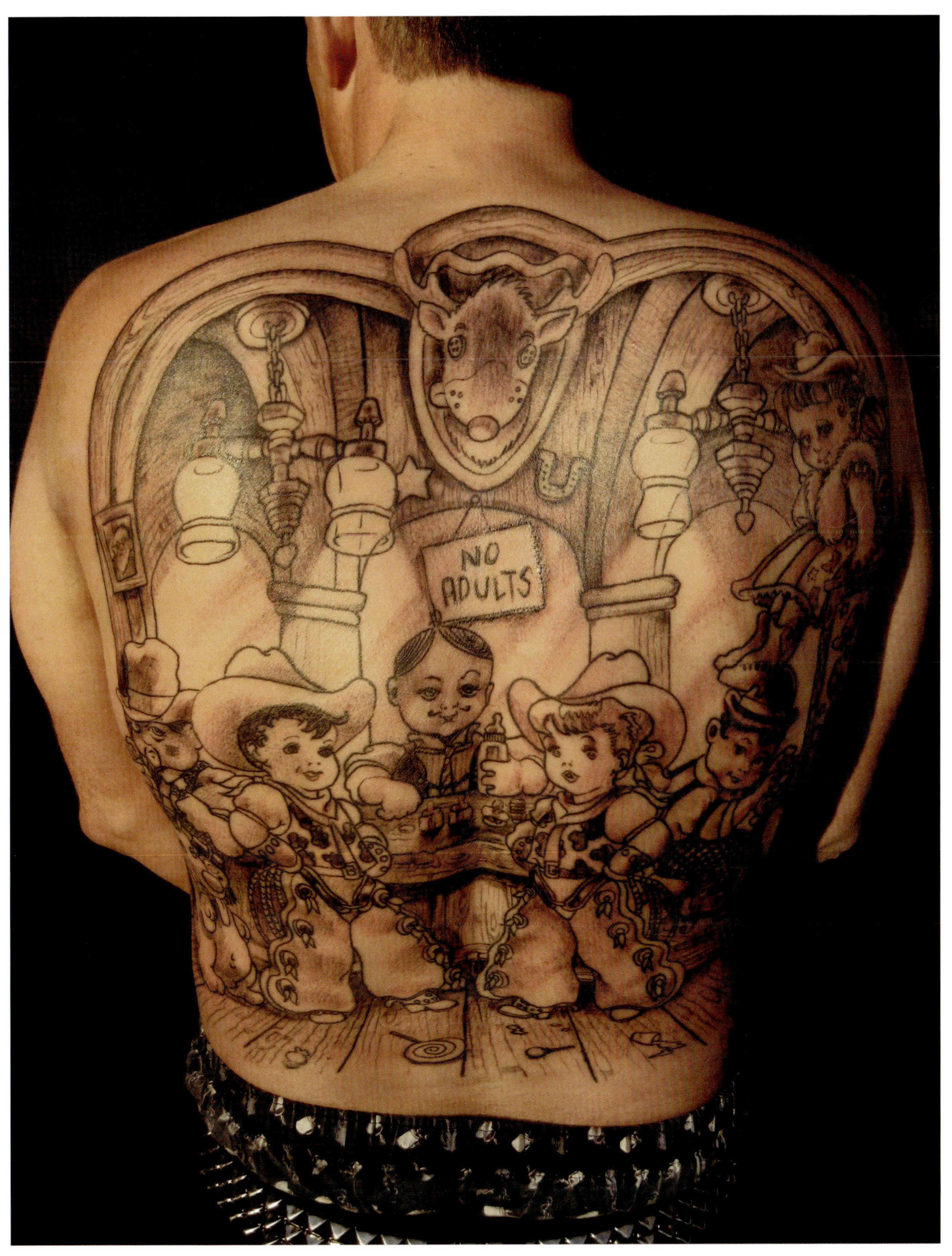
NO ADULTS

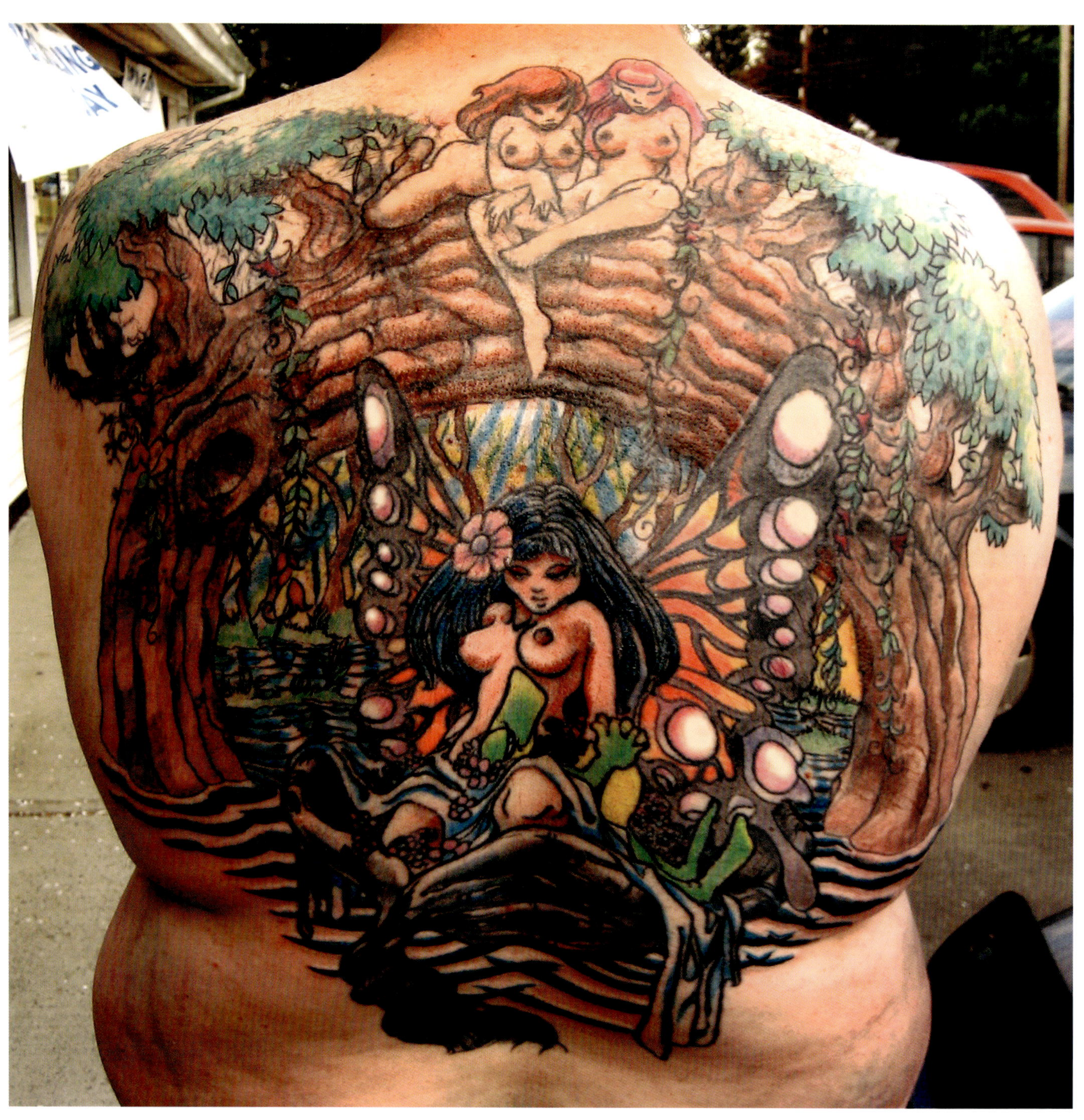

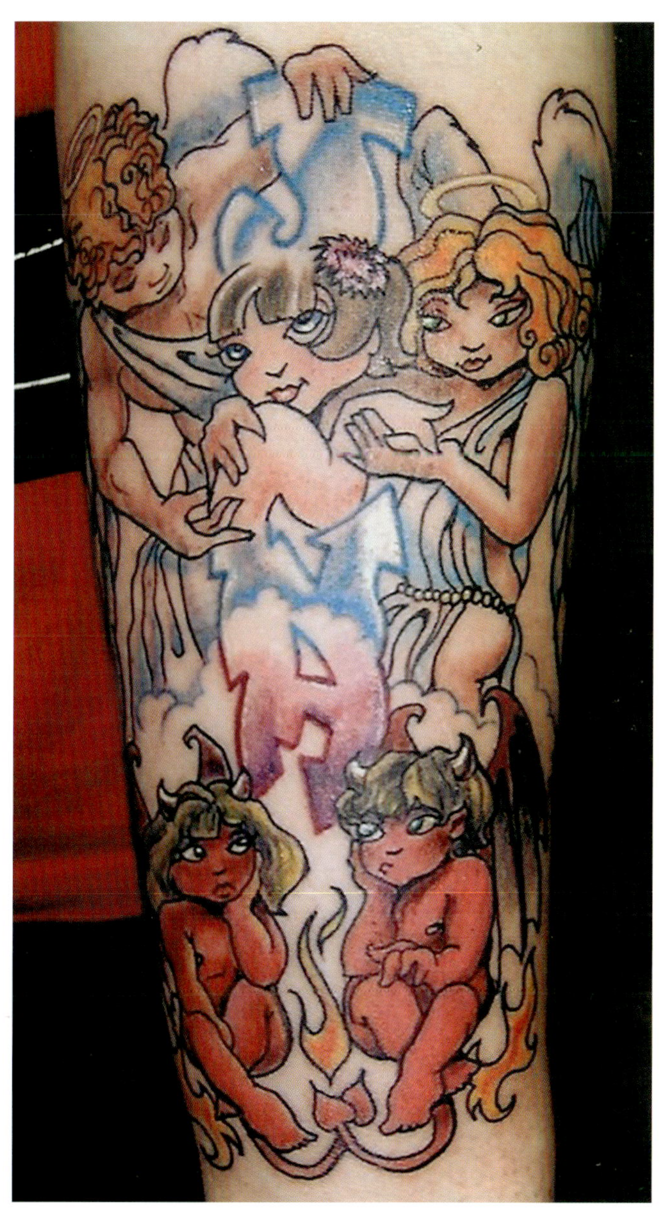

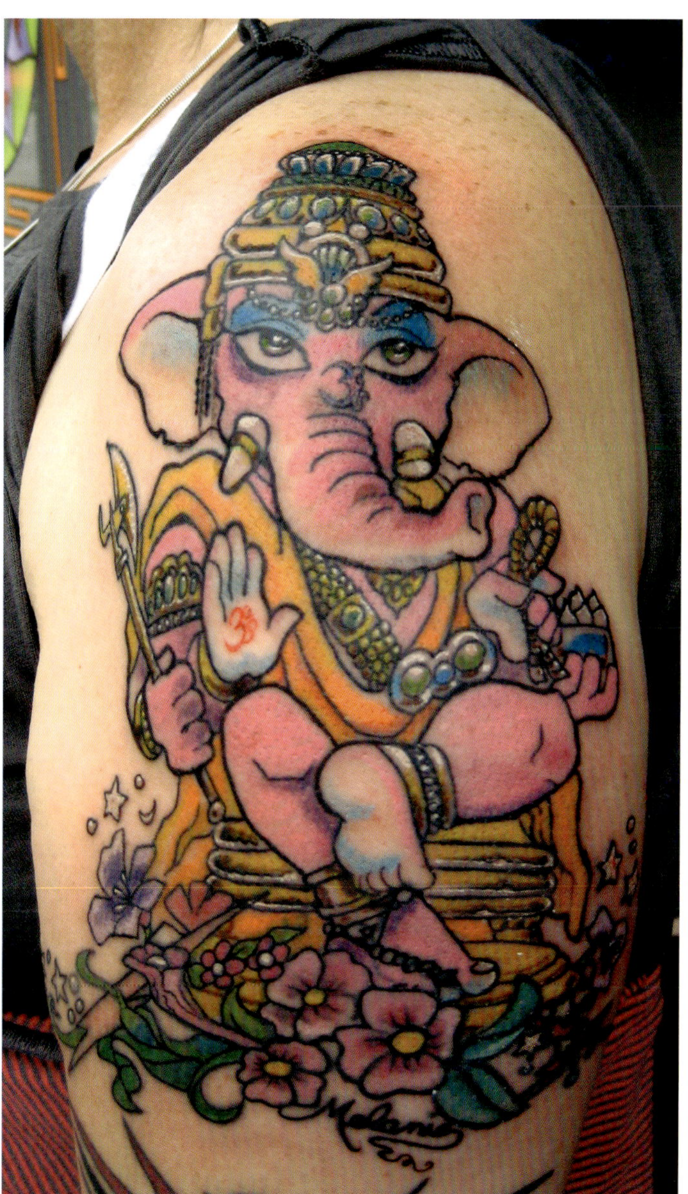
Melanie

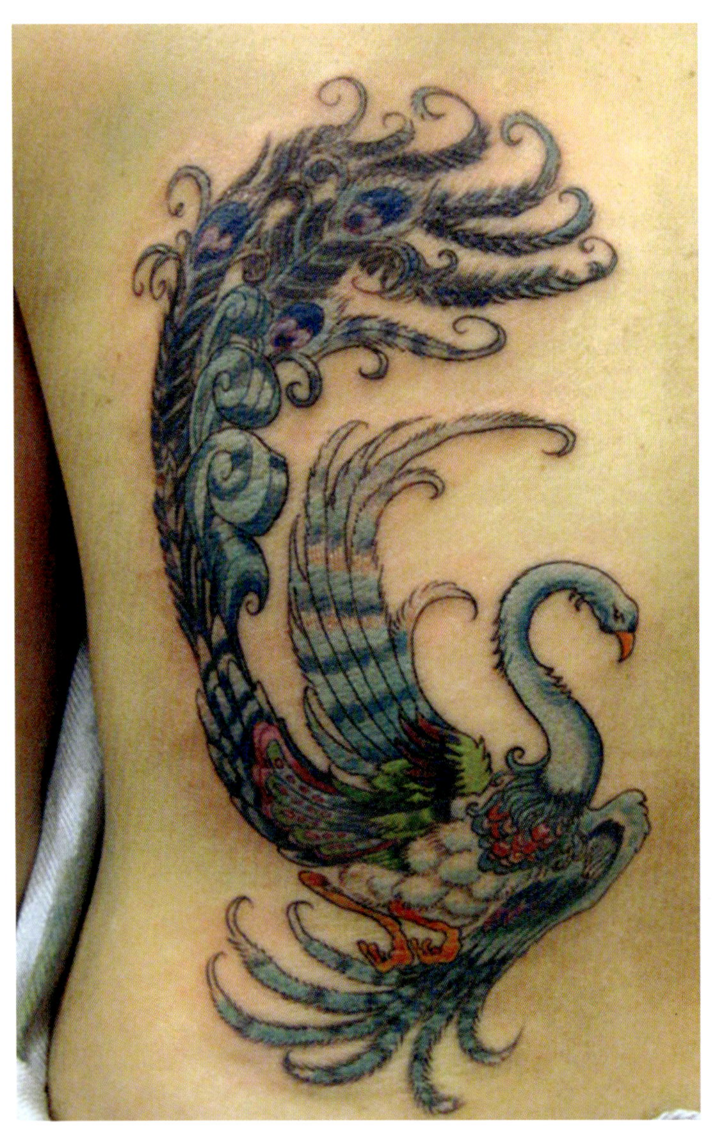

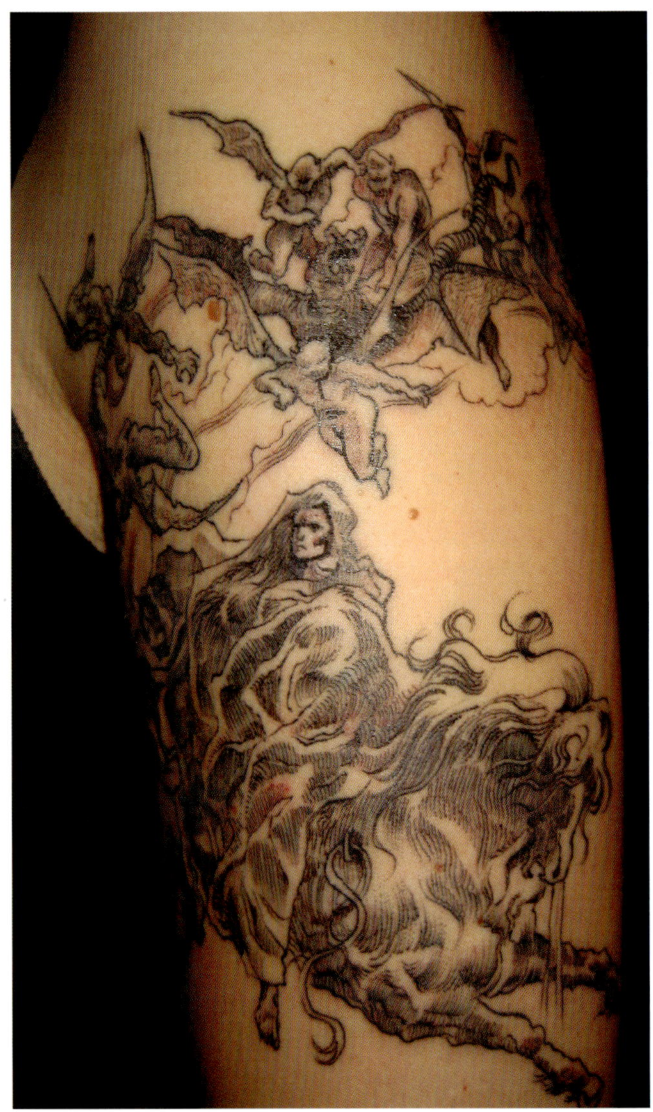

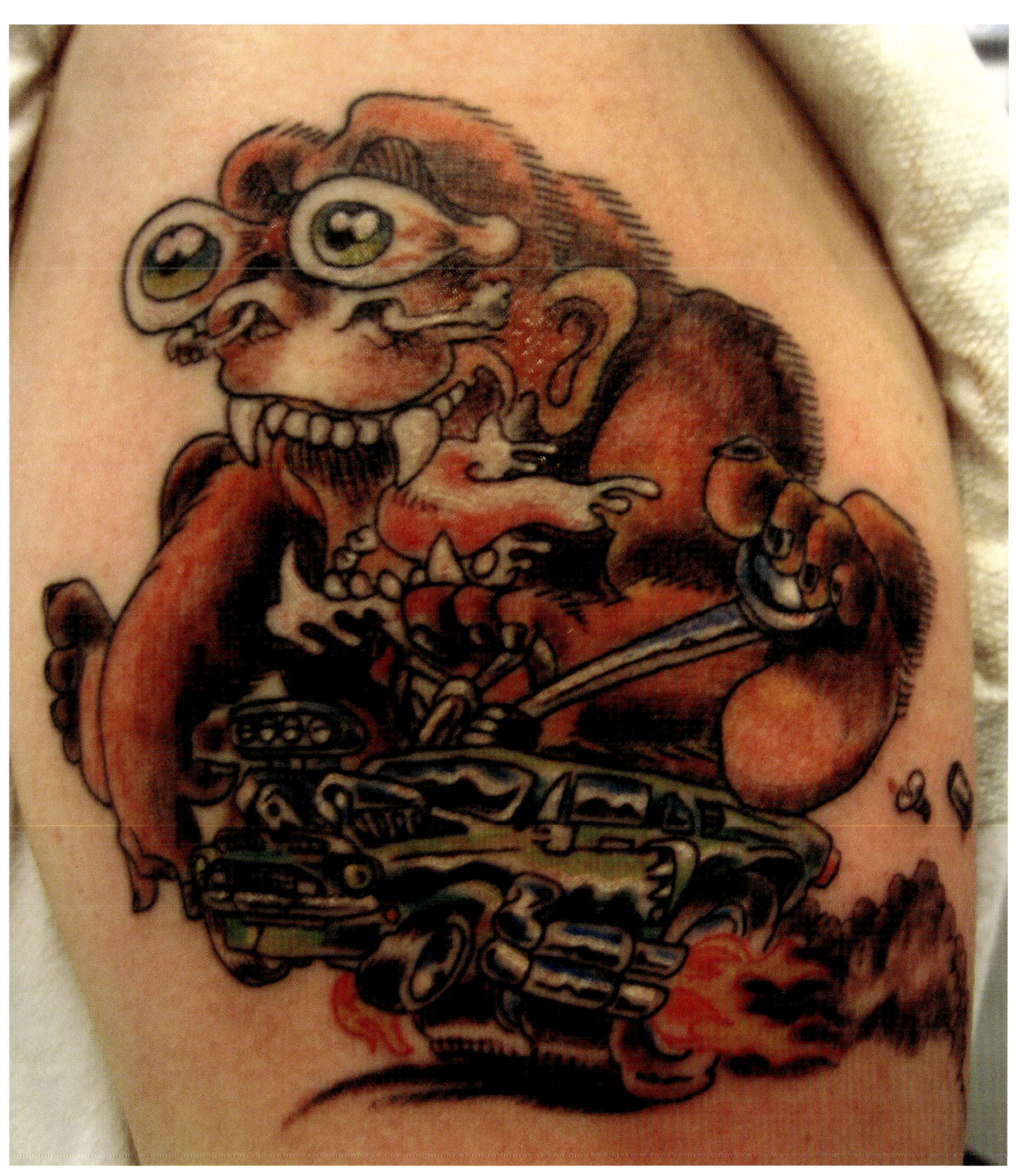

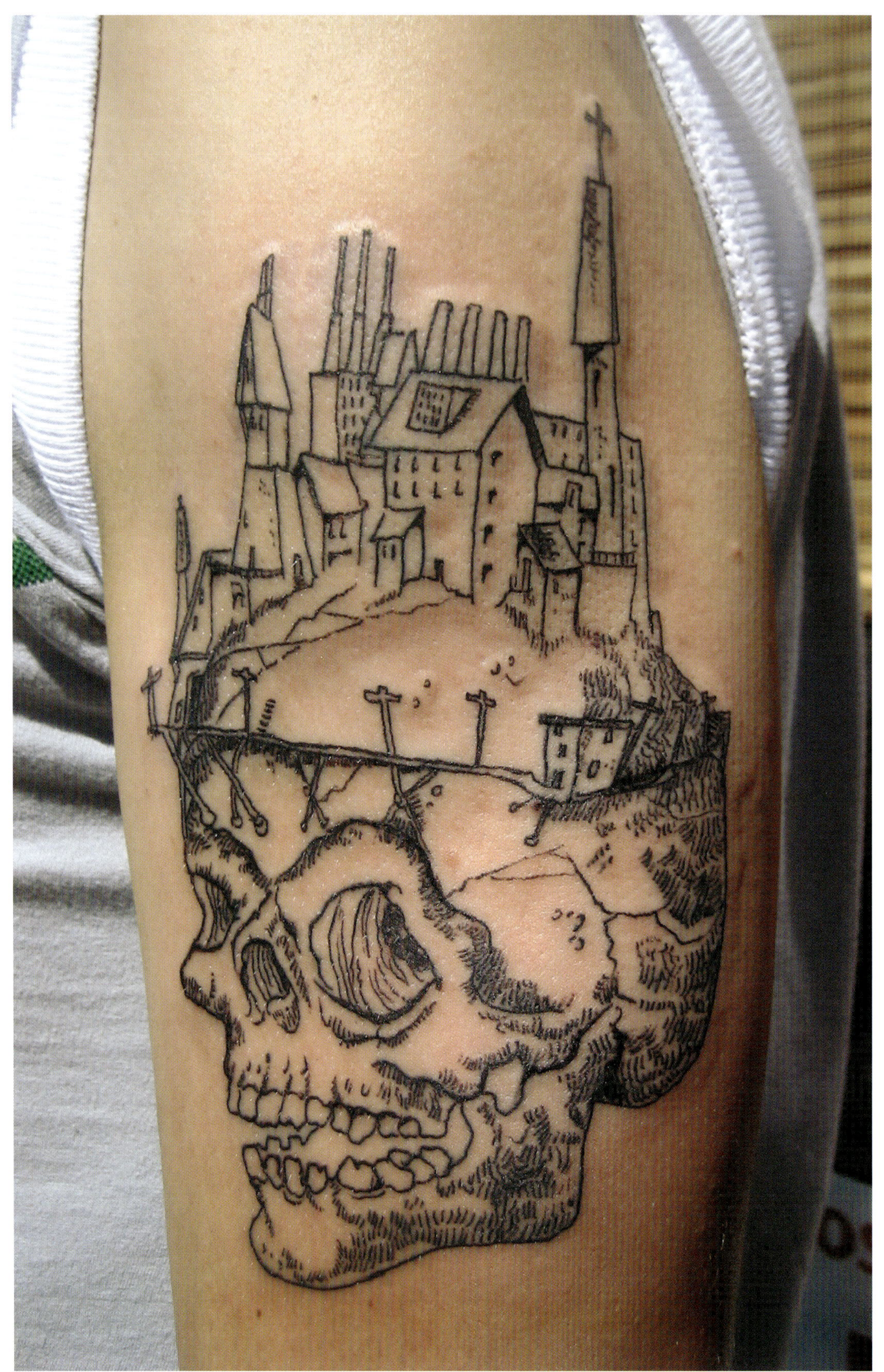

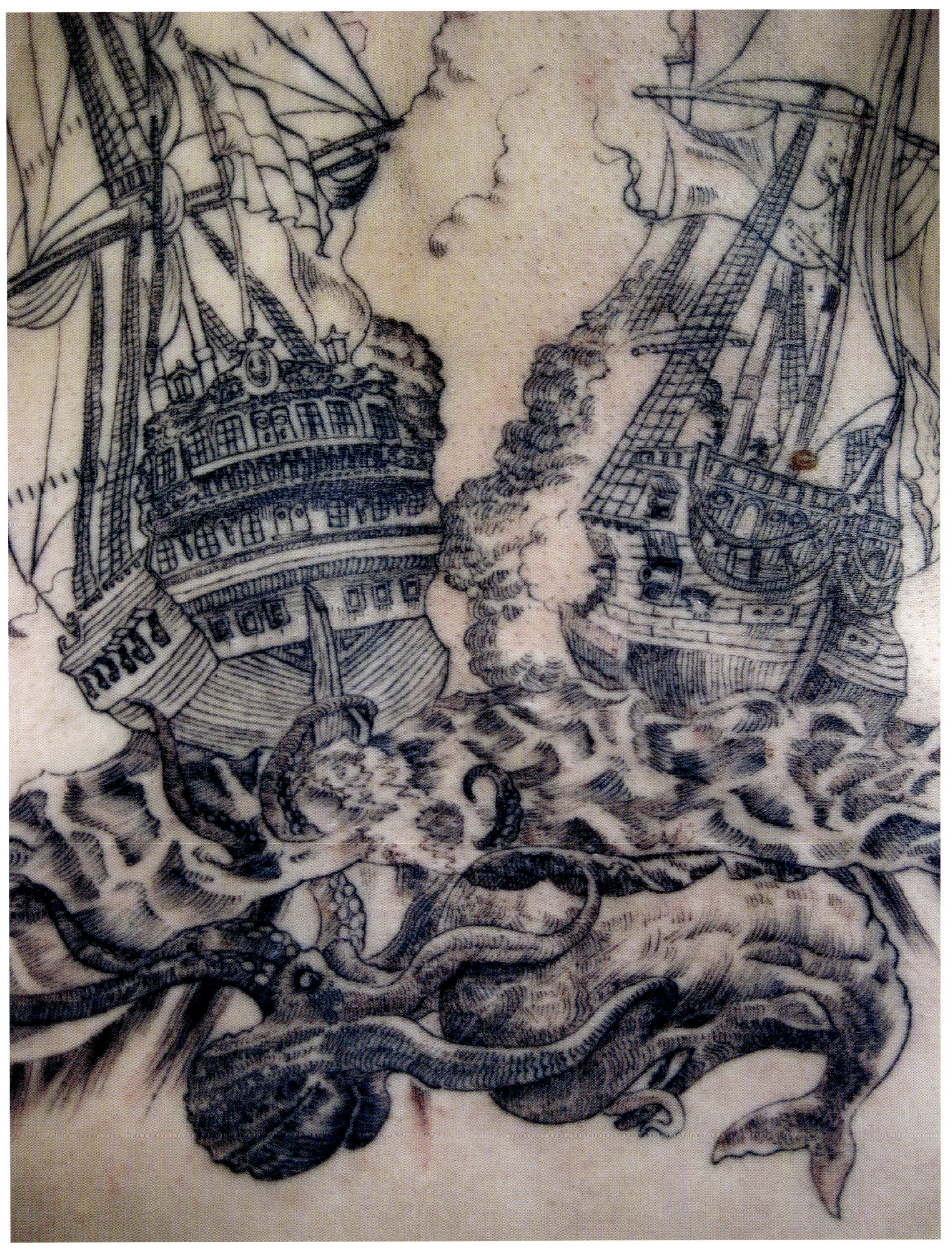

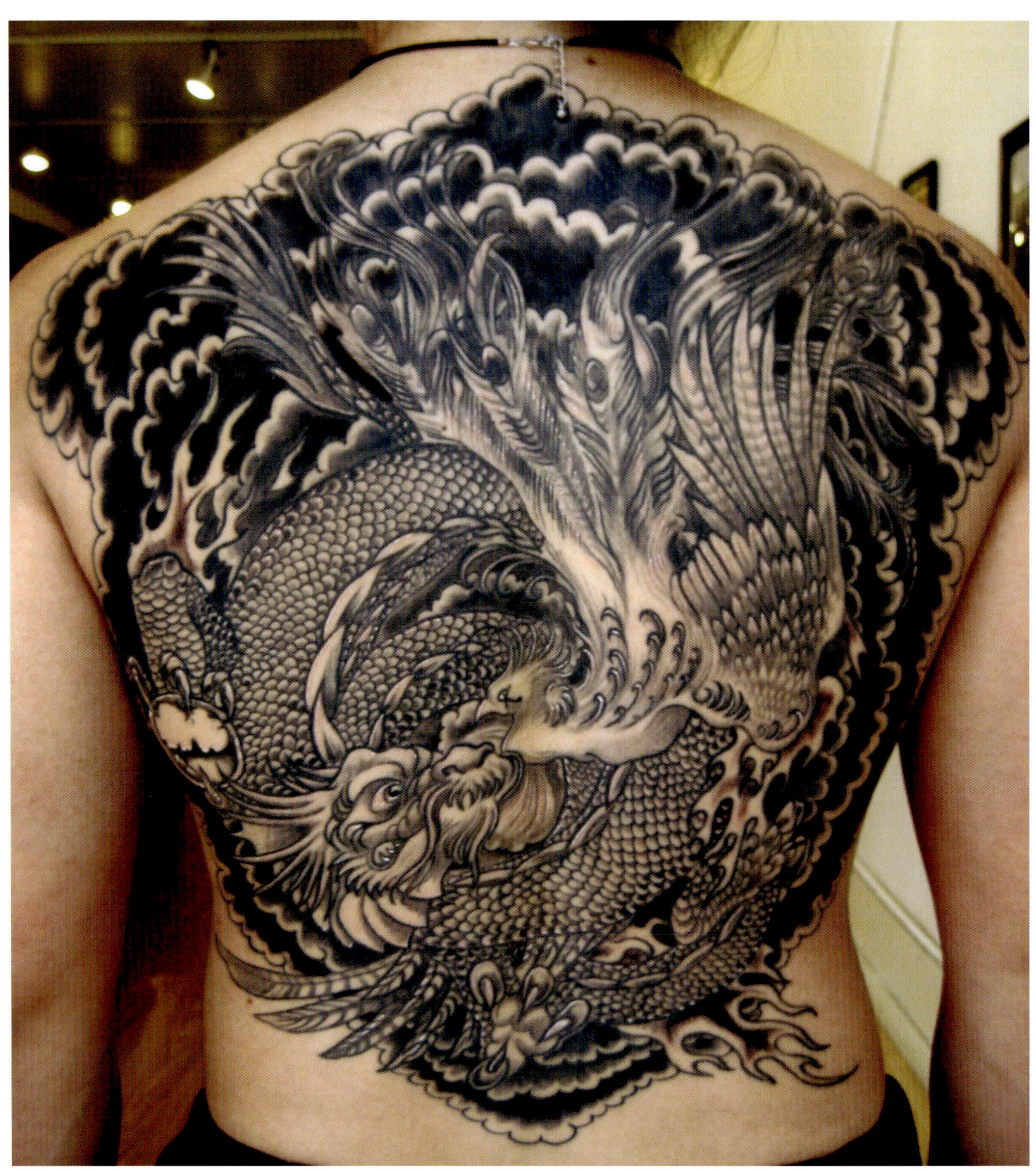

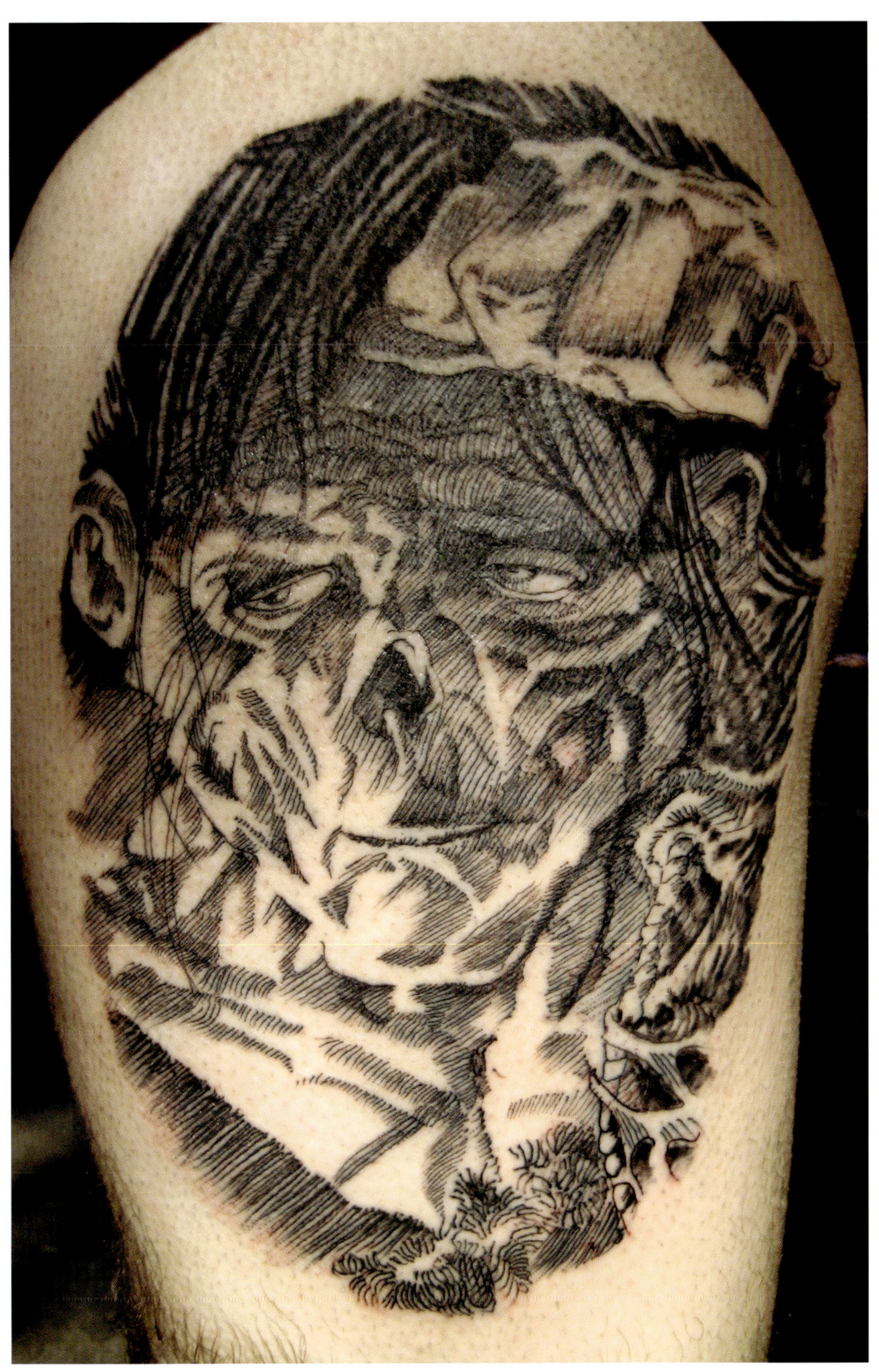

Sunny Buick

I've always considered my style to be original yet traditional. Admittedly, lately my tattoos have taken on a modern twist and have nothing to do with old school tattooing except maybe the strong outline and simplicity. I'm proud to say that I have developed my own signature look. I like to leave lots of open skin and not too much black shading, always thinking "how will the tattoo look in 50 years?" because I love the look of old sailors and circus performers and their "collections" of separated, blurry tattoos.

My first interest in tattooing came through art and my fascination for the circus and sideshows. There were the naturally born "special" and the self-made freaks: the tattooed. This lifestyle choice can be seen as self-mutilation, a primitive impulse, internal feelings expressed on the exterior layer, fashion, a self-esteem barometer, a way to cover our nakedness, eroticism, or an impulse to experience physical pain as a cure for emotional pain. I've been a tattoo artist for 18 years continually trying to understand why people get tattooed. I think it's because we simply like to decorate.

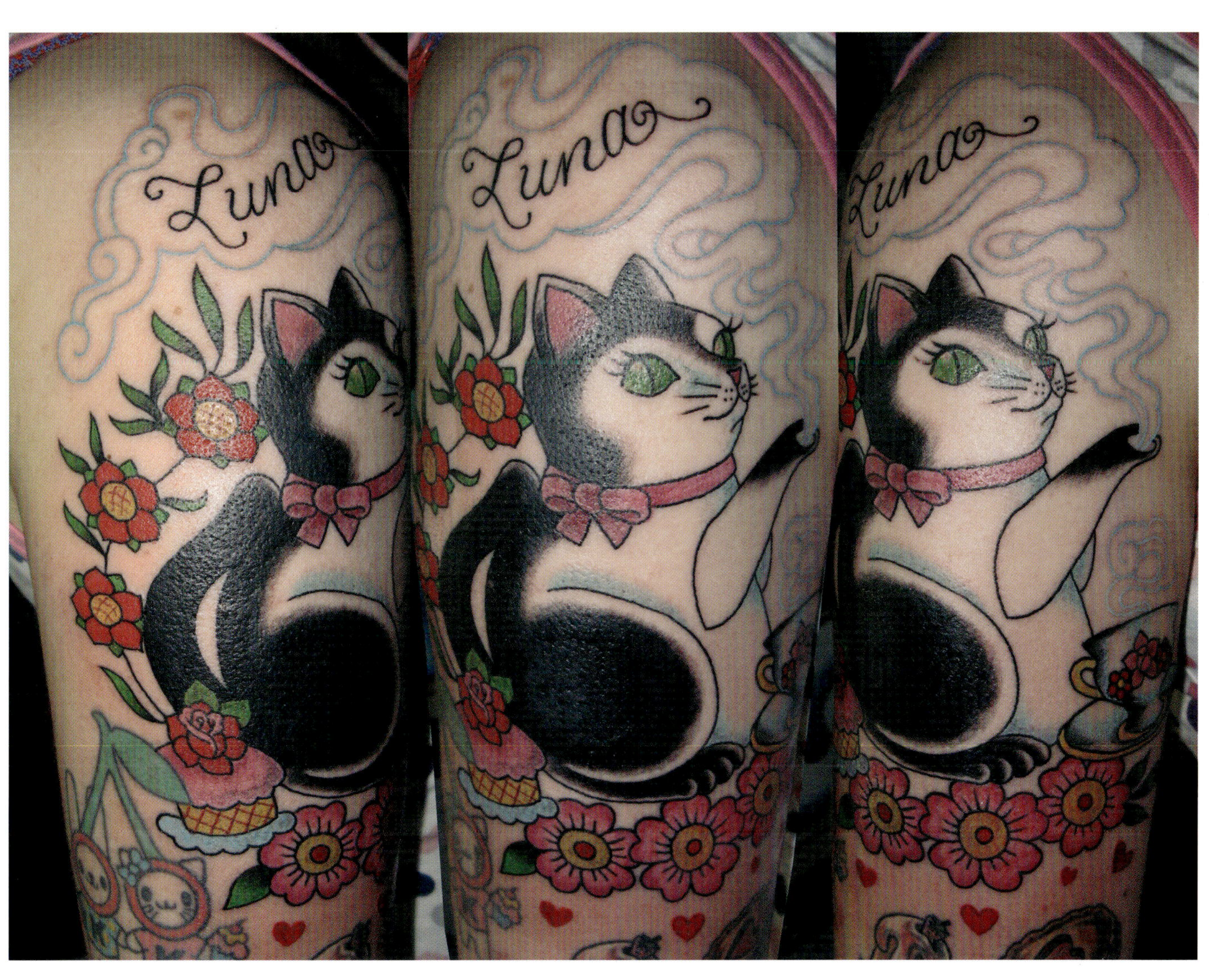
Luna
Luna
Luna

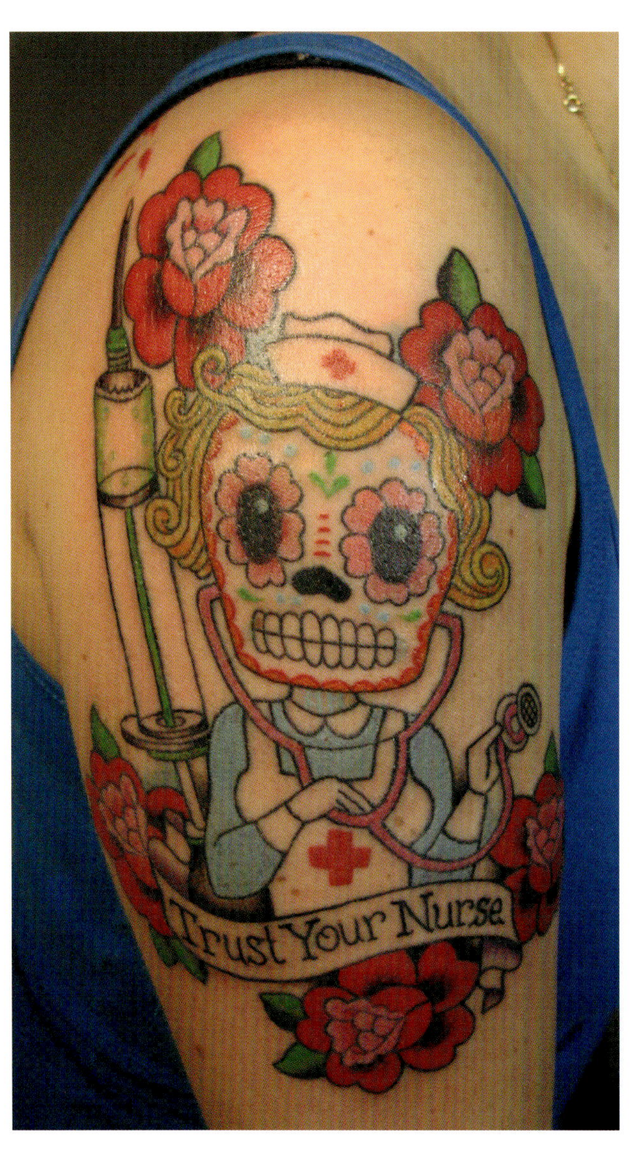
Trust Your Nurse

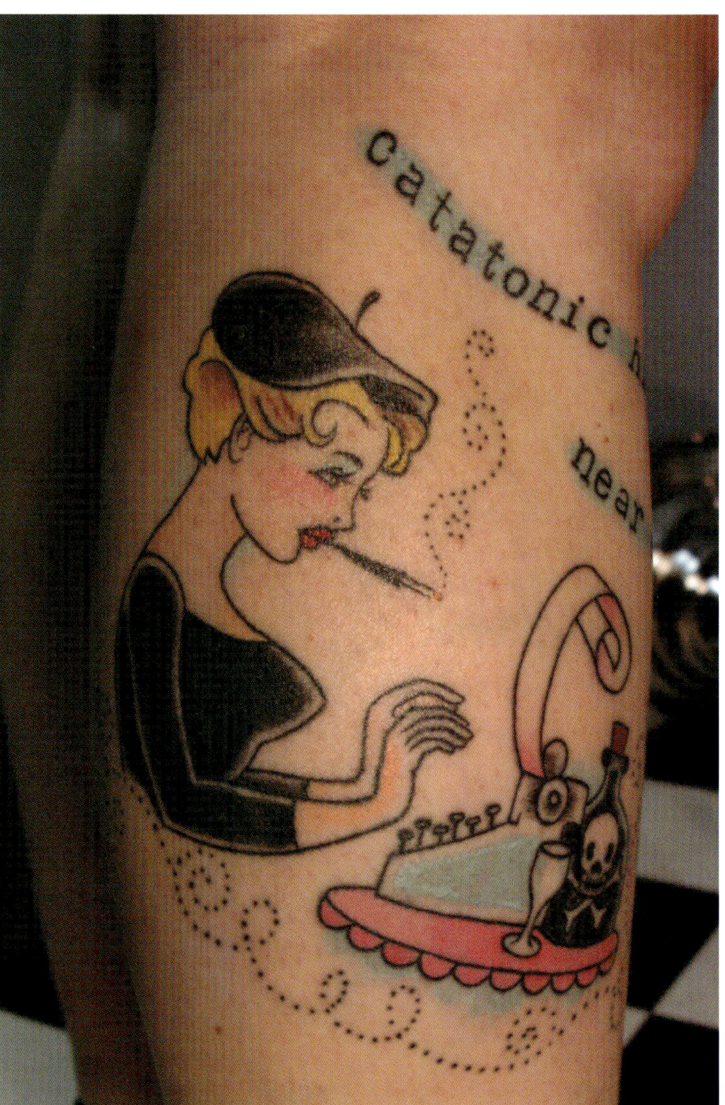
catatonic
near

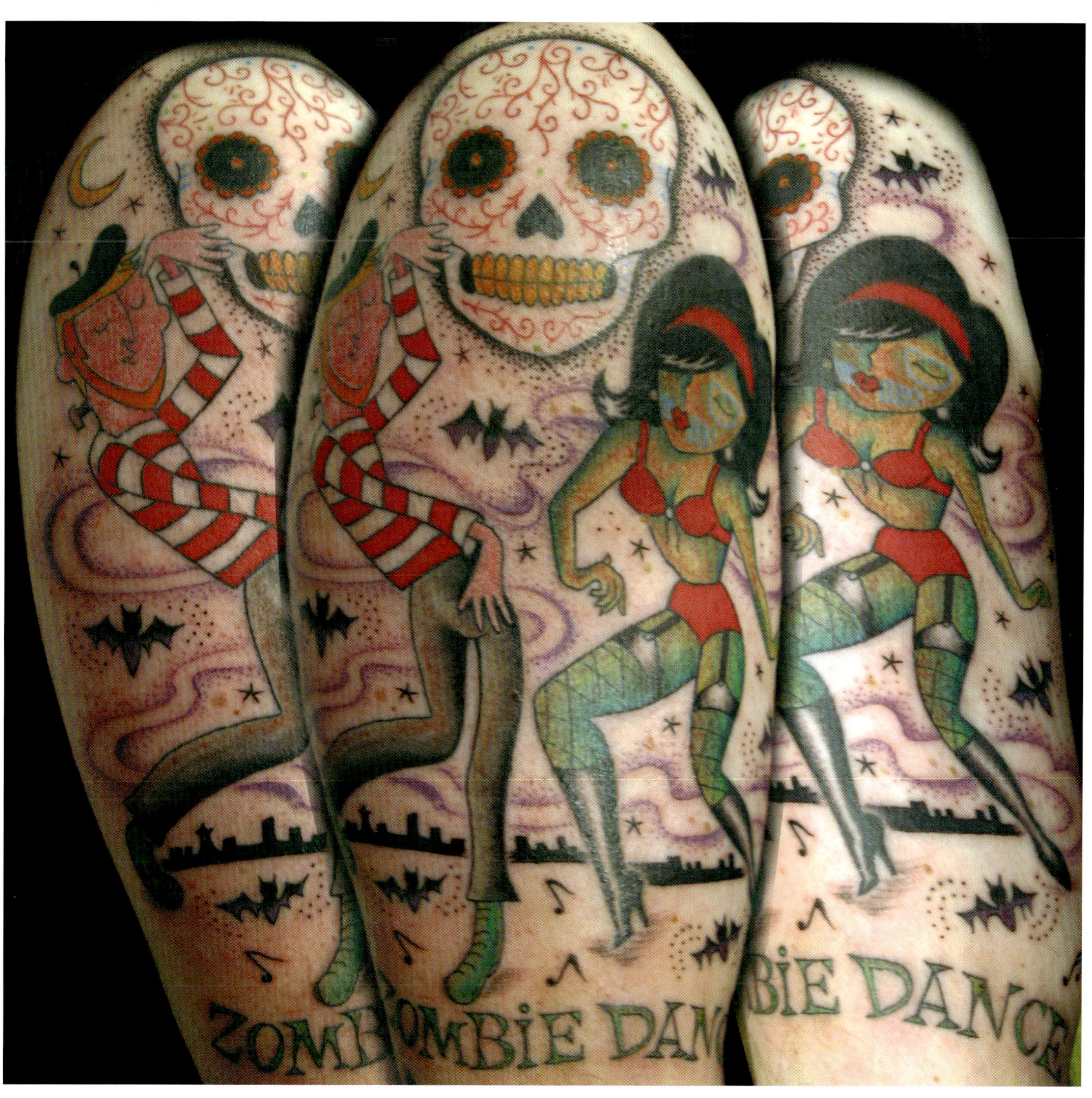
ZOMBIE DANCE

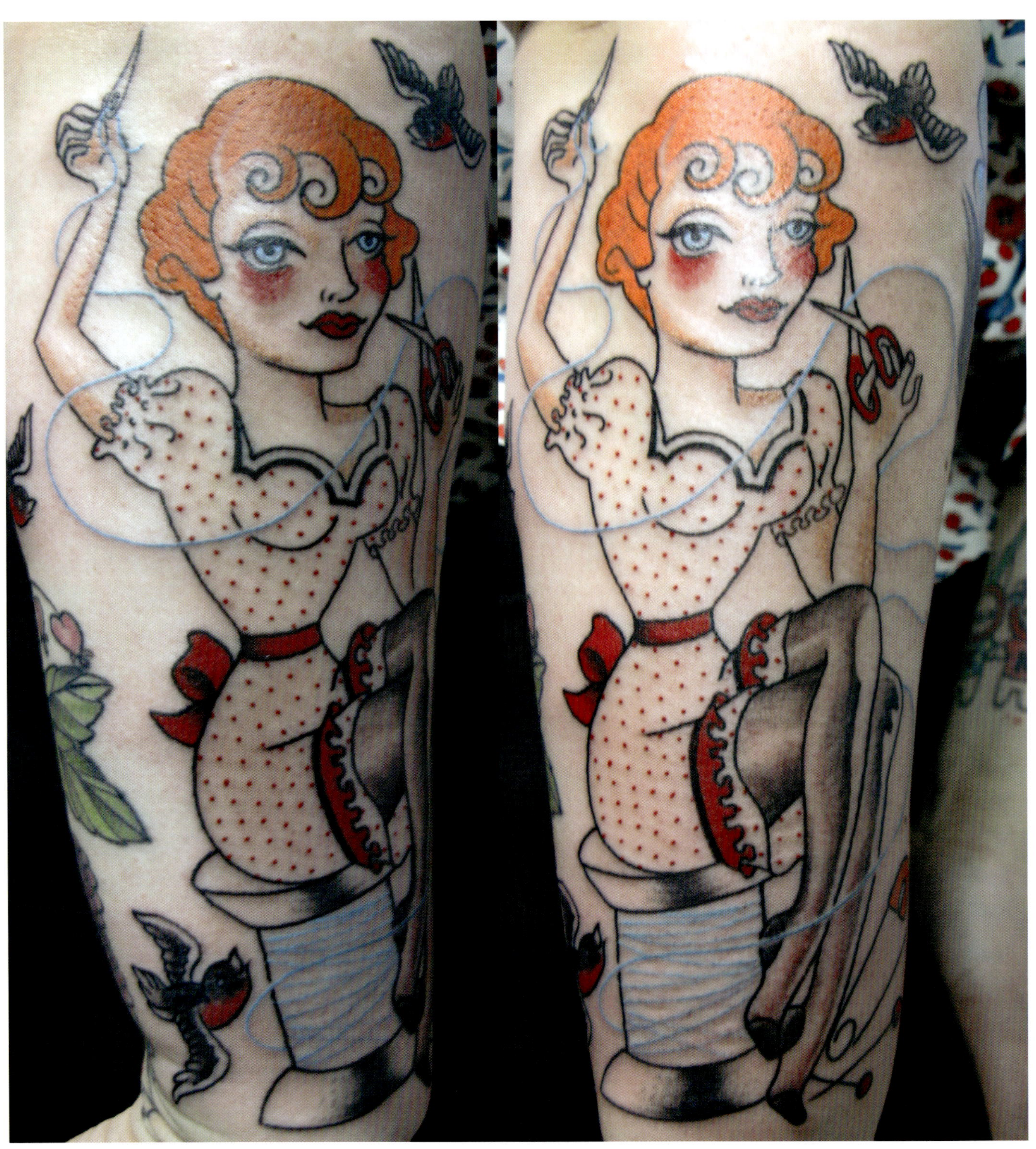

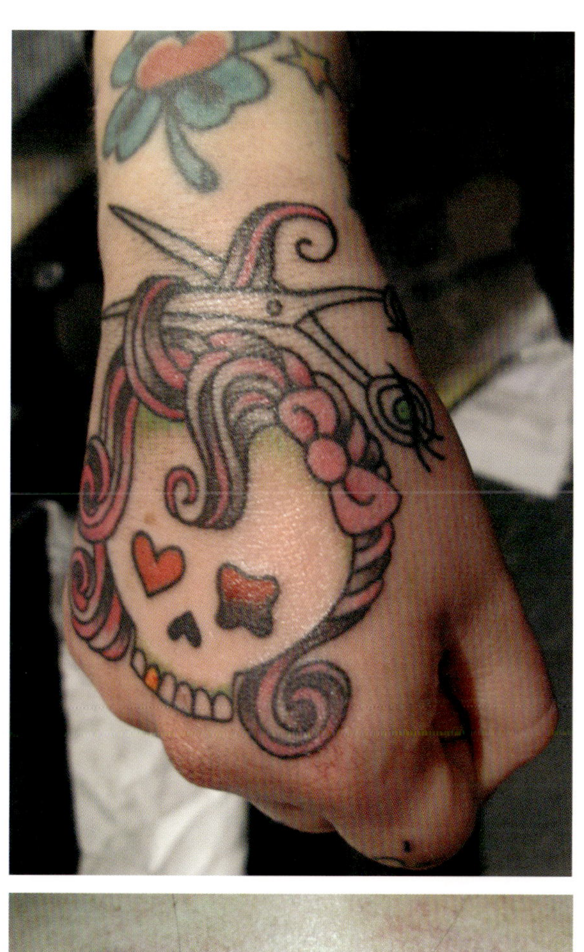

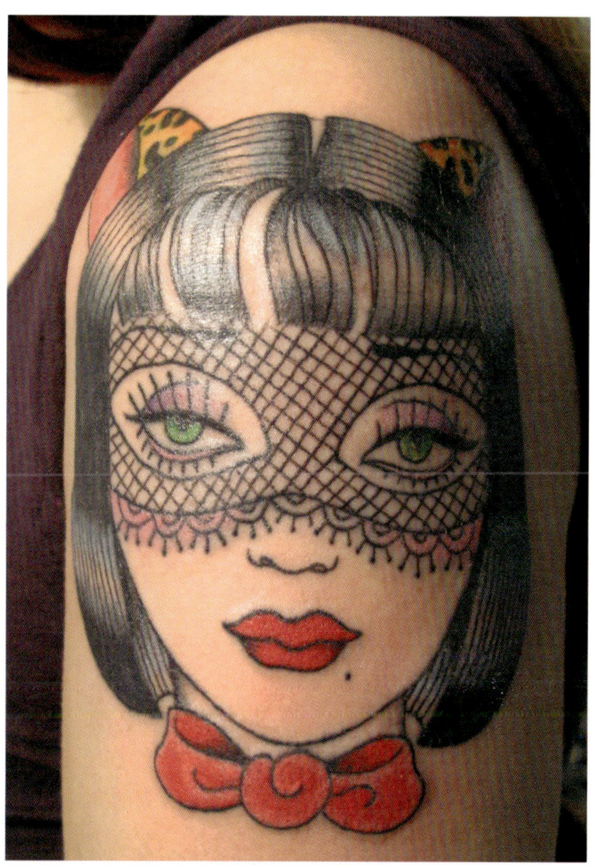

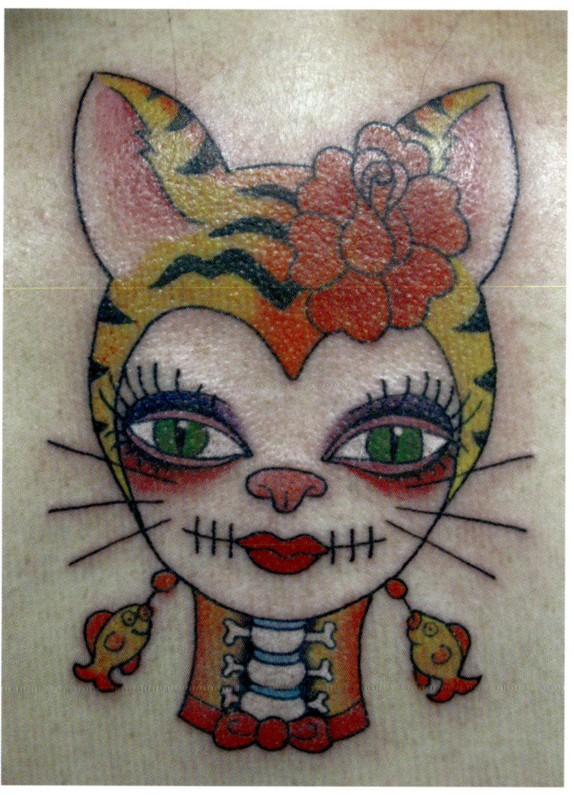

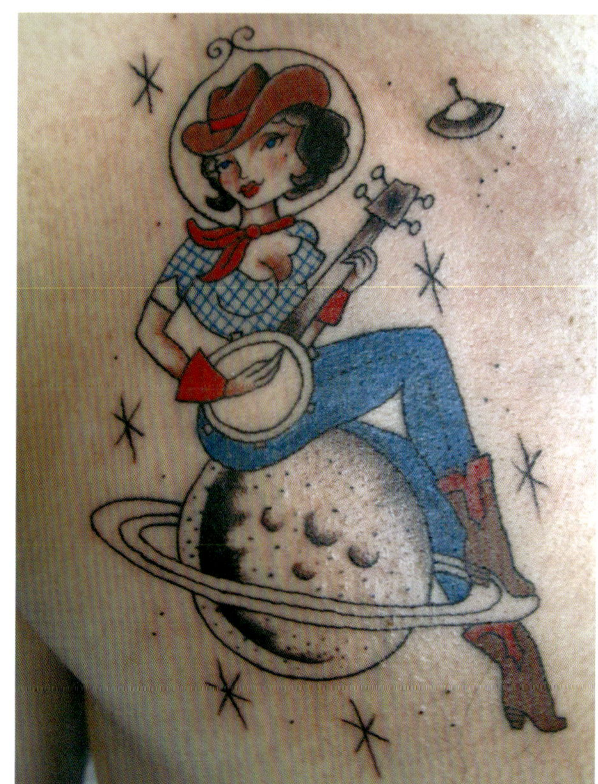

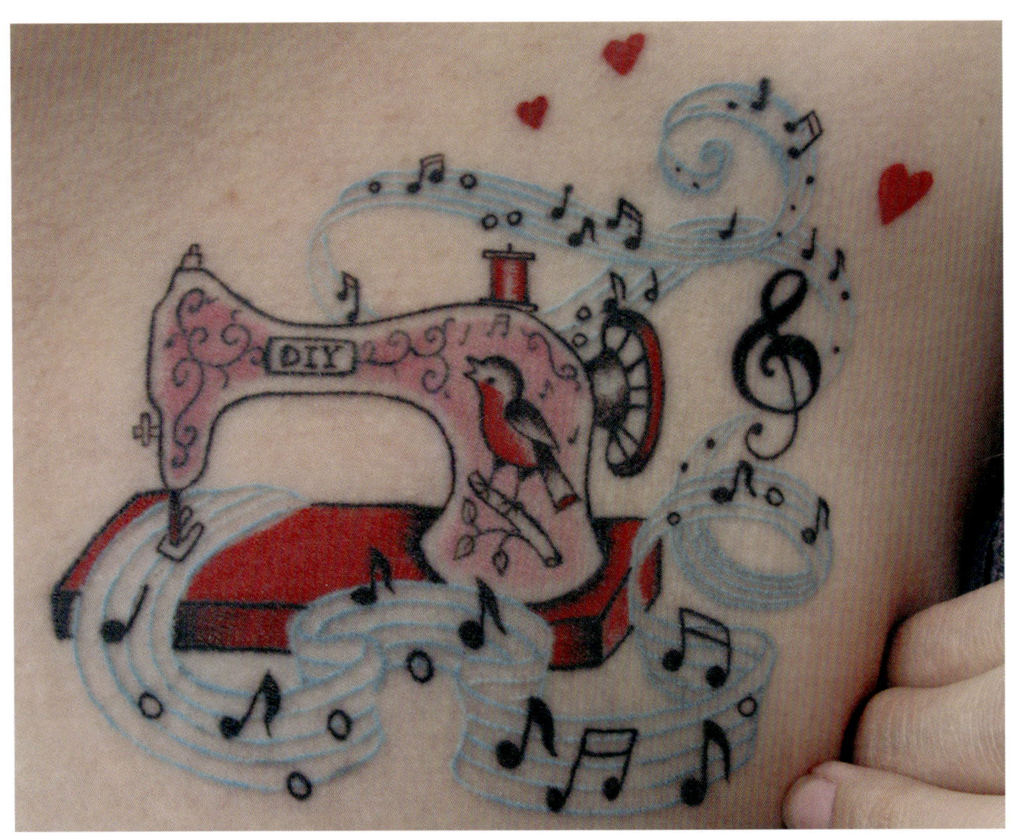
DIY

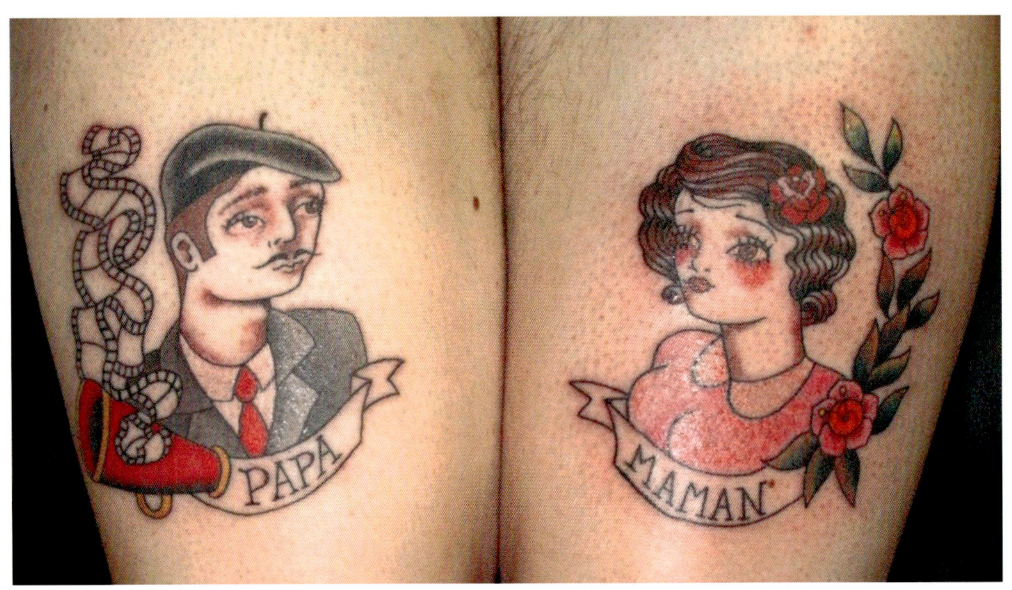
PAPA
MAMAN

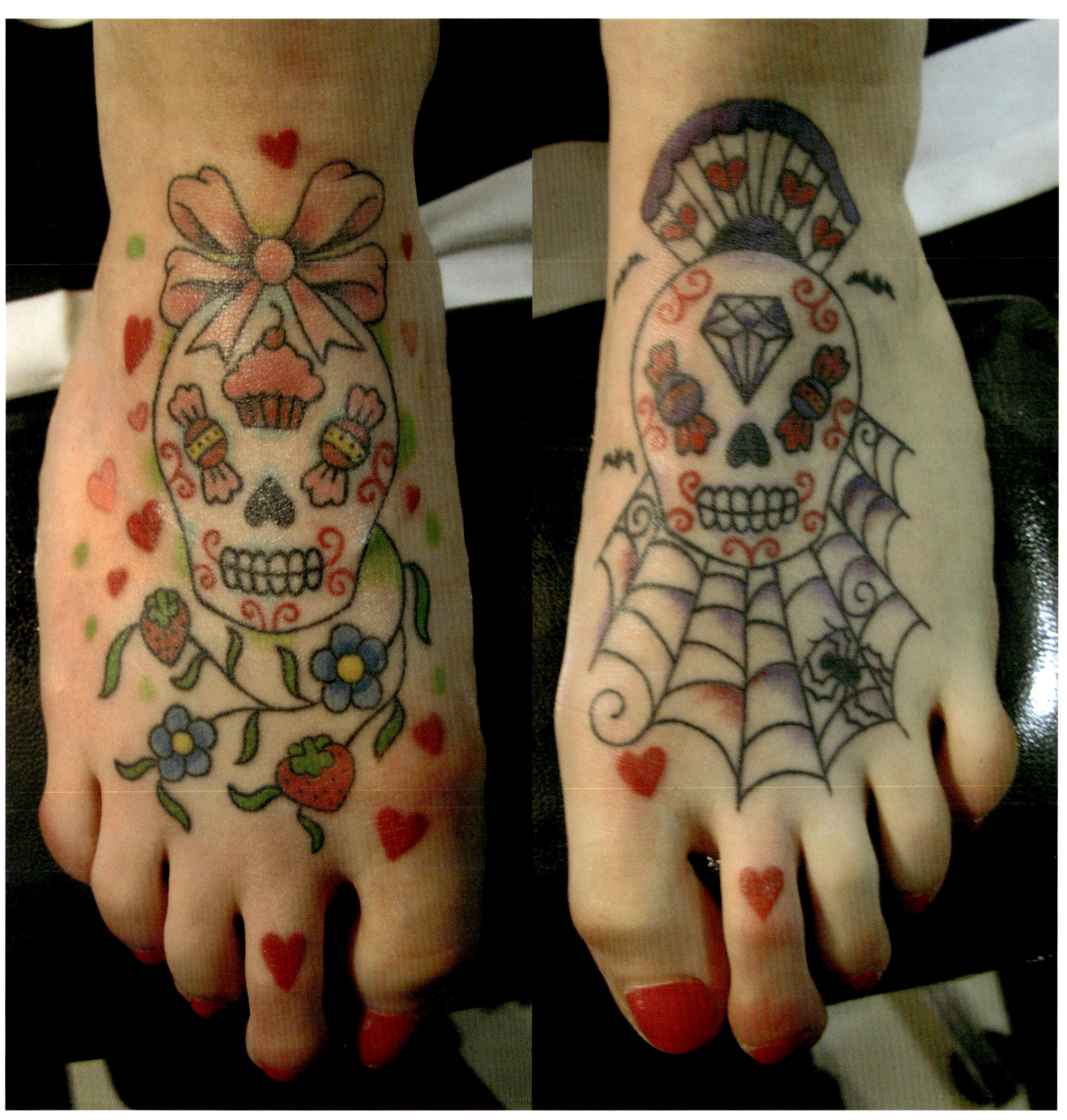

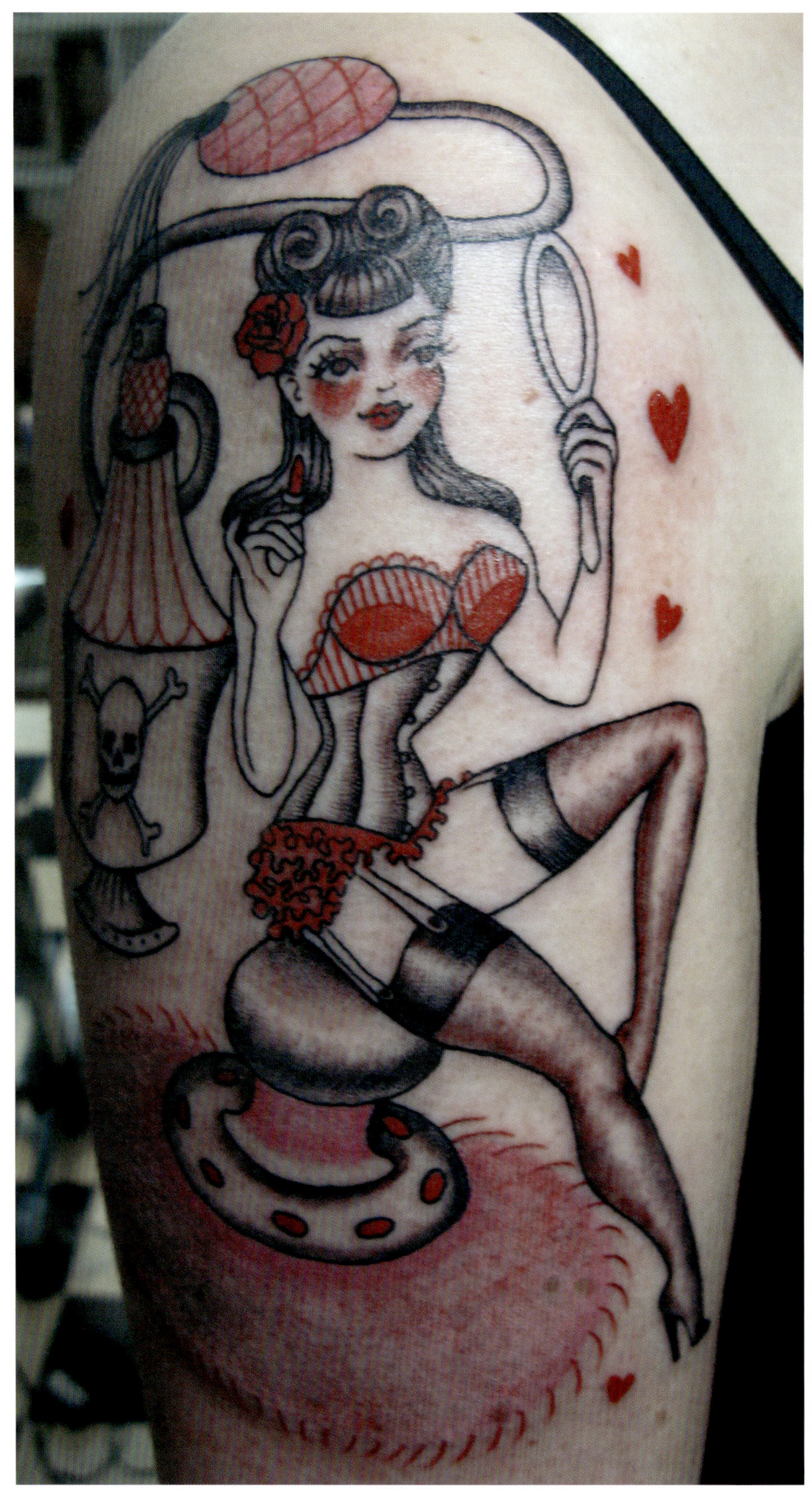

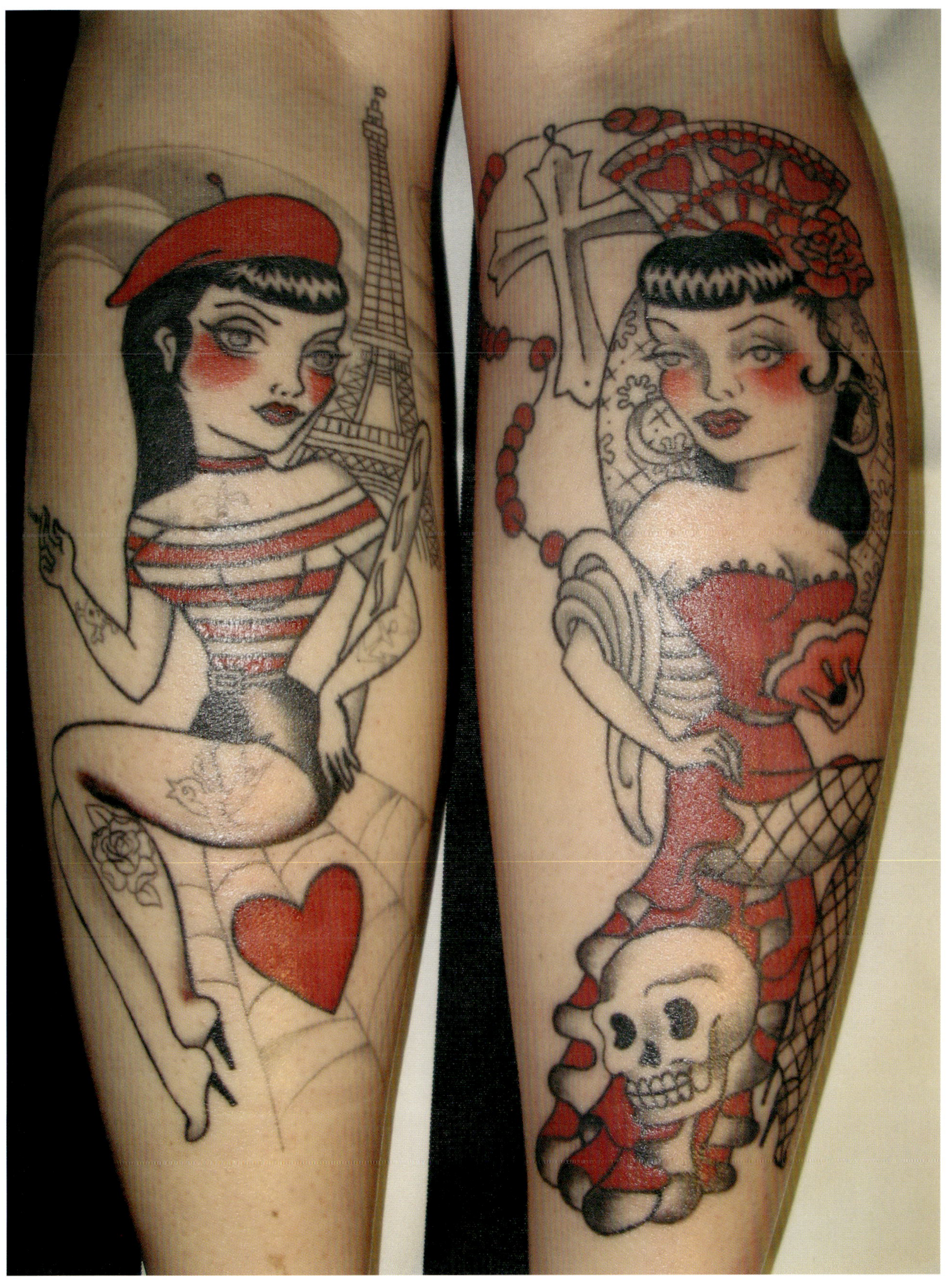

Steve Byrne

After many years tattooing all over the world and extensively throughout my native England, my family and I decided to relocate to the United States in August of 2009.

I currently co-own Rock Of Ages Tattoo in Austin, Texas along with Tony Hundahl.

My love for tattooing has never faltered. The desire to keep moving onwards and upwards has stayed with me throughout.

The desire to surpass my clients' expectations is very important to me, and I'm also very conscious of doing good work that my peers will enjoy seeing.

Being an honest and real tattooer is a matter of pride for me. I've always believed that you're only as good as the last tattoo you did so the pressure is on all the time.

Keep it secret. Keep it safe. S.O.G.G.

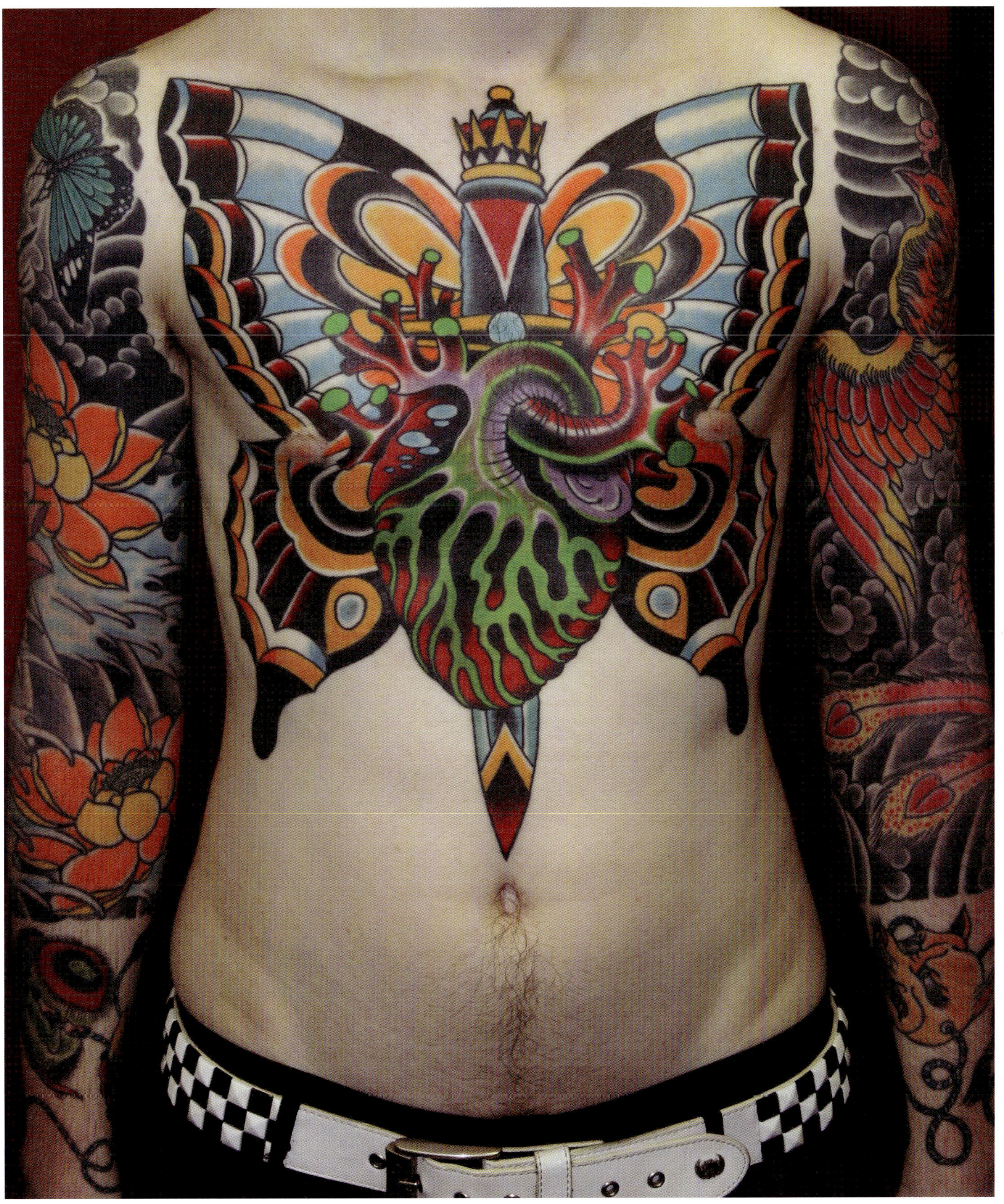

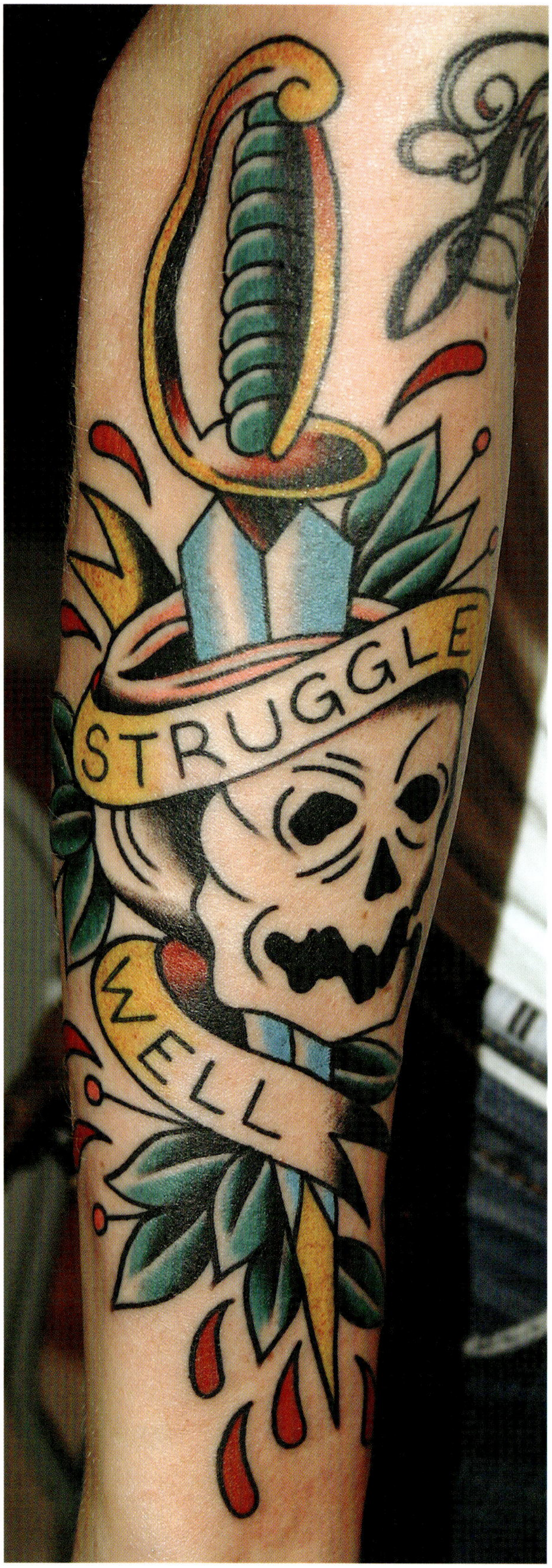

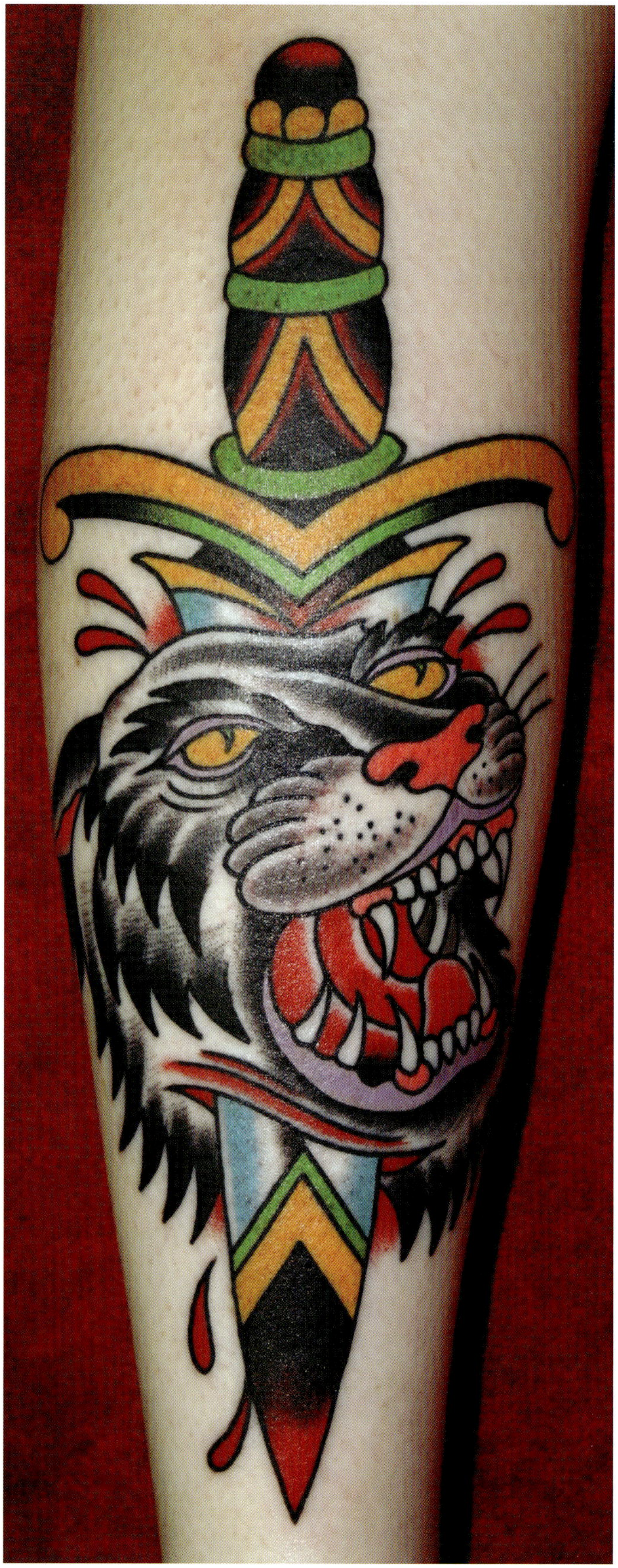

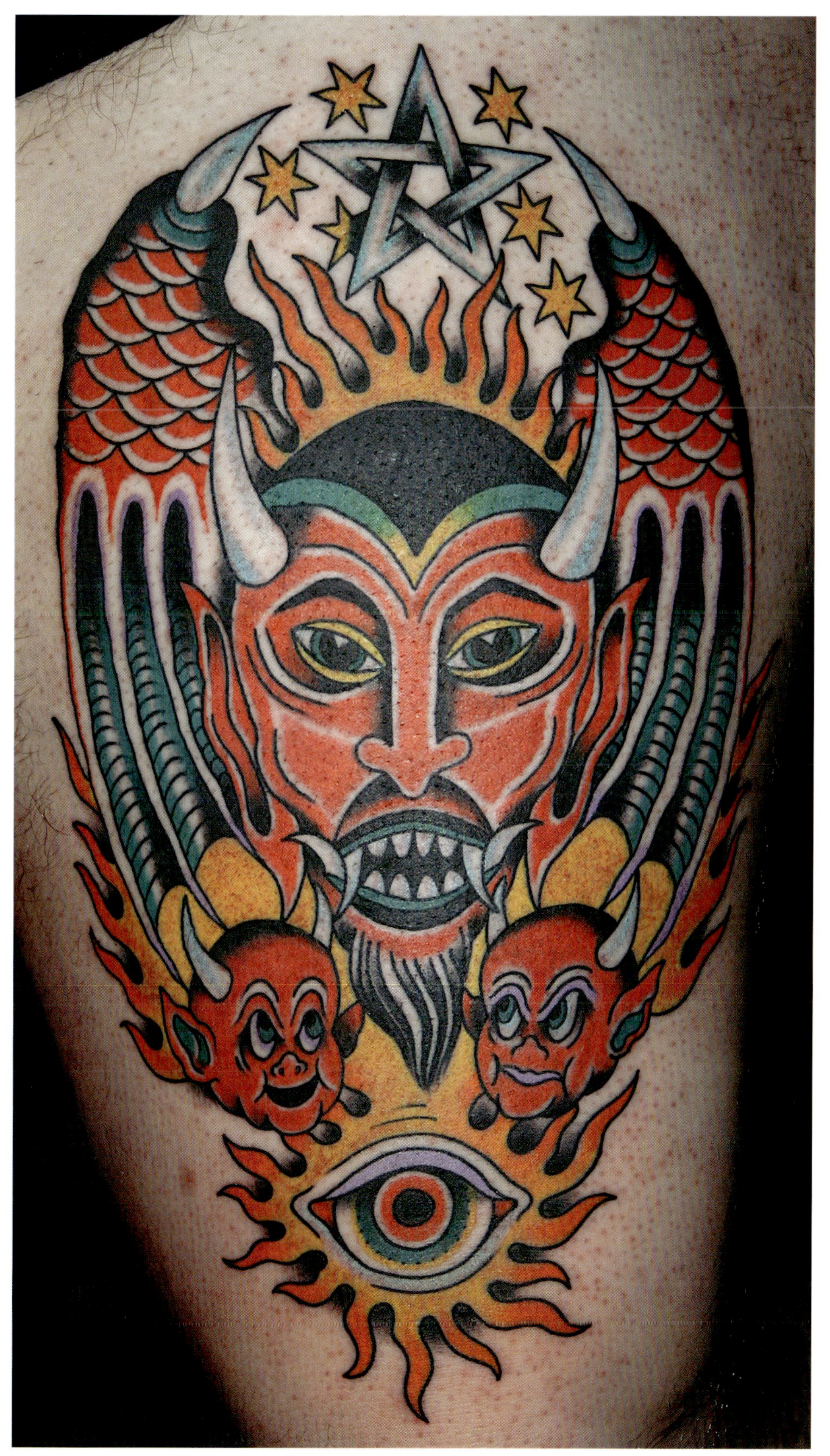

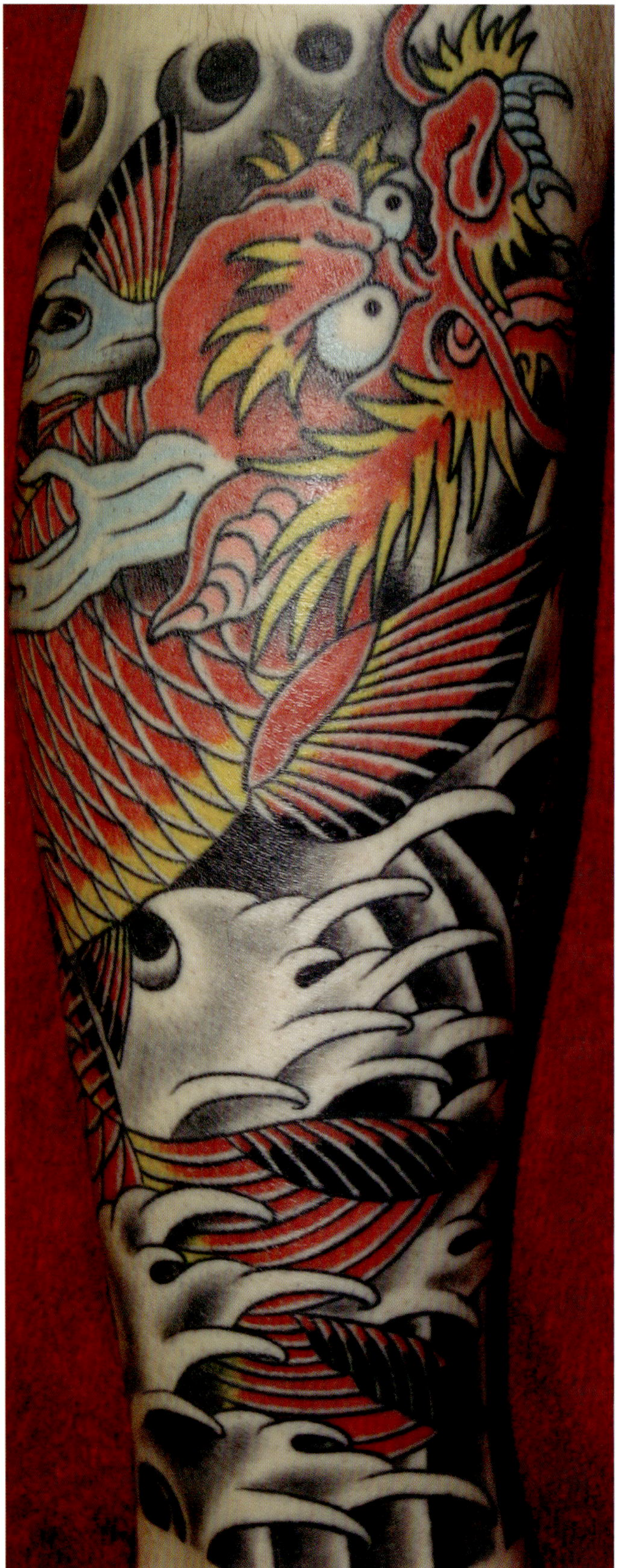

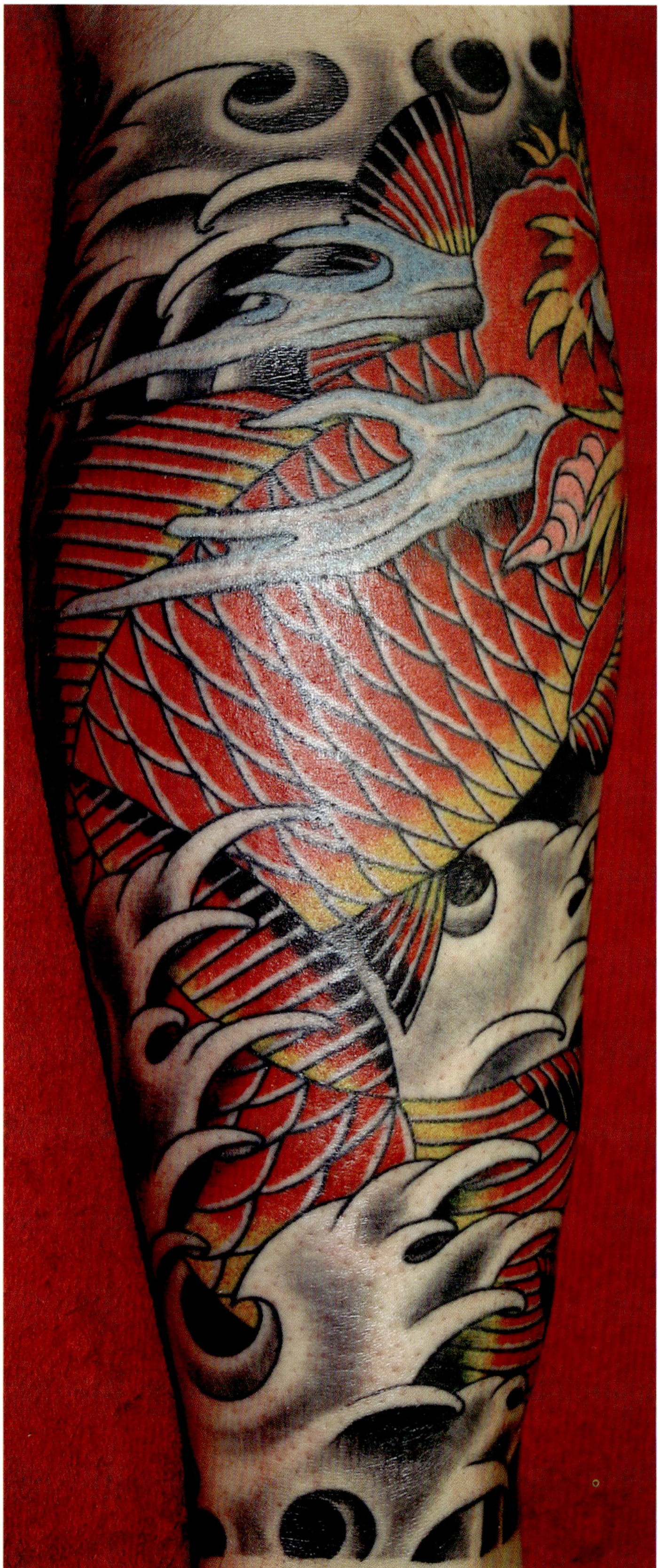

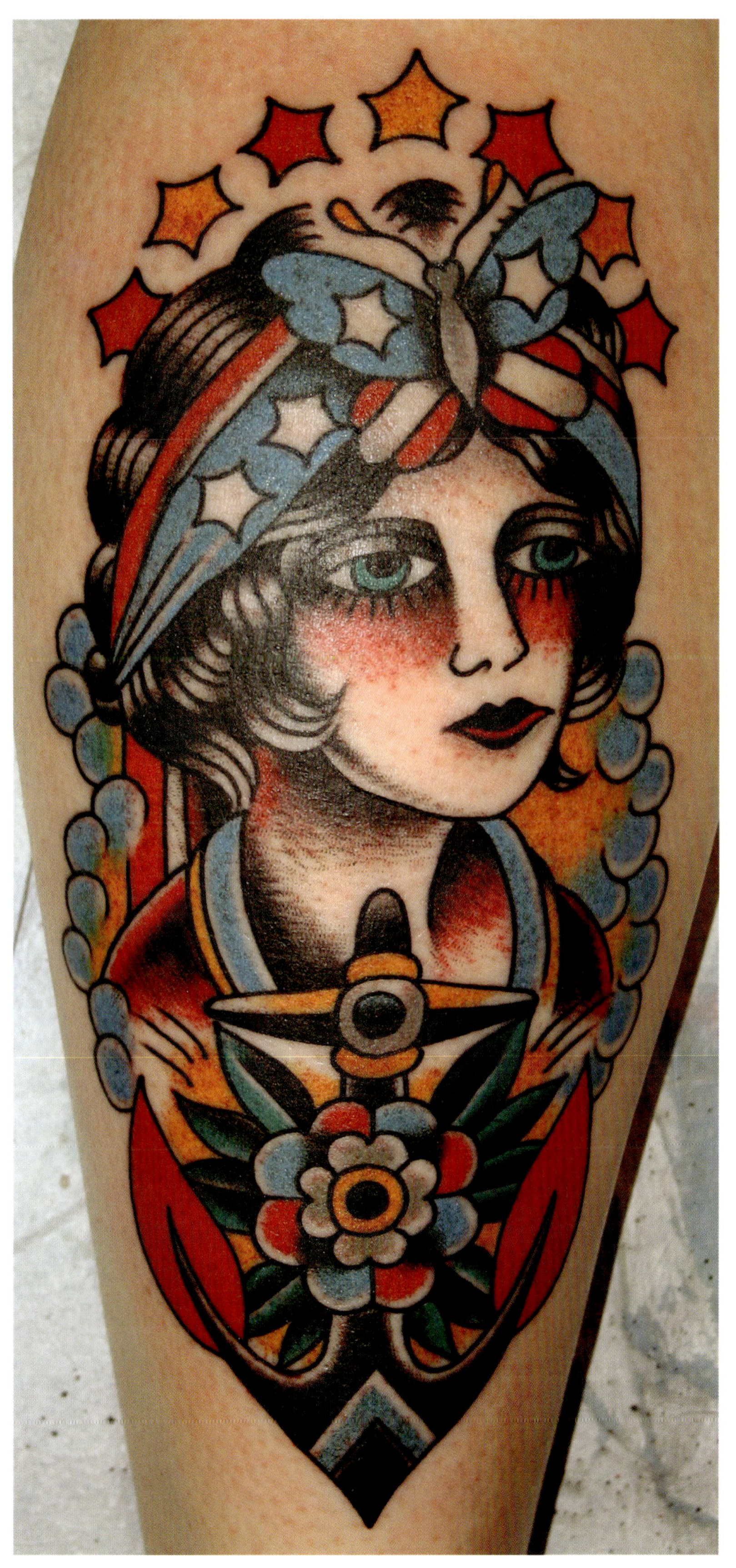

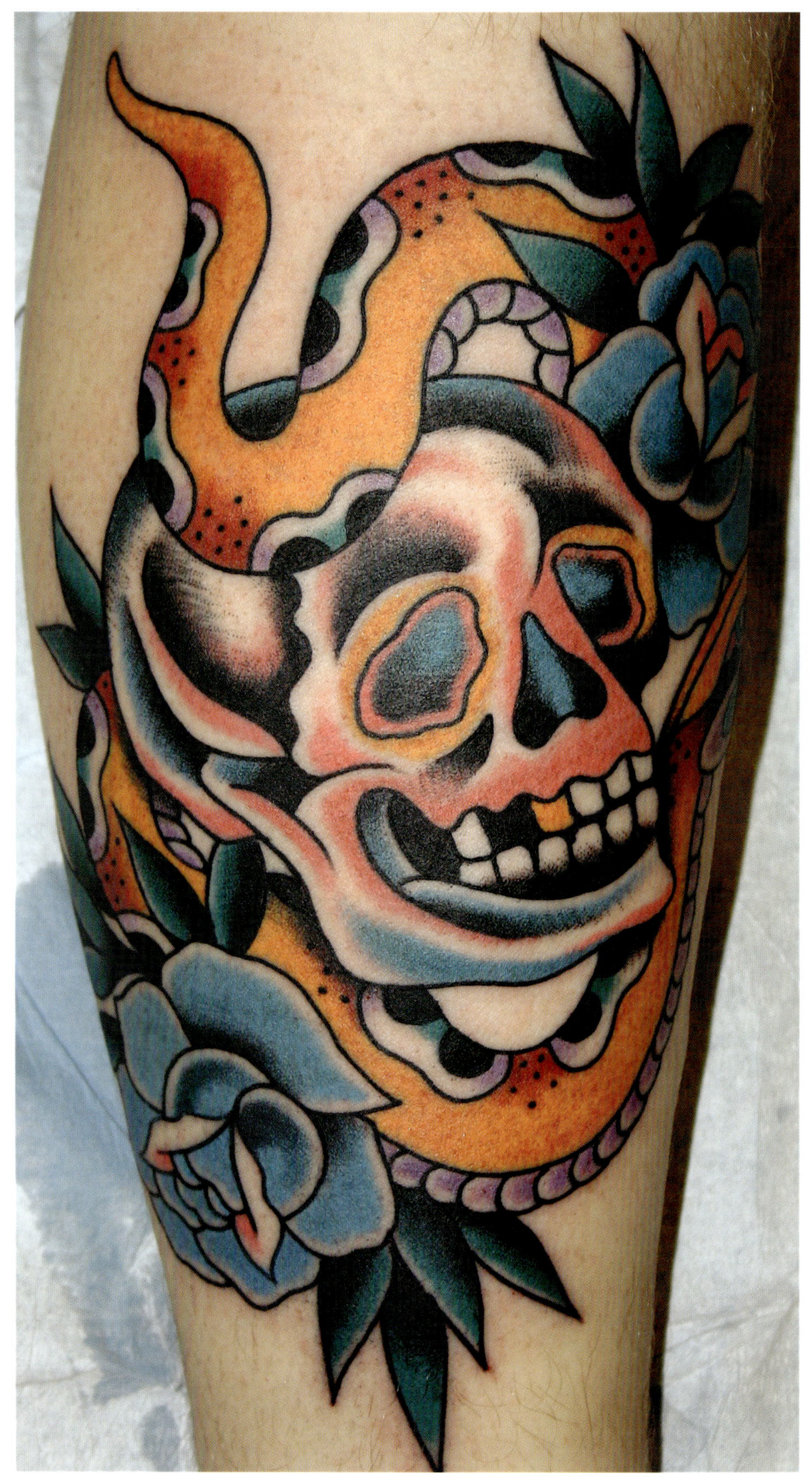

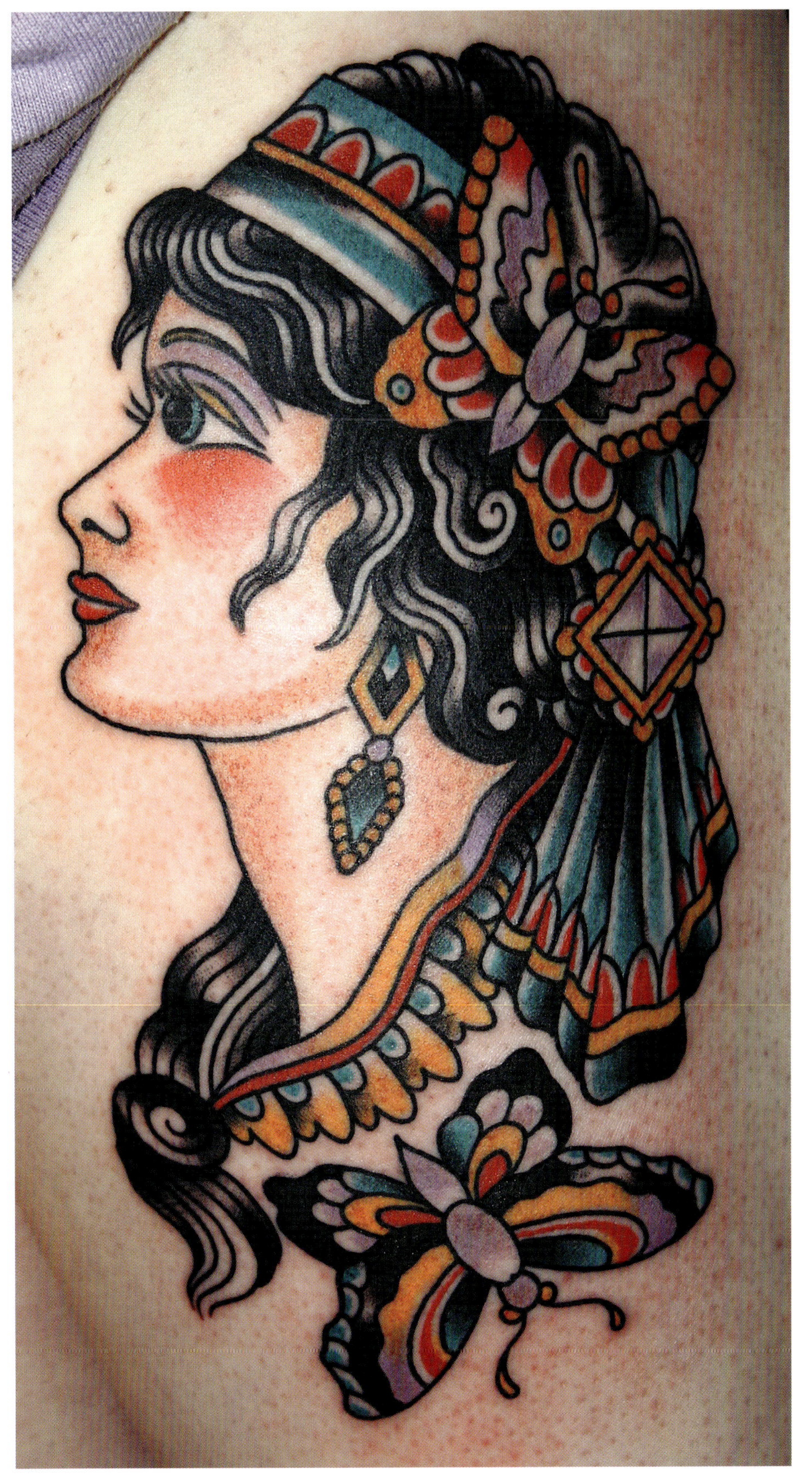

Jun Cha

The focus lies in the basics and foundation. I could never fully relate to being the "tattoo artist"- I'm just an artist. Especially now when that title has so many different qualities attached to it, I always emphasize that the art form still comes from the core skill of traditional drawing.

So my work revolves around the whole. At the center is what, how and why I choose to perceive things the way they are. Whatever is being used to communicate with the viewer or client in order to start a dialogue, whether it's a tattoo machine, paintbrush, or pencil, is just a difference in tools. For me, the ideas and thought process come from the same source.

Just as I feel a foundation in art is important to tattooing, I also feel that the history behind the tattoo culture is important. As the community youngster, I was fortunate to be educated and disciplined by pioneers like Baby Ray and Jose Lopez, who've spent their lives demonstrating the responsibility to contribute to both the art and culture behind tattooing.

This responsibility is one that the younger generation of tattooists can focus on and continue.

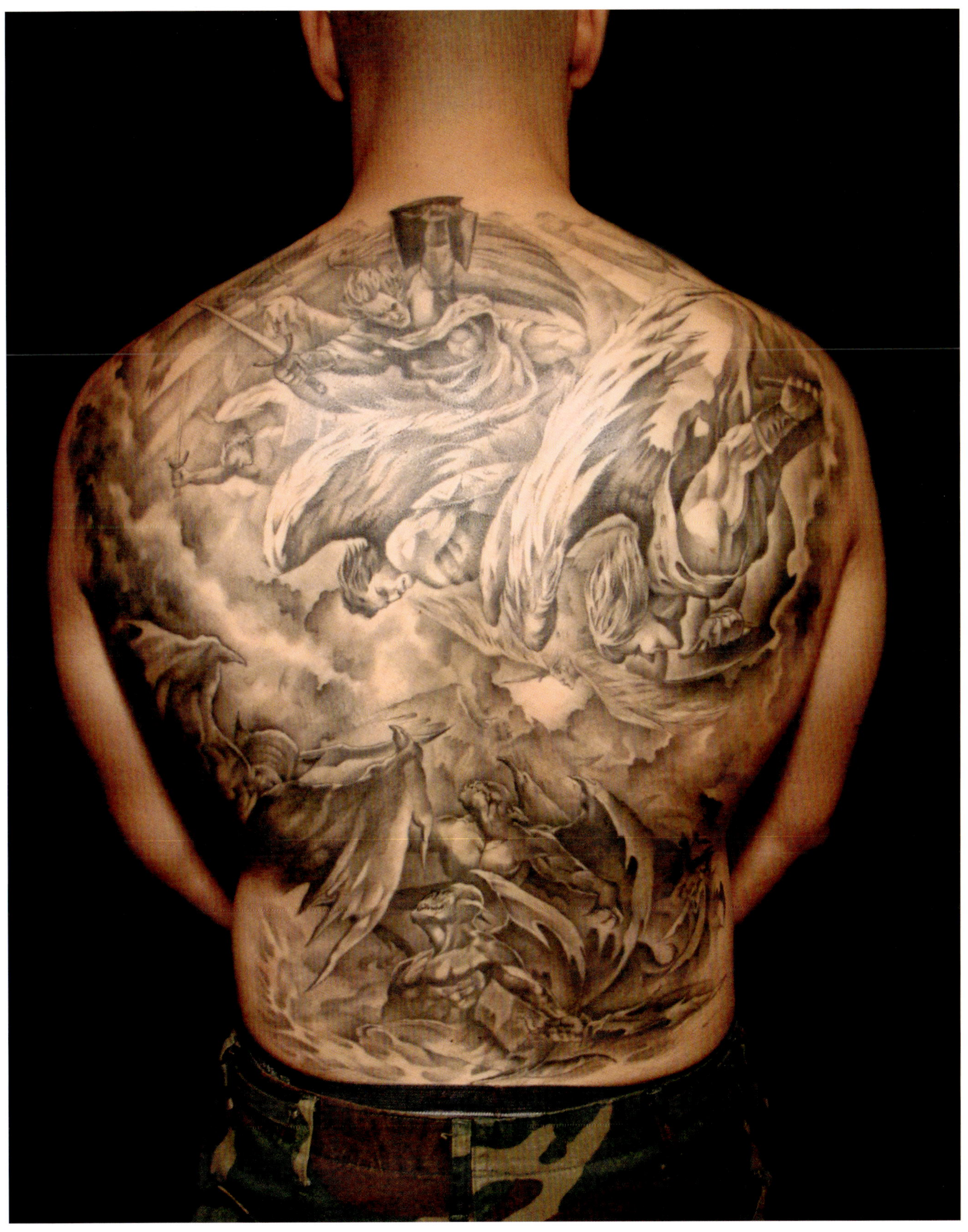

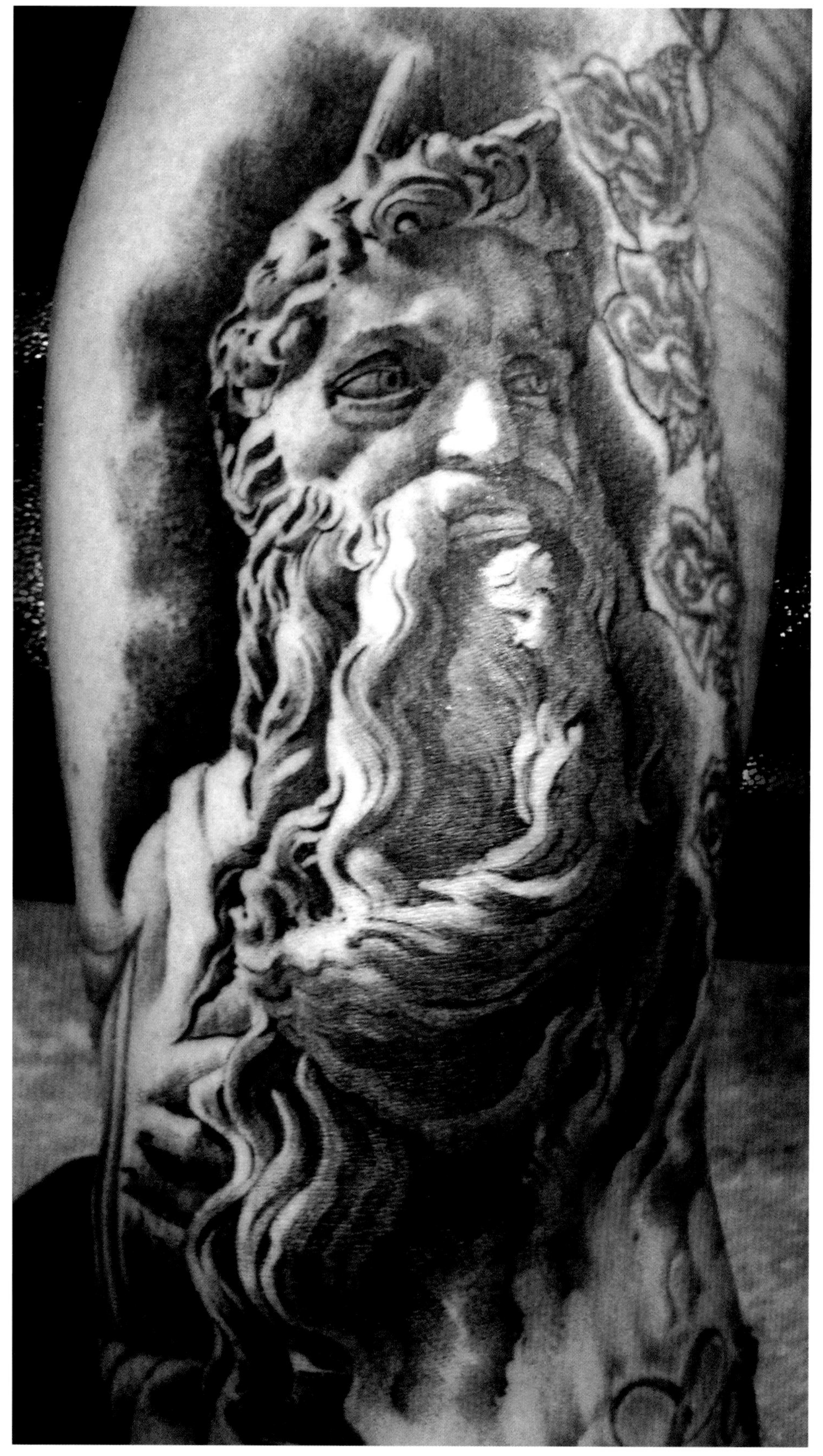

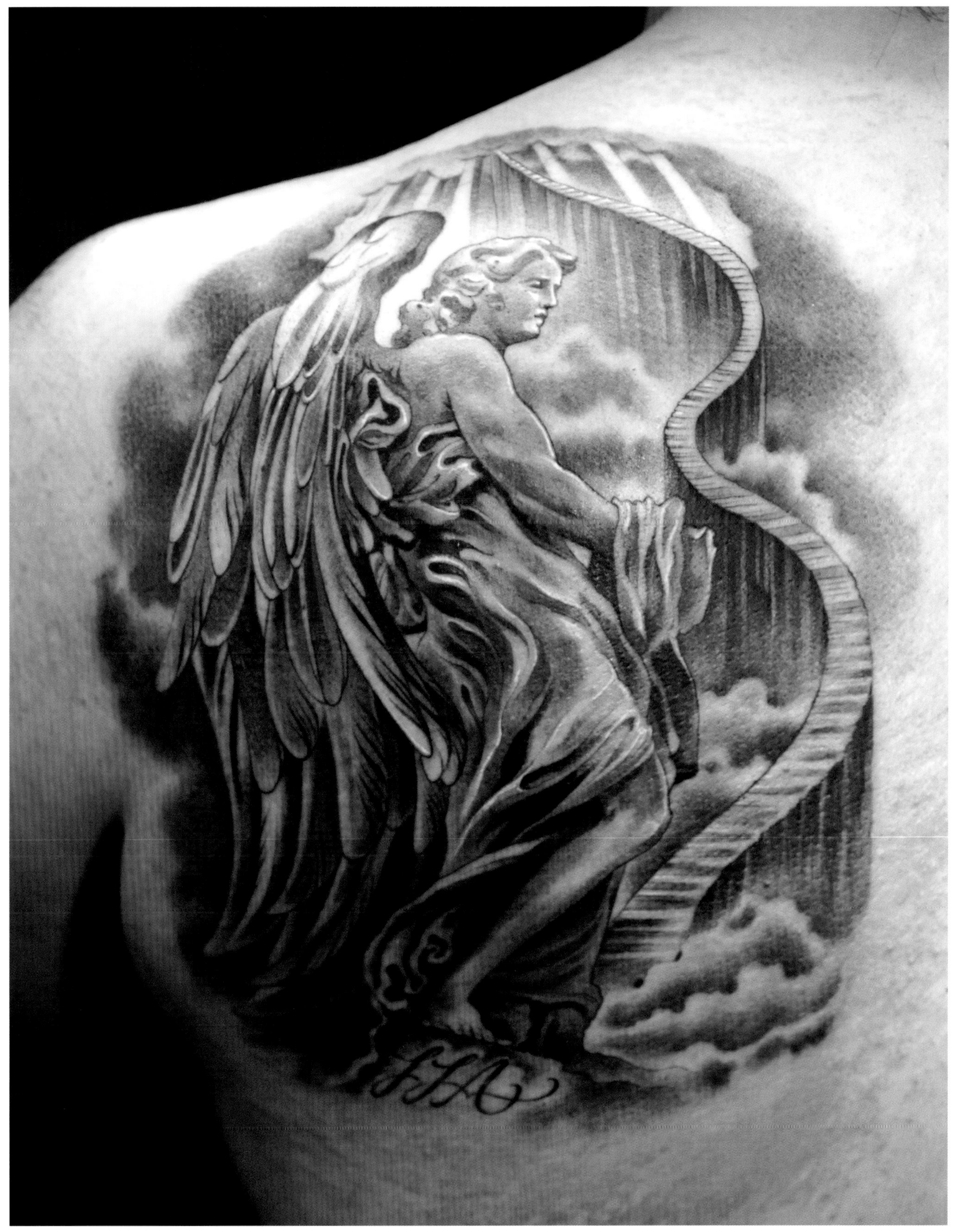

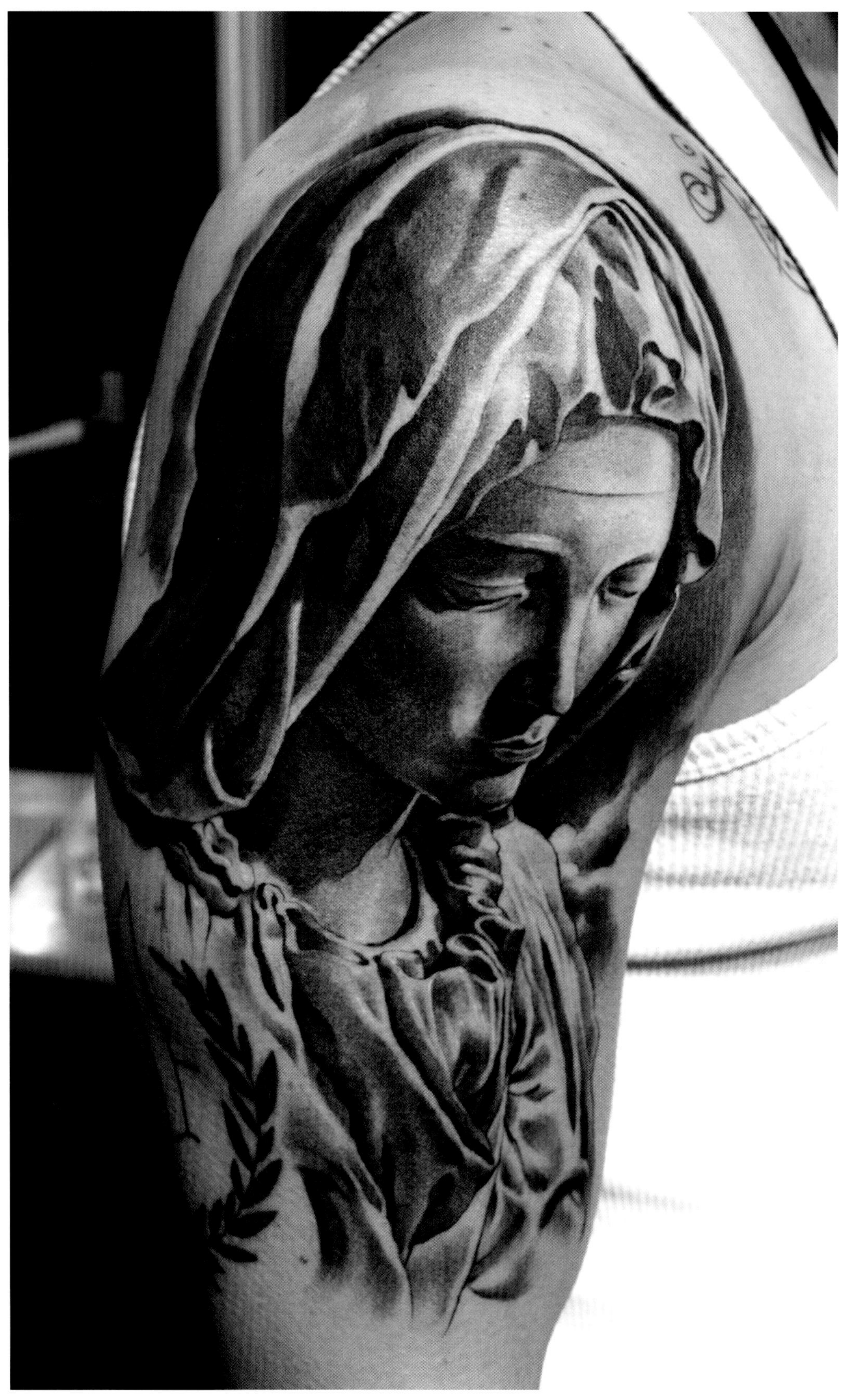

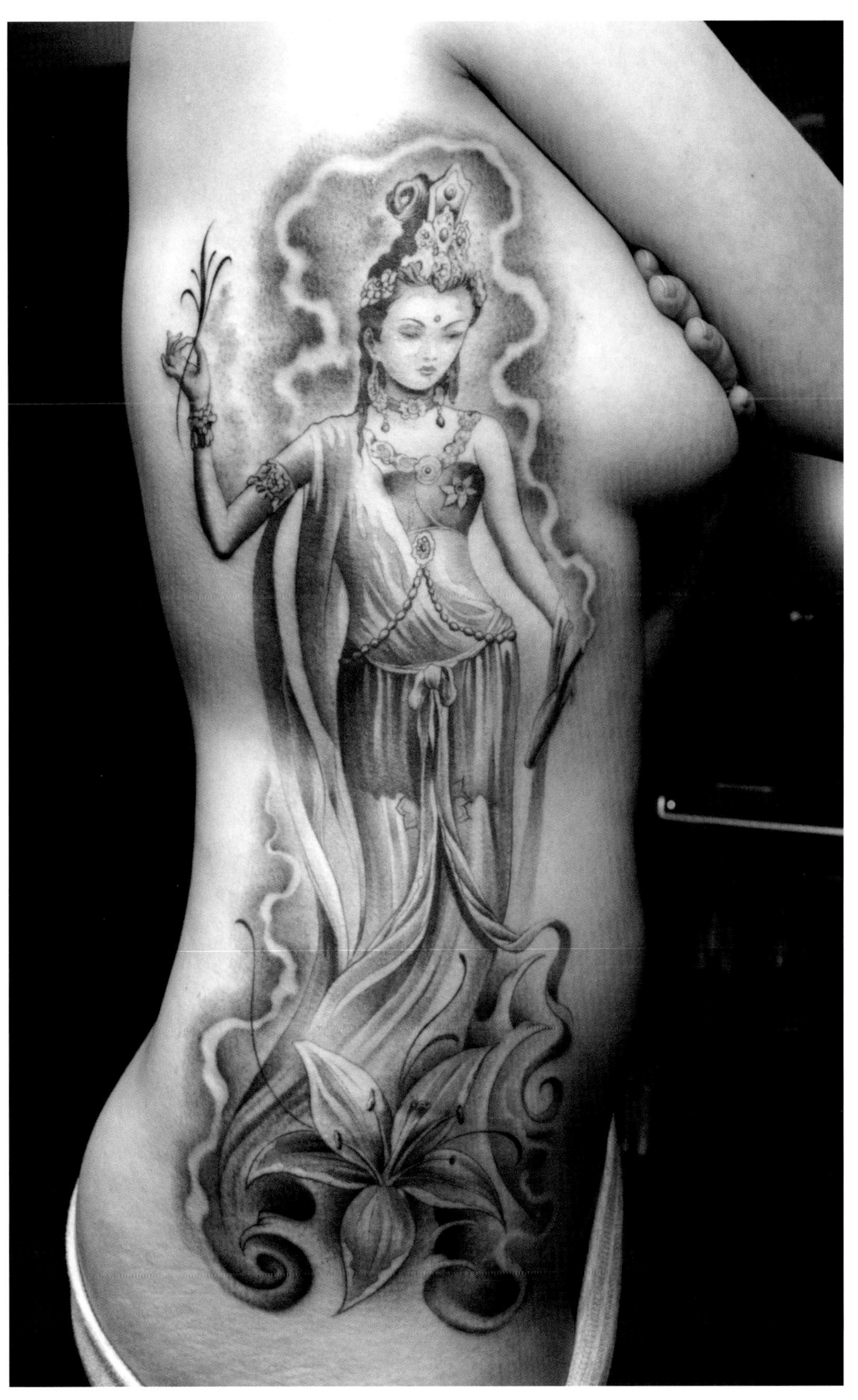

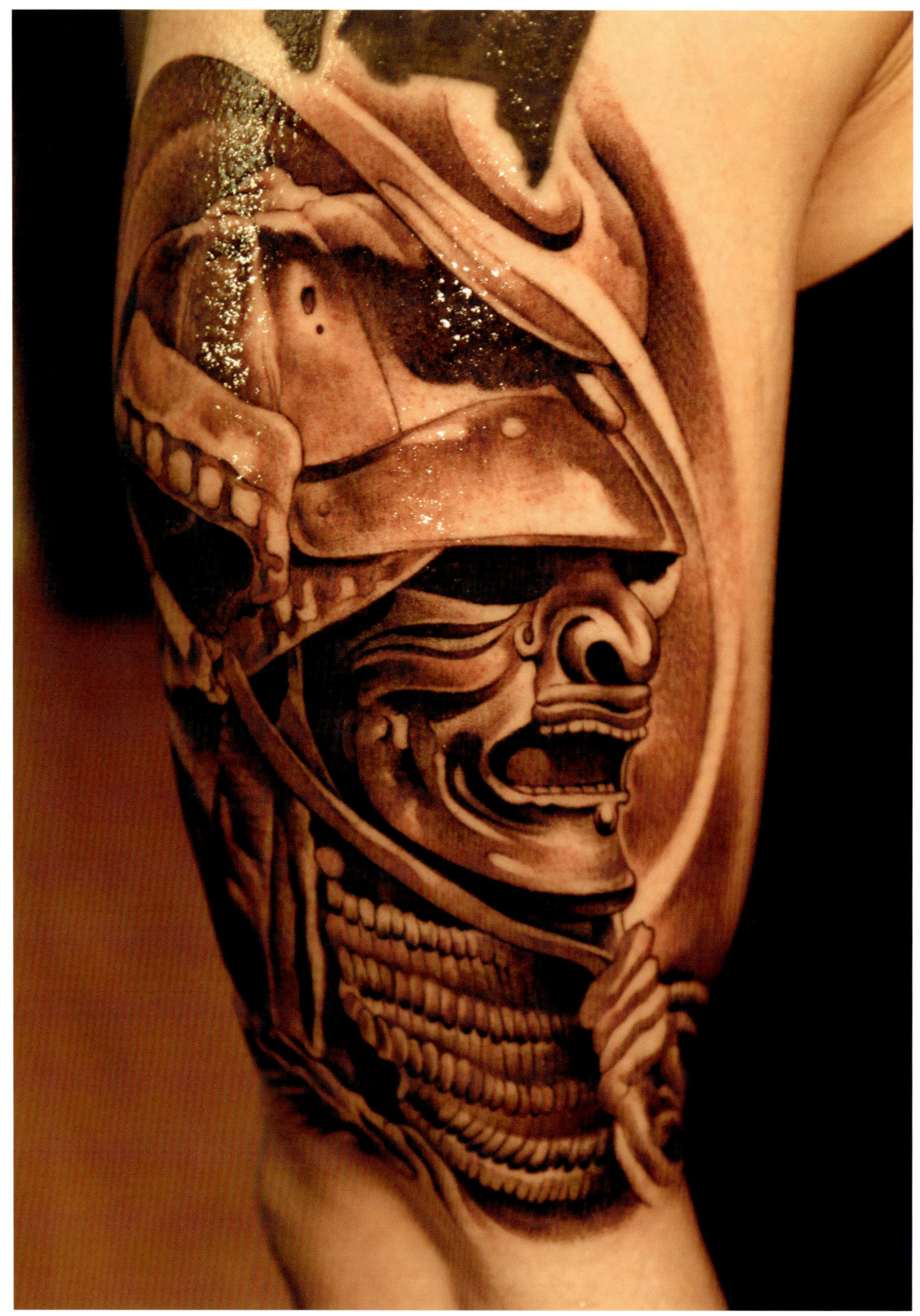

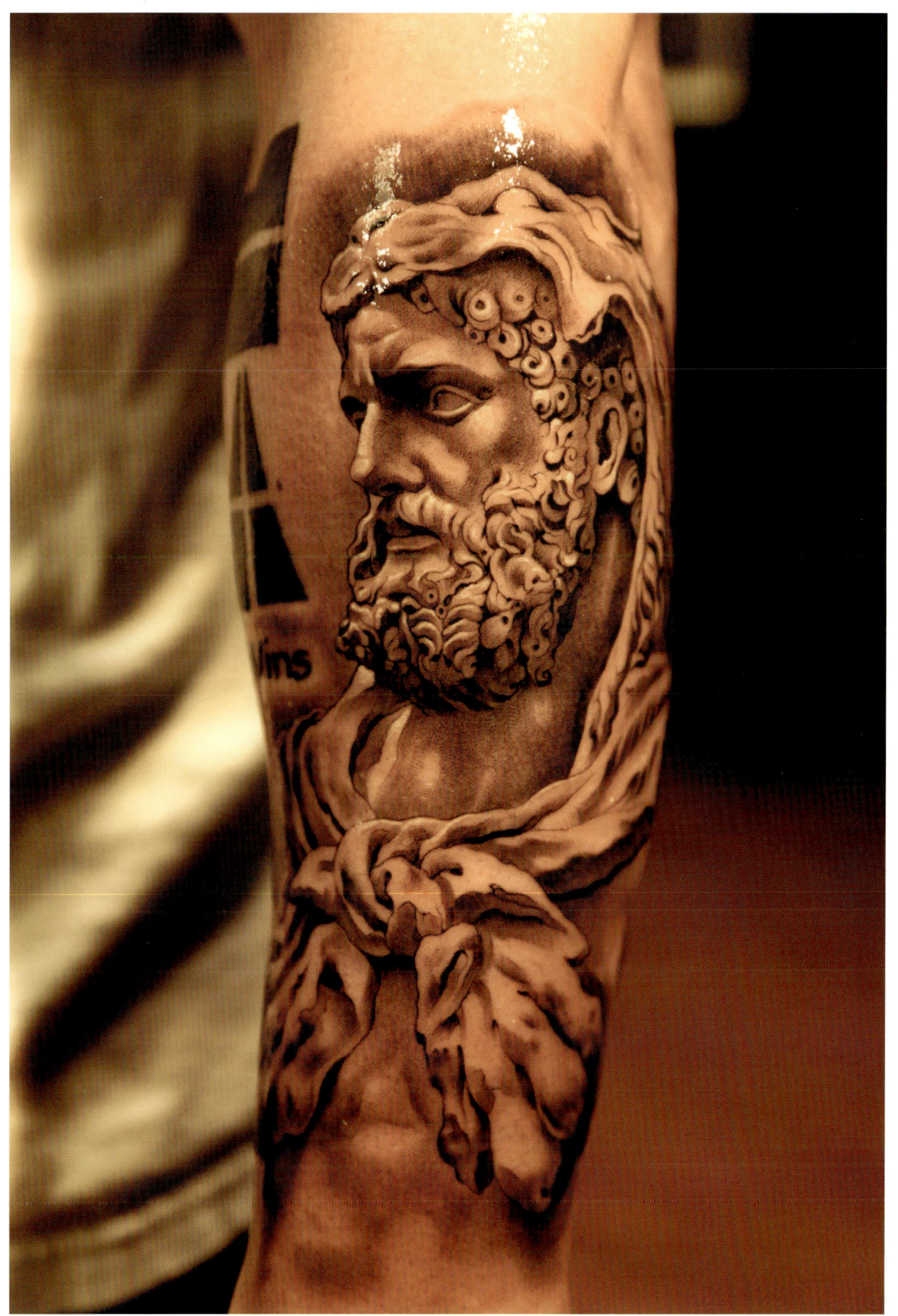

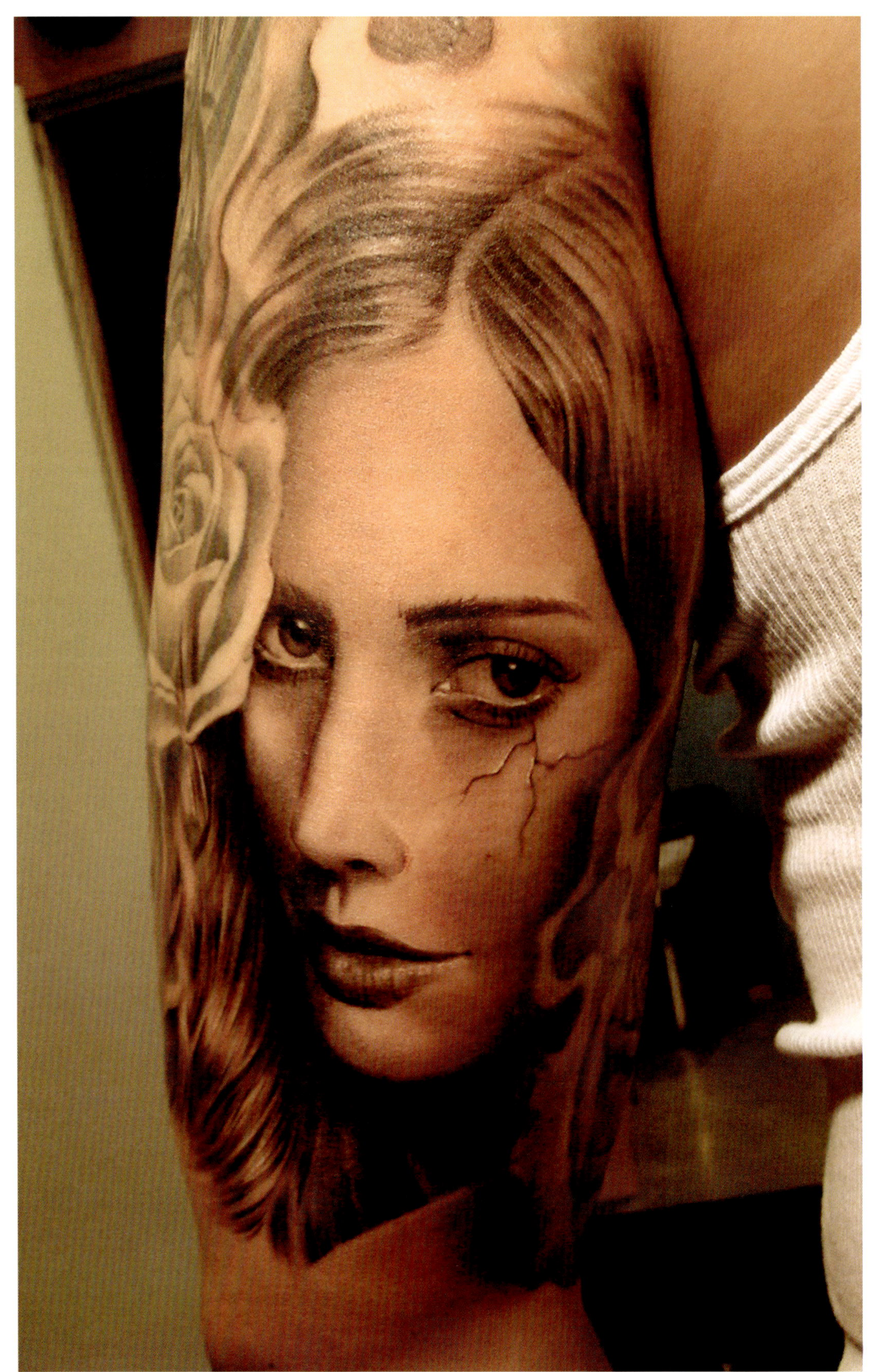

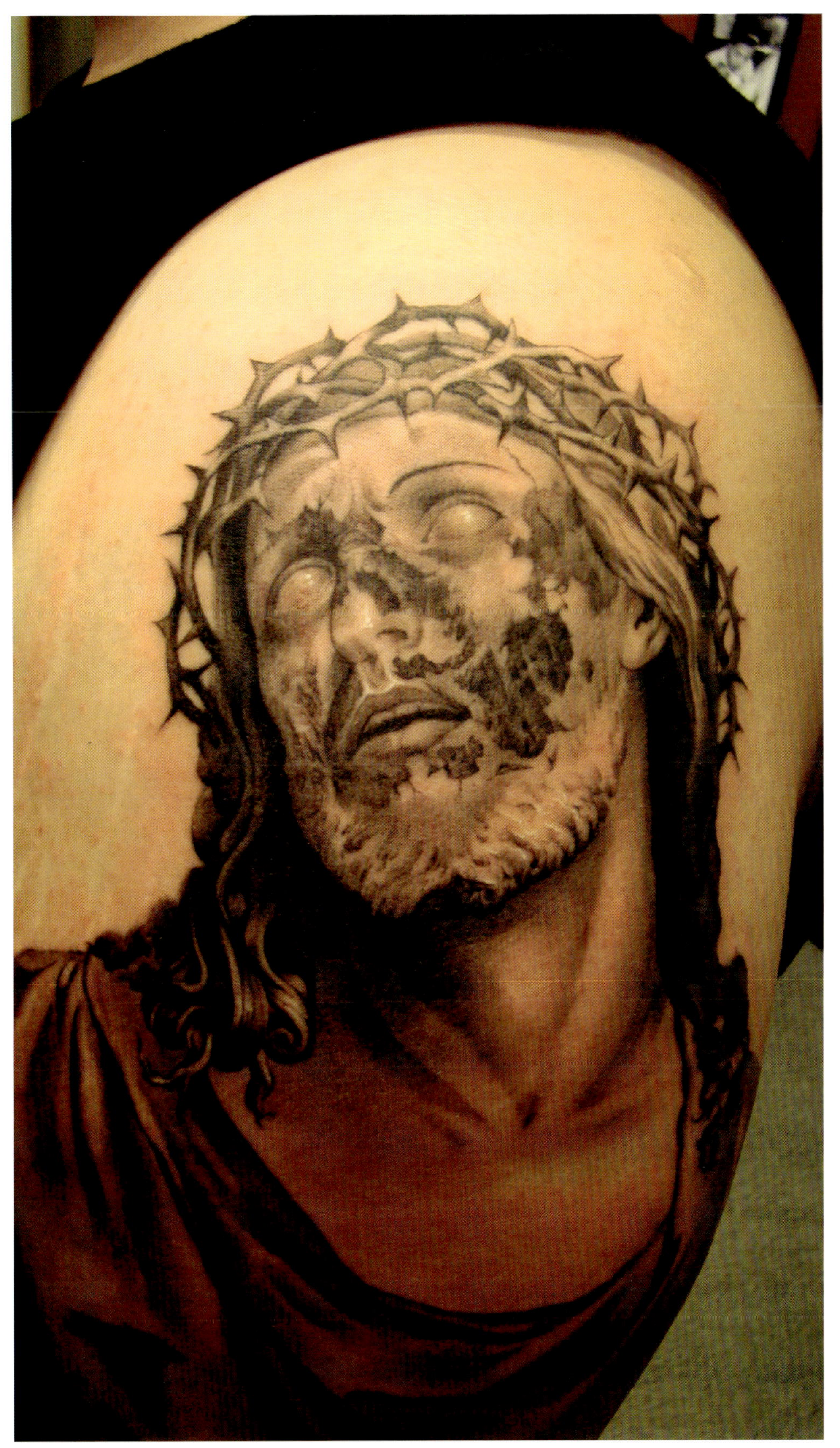

Virginia Elwood

"I, Leonard "Stoney" St Clair, am in the business of rendering a service to this community for the small group of people who choose to have their bodies decorated in some way or another...

I choose to pursue my profession with intelligence and skill, wishing not to offend anyone, but instead do what I can with my love of mankind before I die."

-Leonard L "Stoney" St Clair
Tattooist of the old school...since 1928

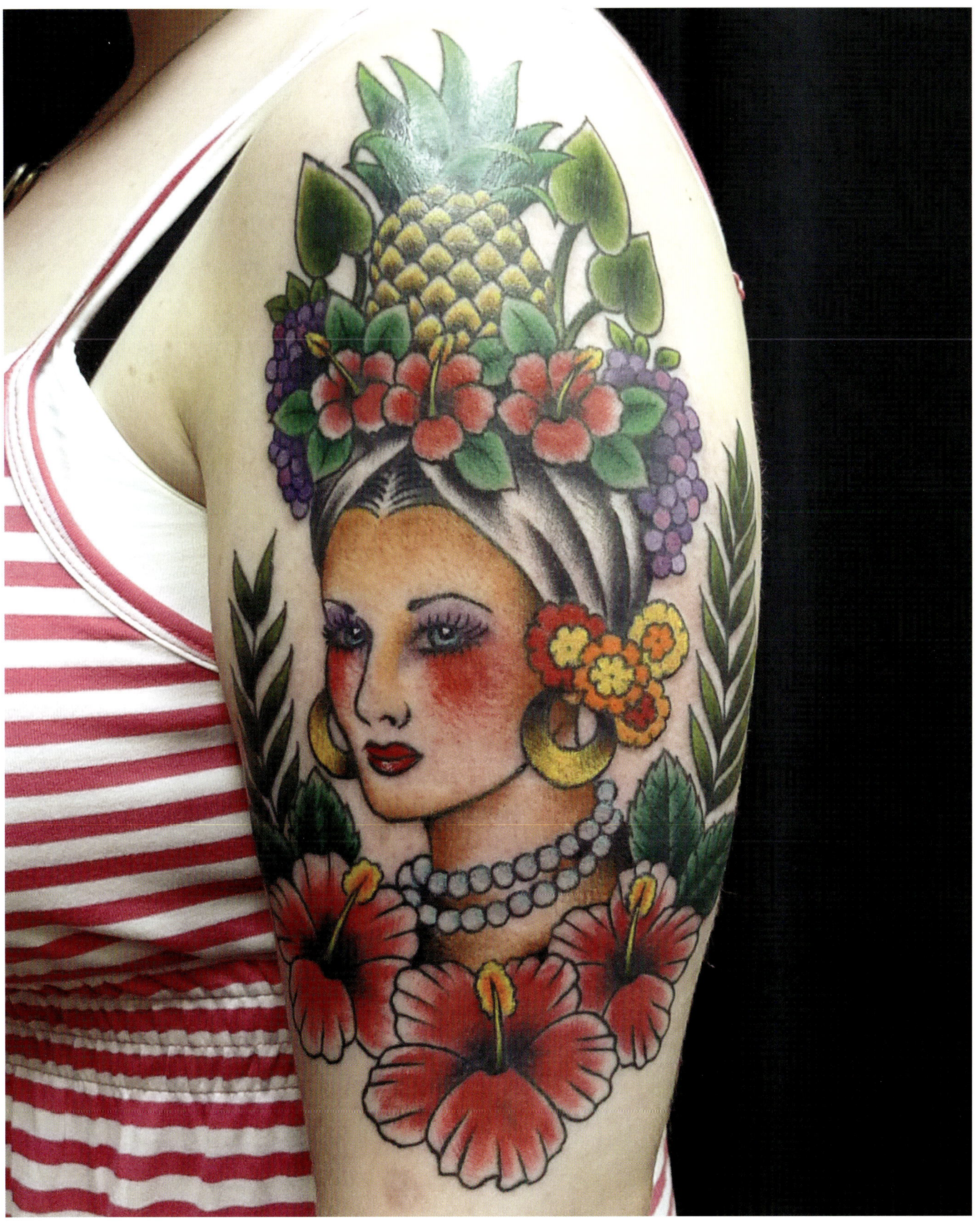

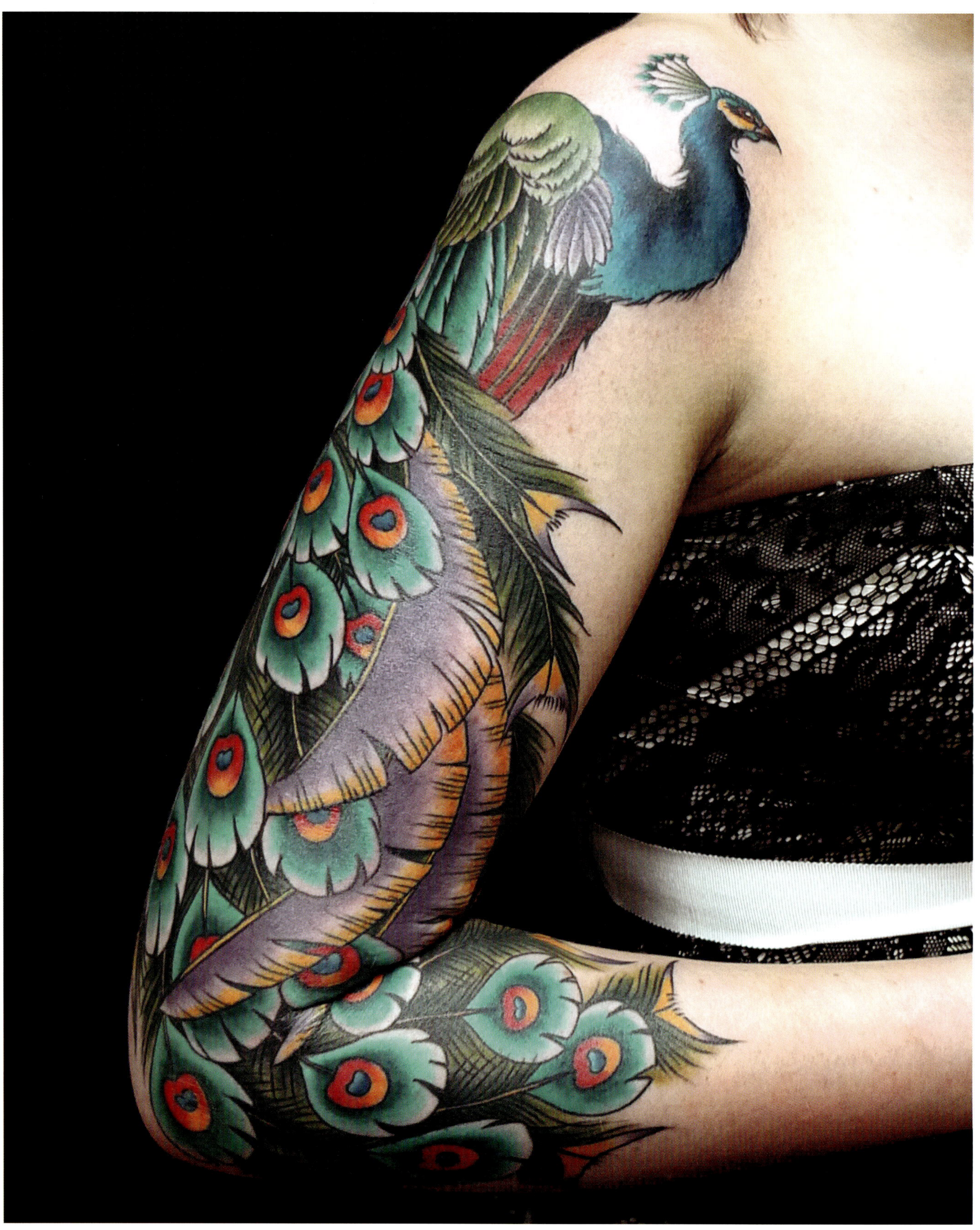

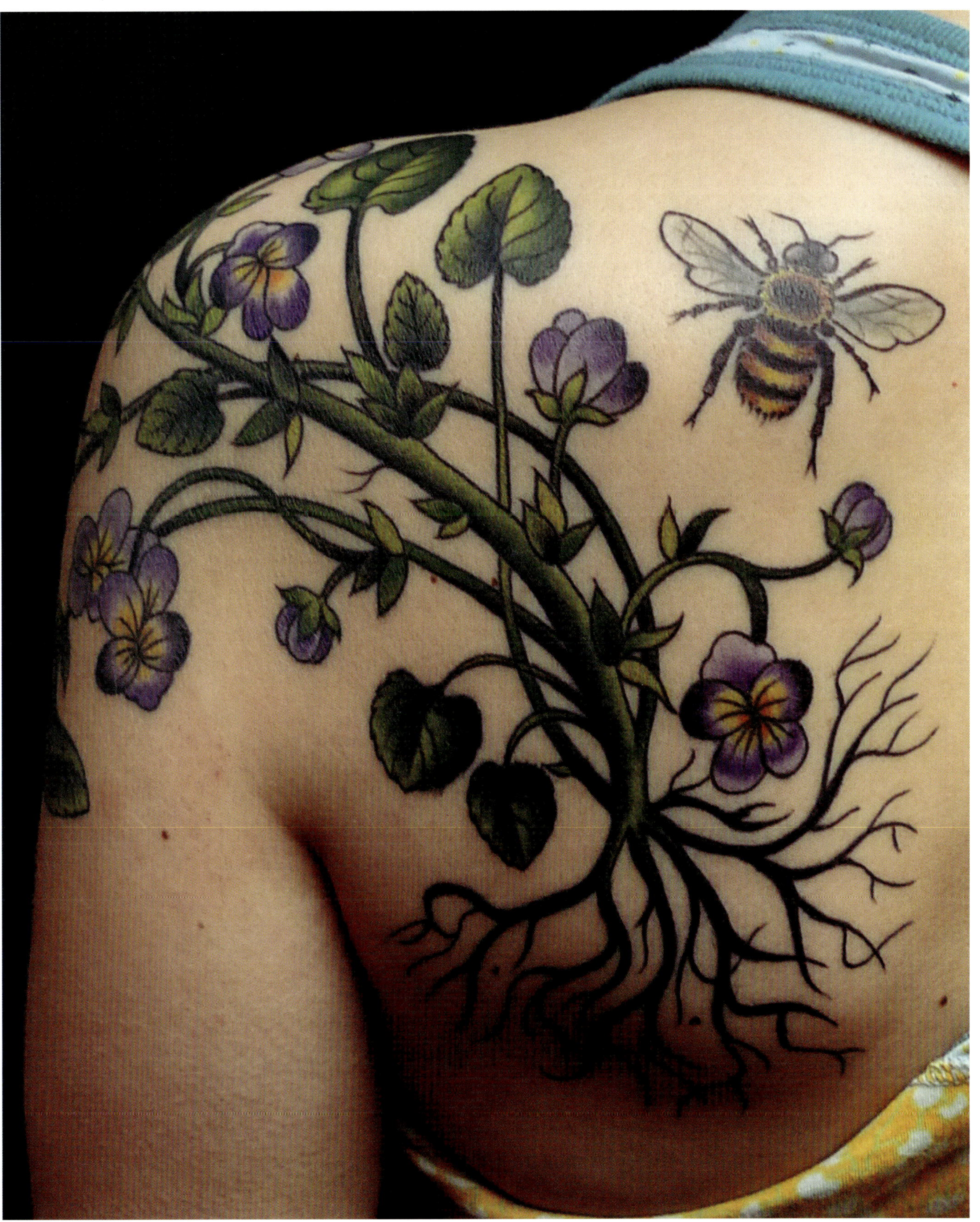

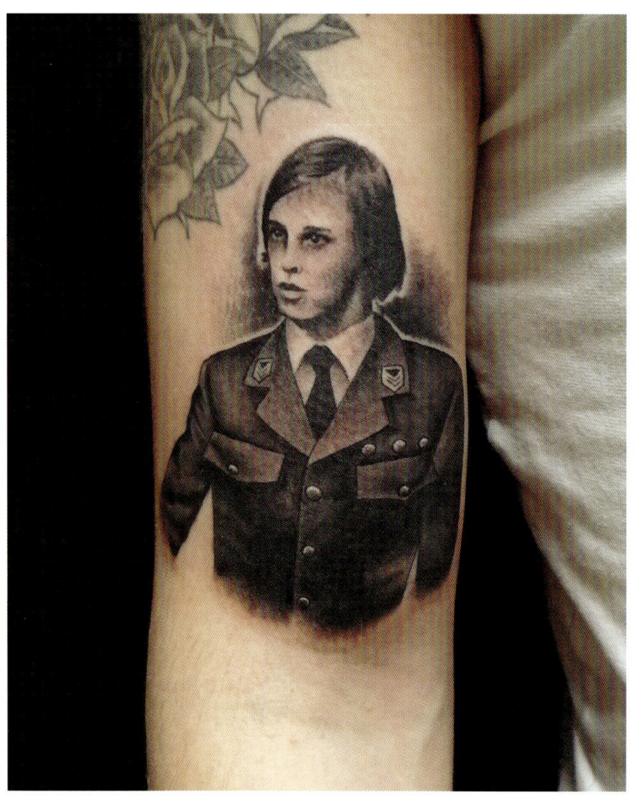

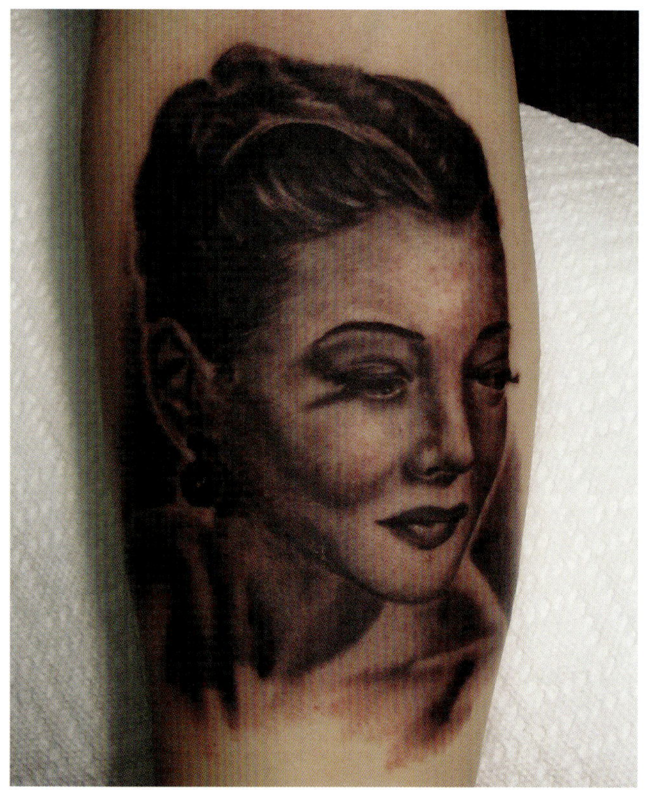

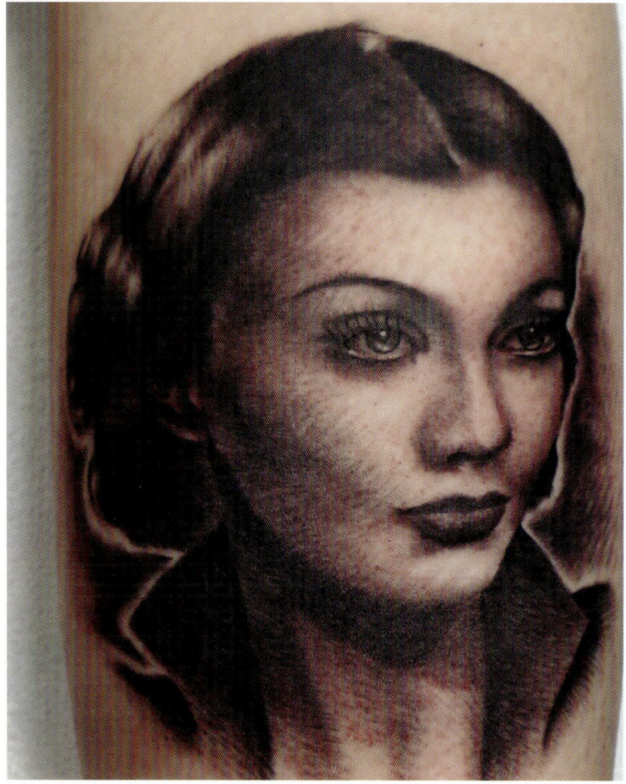

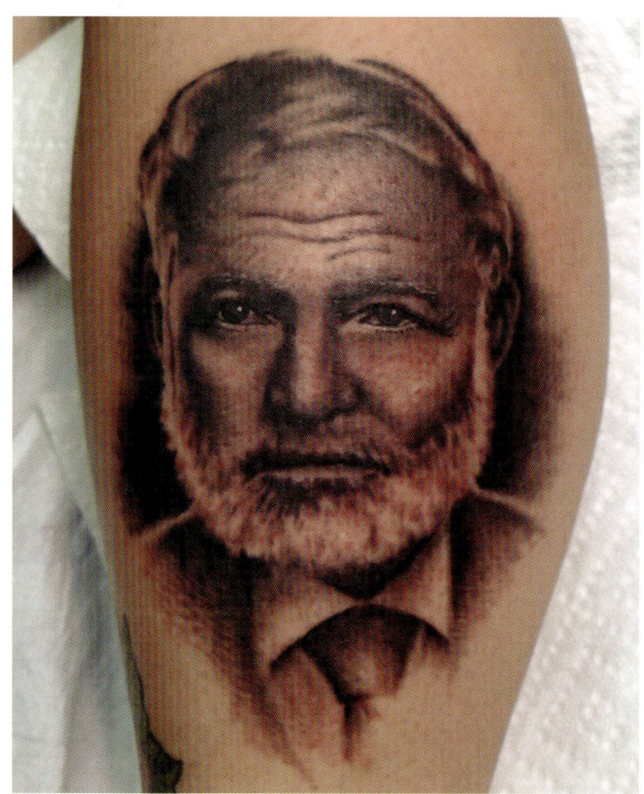

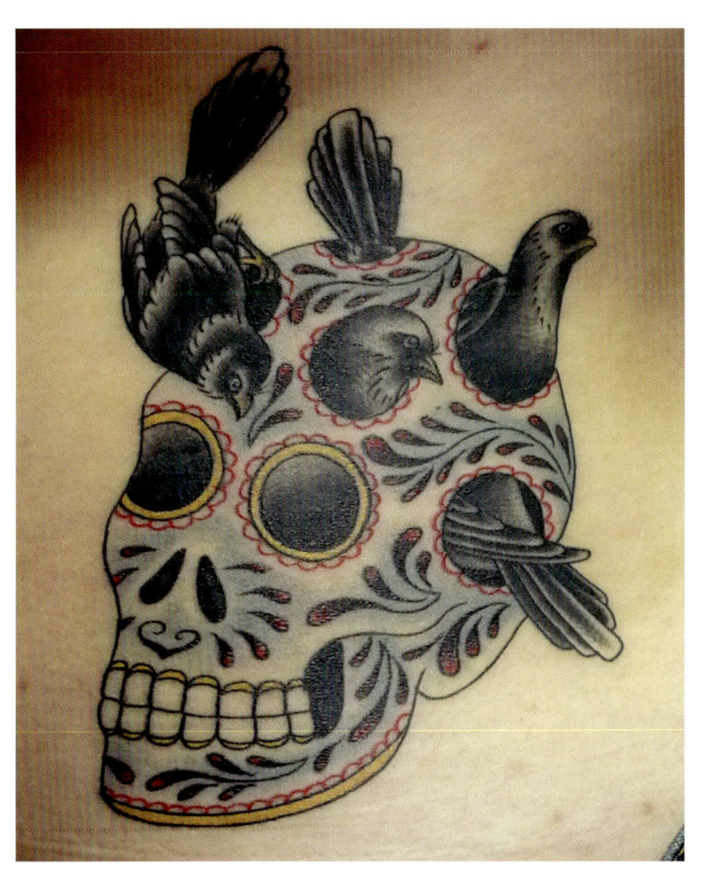

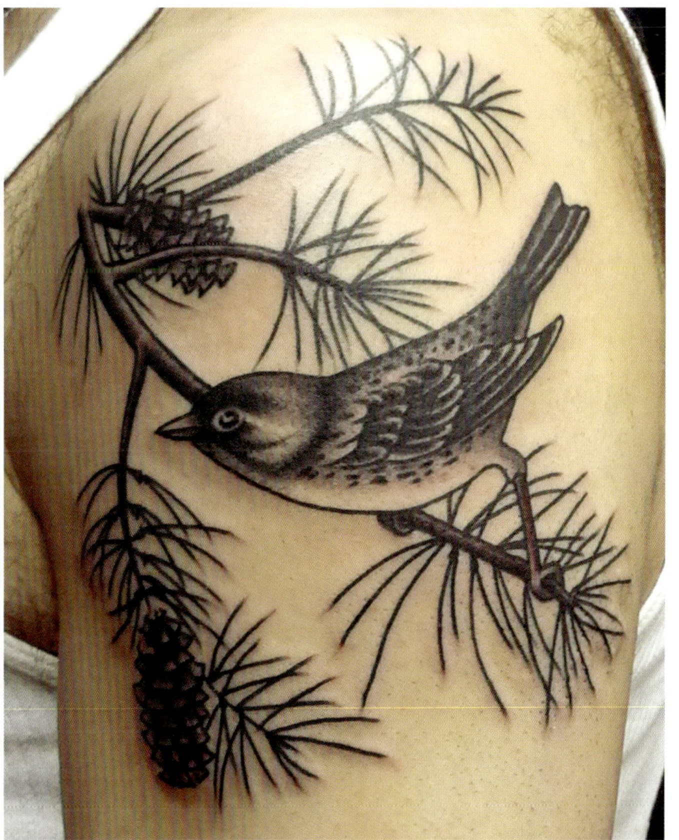

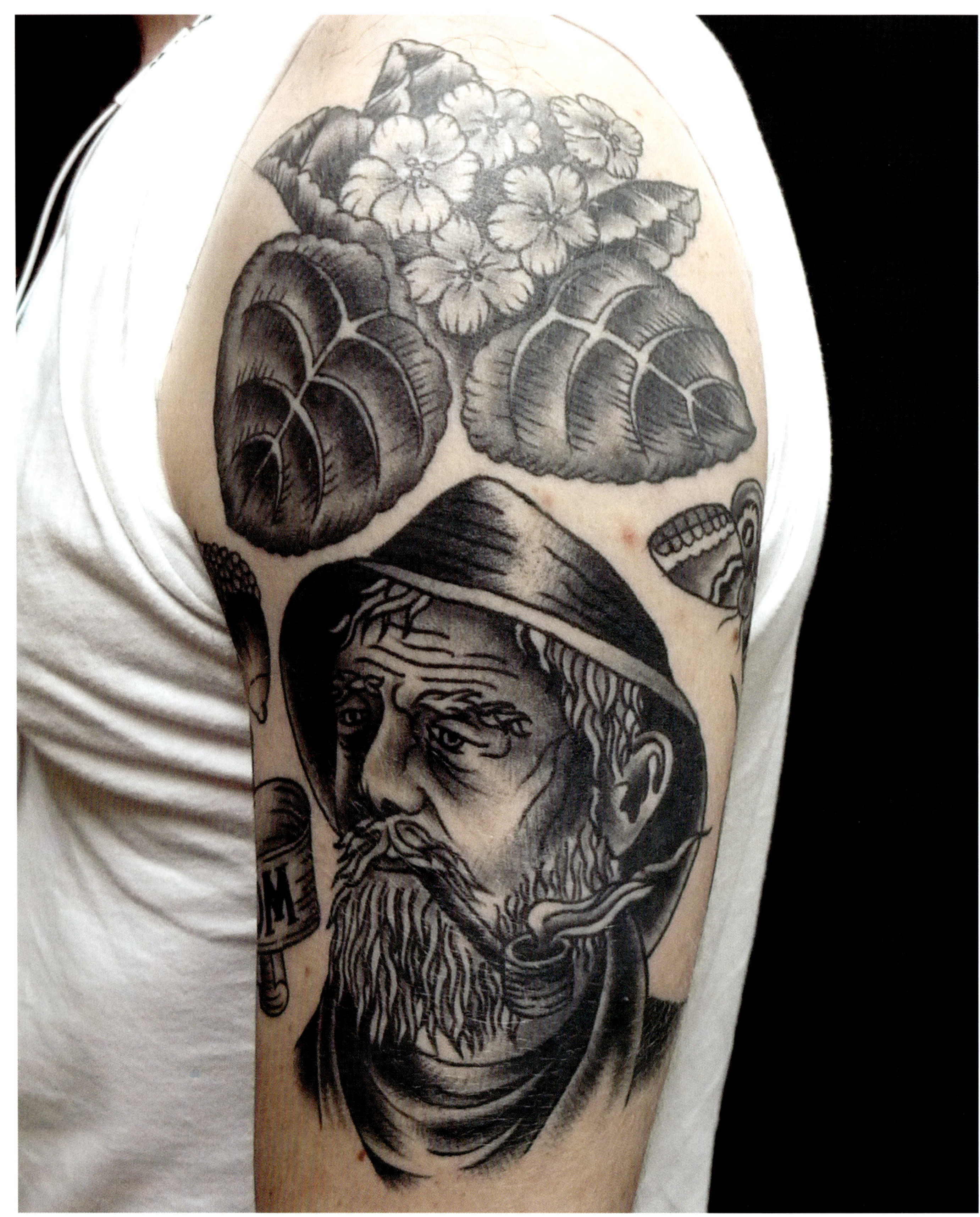

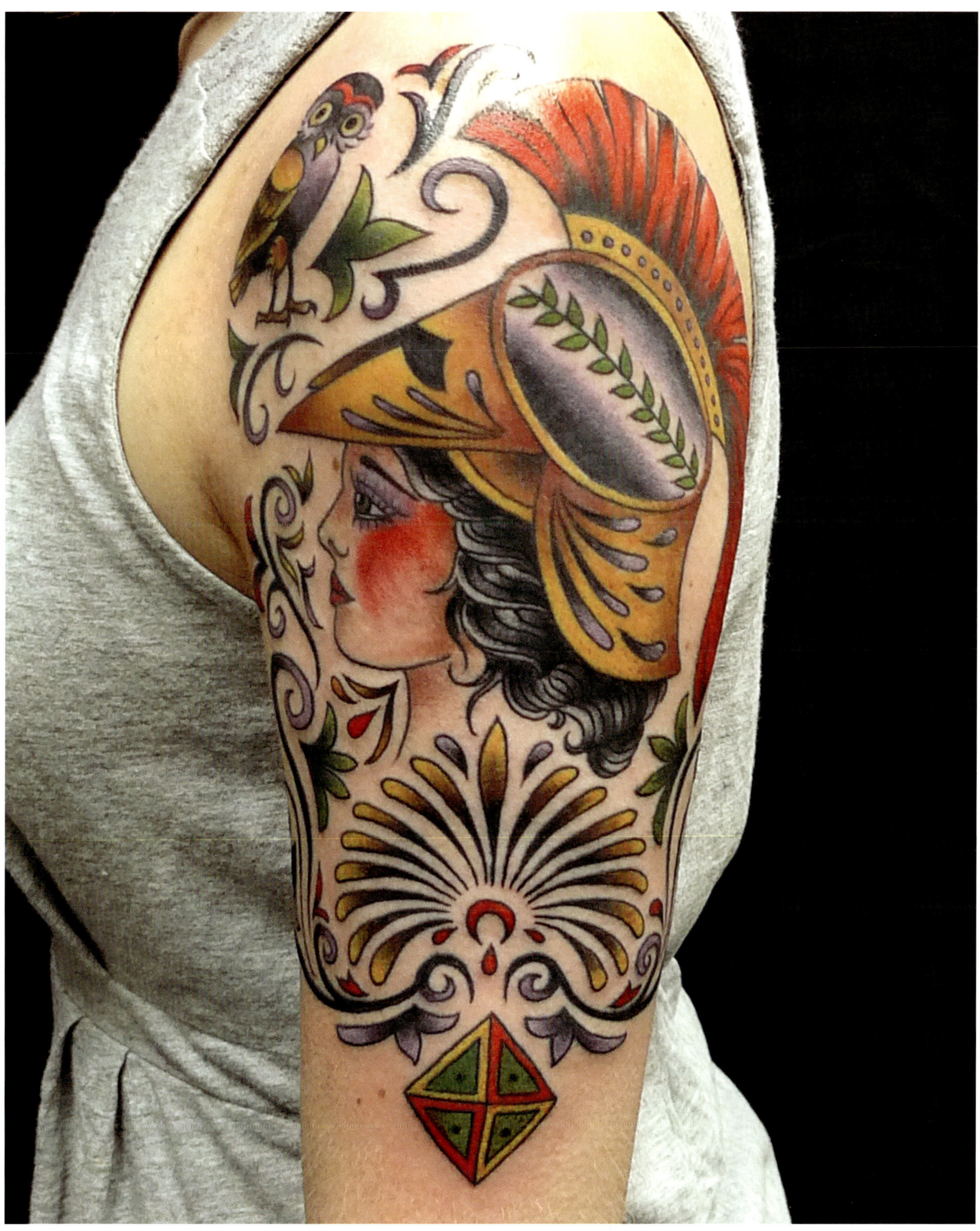

Liz Gruesome

Once upon a time, there was a sweet innocent little girl, who spent her days drawing and daydreaming. One day, she met a surly looking young man covered in colorful drawings who invited her into his world. She was frightened and intrigued and chose to follow him. When they arrived in his world there was a great sign that read "Smokin' Guns Tattoo and Piercing." She was greeted by all sorts of strange creatures: a gator dressed as a man, a man with a chicken leg for an arm and many people adorned with glittering metals and jewels on their faces and drawings covering their entire bodies. The Gator took her hand and her fears melted away. "What is this place?" she asked... the Gator just smiled. The answer was clear... She was in heaven...

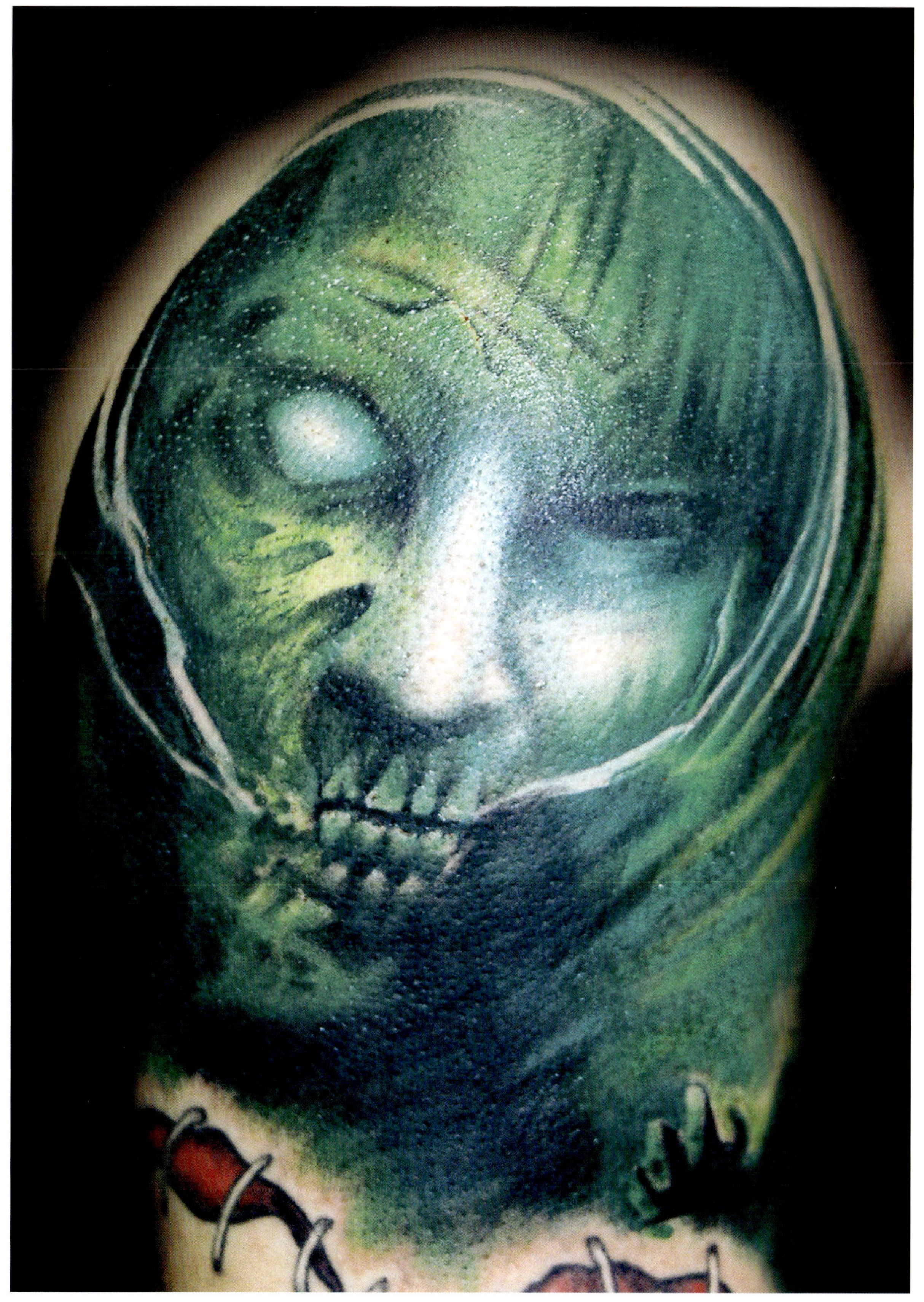

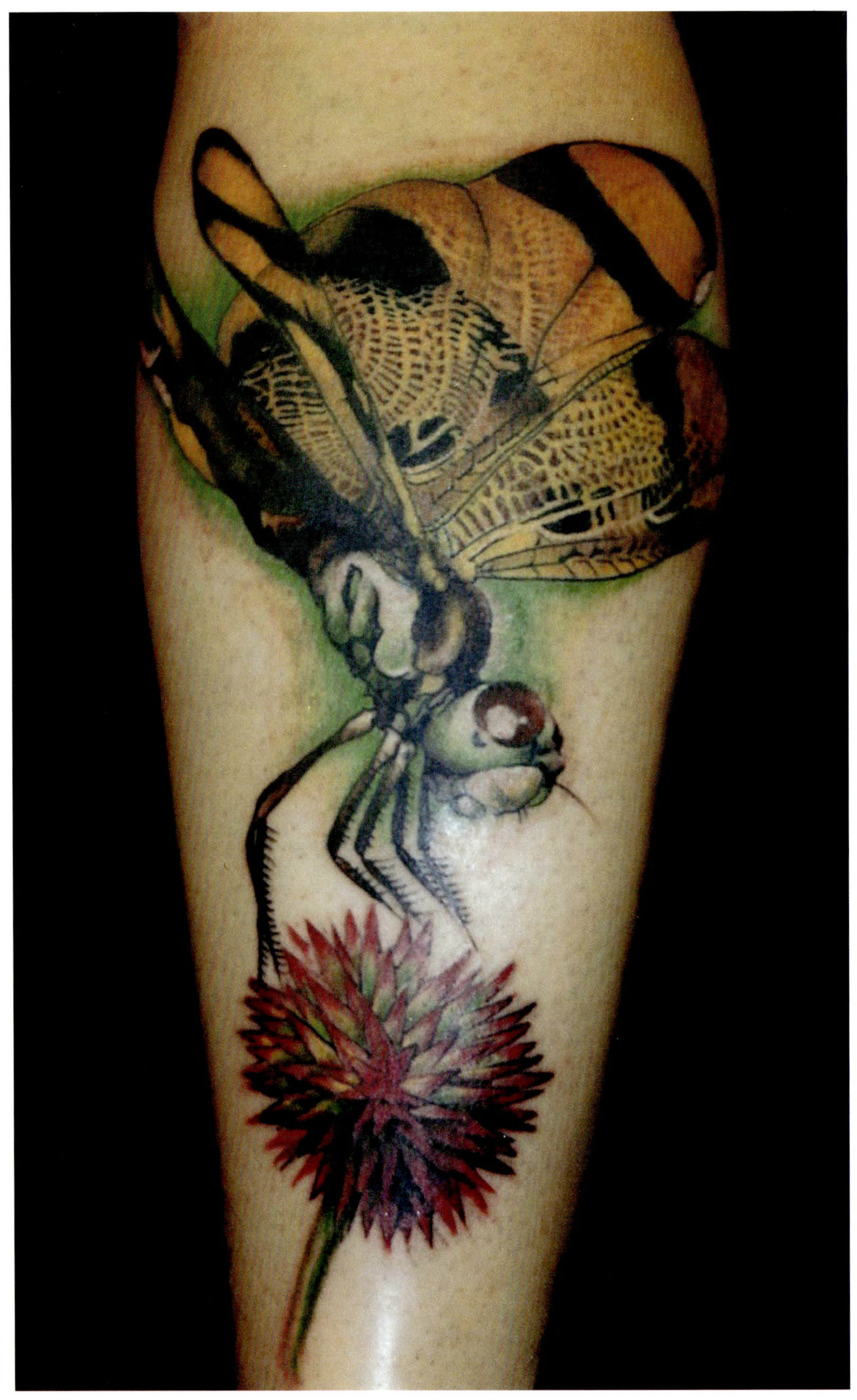

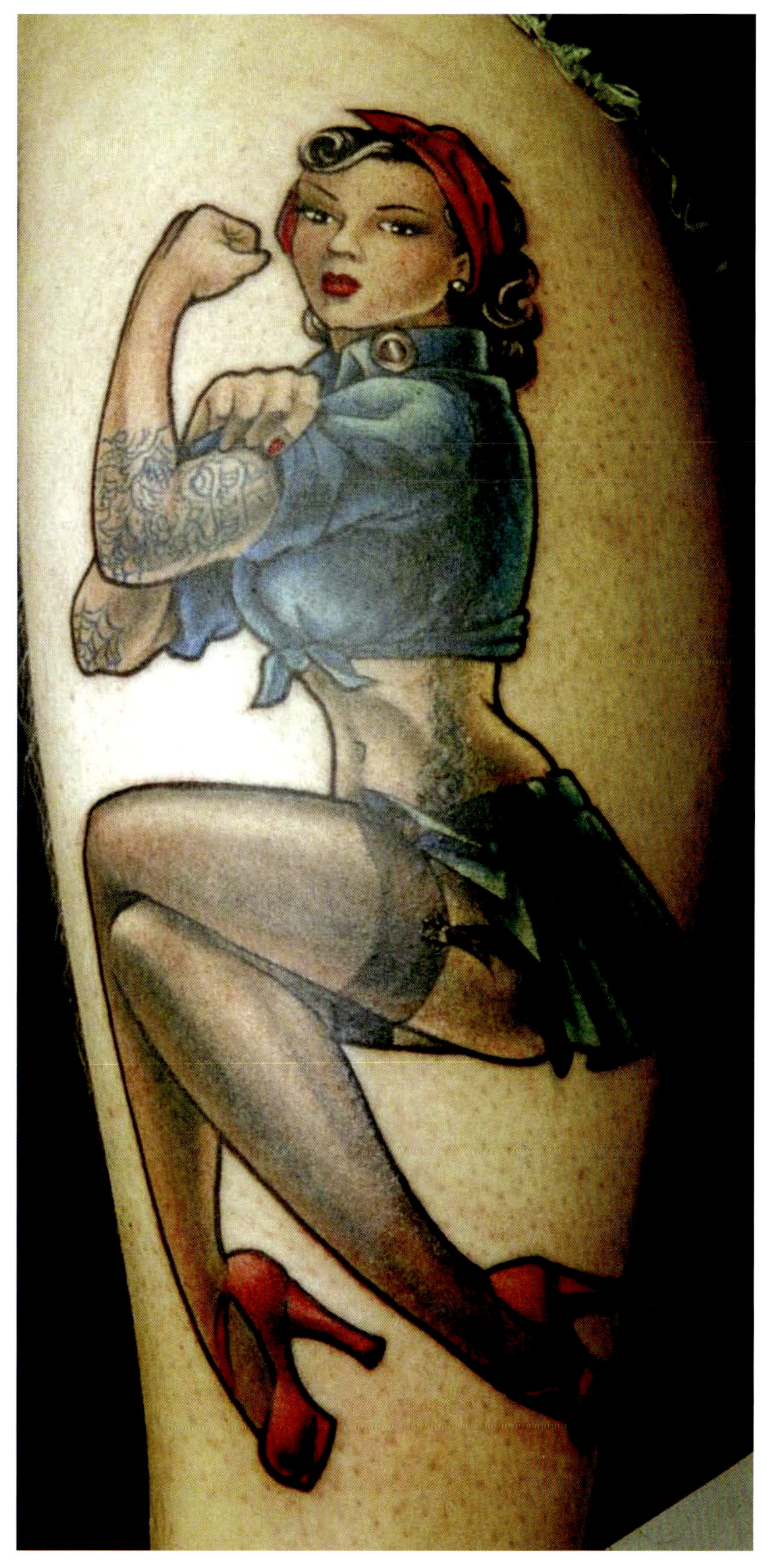

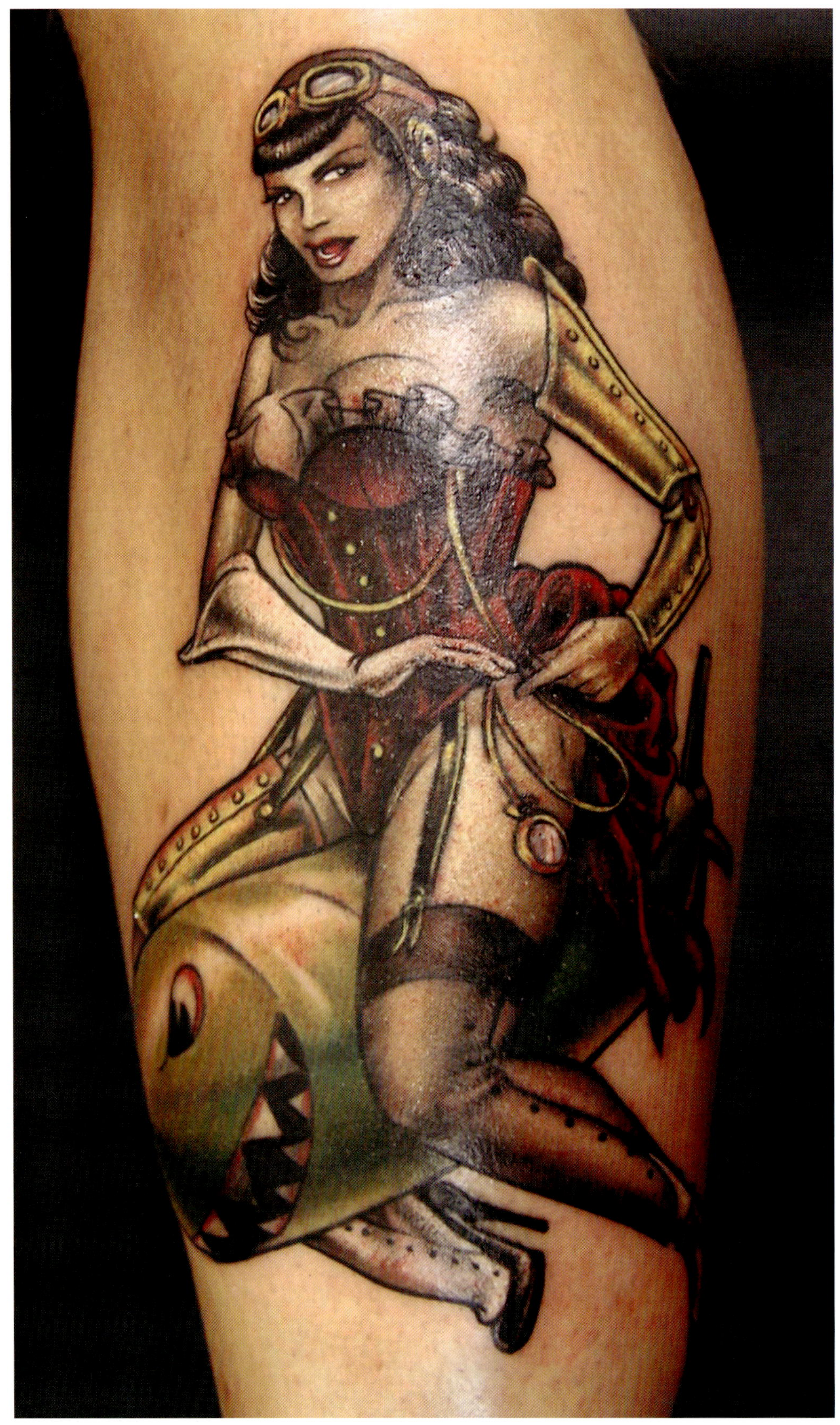

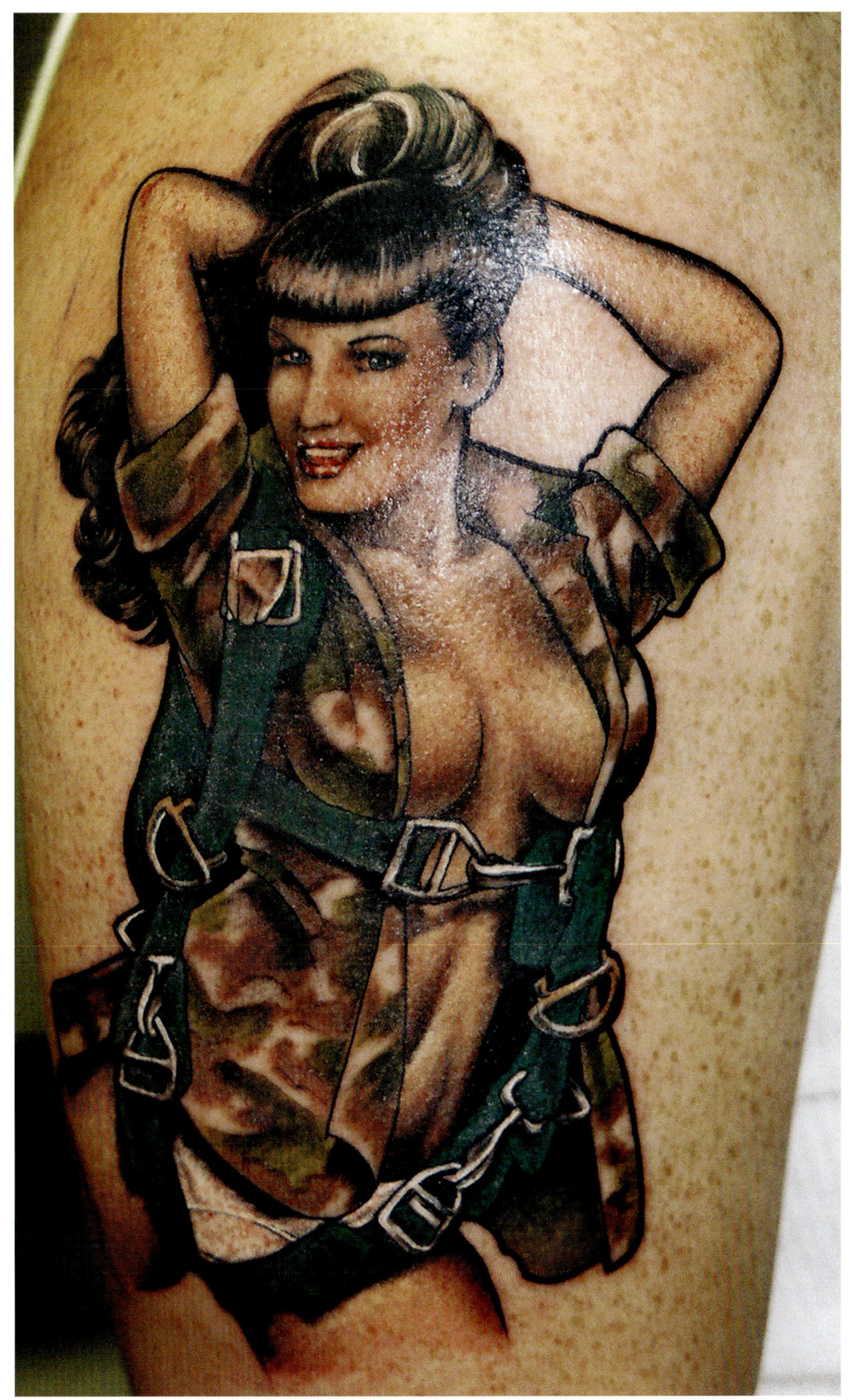

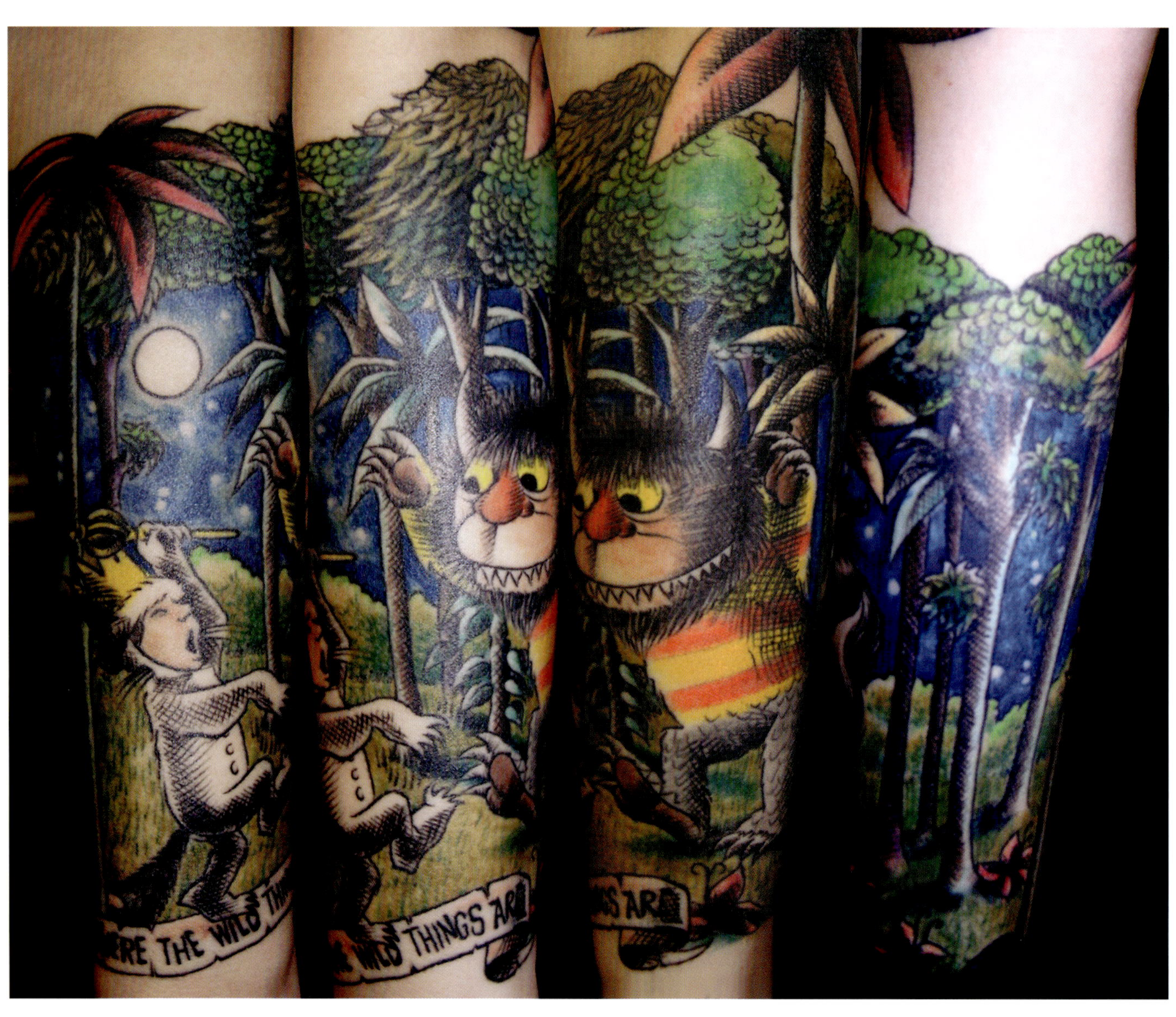
ERE THE WILD TH
WILD THINGS AR
GS AR

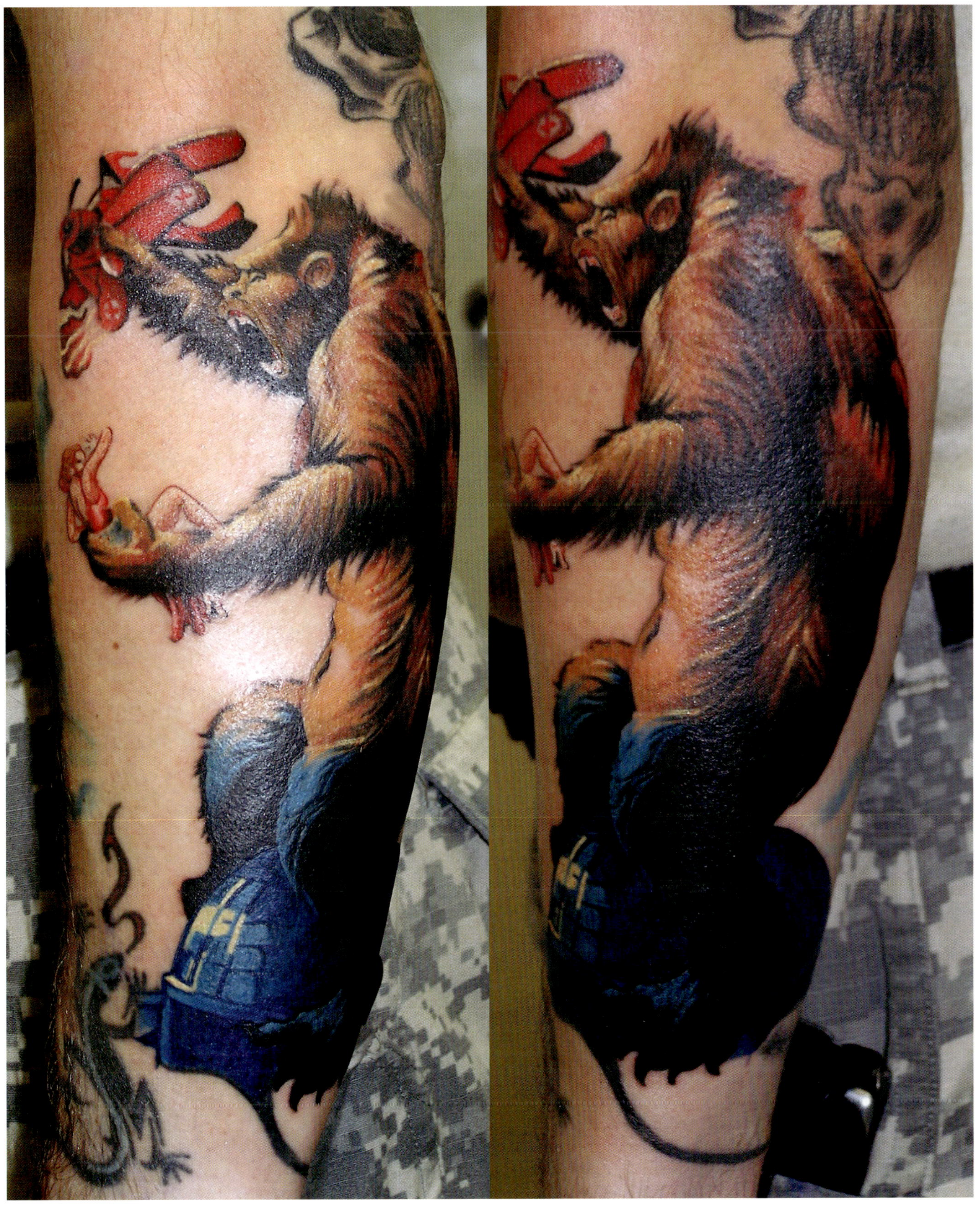

Mark Heggie

As a young boy, I collected butterflies and listened to Barry Manilow. With youthful enthusiasm, I built snowmen and they melted. I built sandcastles and the tides washed them away. It was in these formative years, which ultimately led to the development of a socially adroit misanthrope, that I realized the need to make lasting impressions.

To aid the ever-expanding contingent of persons looking to spend as little money as possible on a lifetime investment, I then leaped at the opportunity to serve the people by joining the tattooing community as a naive fledgling.

Many moons later, I still continue to etch it and permanently sketch it. My fervor and integrity have since matured.

Consistently unable to pigeonhole myself stylistically, I continually strive to illuminate the beauty I have come to know and love as a spectator of life and its fireworks.

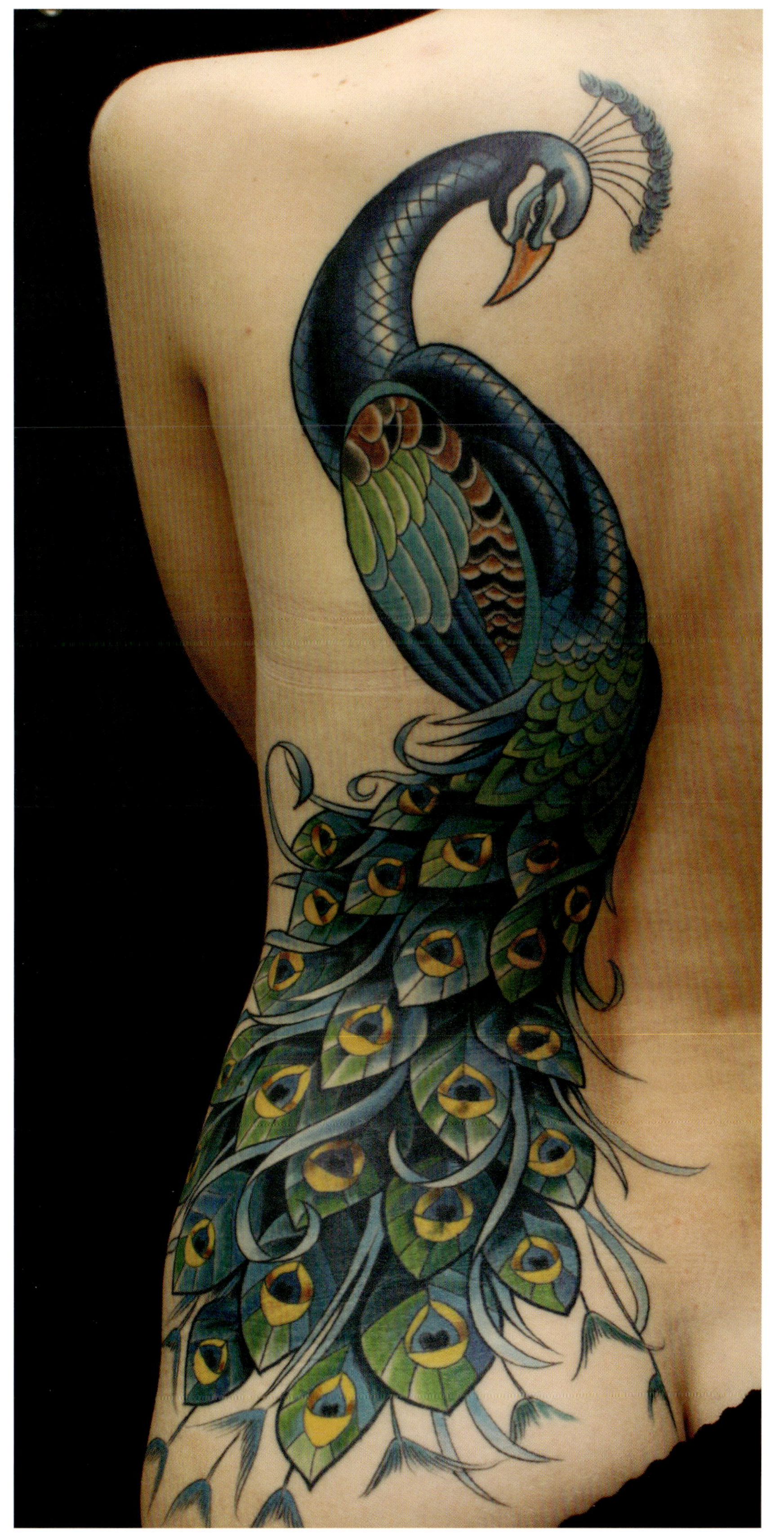

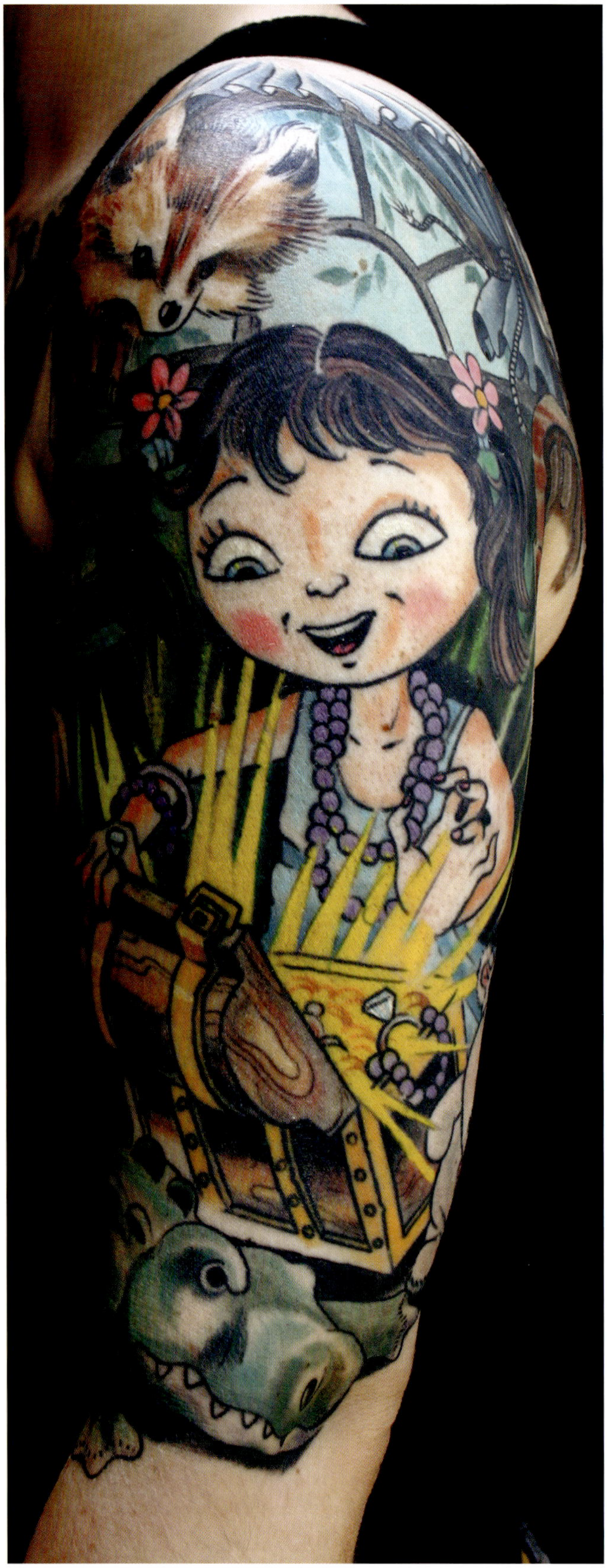

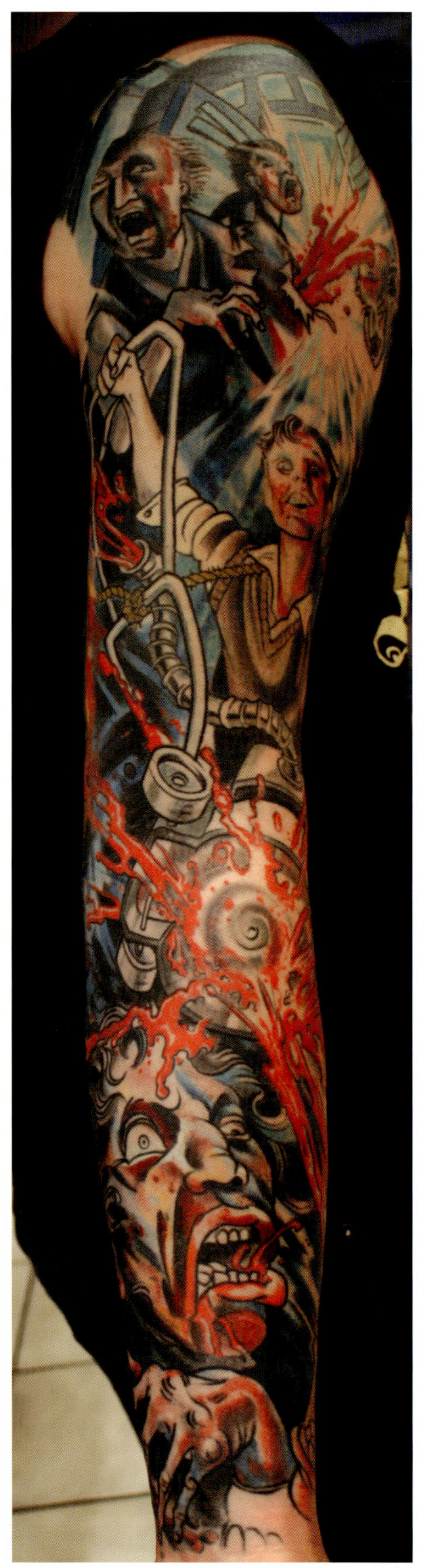

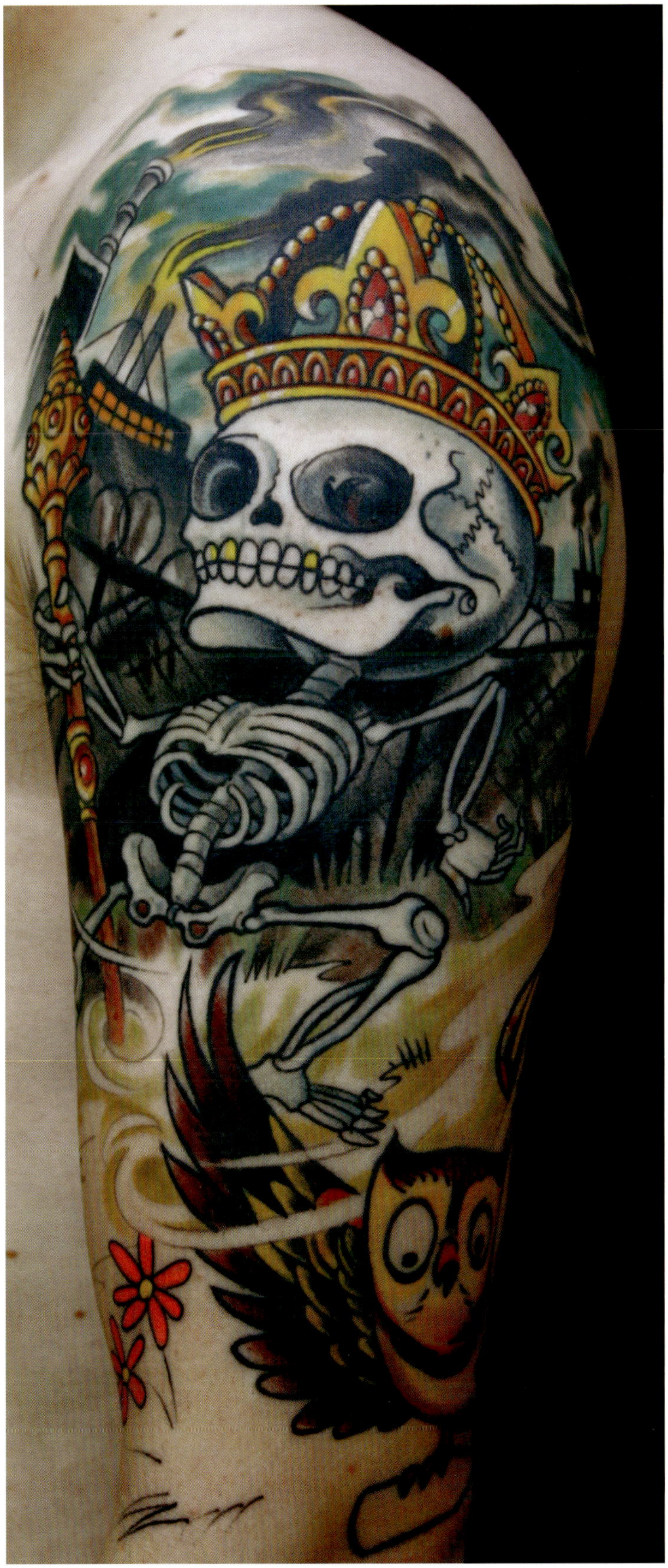

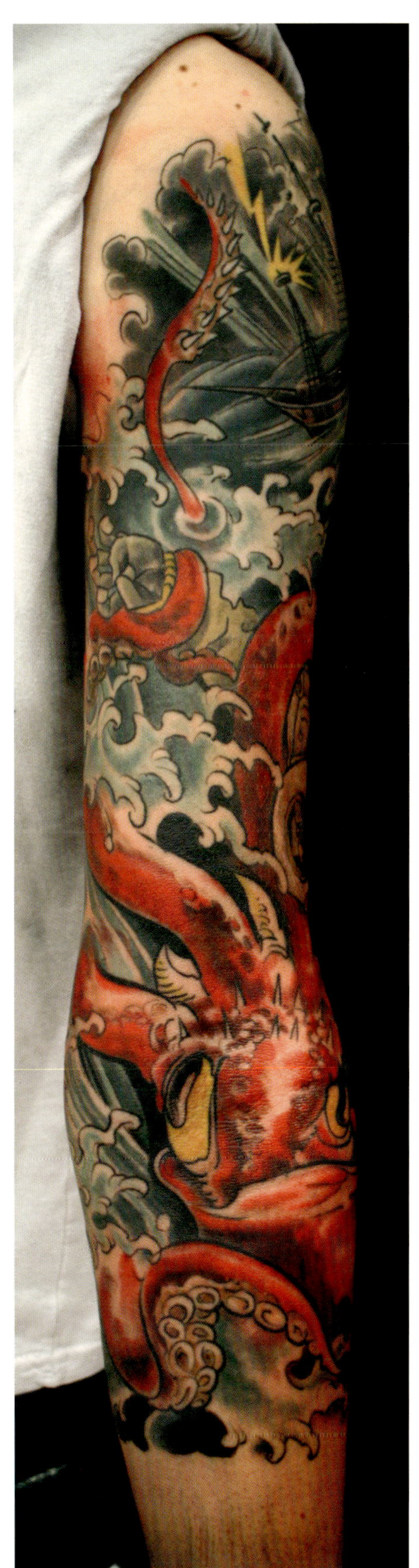

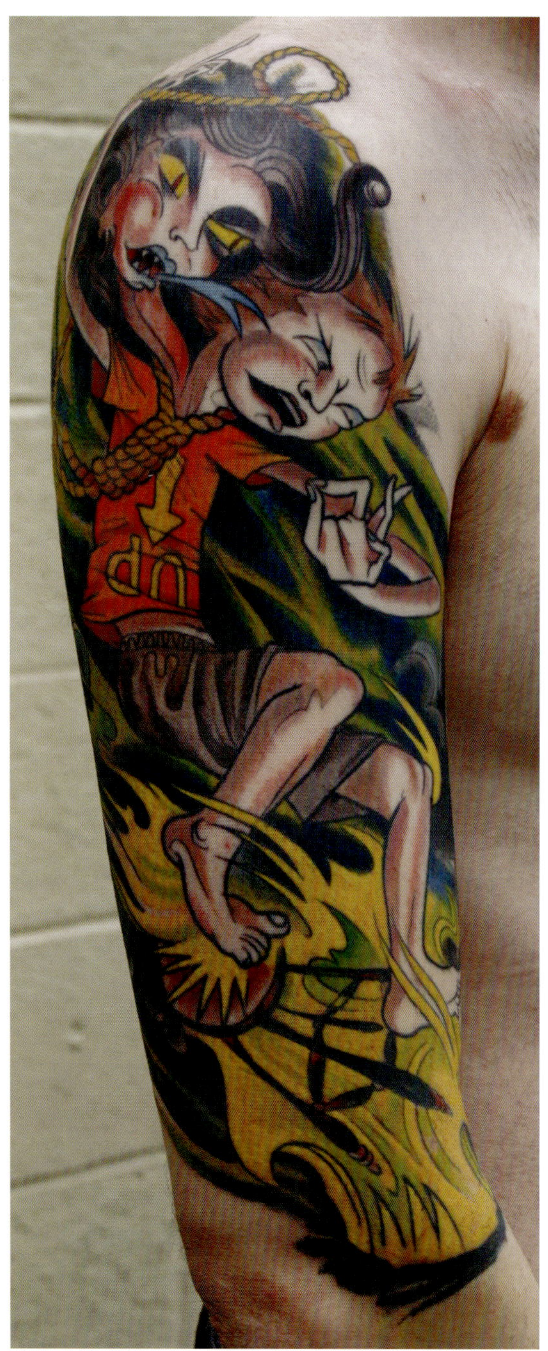

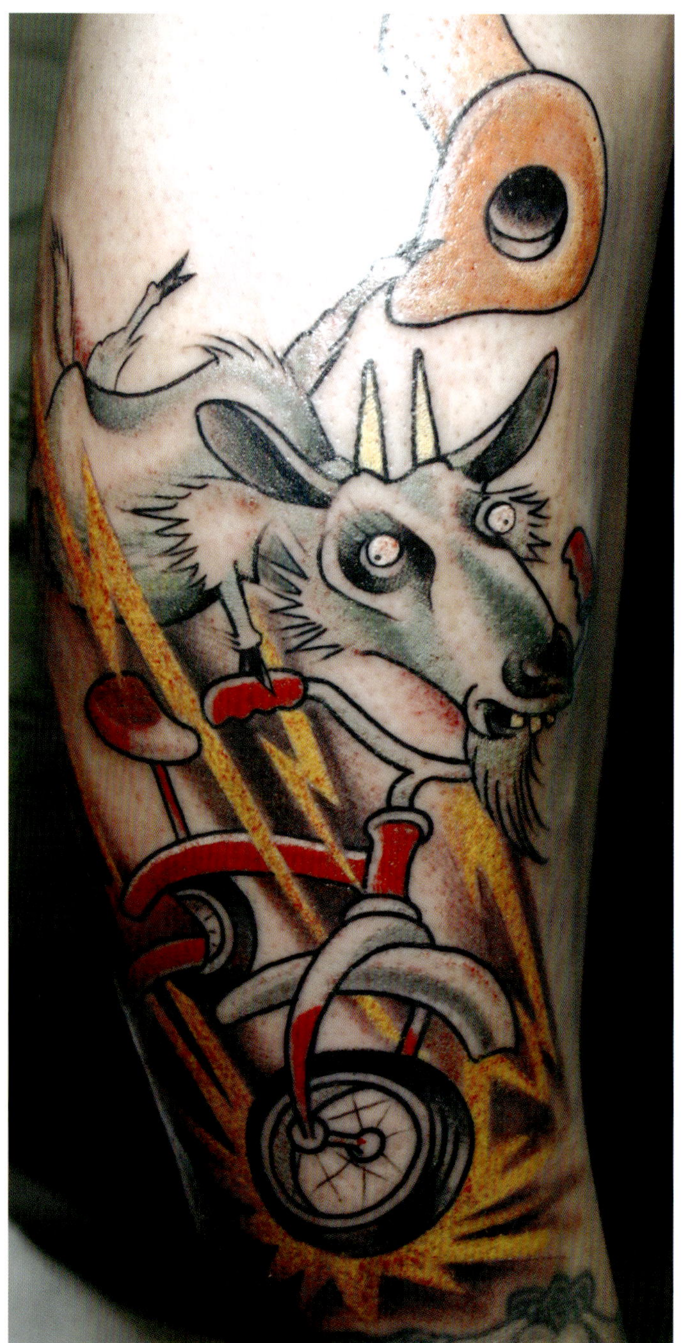

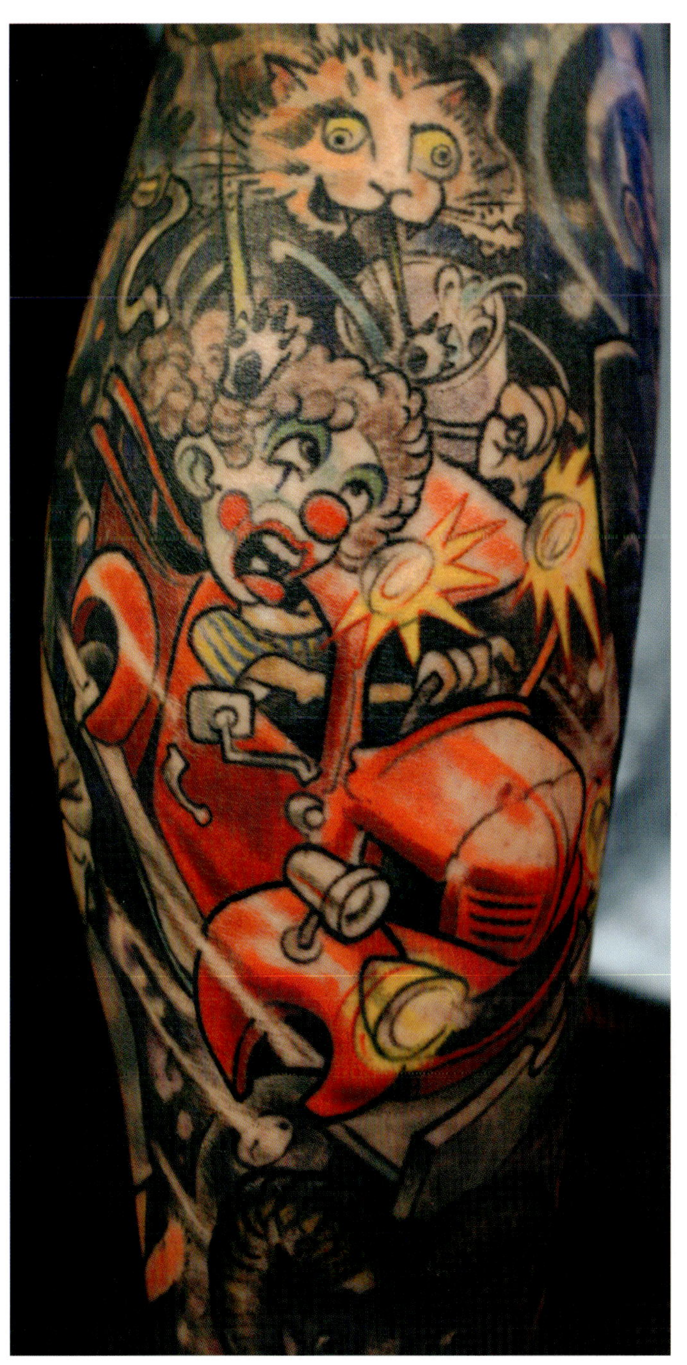

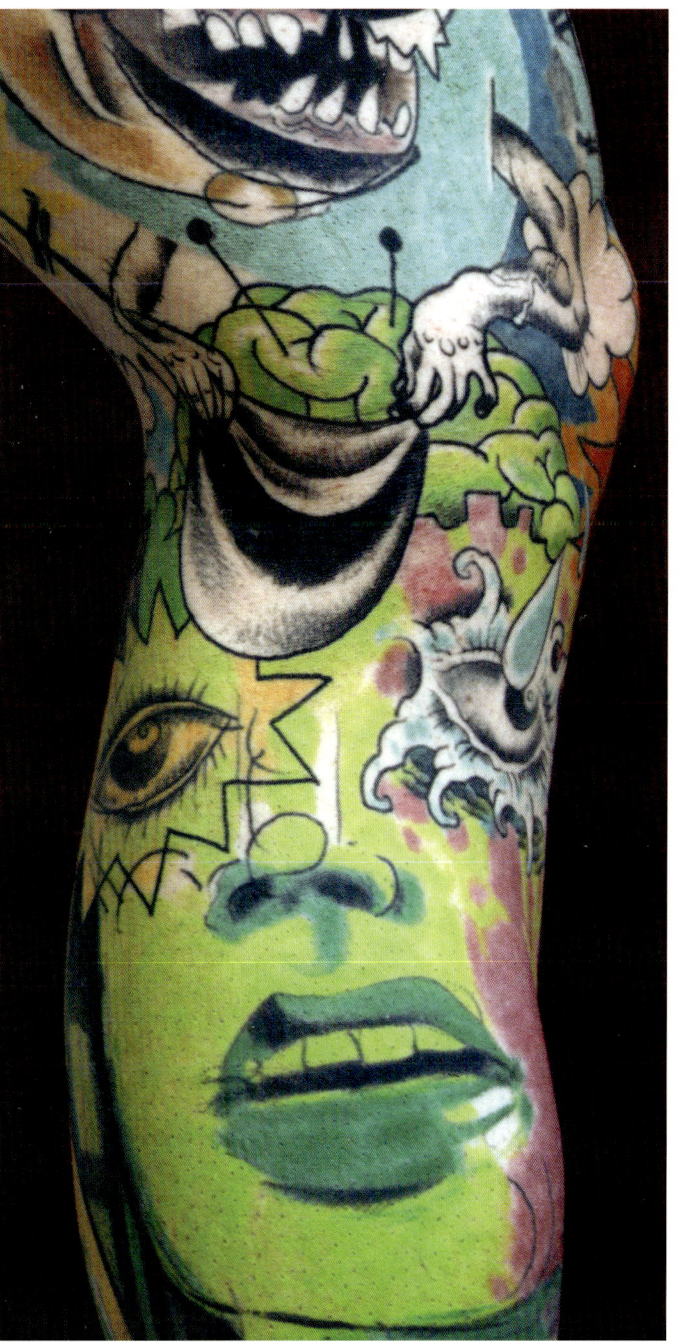

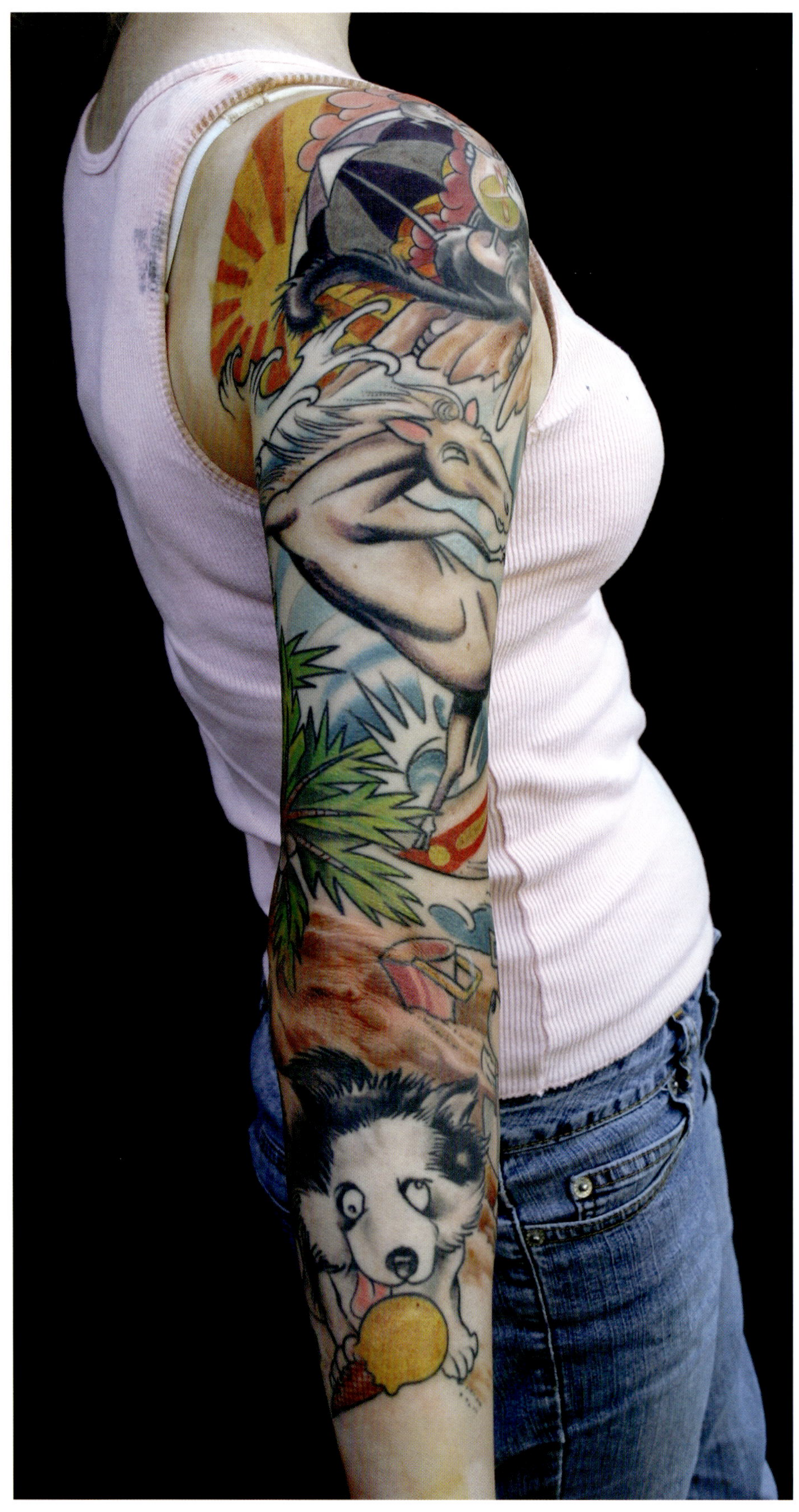

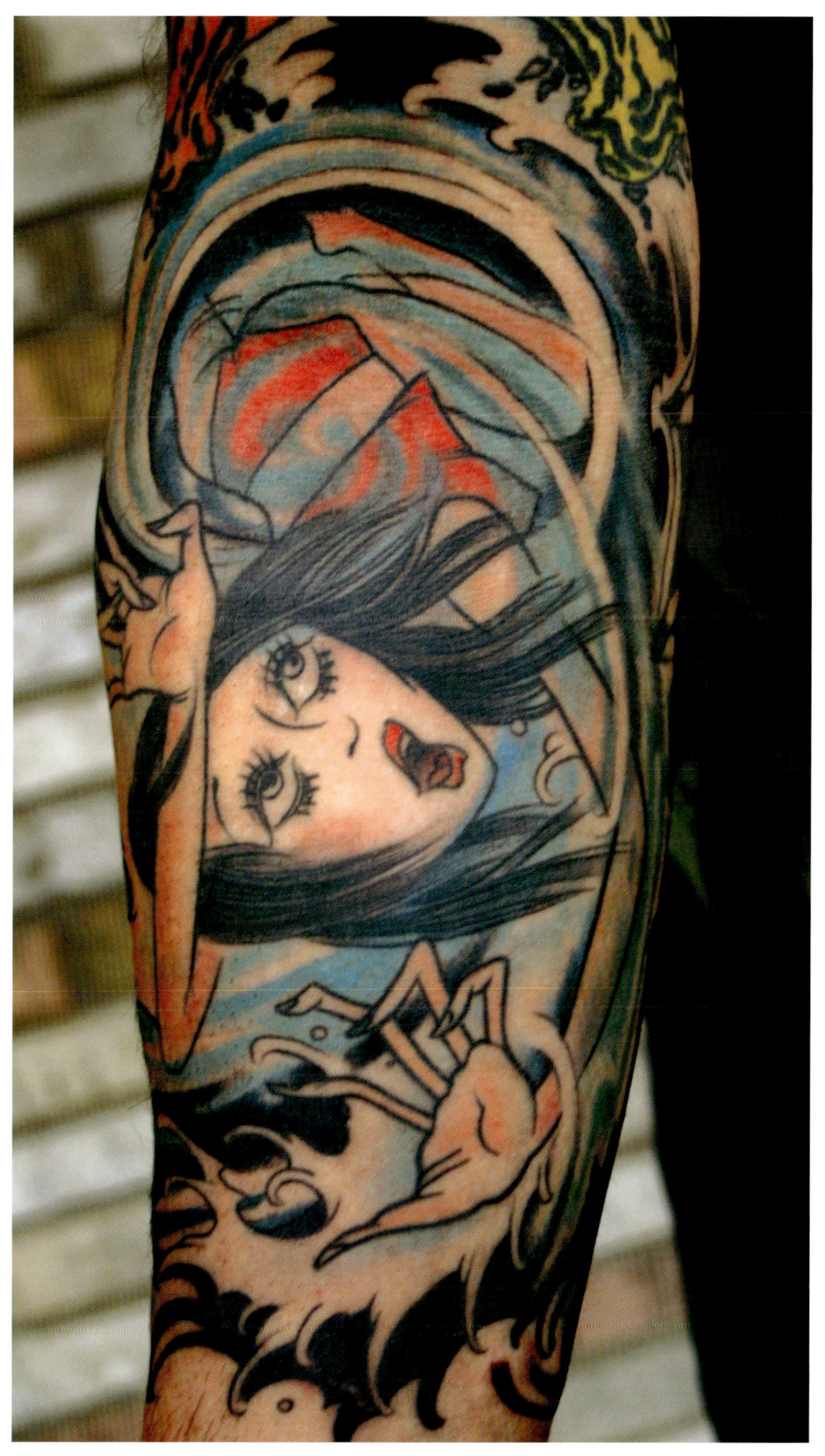

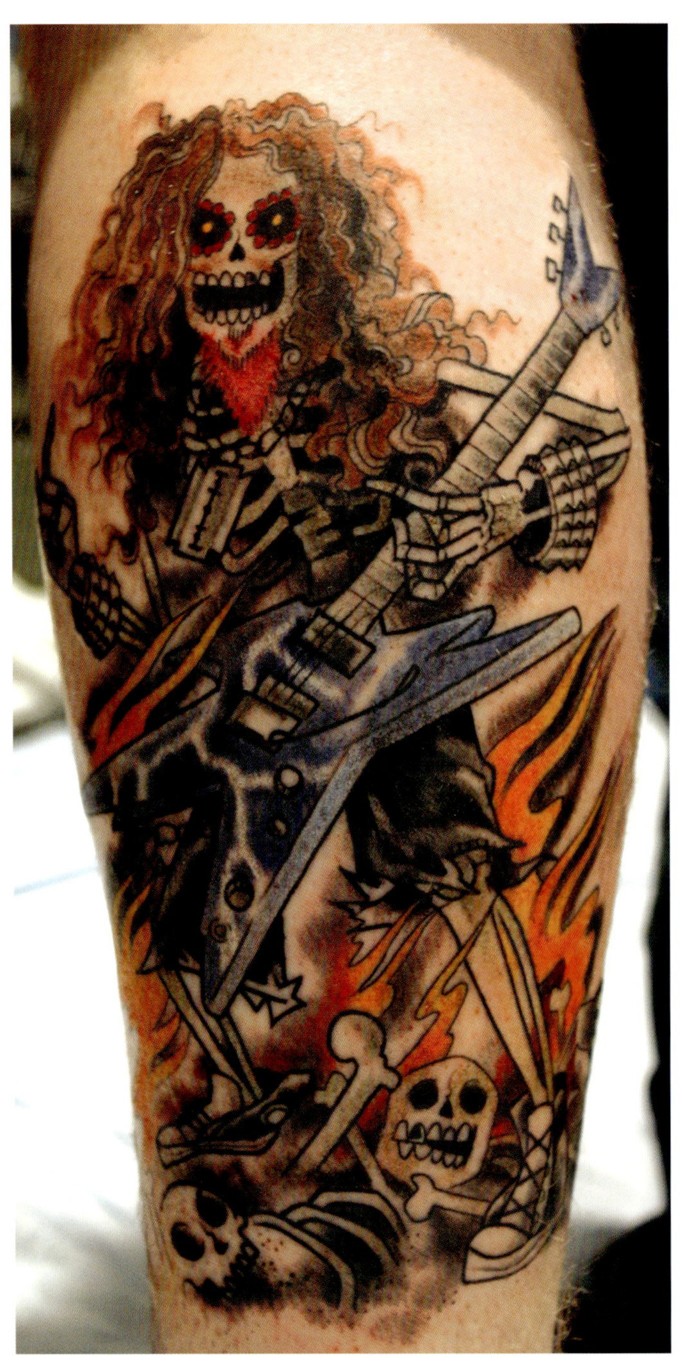

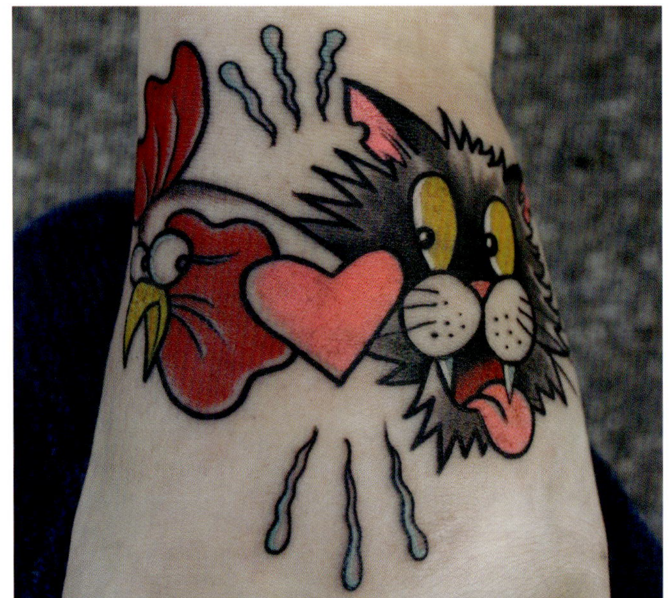

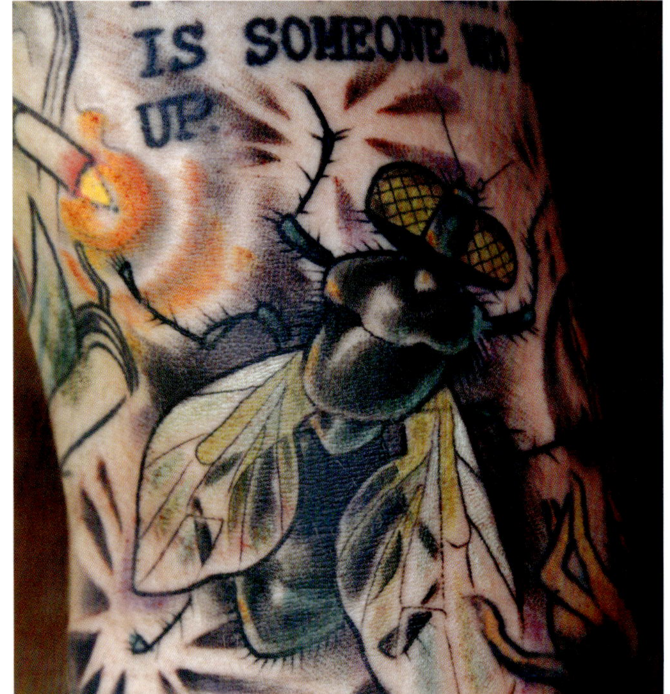
IS SOMEONE
UP.

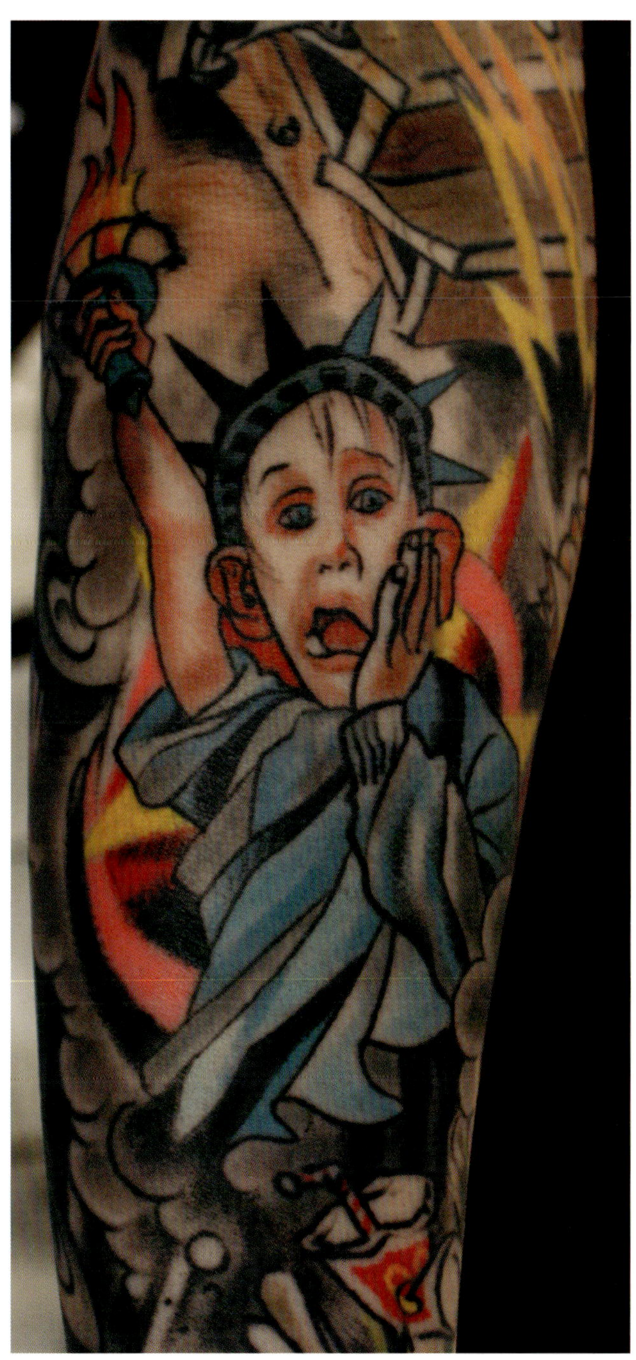

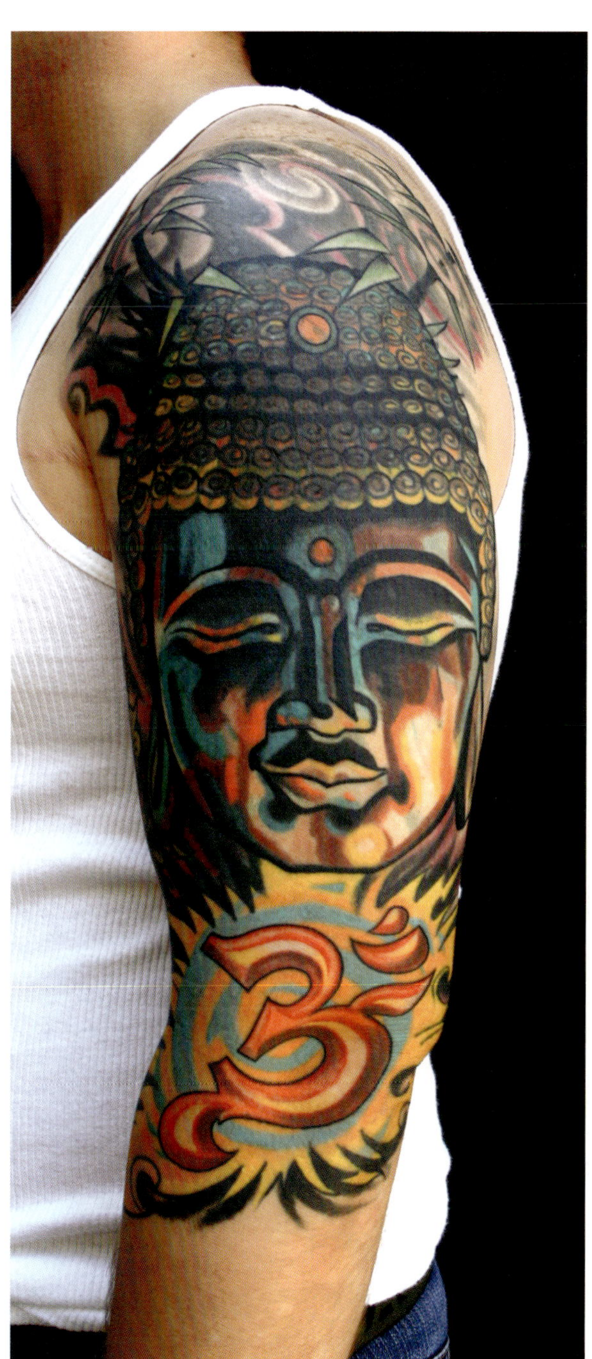

Angelique Houtkamp

The typical old school snake and dagger was a tattoo that my uncle sported on his forearm. I remember I used to stare at it as a kid and thought it was magical, partly because snakes are very rare where I'm from and daggers seem like such an ancient weapon. This tattoo was the only one I ever saw up close throughout my whole youth. My uncle used to tell me to never get a tattoo 'cause he regretted it very much, which, of course, only made it more appealing to me. I now think that it was this tattoo that forever instilled in me a love for old school imagery and tattoos.

They give me a feeling of adventure, freedom and a secret mystery passage into the dark narrow alleyways of harbours and sunsoaked Pacific islands.

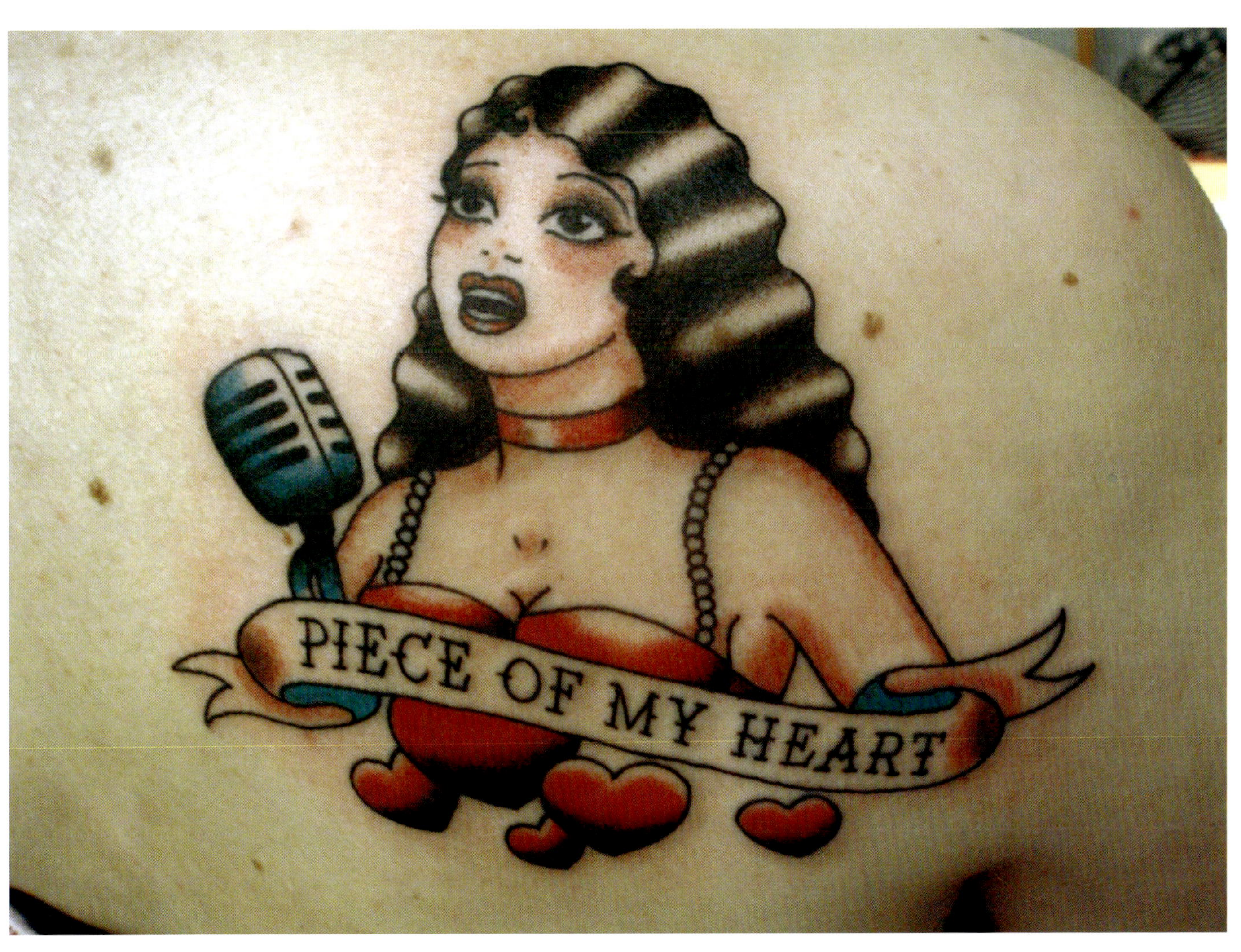
PIECE OF MY HEART

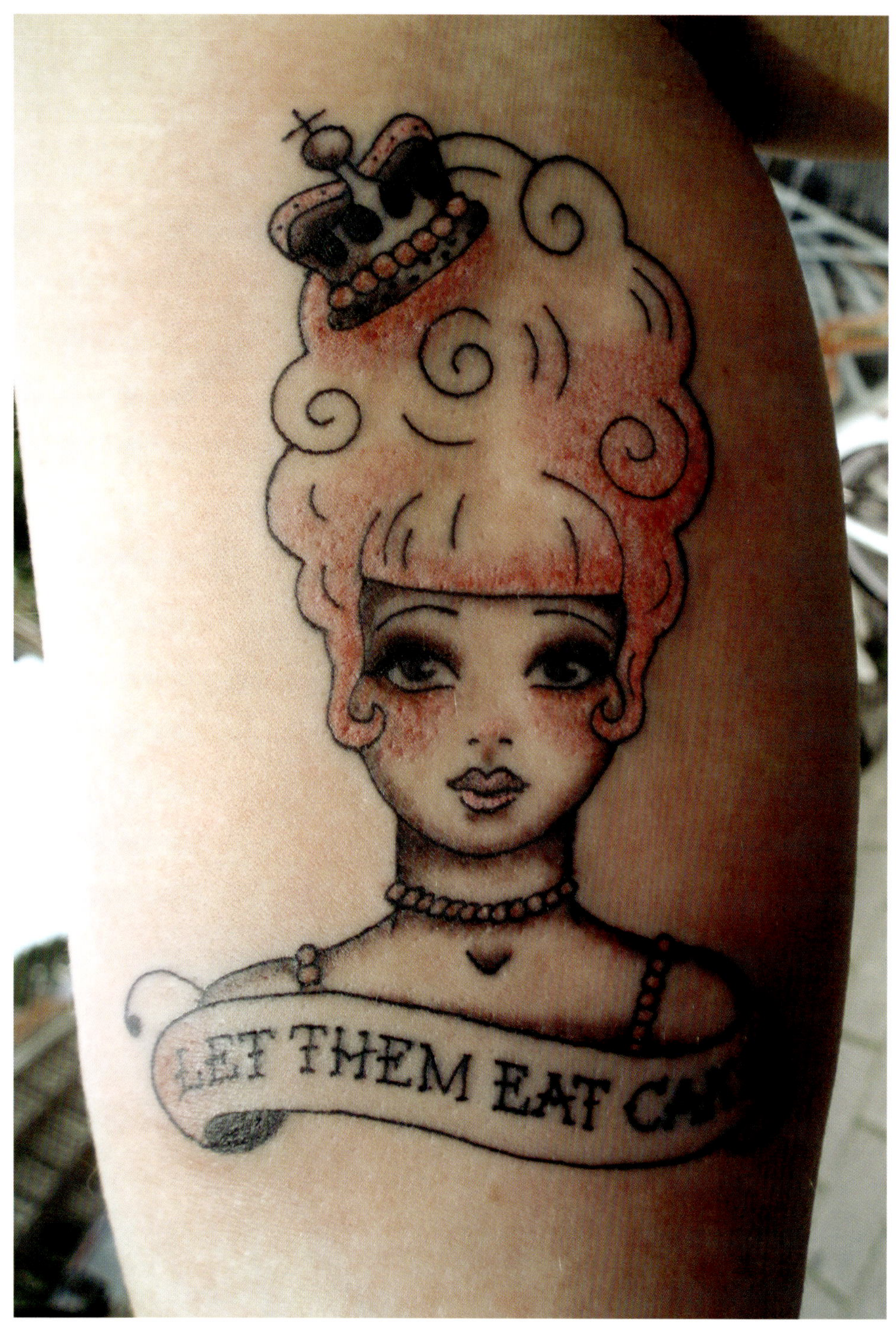
LET THEM EAT CA

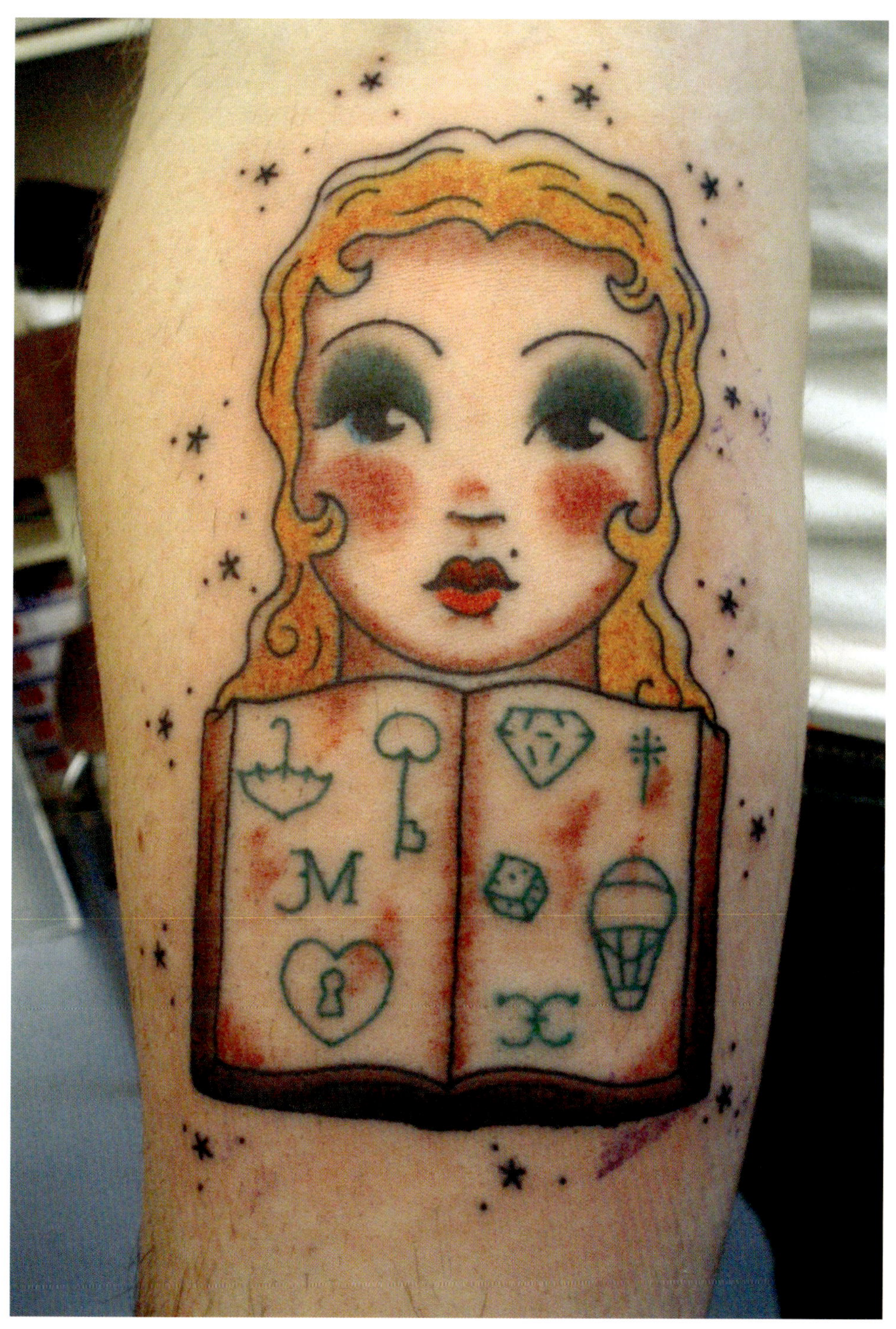

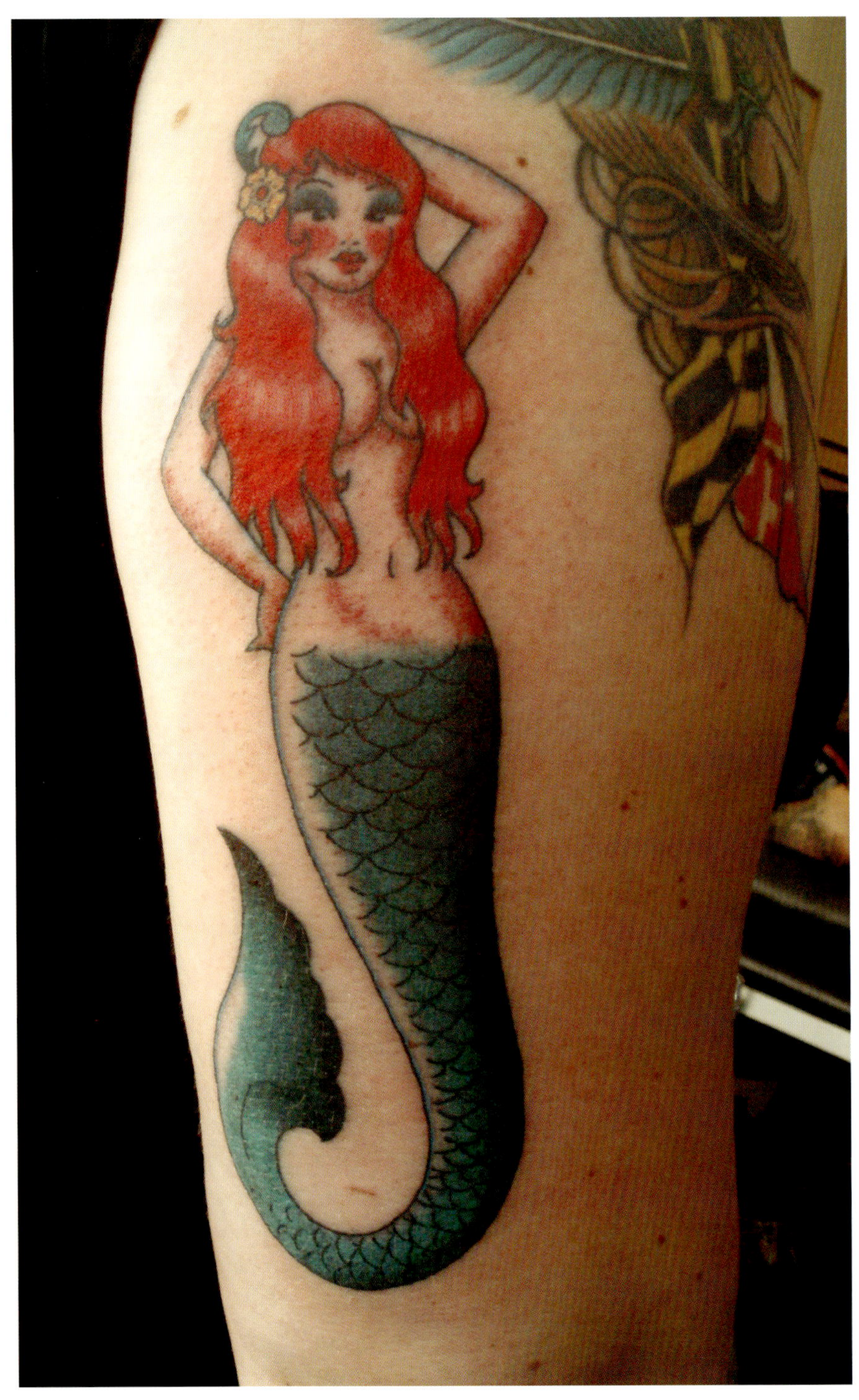

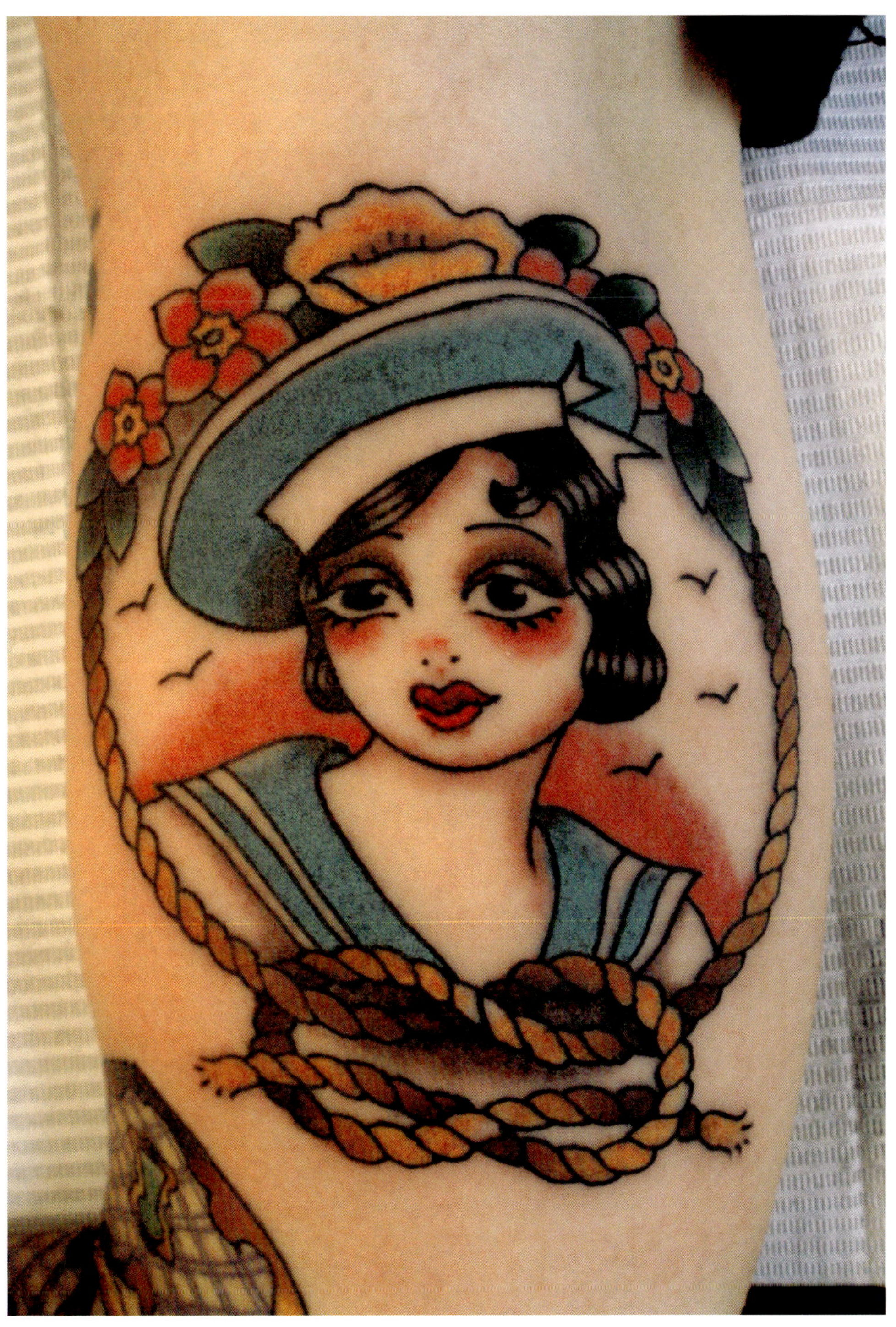

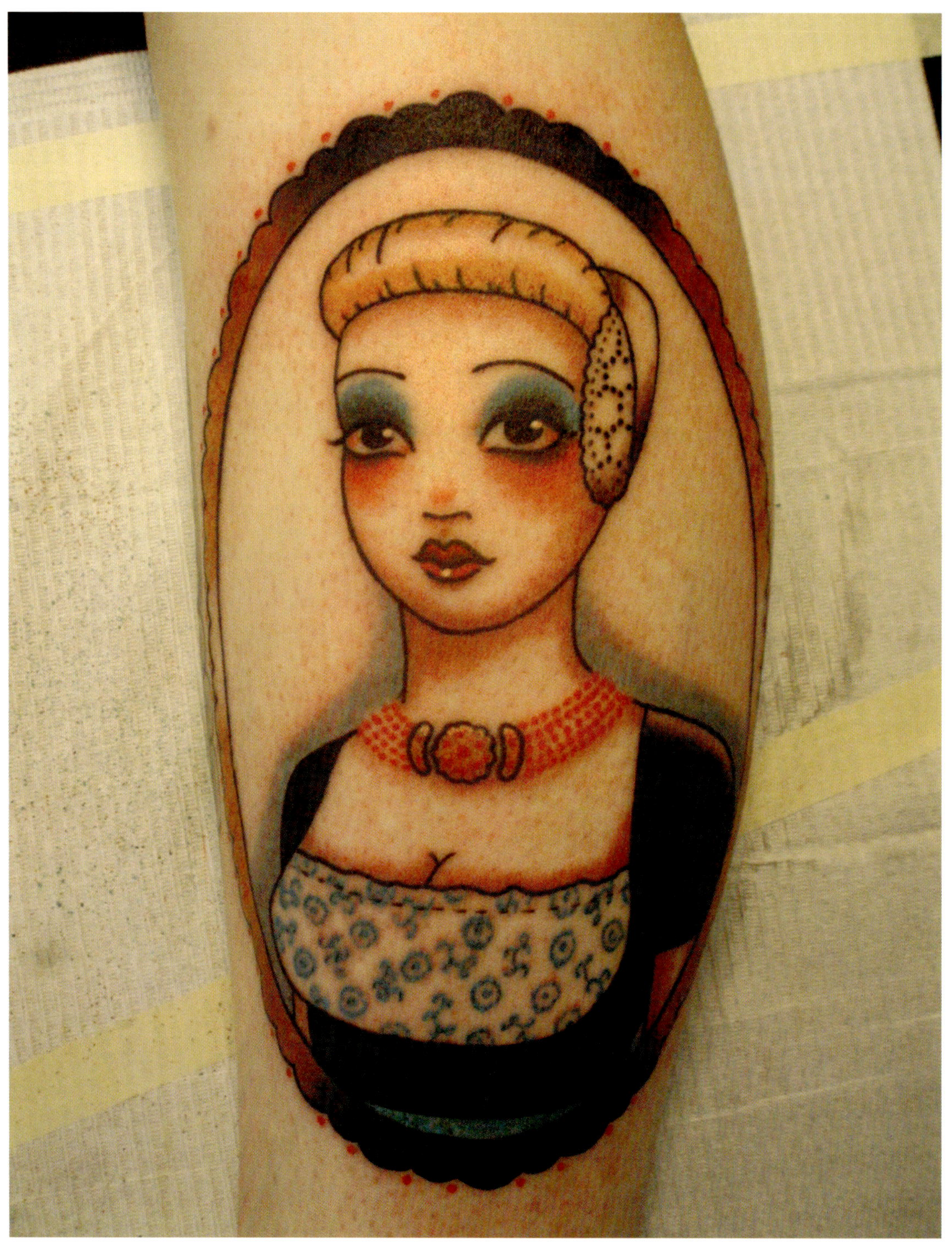

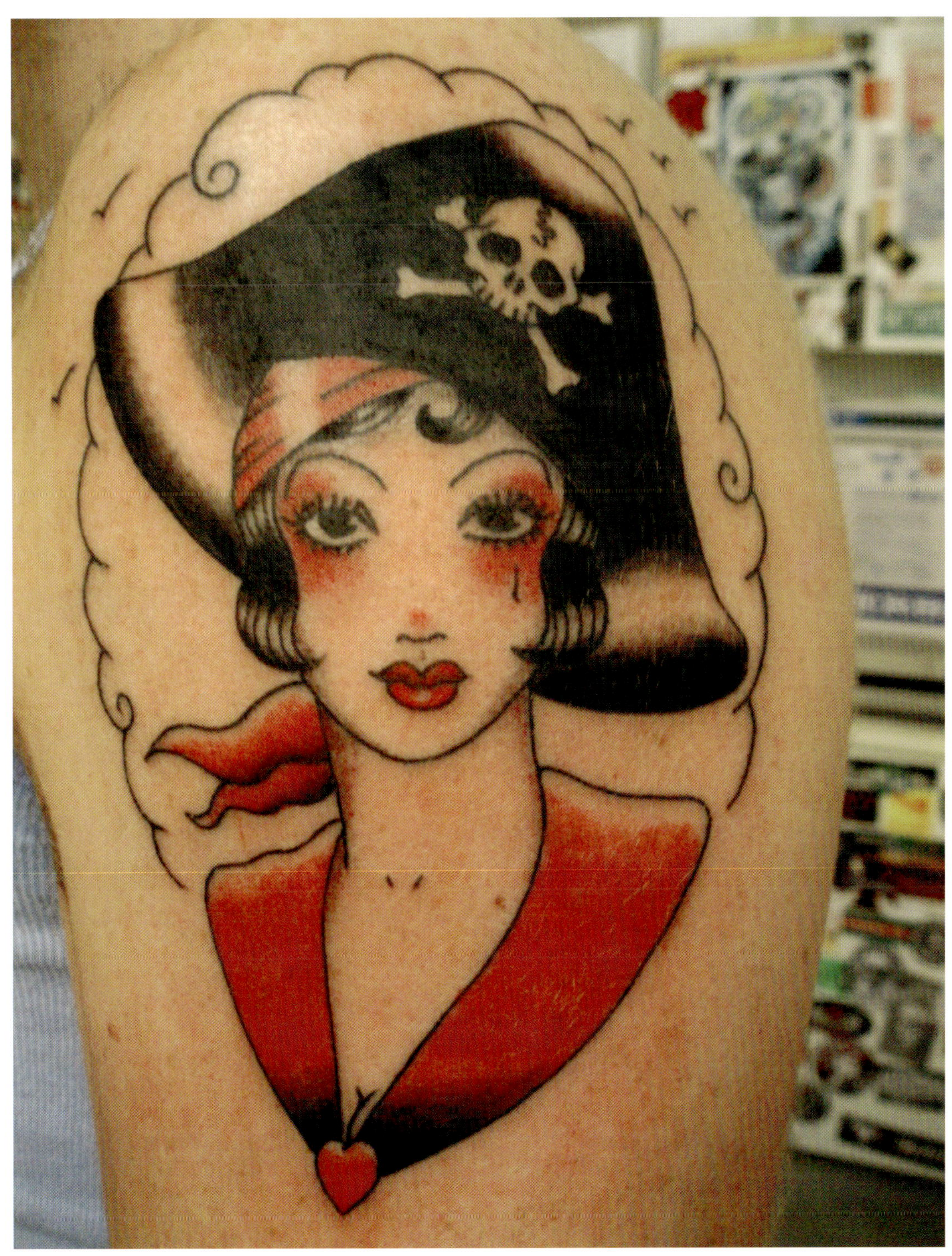

Eva Huber

I'm not really too sure what provokes the chemical development in the brains of individuals who then pursue visual creation their entire lives. I do know, however, that I appreciate such an odd and unique happening on this planet.

Before I got started in the skin engraving business, I never saw it coming. That was seven years ago.

Young girls running away from the safety of their suburban upbringing to join the Motley Crue world of circus style tattoo-life — I never saw it coming. And now I couldn't see myself in too many other places. I do my best to stay away from things that distract me from staying in touch and connected to the real world. I haven't watched much television over the past nine years. I like to spend some of my free time researching the news, contemplating martial arts movement, and meditating.

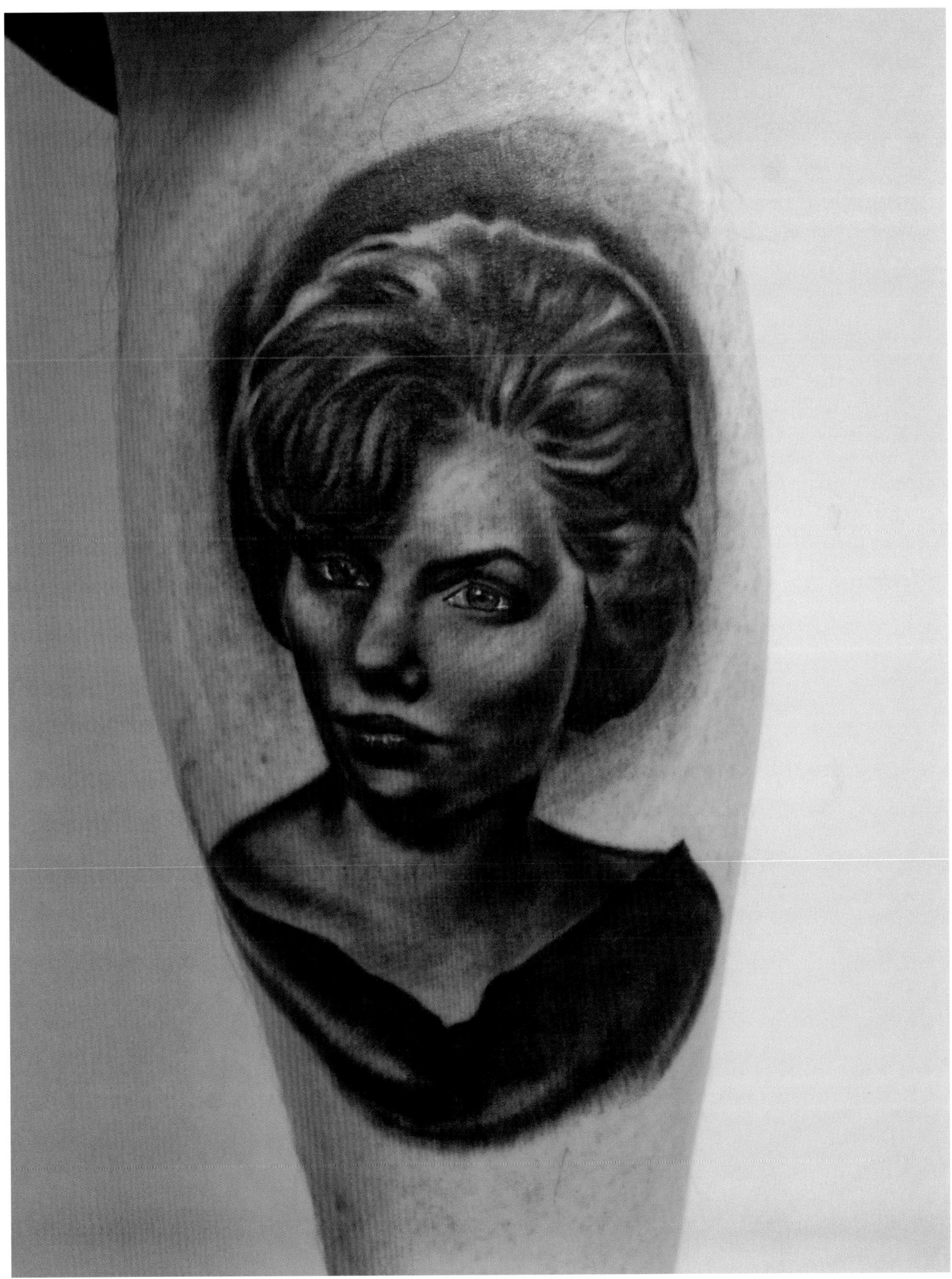

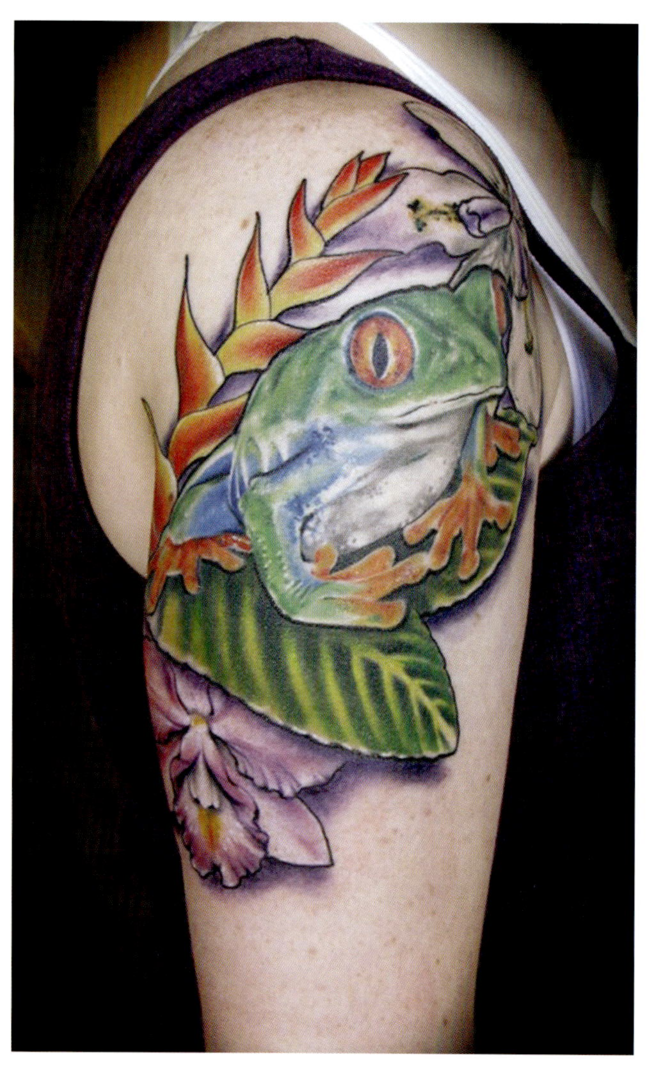

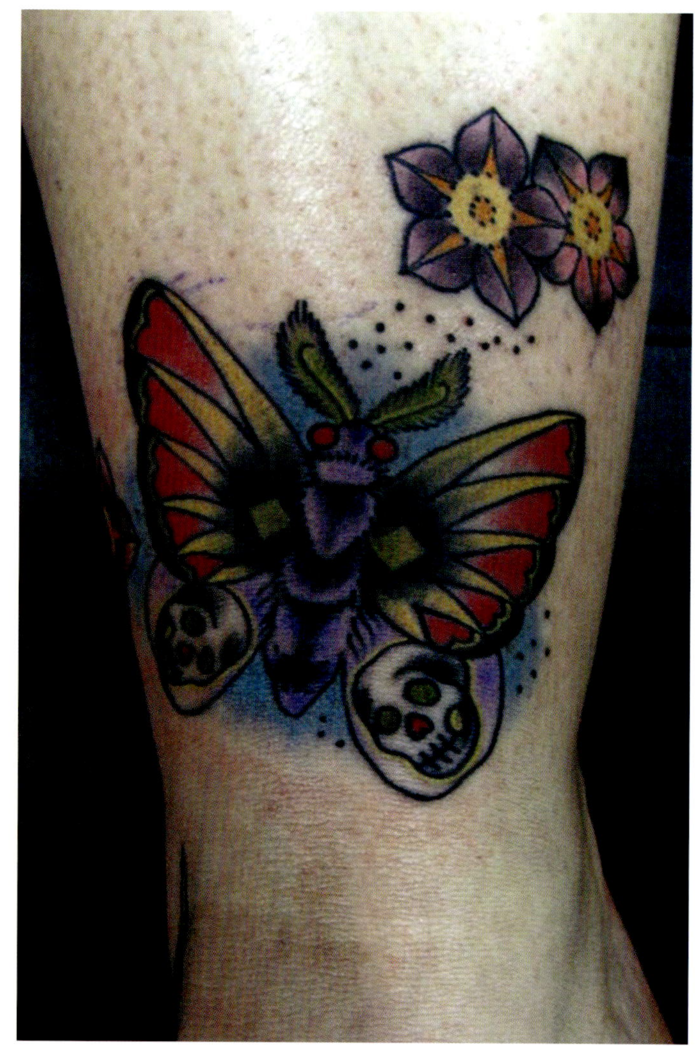

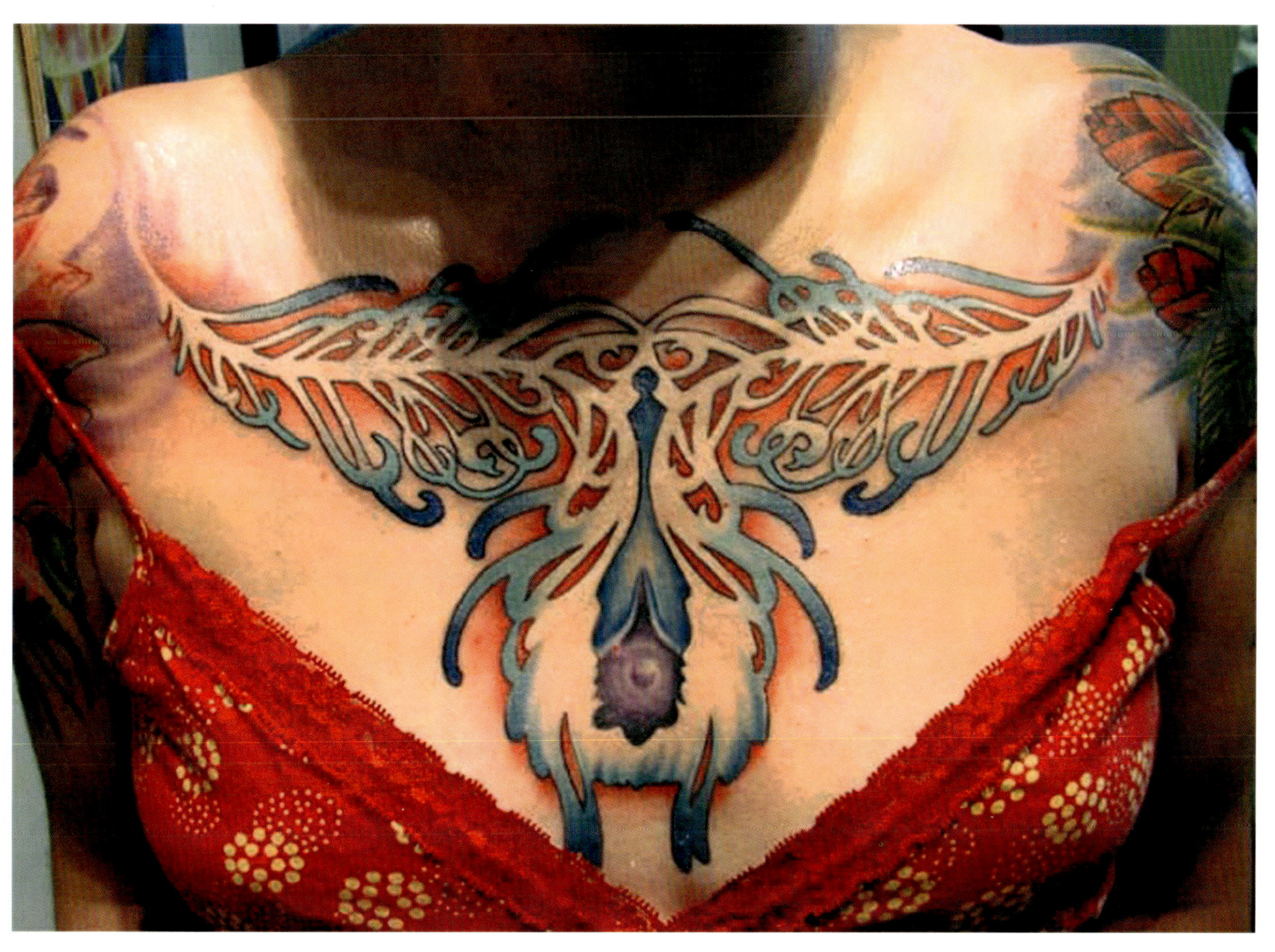

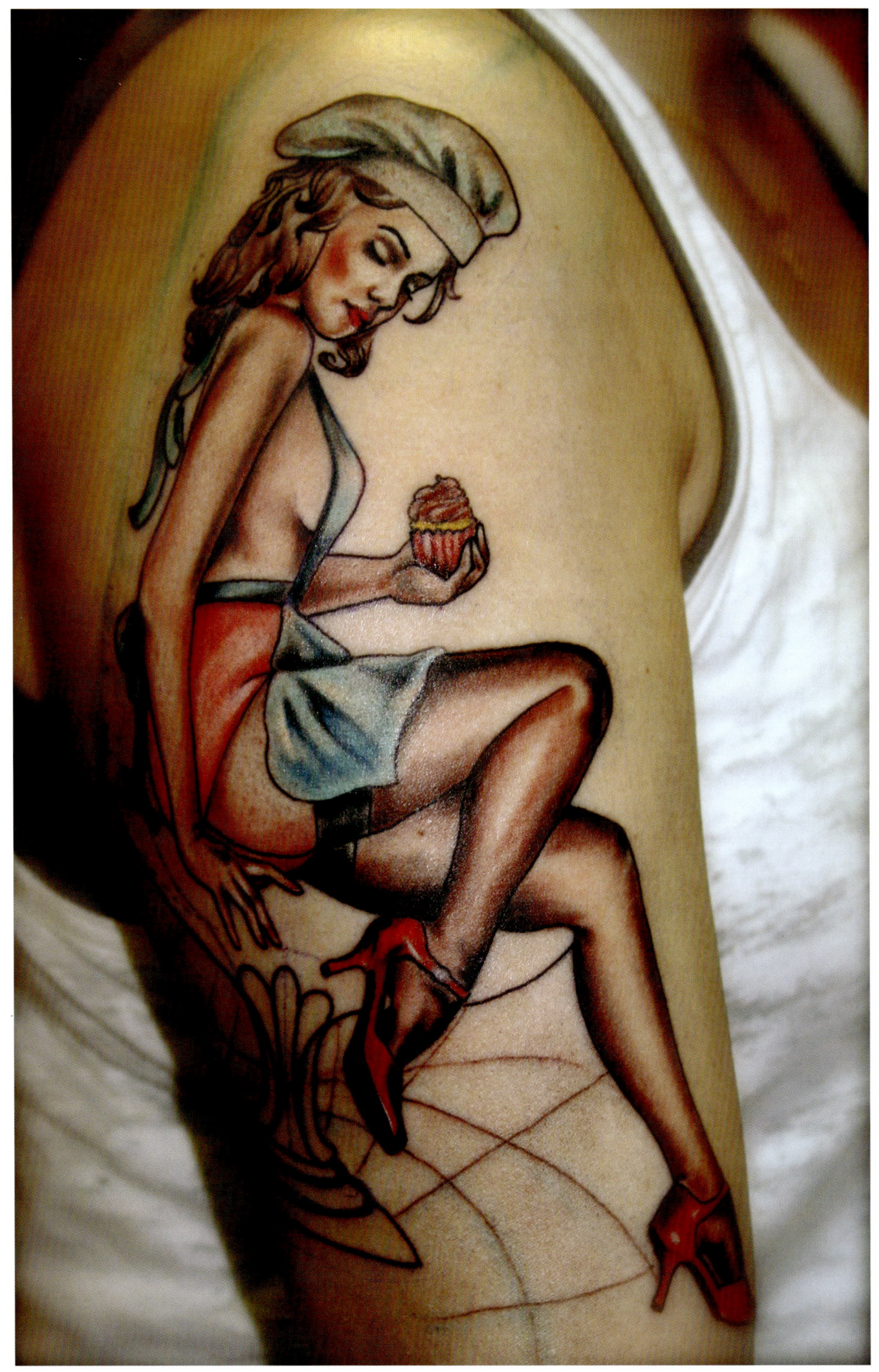

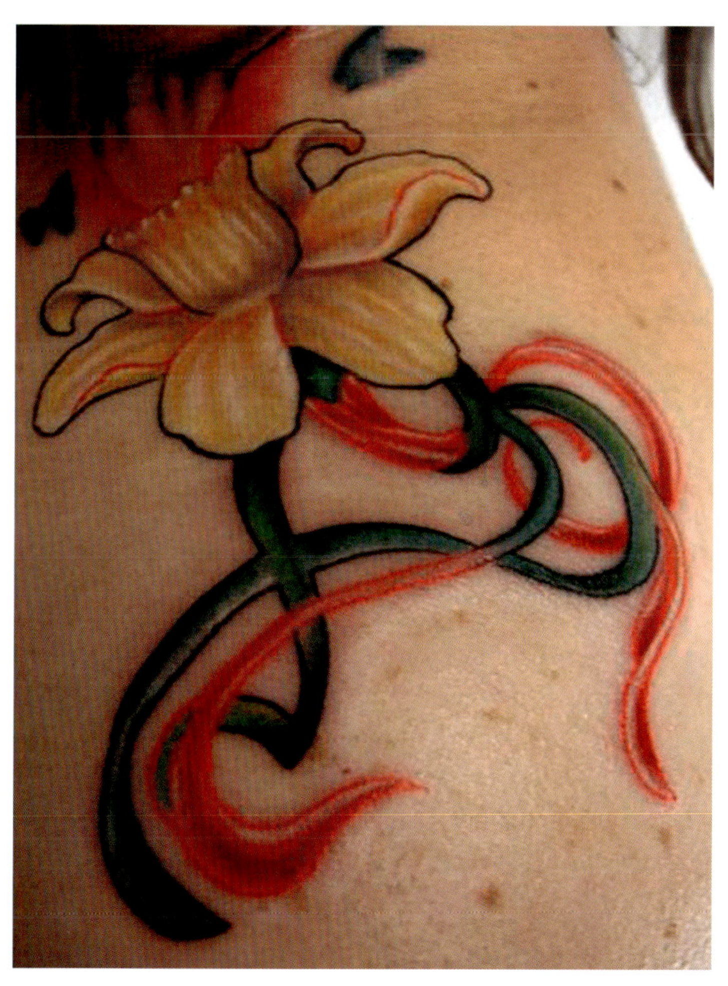

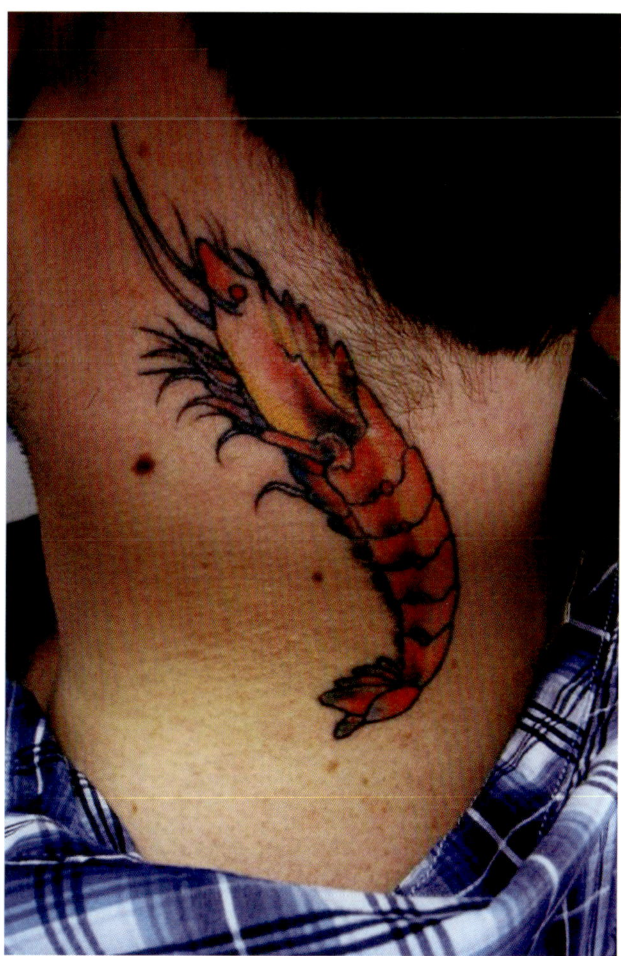

Nathan Kostechko

Being your own worst critic is something I don't wish upon anyone. It keeps me up at night, makes me distant from everyone, and I have a feeling it's what made my teeth start to rot. Or maybe that's smoking? Constantly trying to recreate myself and out-do the last thing I created. Not having a permanent home and always living out of a bag. Trying to see a new place every day. Living life like I'm twelve but with a bit more permanence to my actions. SLAYERRRRR!

I guess this is what keeps me going...

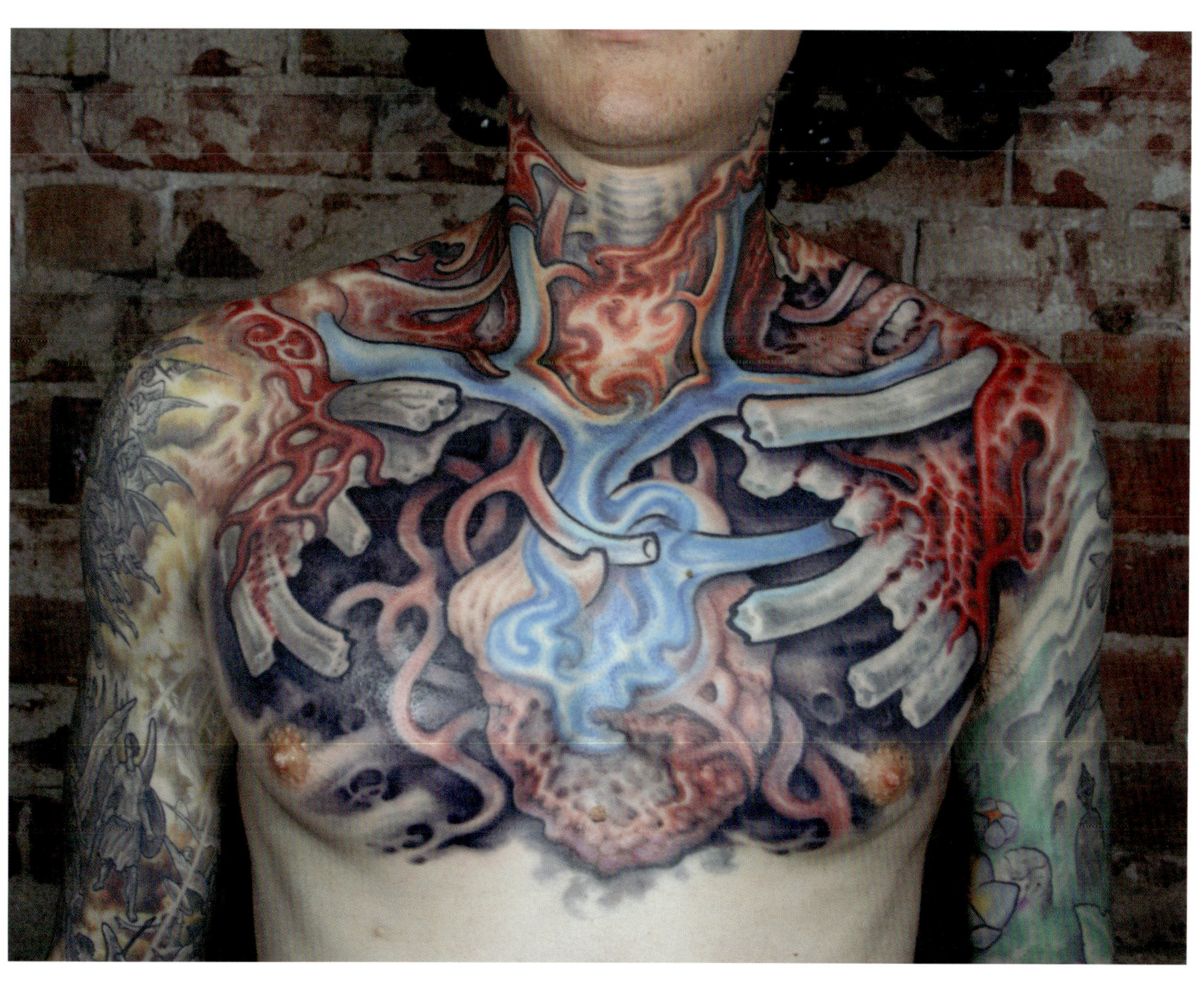

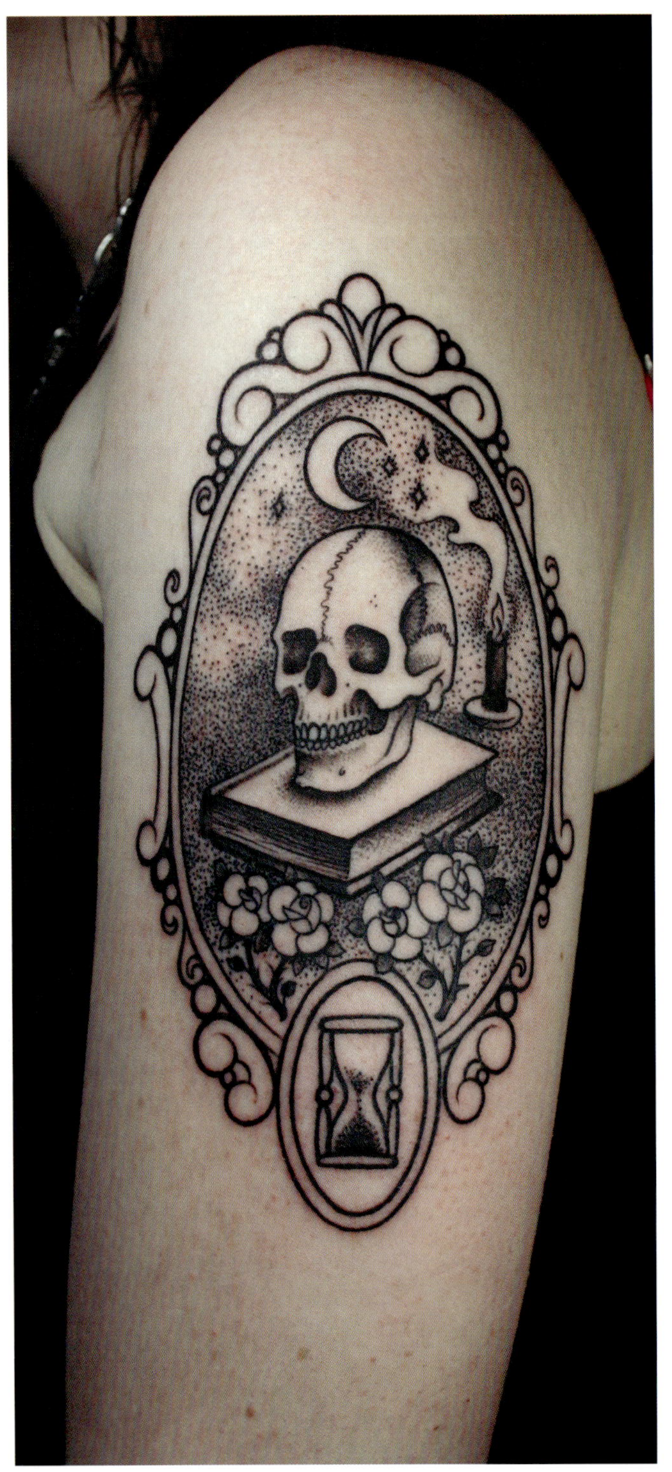

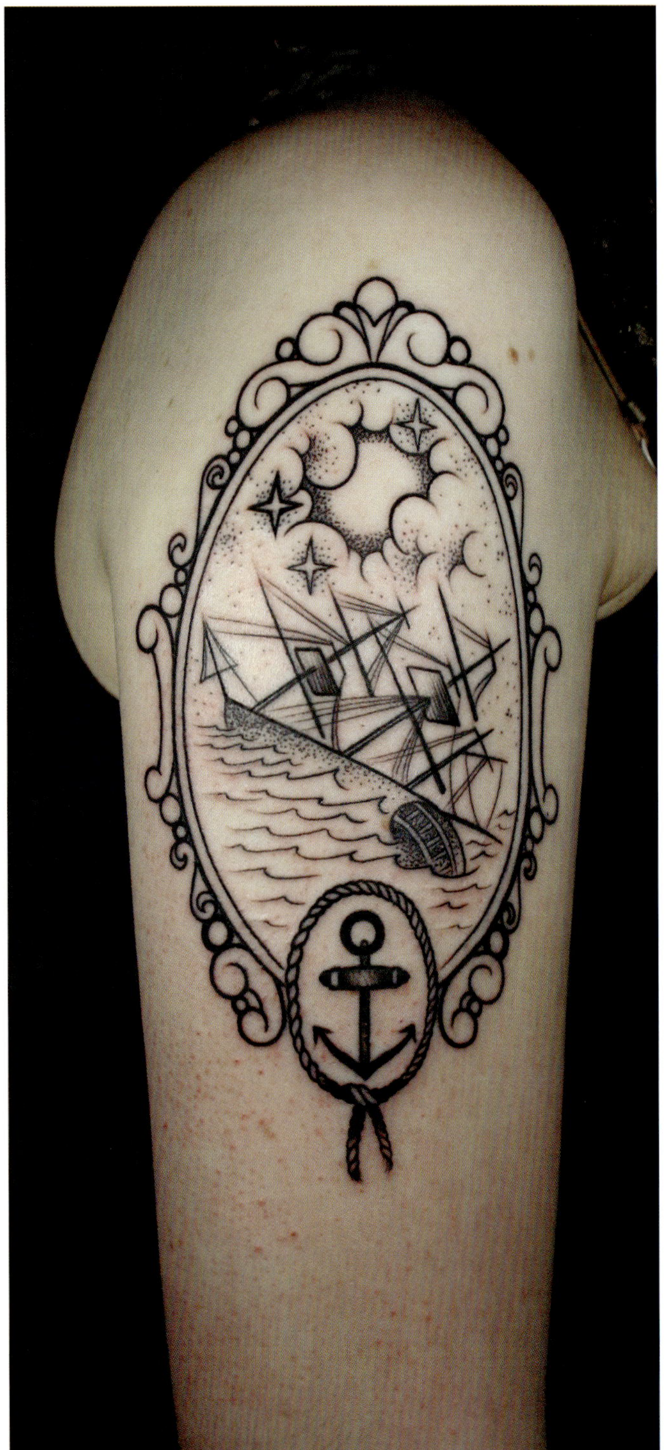

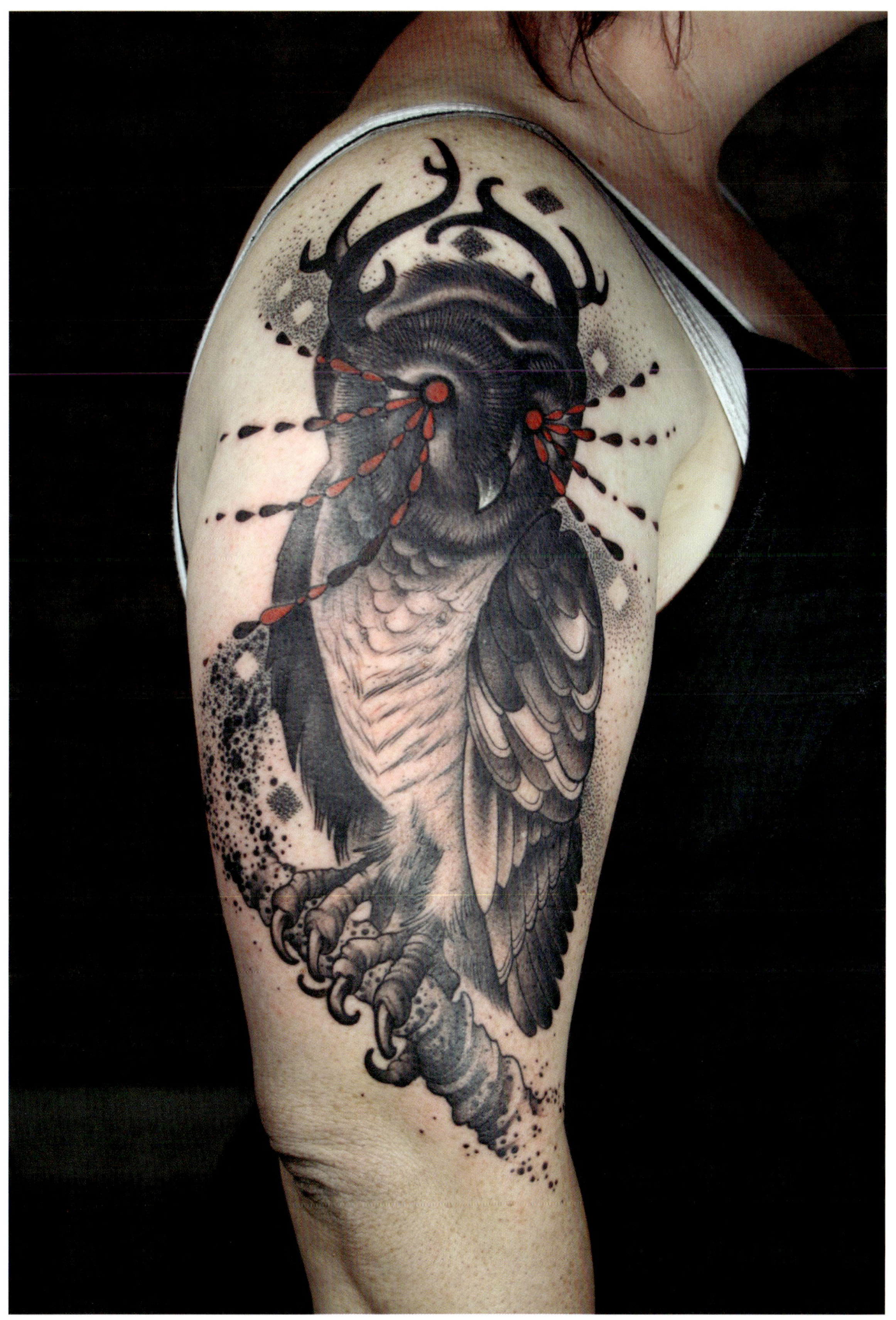

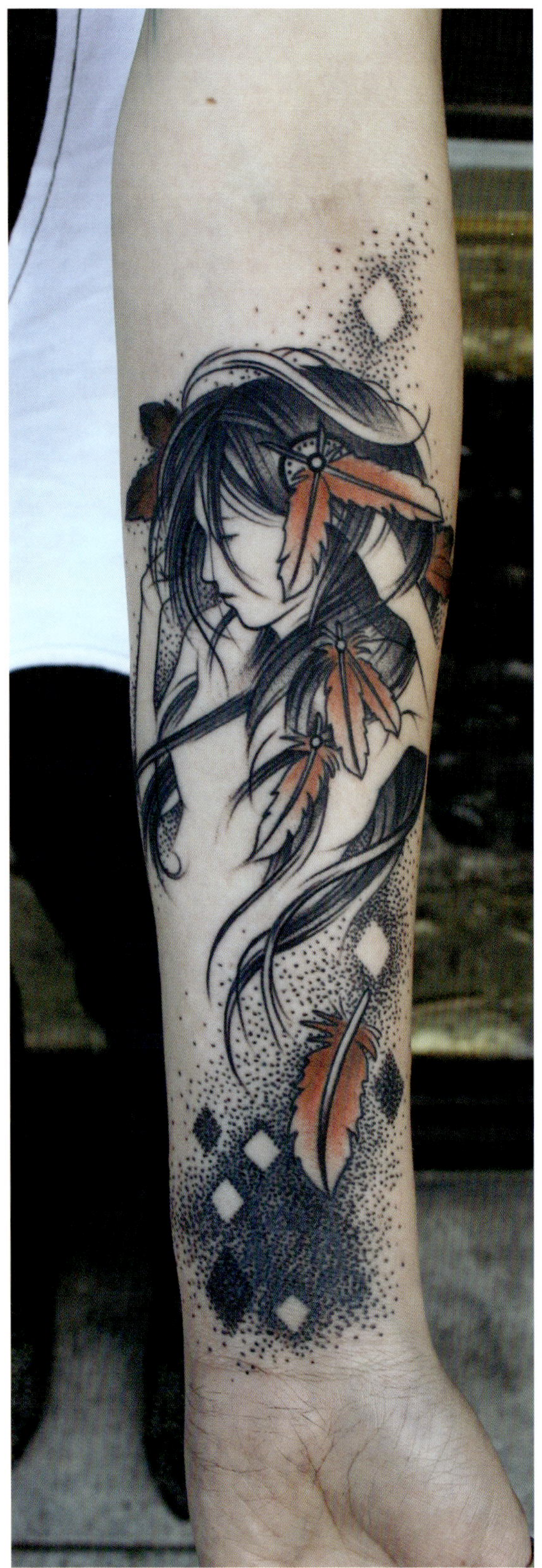

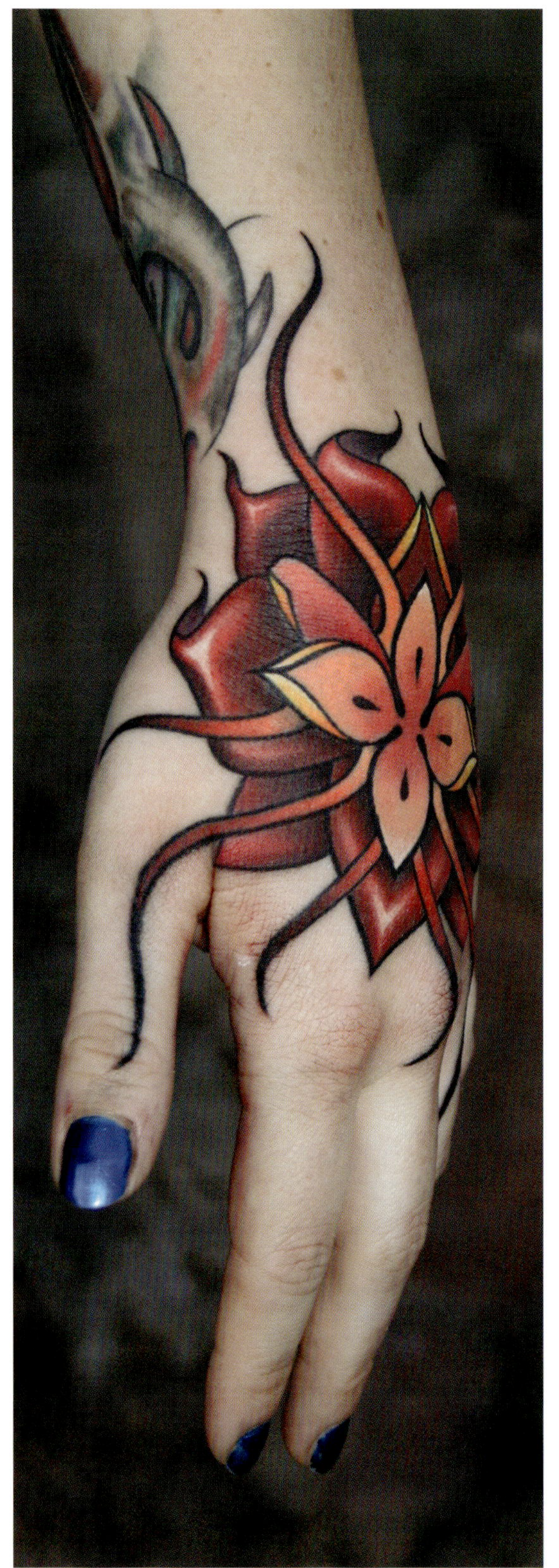

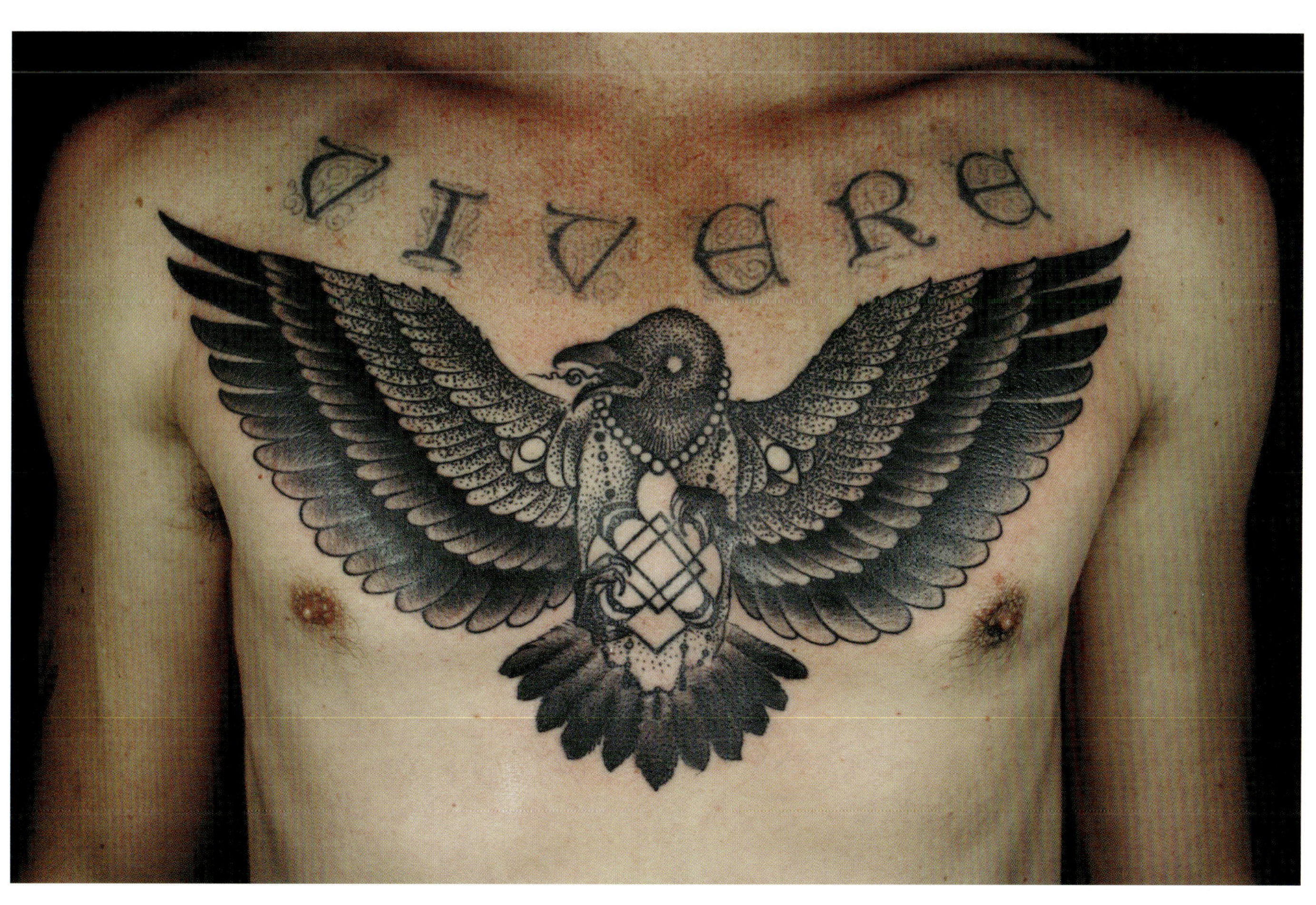
VIVERE

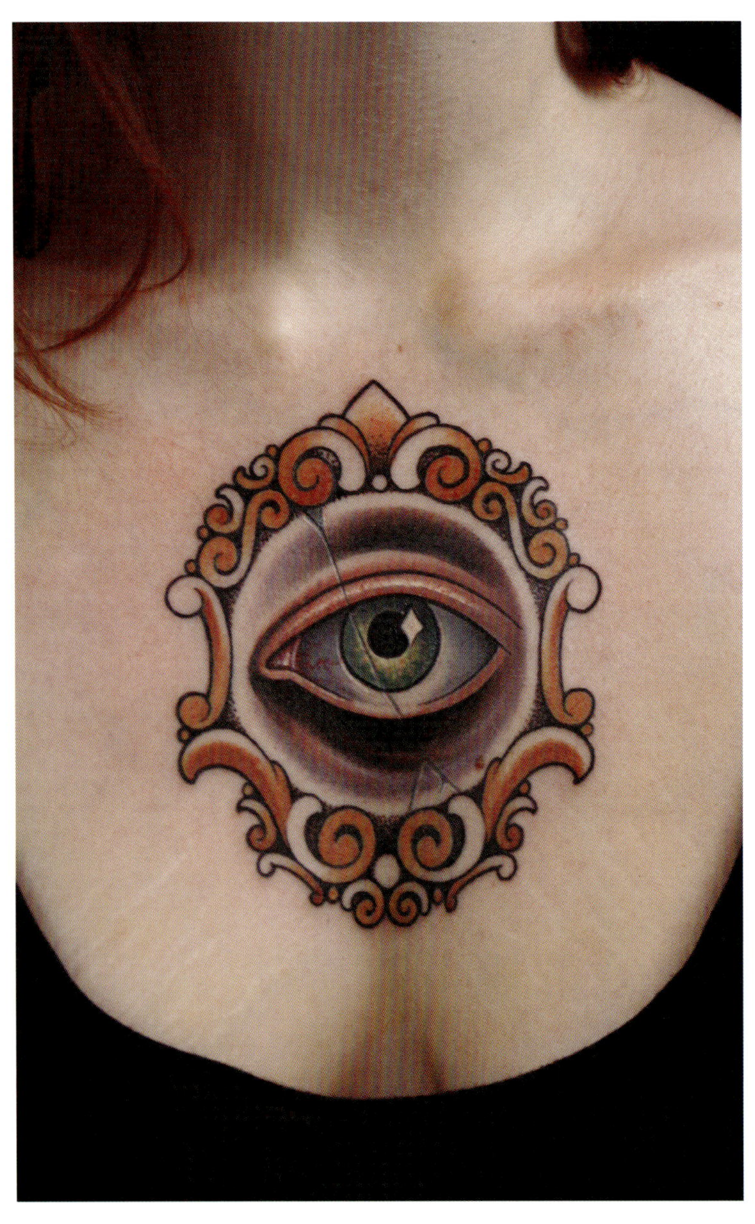

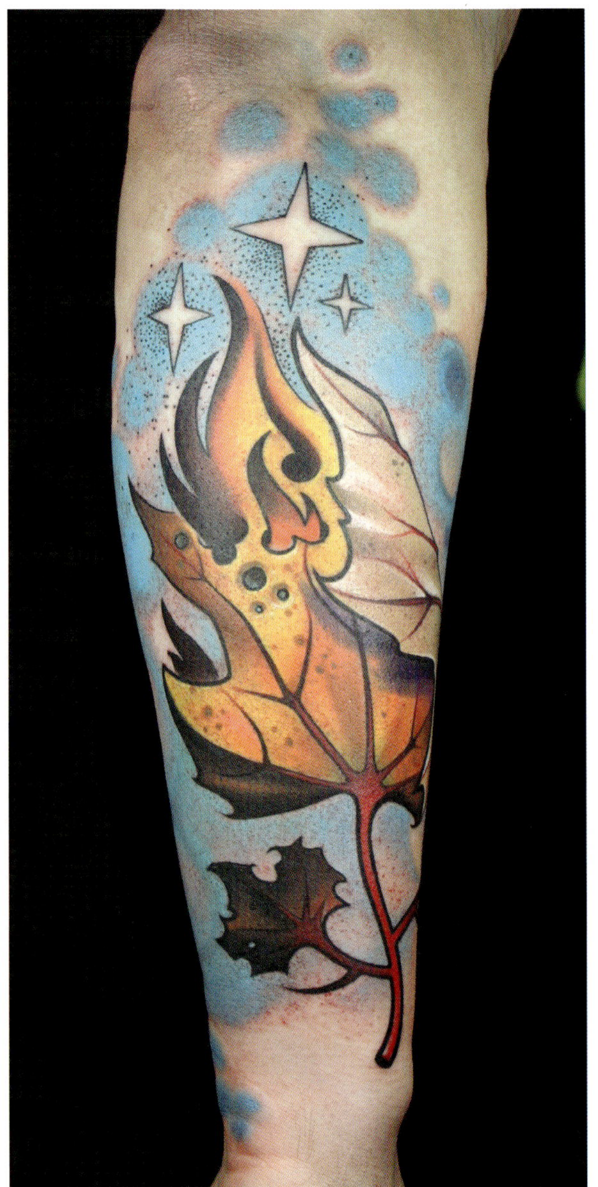

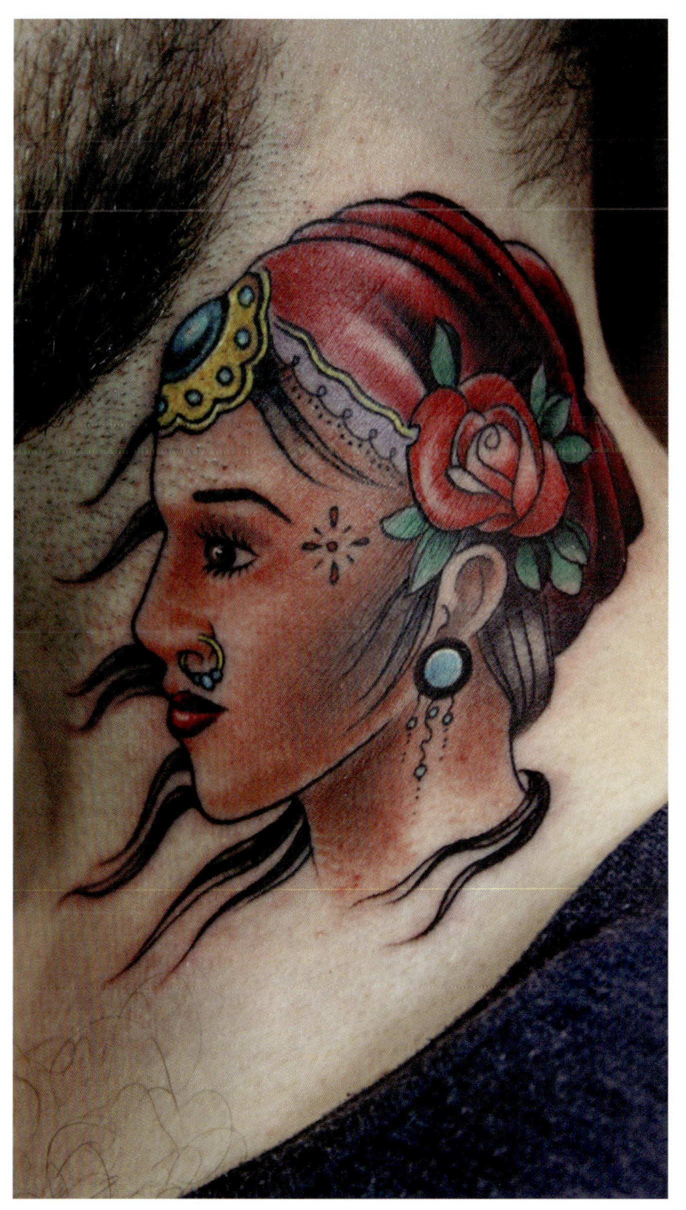

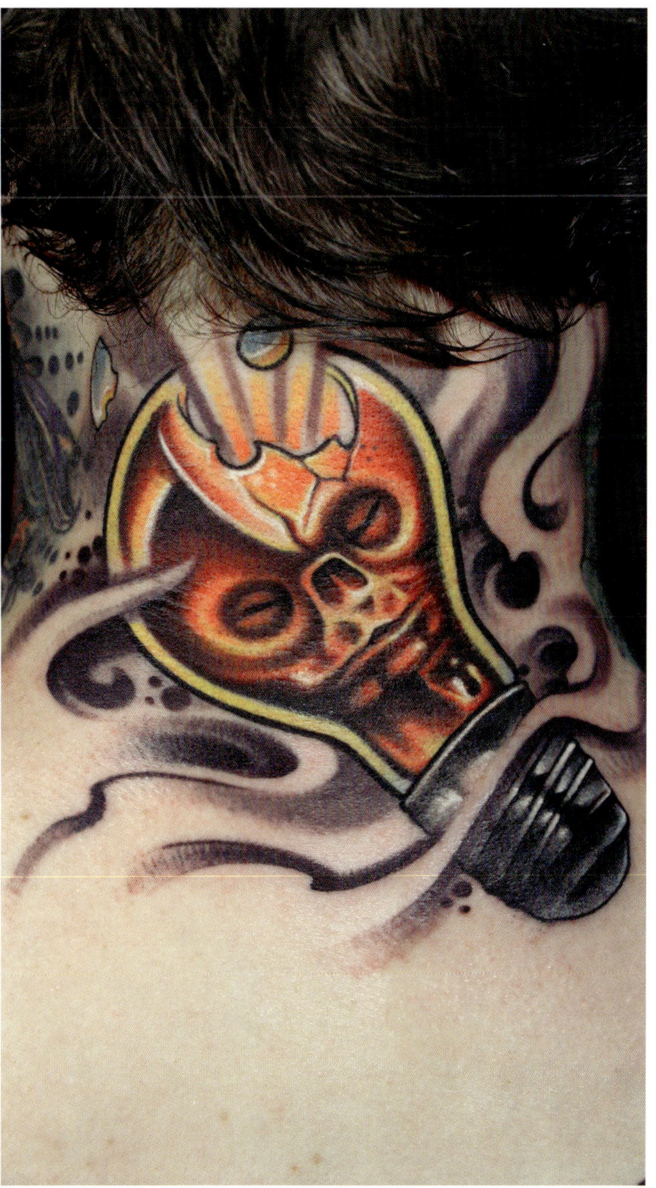

Mike Ledger

My father didn't tell me how to live — instead, he lived and let me watch him do it. He gave me the greatest gift anyone could give another person... he believed in me.

My life is now dedicated to my two sons, Mana and Micah, and my beautiful wife, Tina. It's been nothing but working hard and being a good dad. I still strive constantly to grow as a tattoo artist and painter, and work hard to be the best husband and father that I can be.

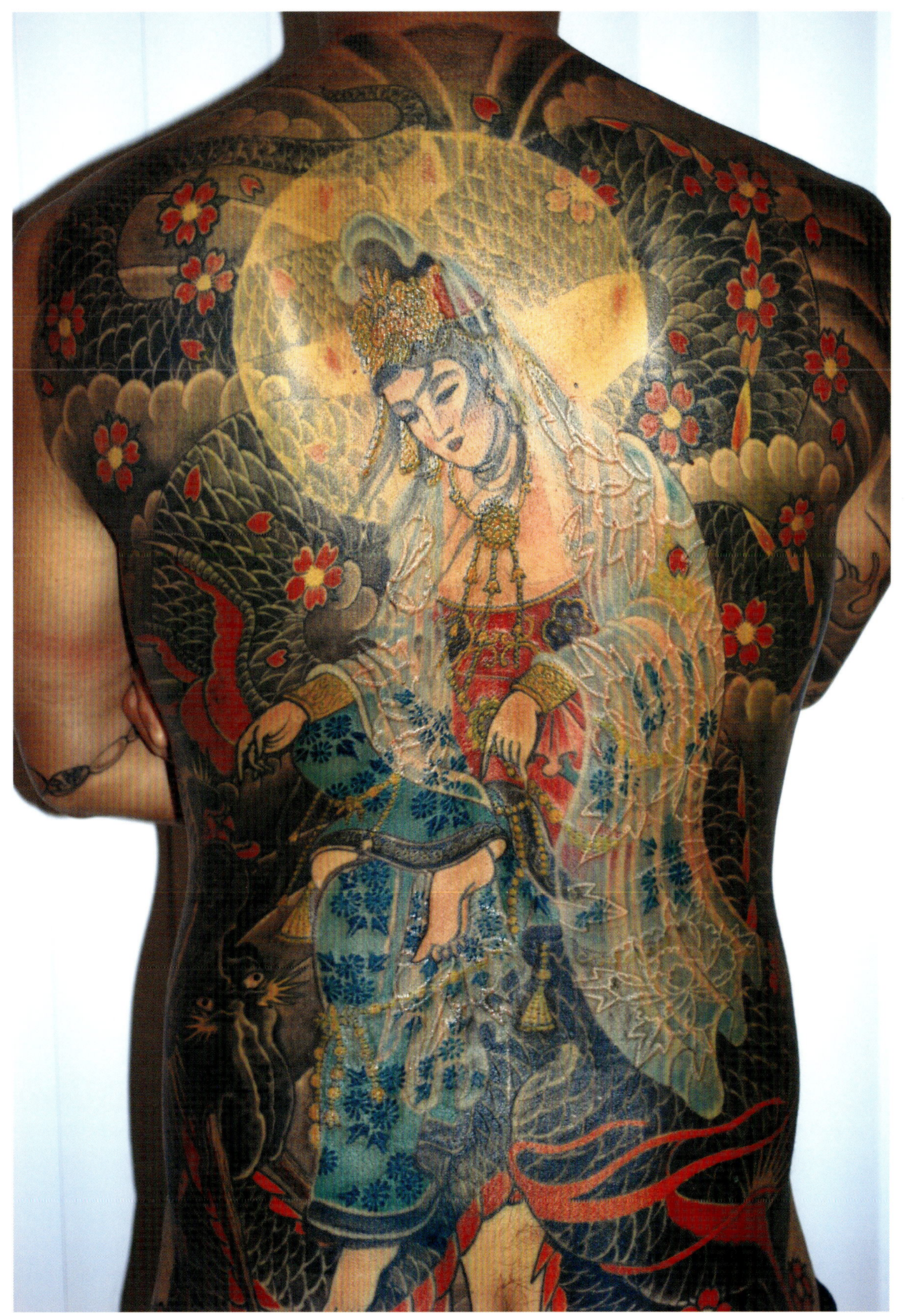

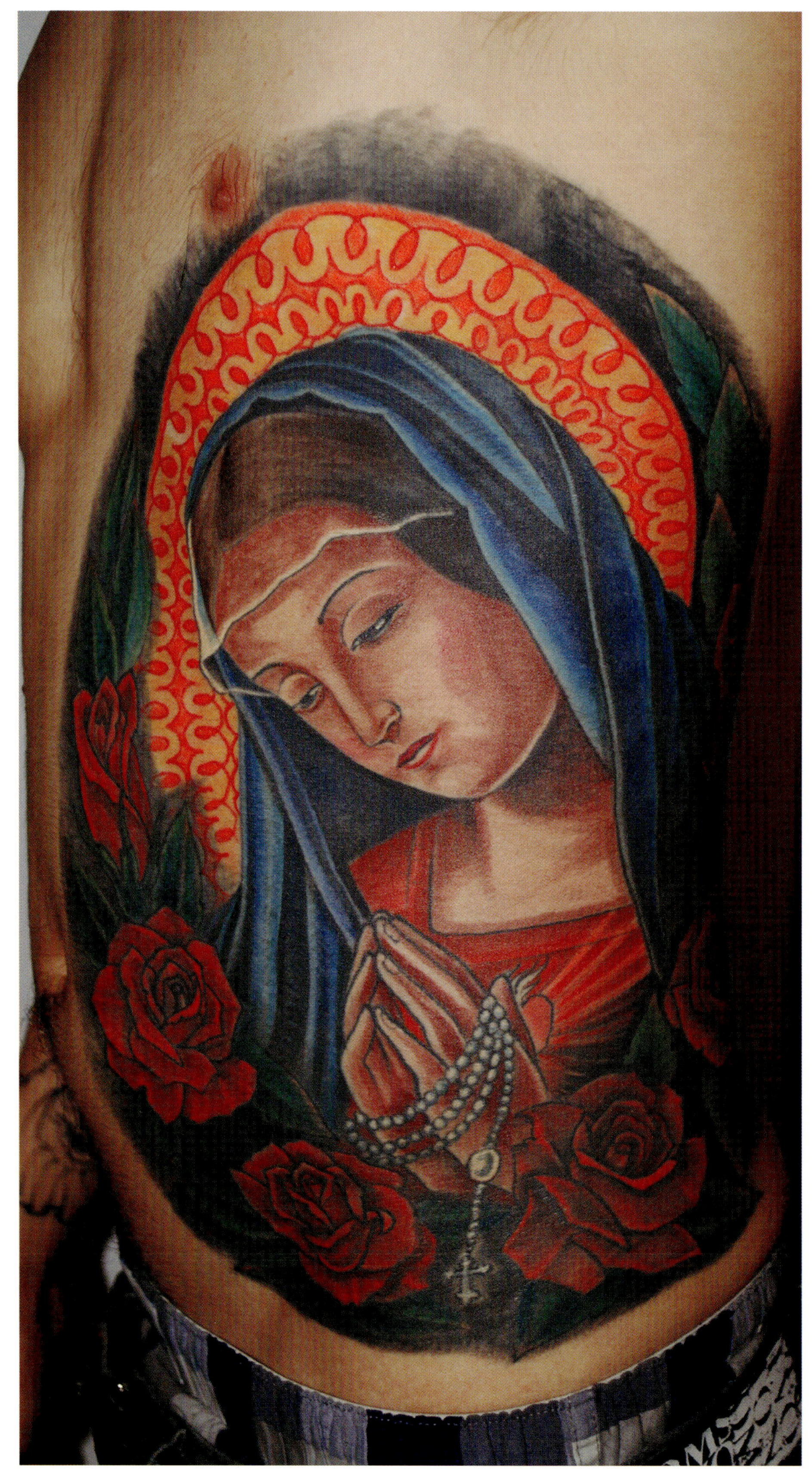

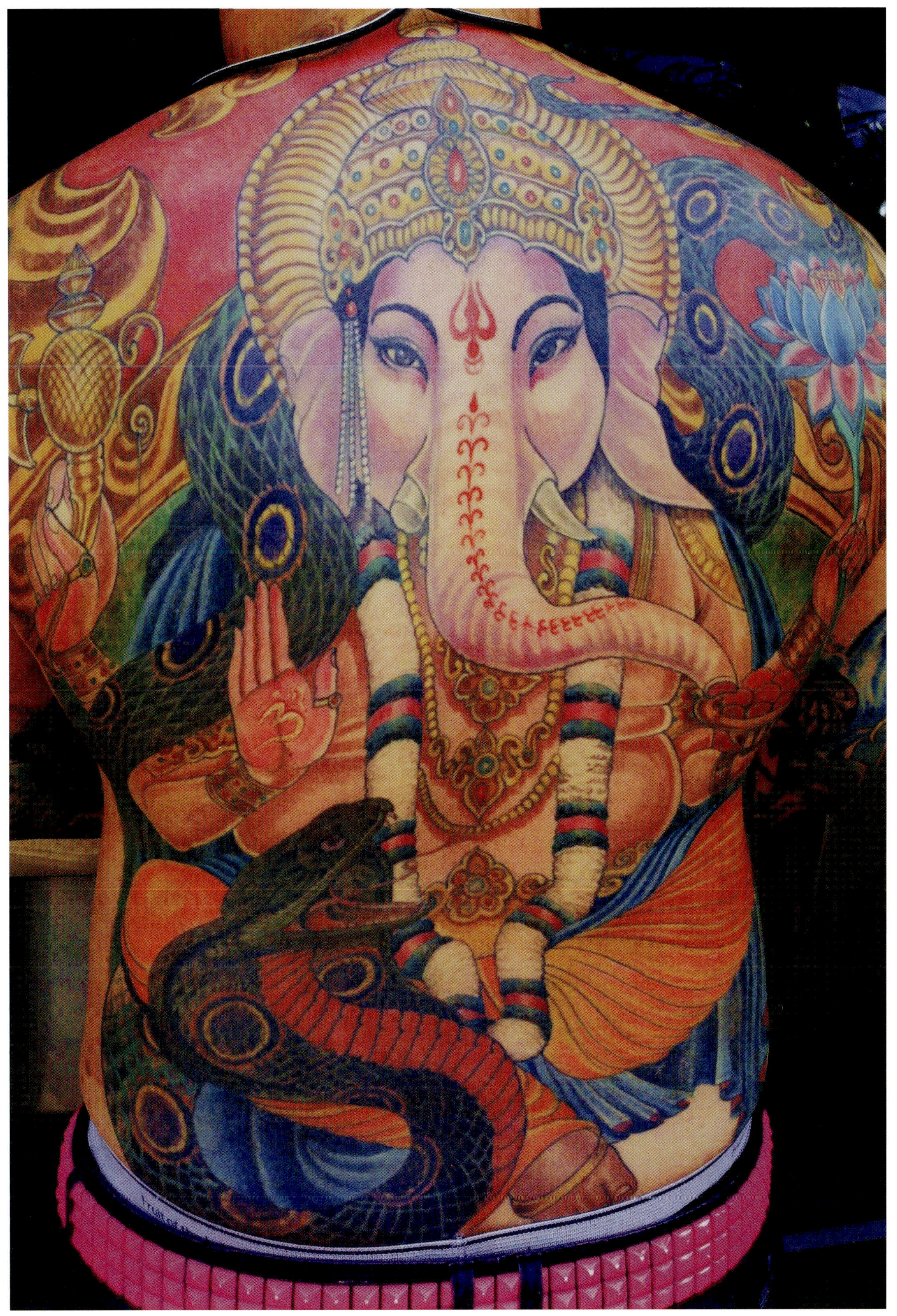

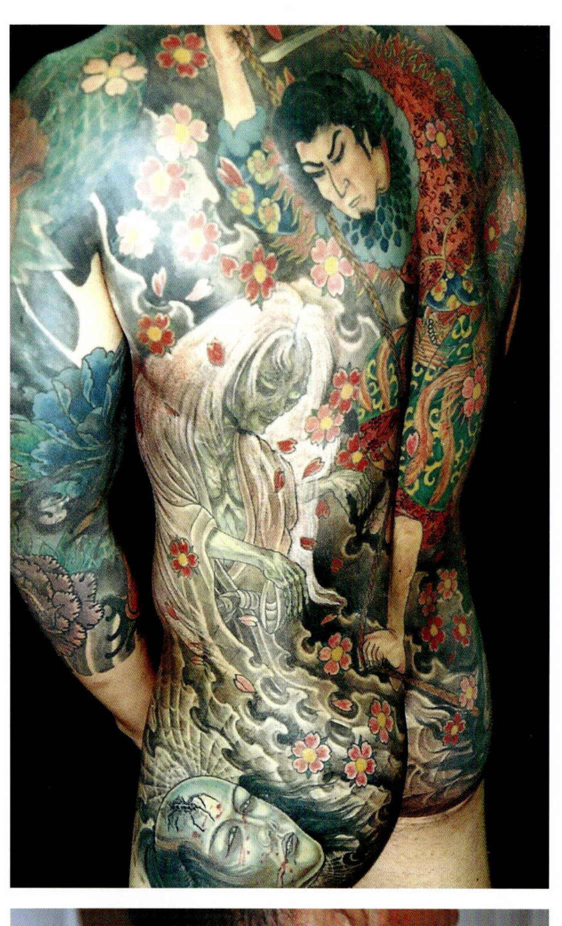

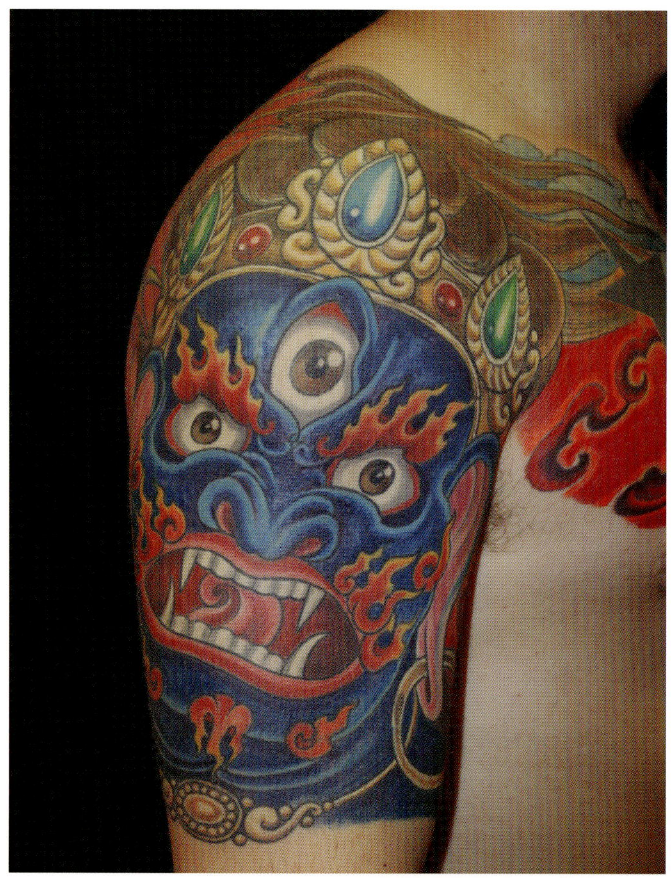

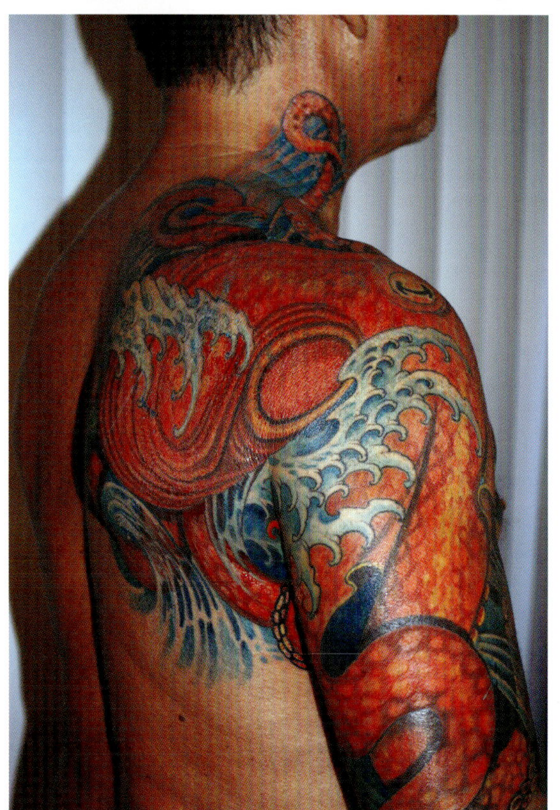

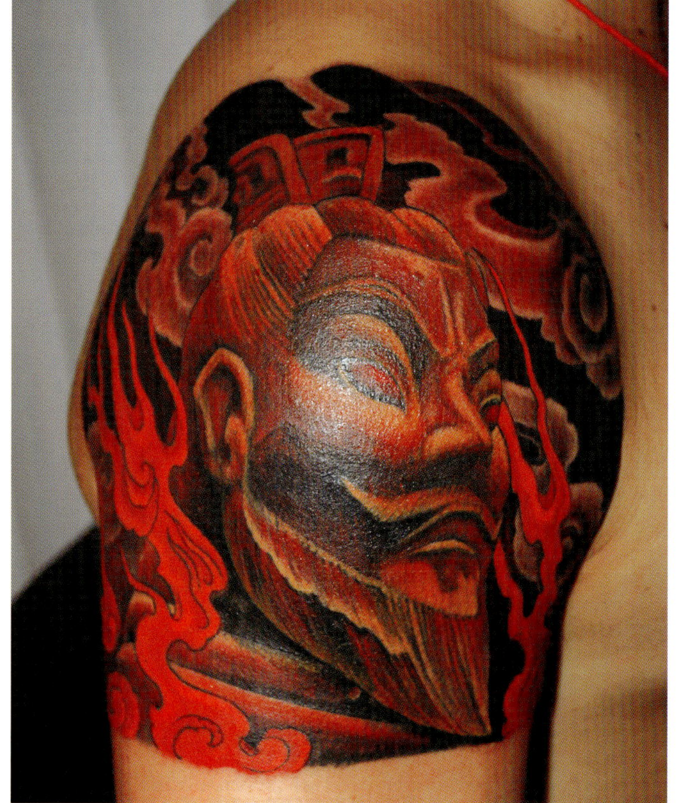

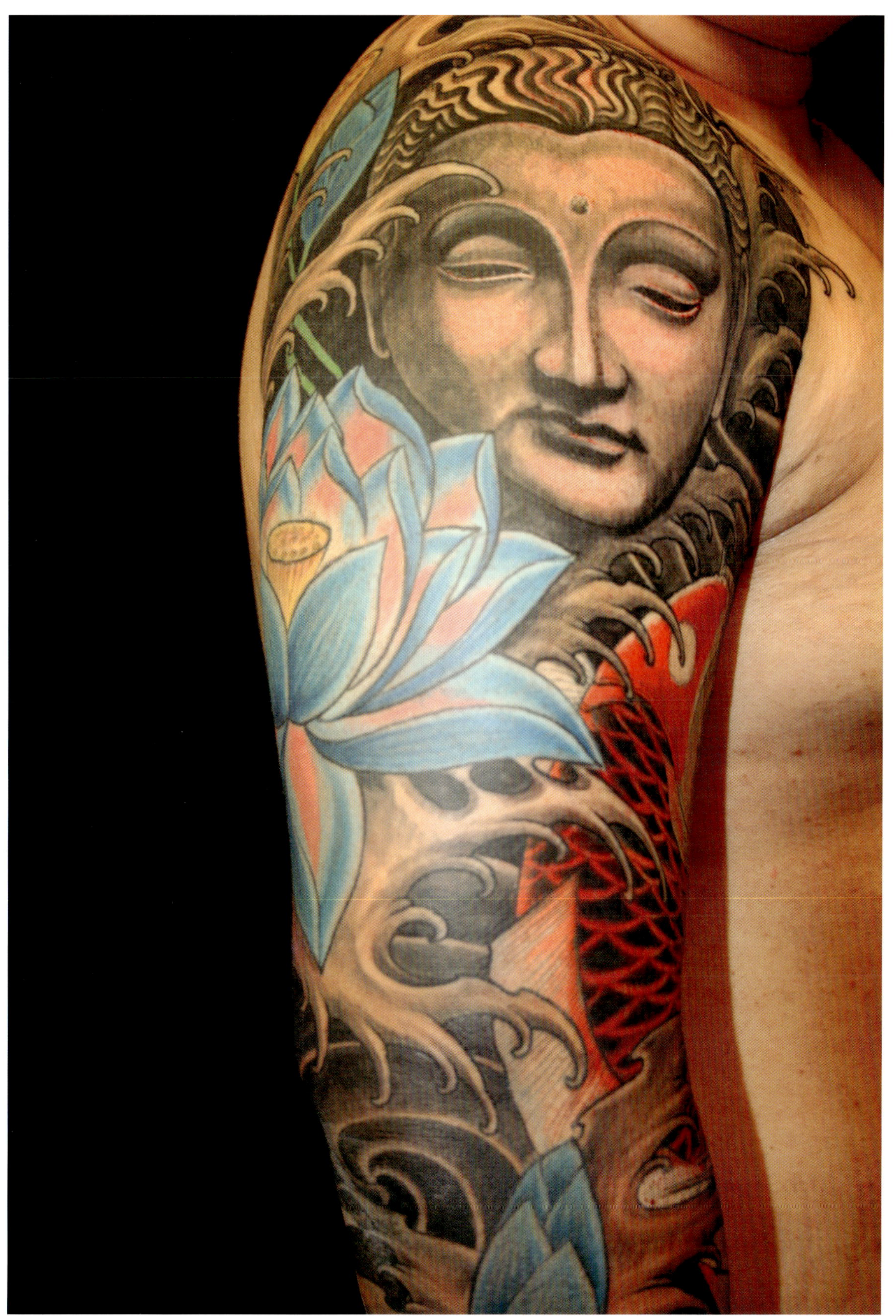

Jime Litwalk

Art has always been a part of my life ever since I was a kid. That's always what I wanted to do; draw, paint or just scribble on whatever! Being an artist truly has been a lifelong dream come true - along with being with my family, my wife and kids. Tattooing and art will always be a part of who I am.

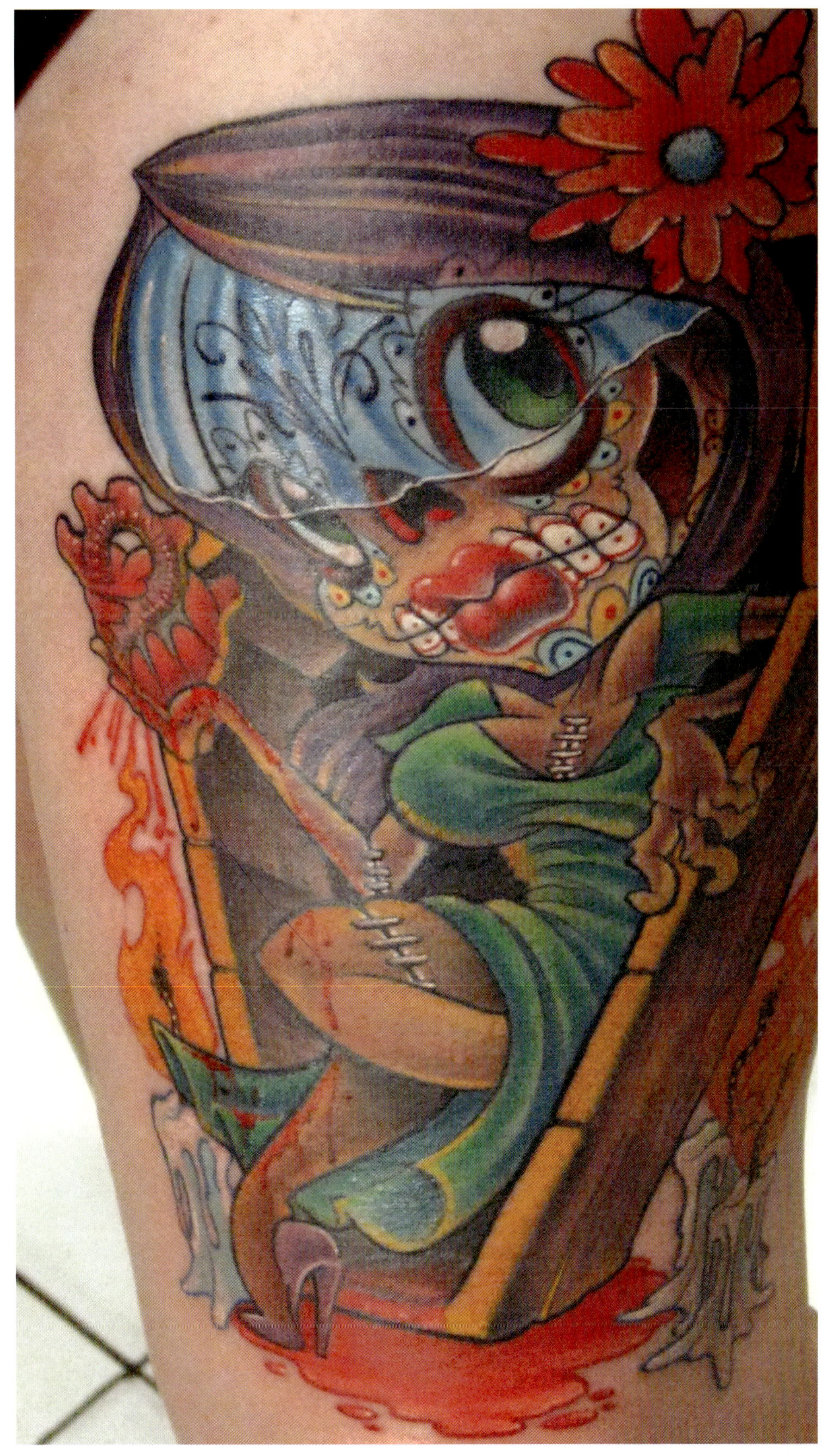

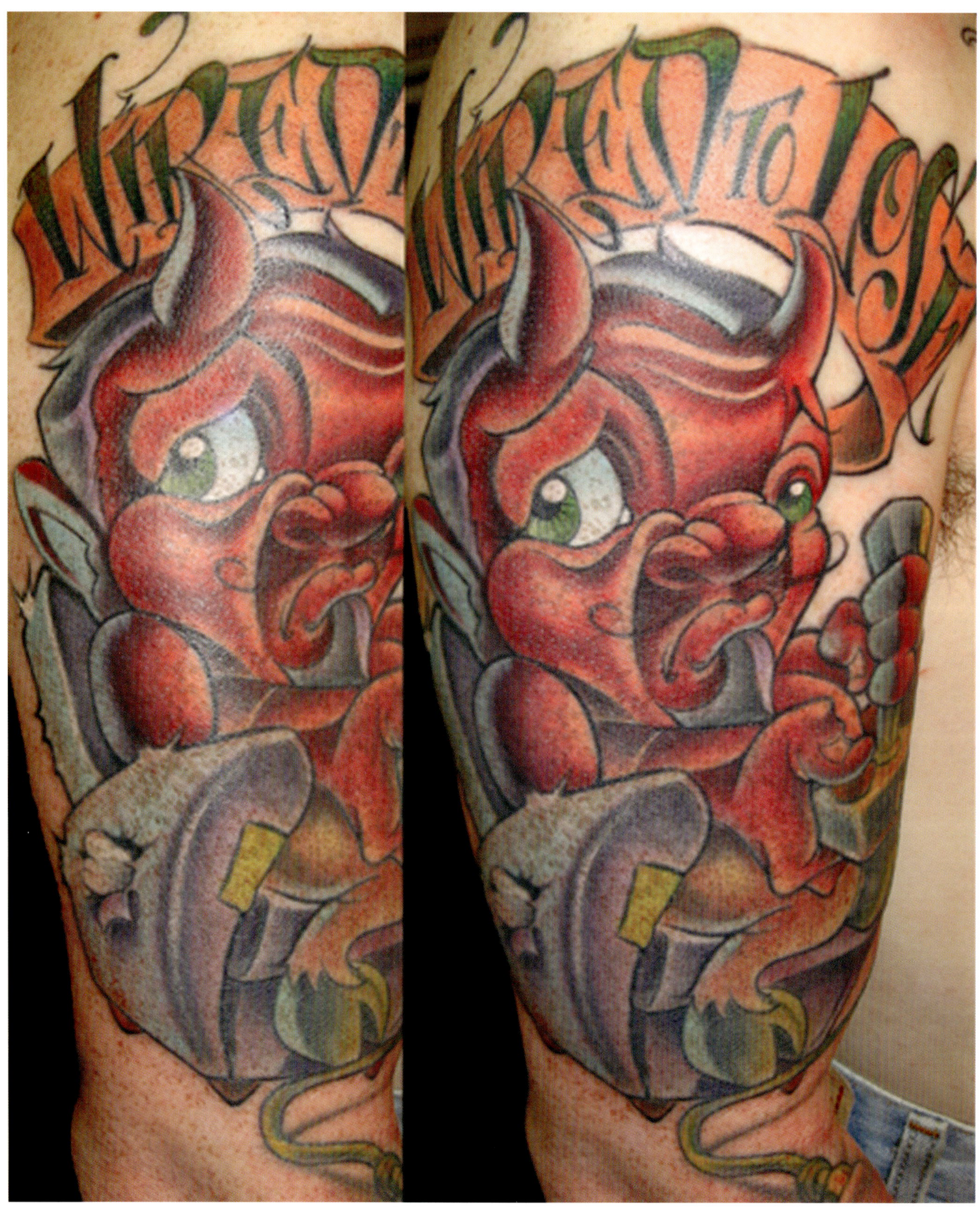

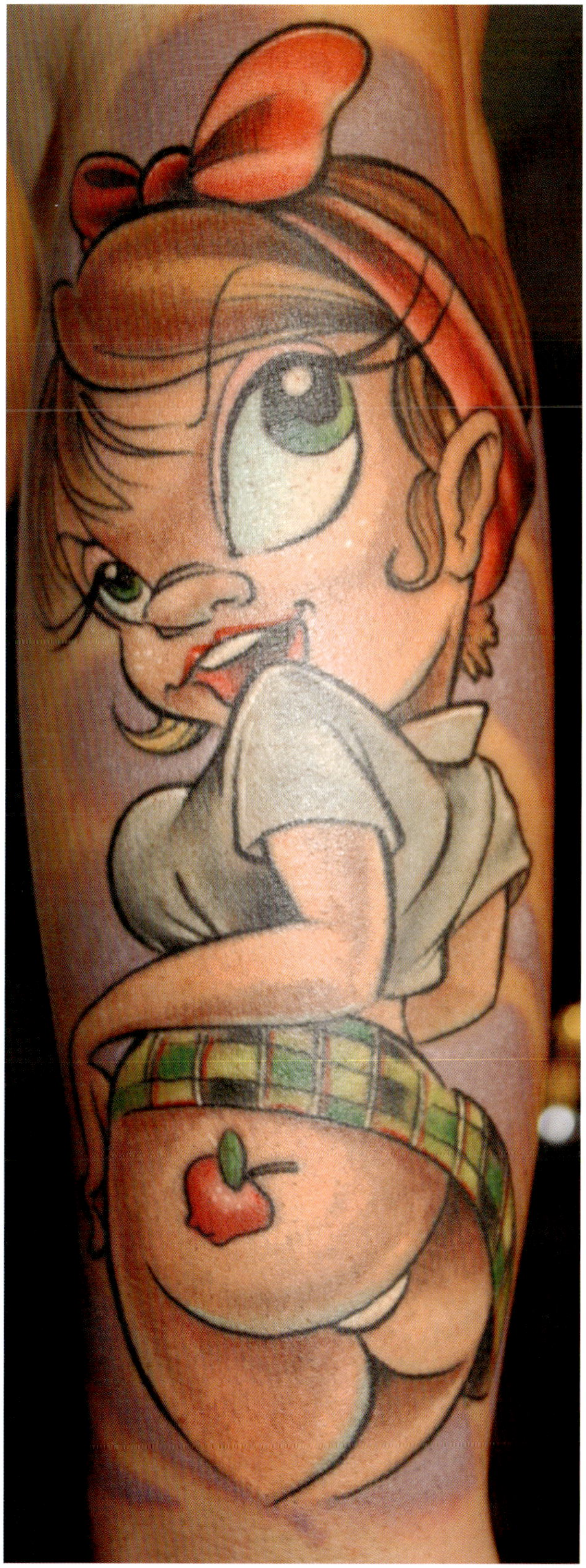

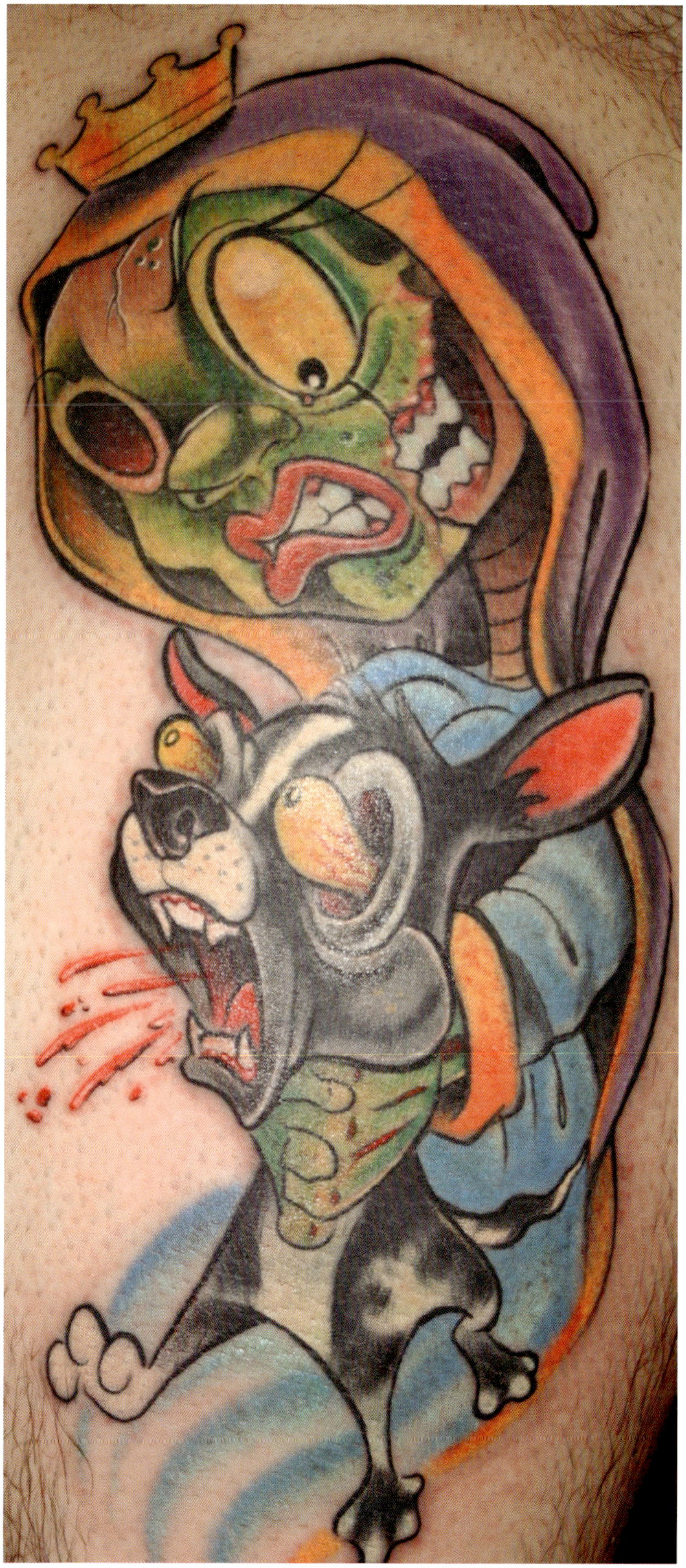

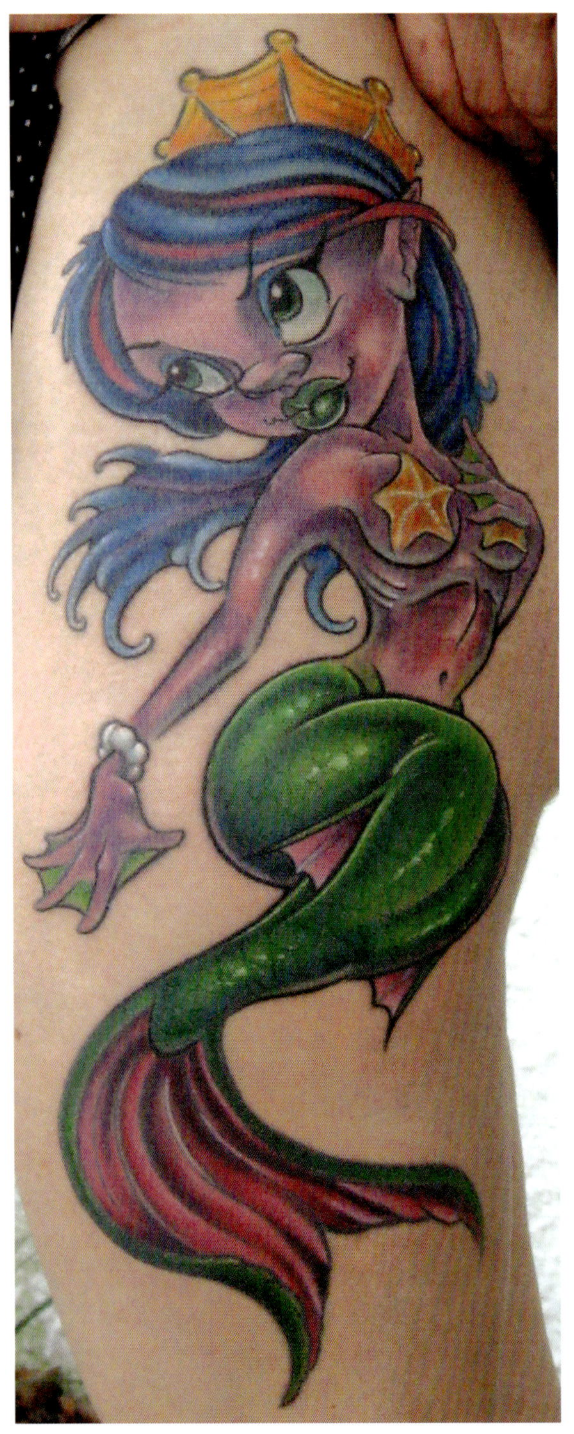

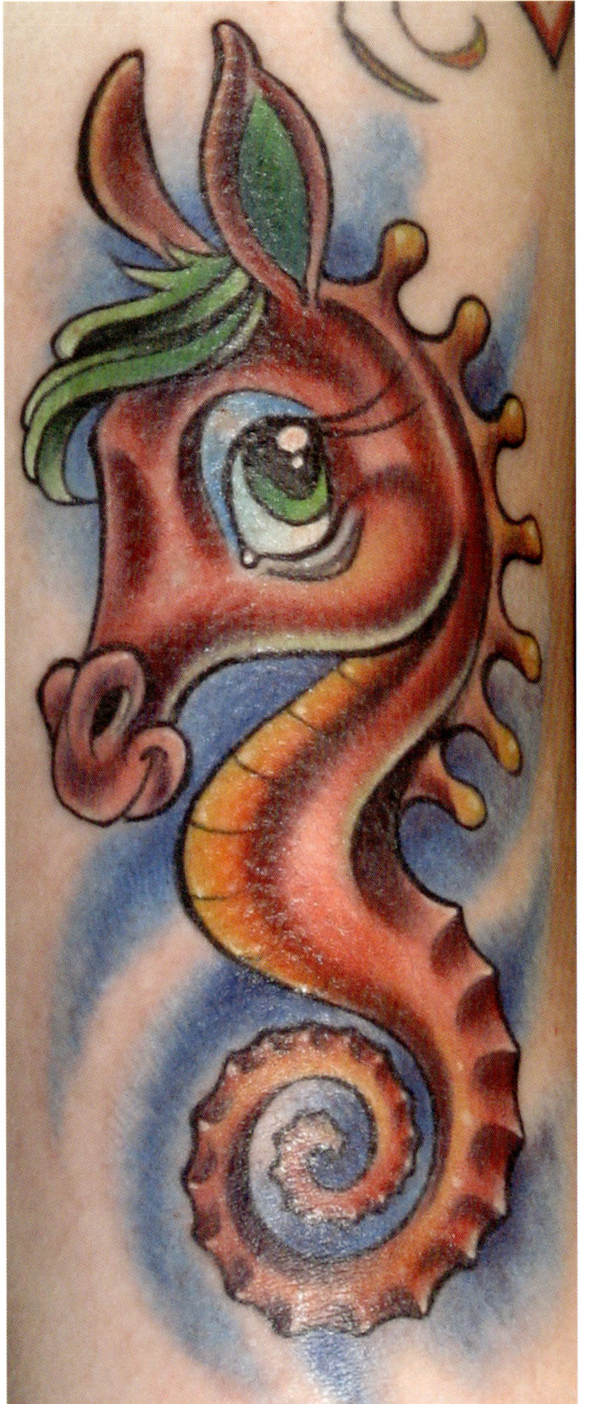

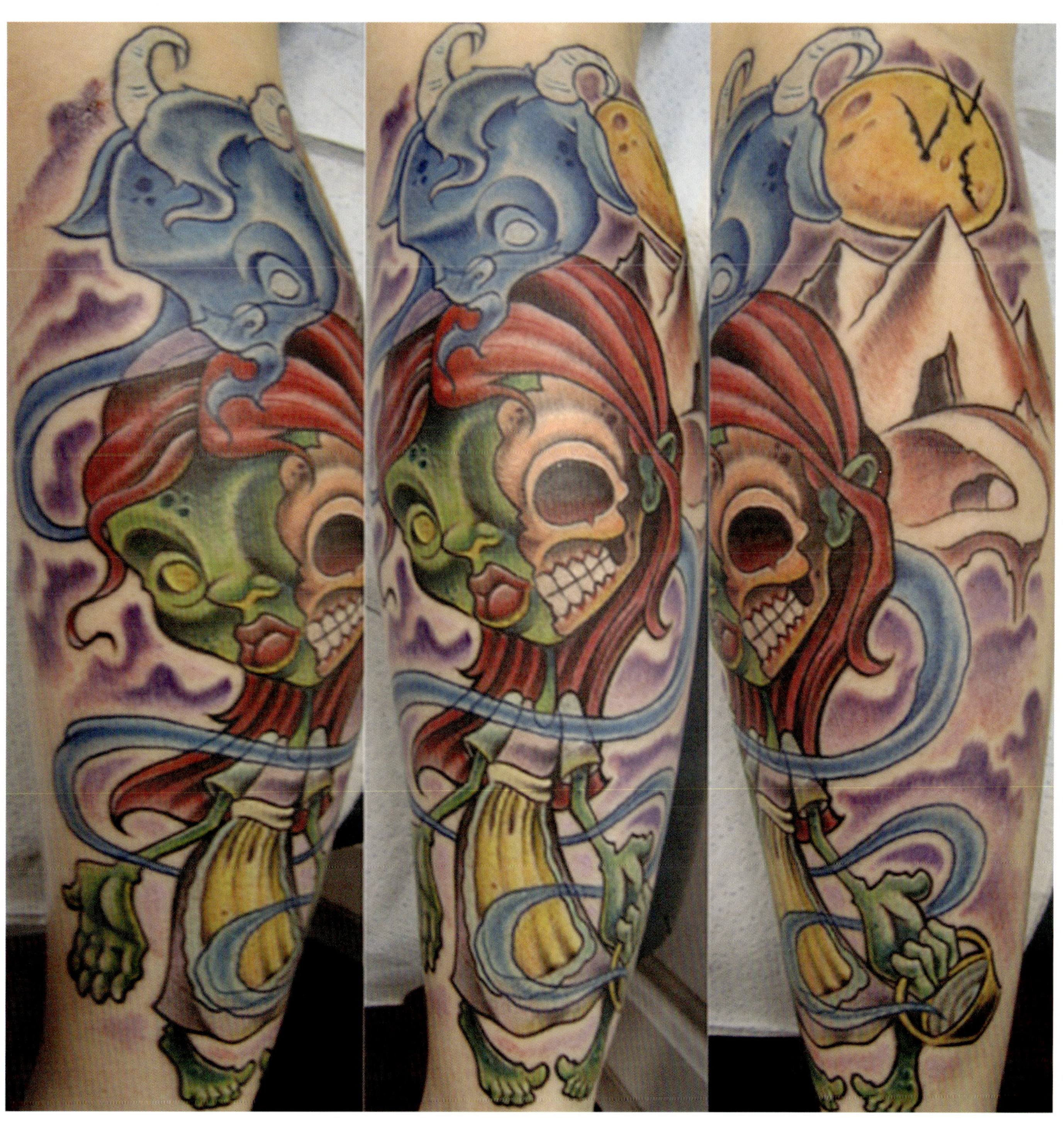

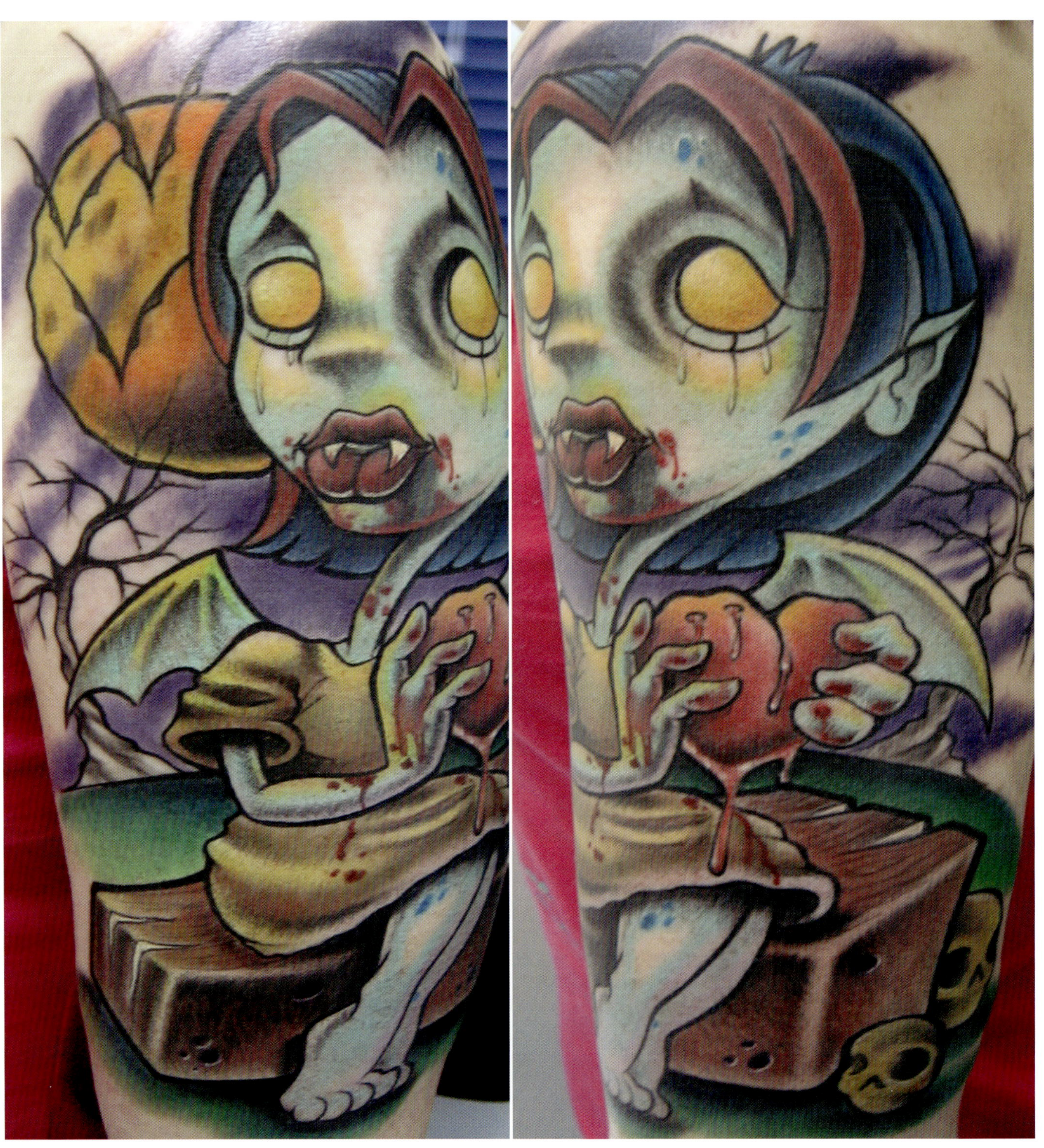

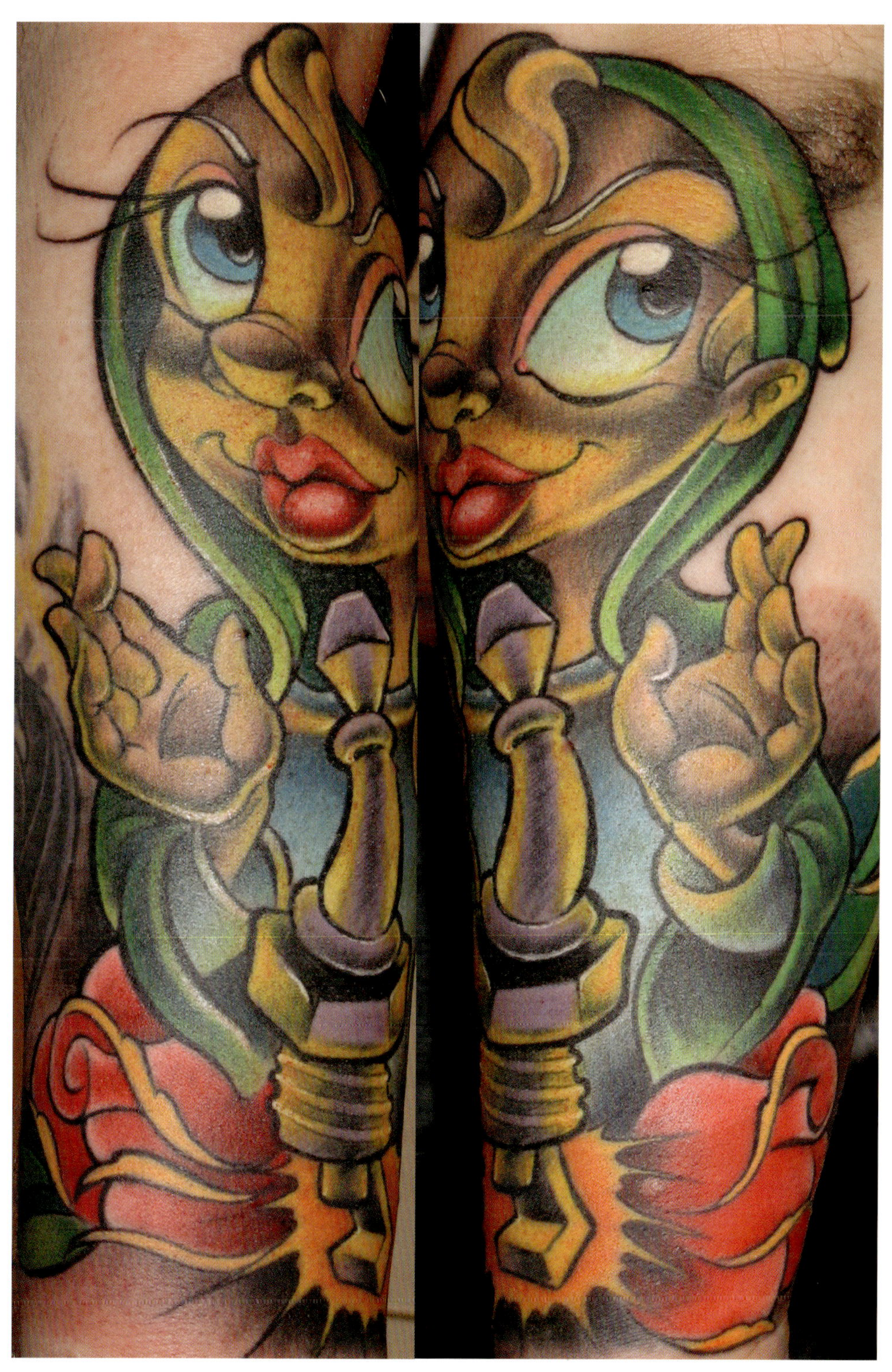

Jose Lopez

"TATTOOS SAVED MY LIFE"

It was about a week ago while doing a tattoo that I heard this expression. I was tattooing my boy Klown, one of the up and coming tattoo artists, when he said this to me — "Tattoos saved my life." I started to think of how many struggles I've been through and it made a lot of sense. I want to acknowledge what my boy Klown put so simply, making me realize the truth of the statement — tattoos have in fact played a huge part in my life and have saved me from so many horrible things I could have done. I hope that everyone who tattoos or who is getting into tattooing also goes through this life-changing experience and learns to appreciate and respect this profession. Thanks for the support.

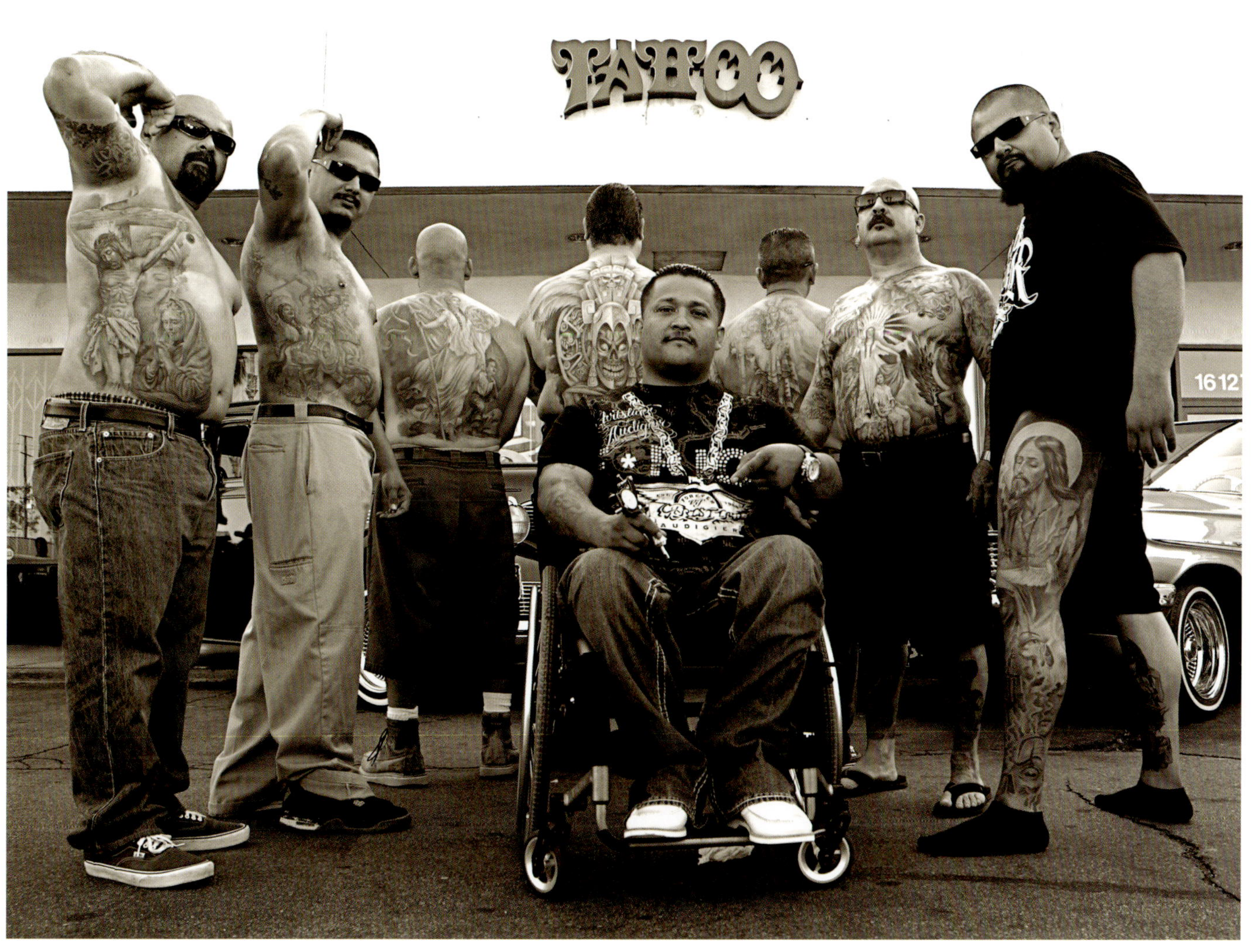
TATTOO

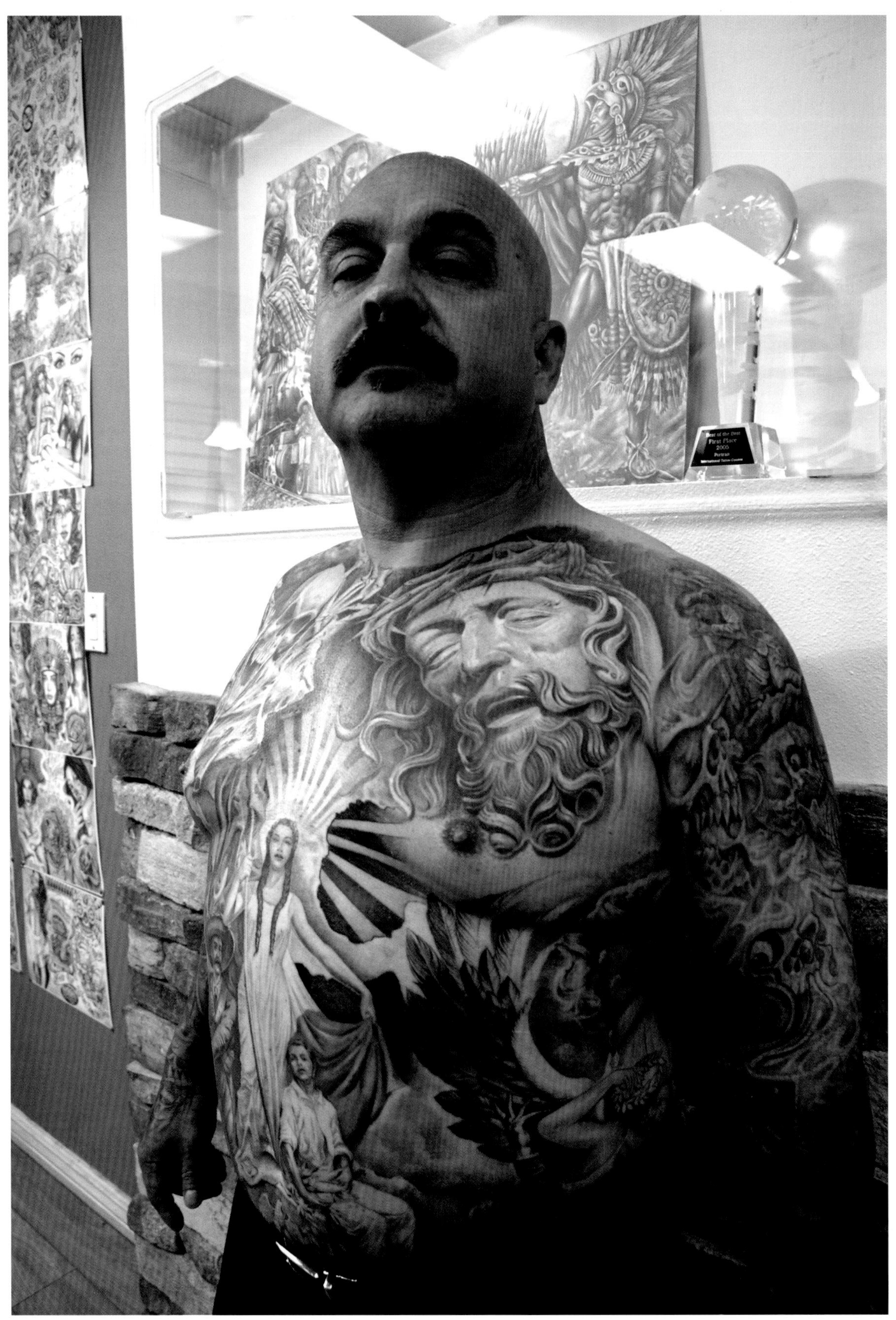
First Place

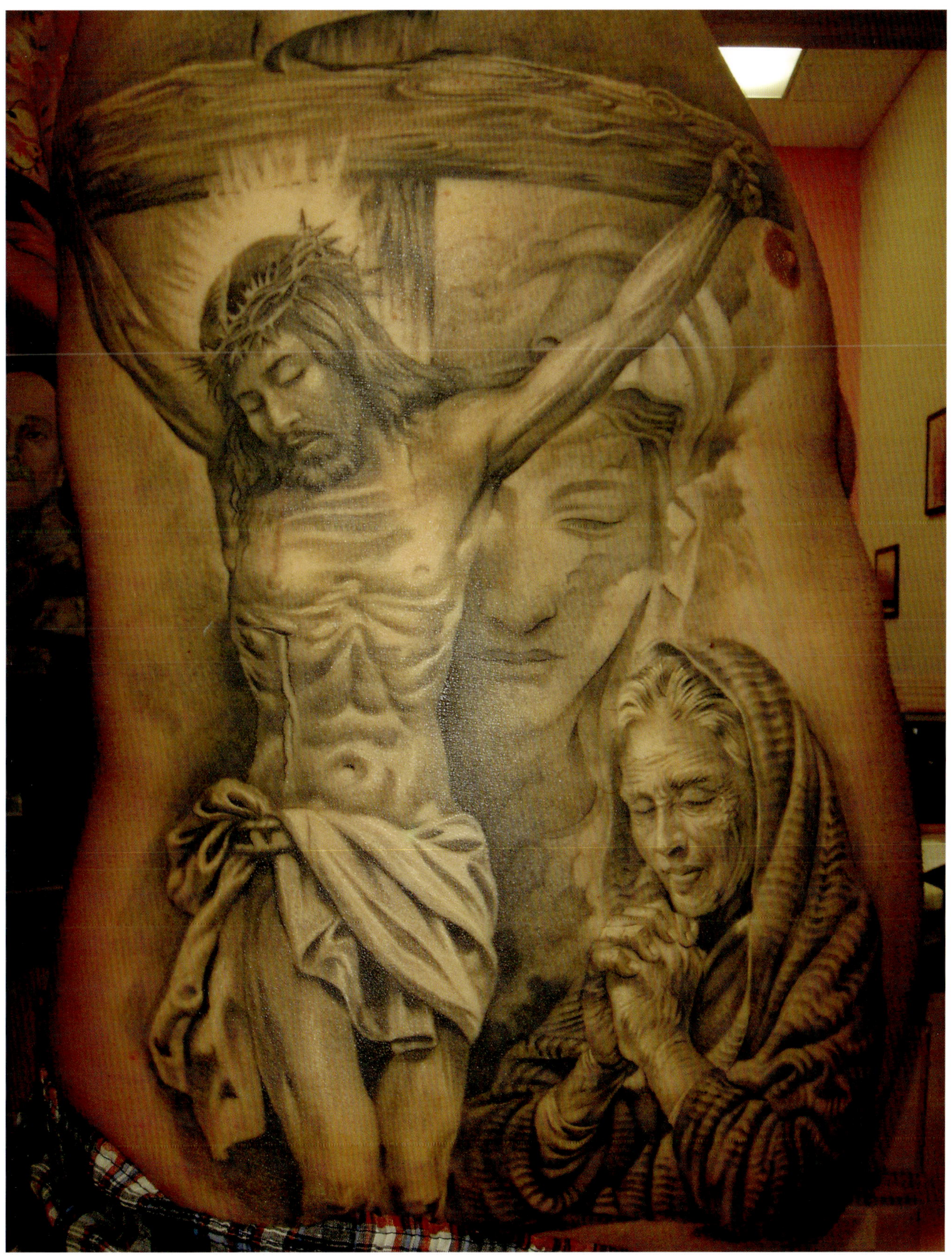

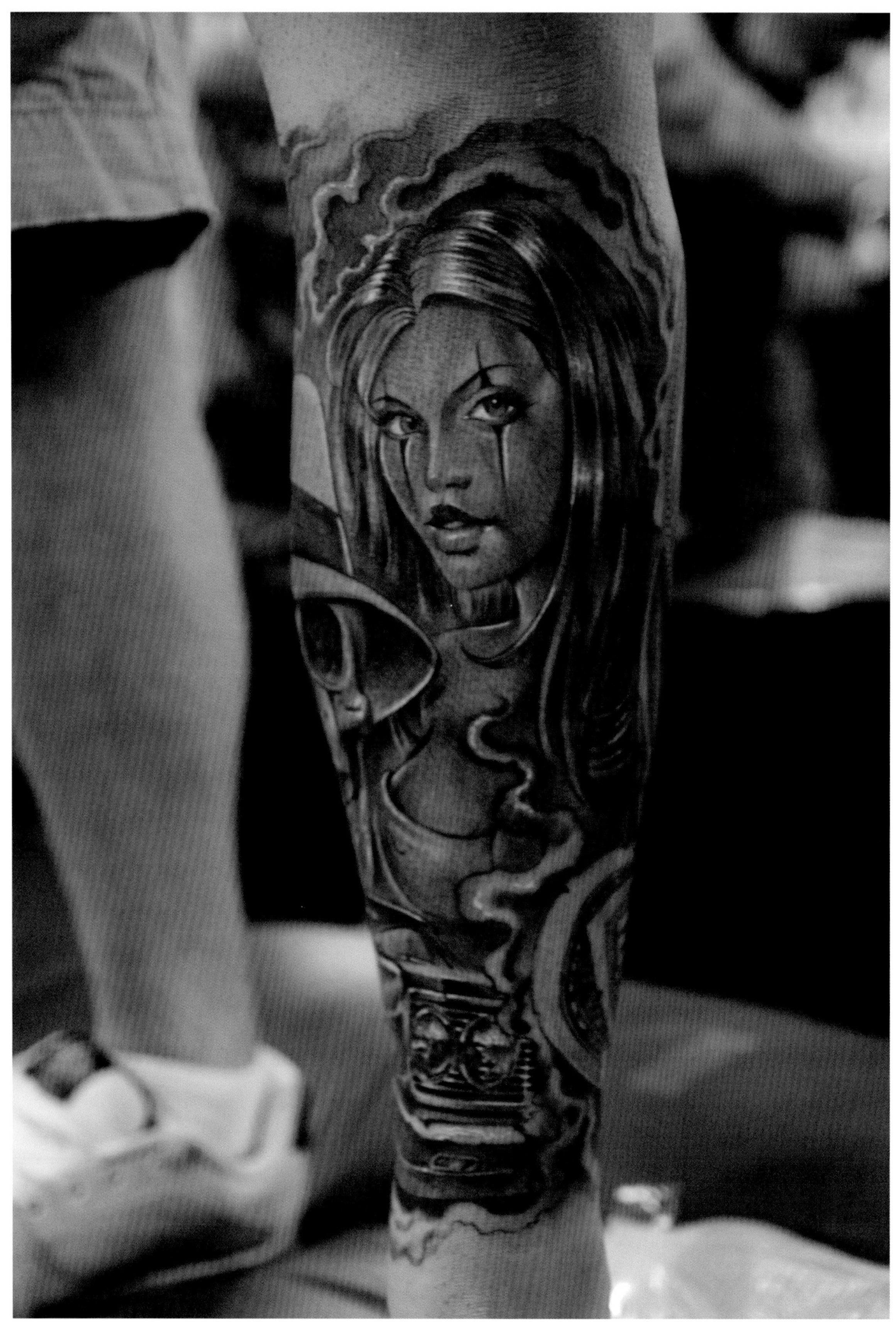

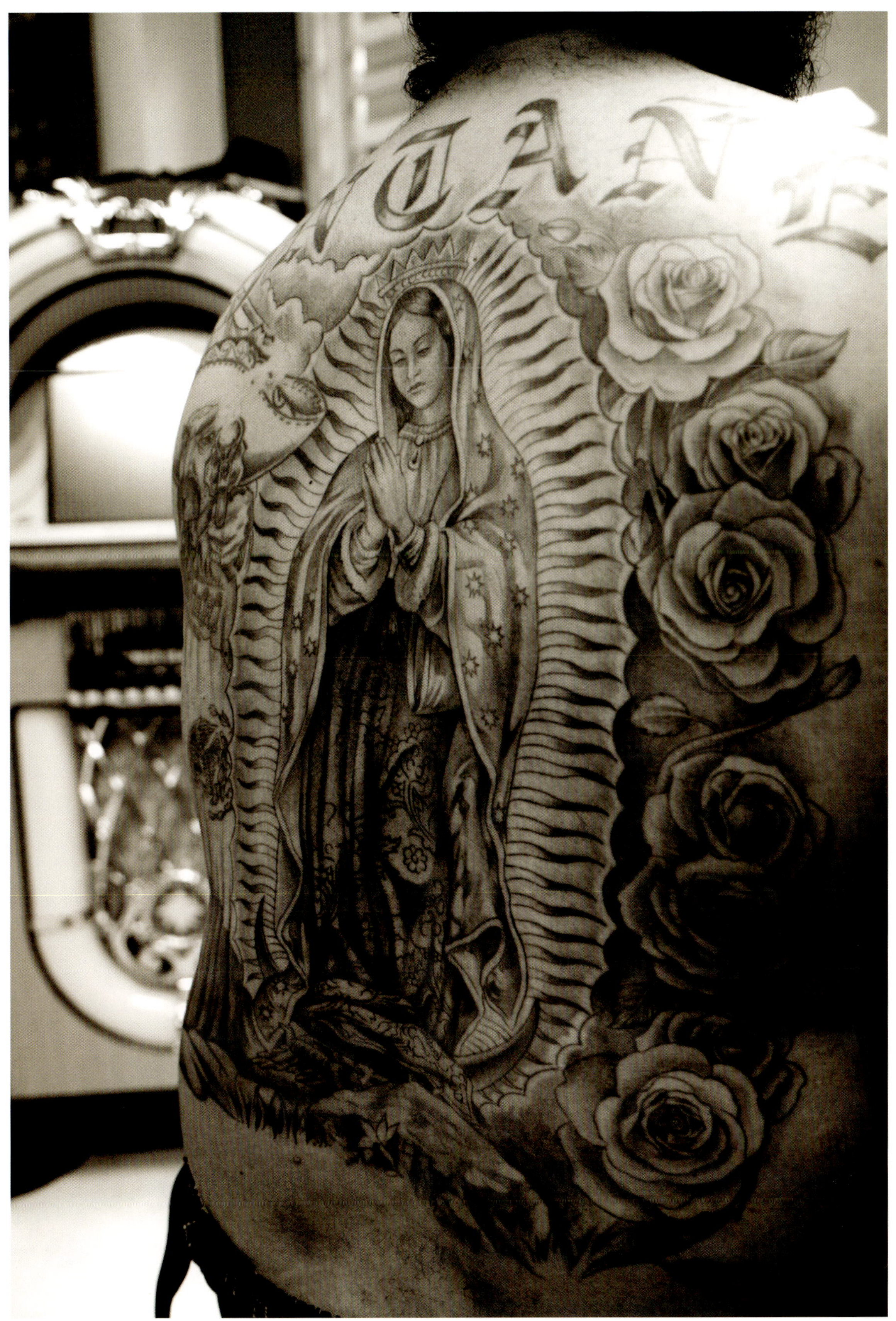

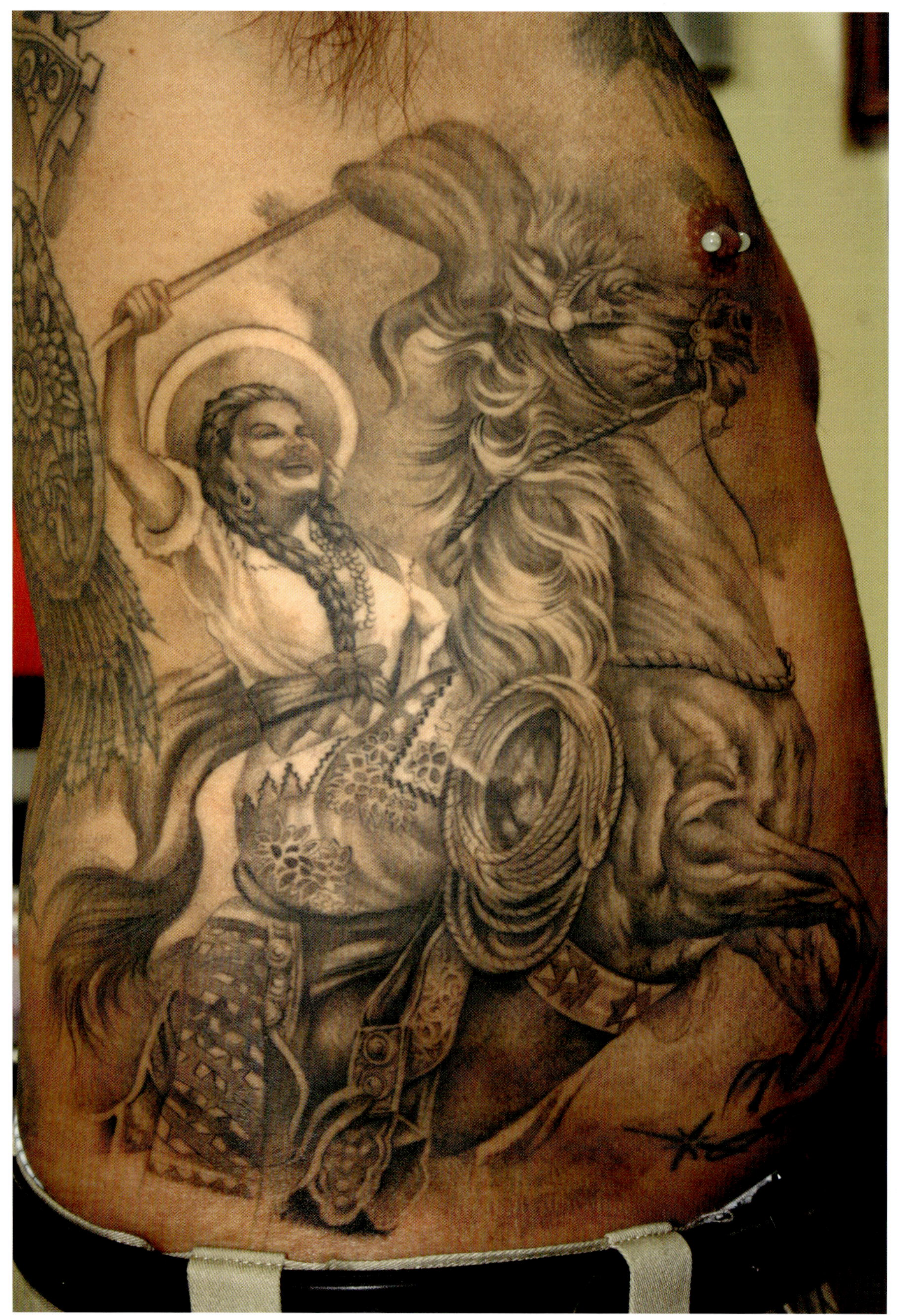

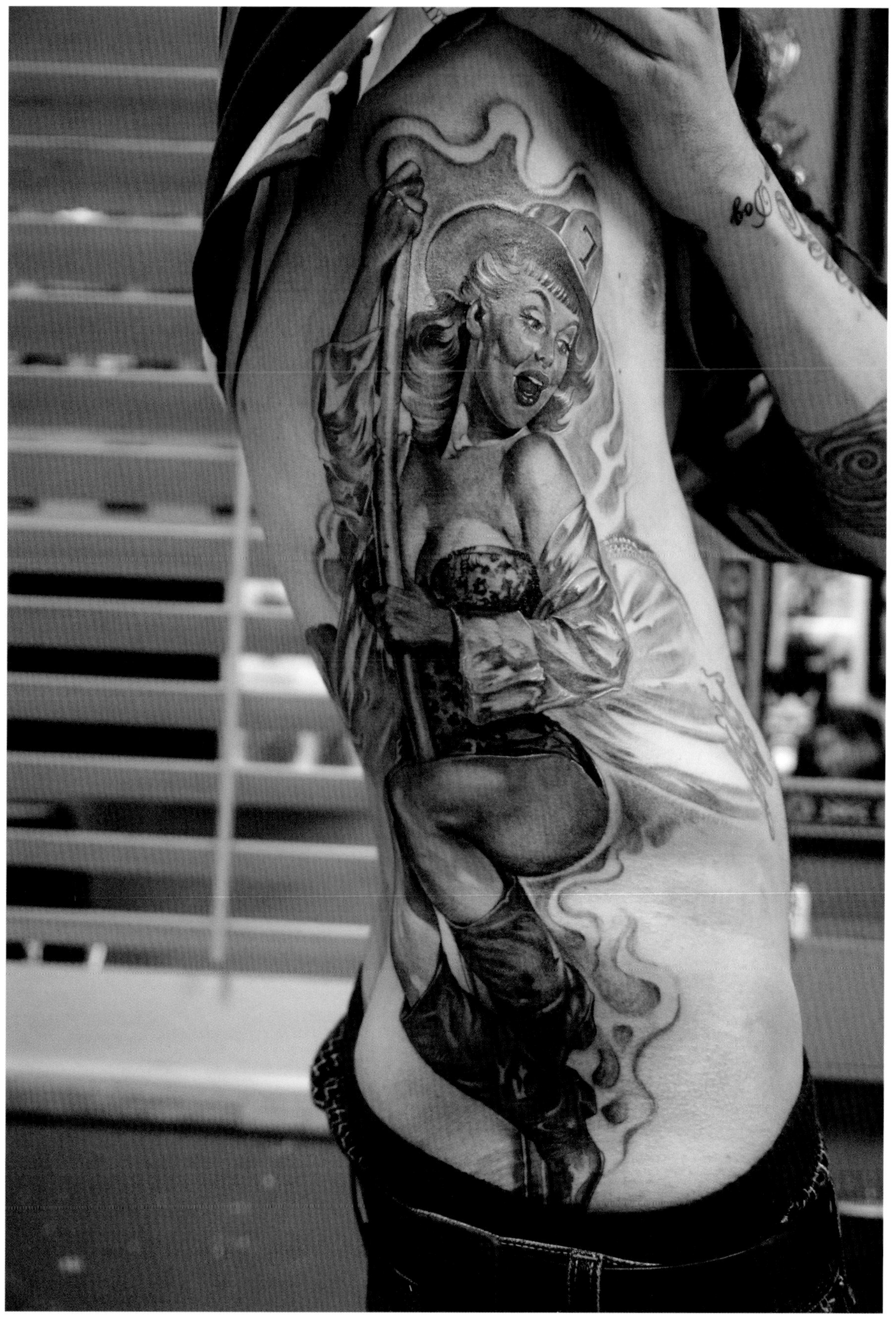

Jon Mirro

'When your average short, Napoleon-type decides it's his time to show the world just how tall he wants to be, he buys a stupid car or tries to kick your ass at a bar. Jon, being a short man with Napoleonic tendencies, compensates instead by staying awake all night and drawing. Don't get me wrong, his last car was an Escalade and he broke his tattooing hand twice throwing punches, but he puts in the work where the work matters and that's what made him the tattooer he is today. While the tall and confident among us are logging hours in zzz, Jon is building himself an empire out of blood and tracing paper.' — Kyle Hollingdrake

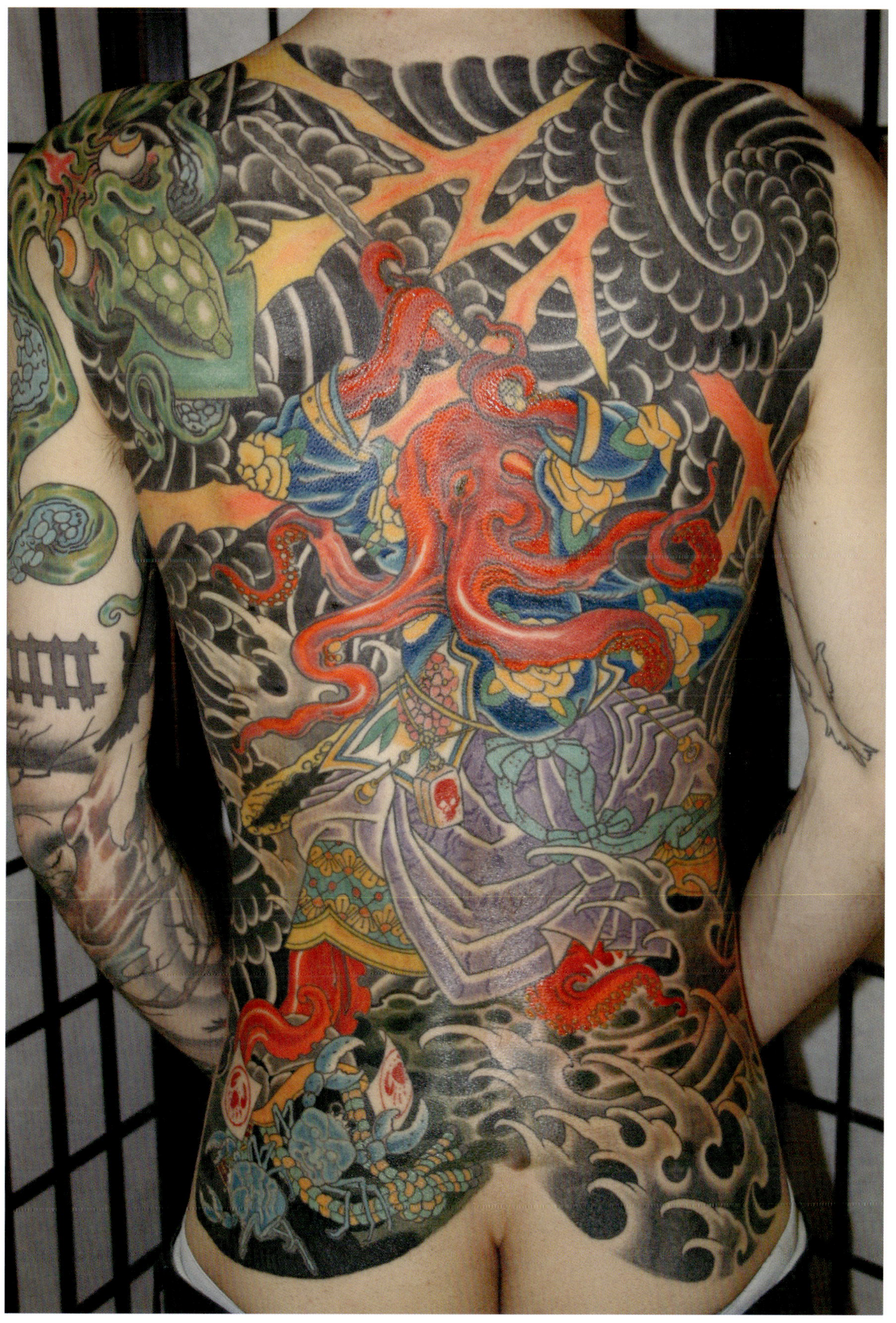

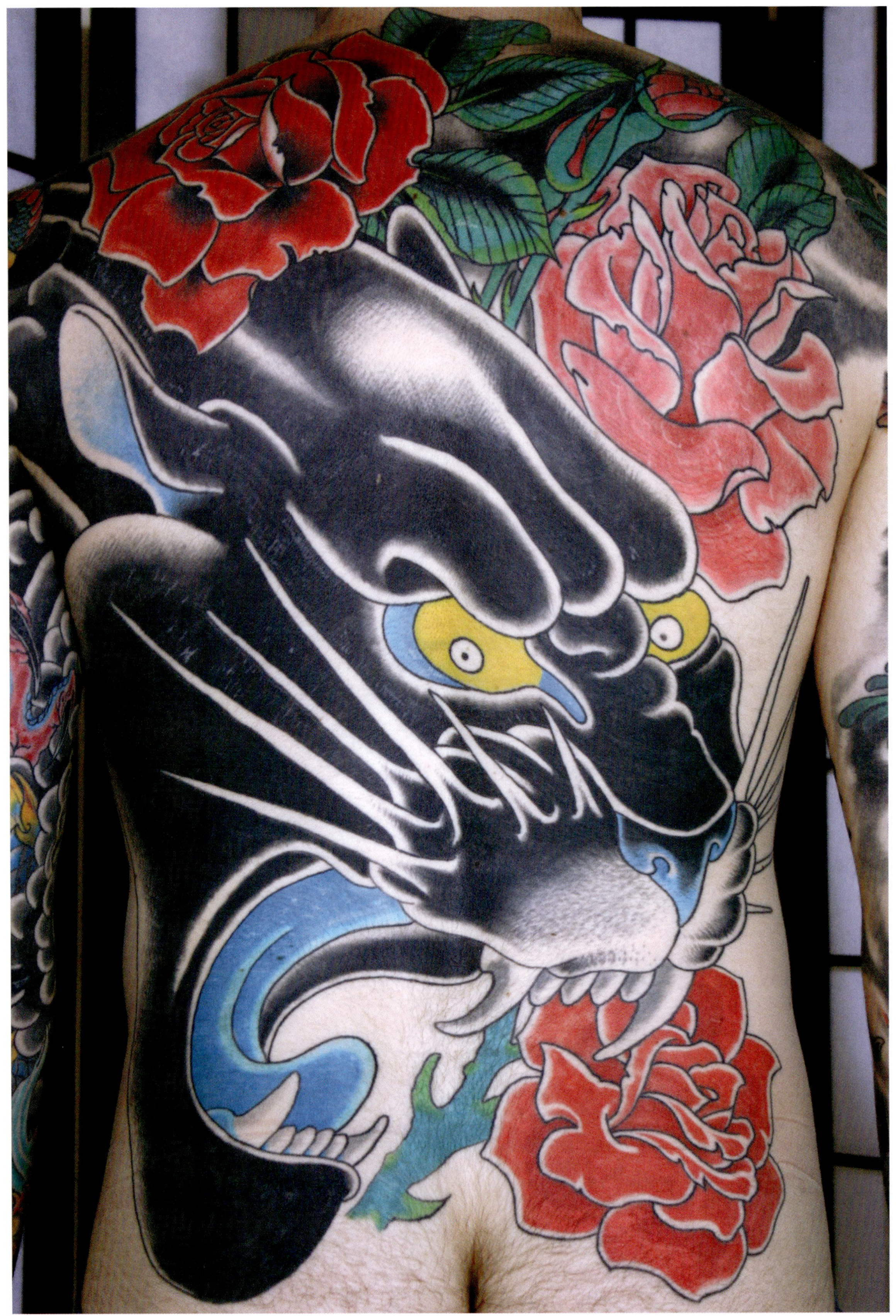

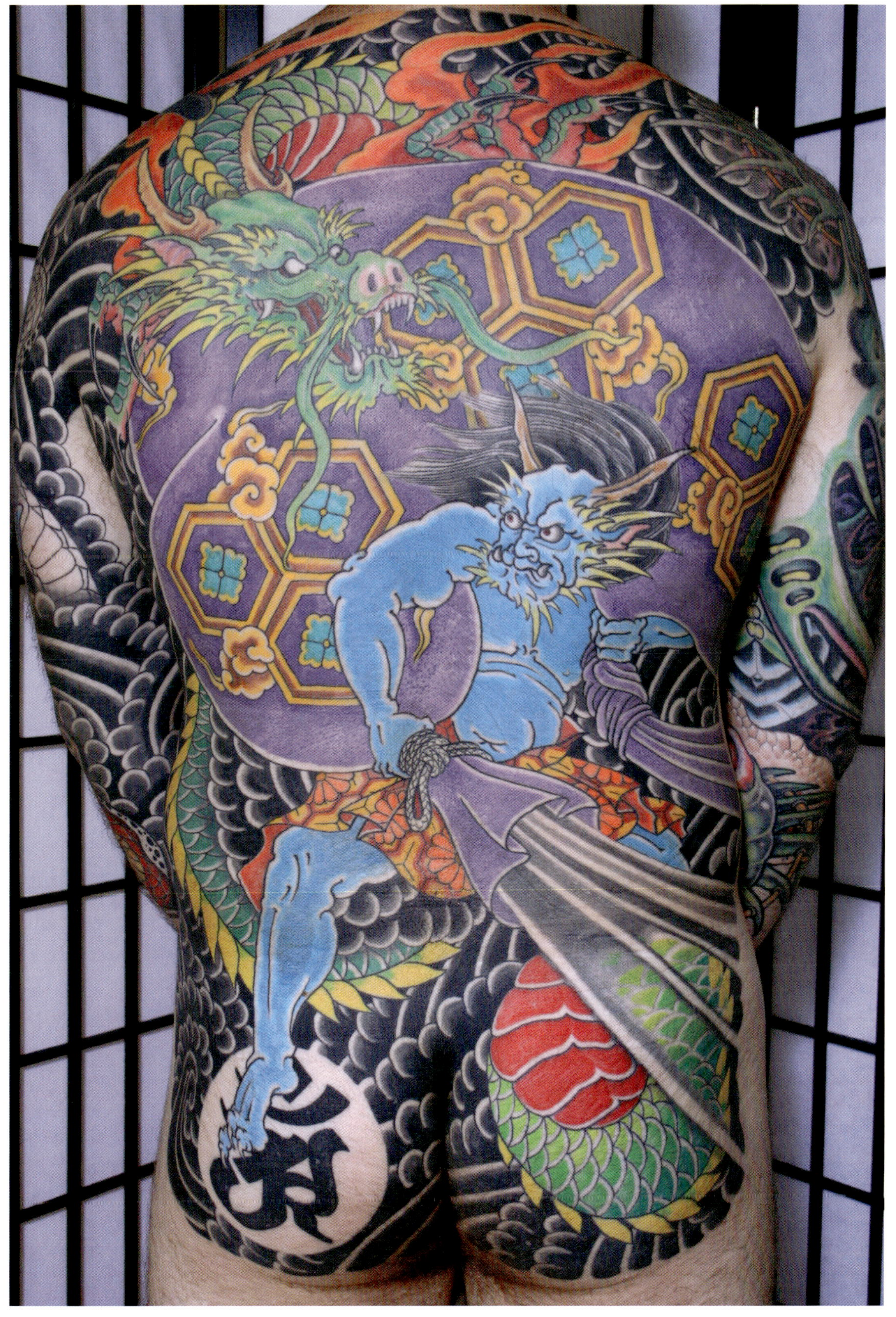

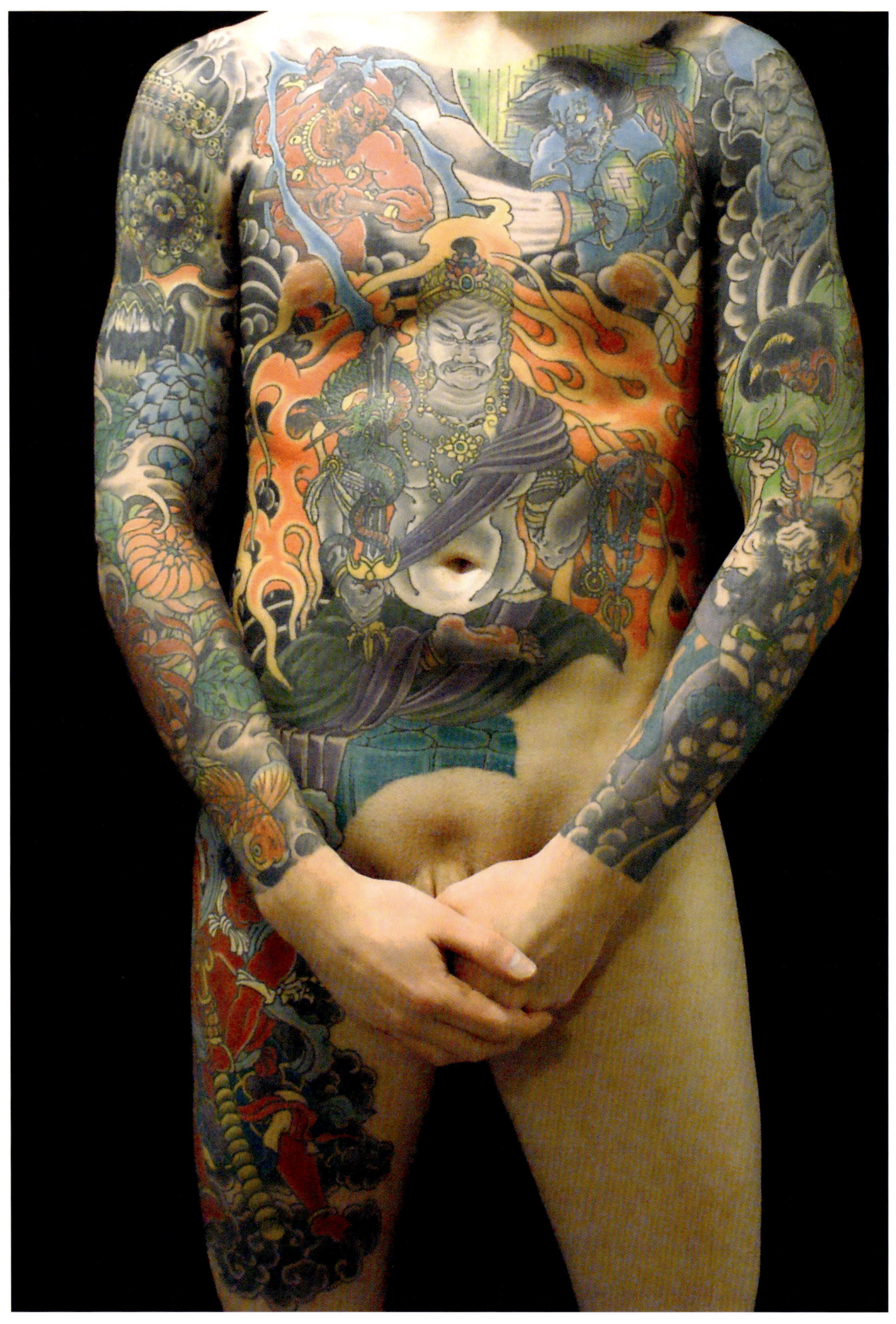

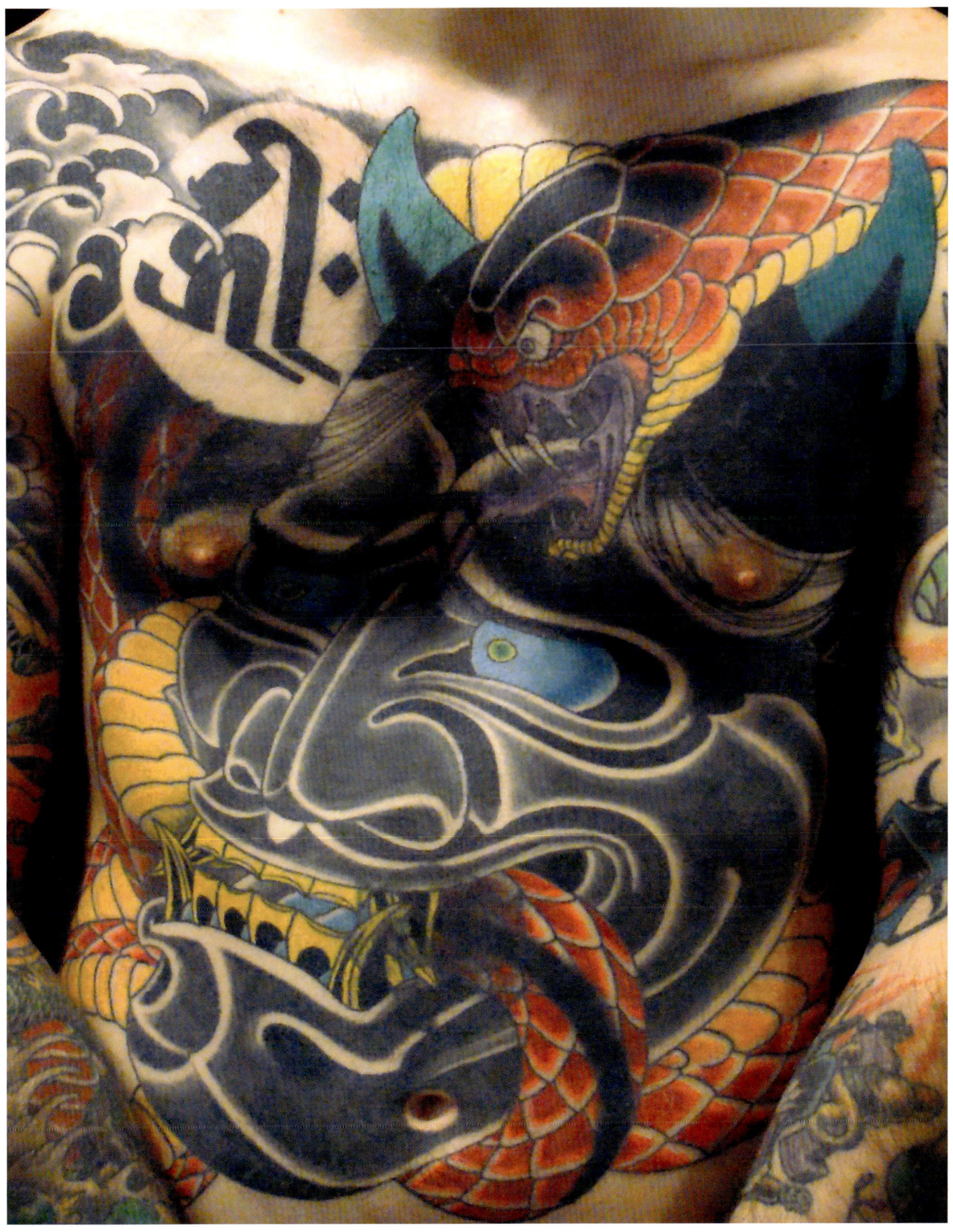

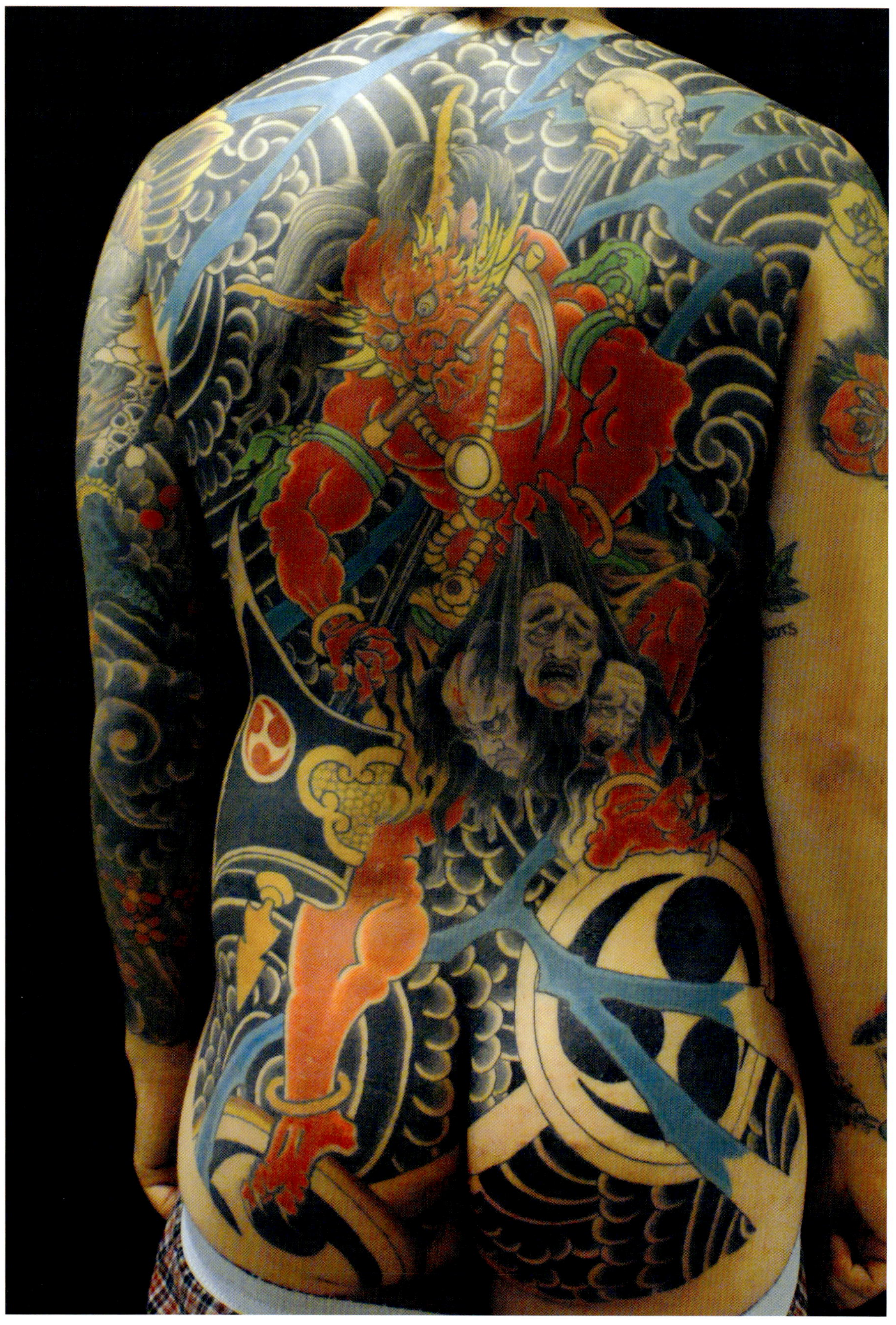

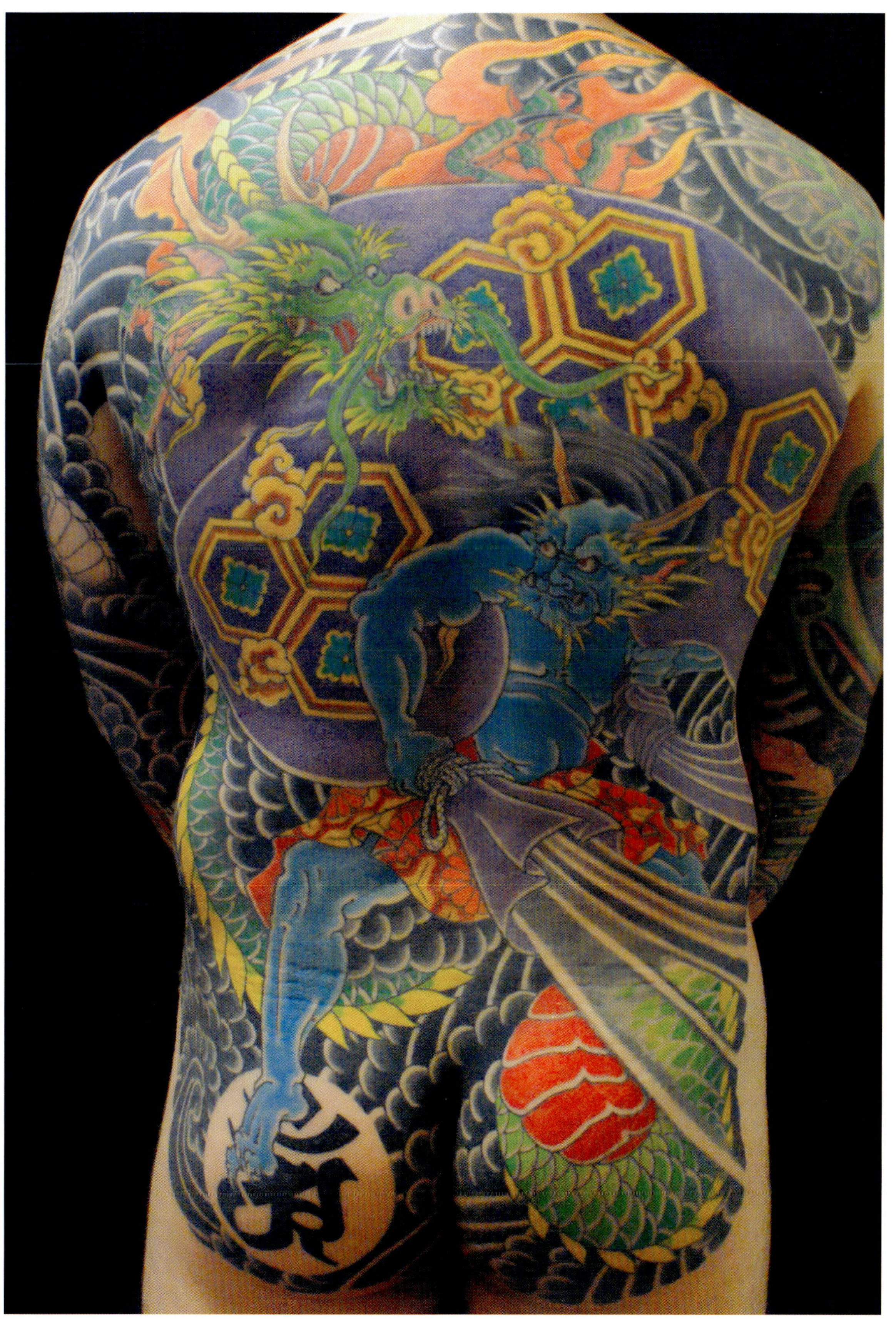

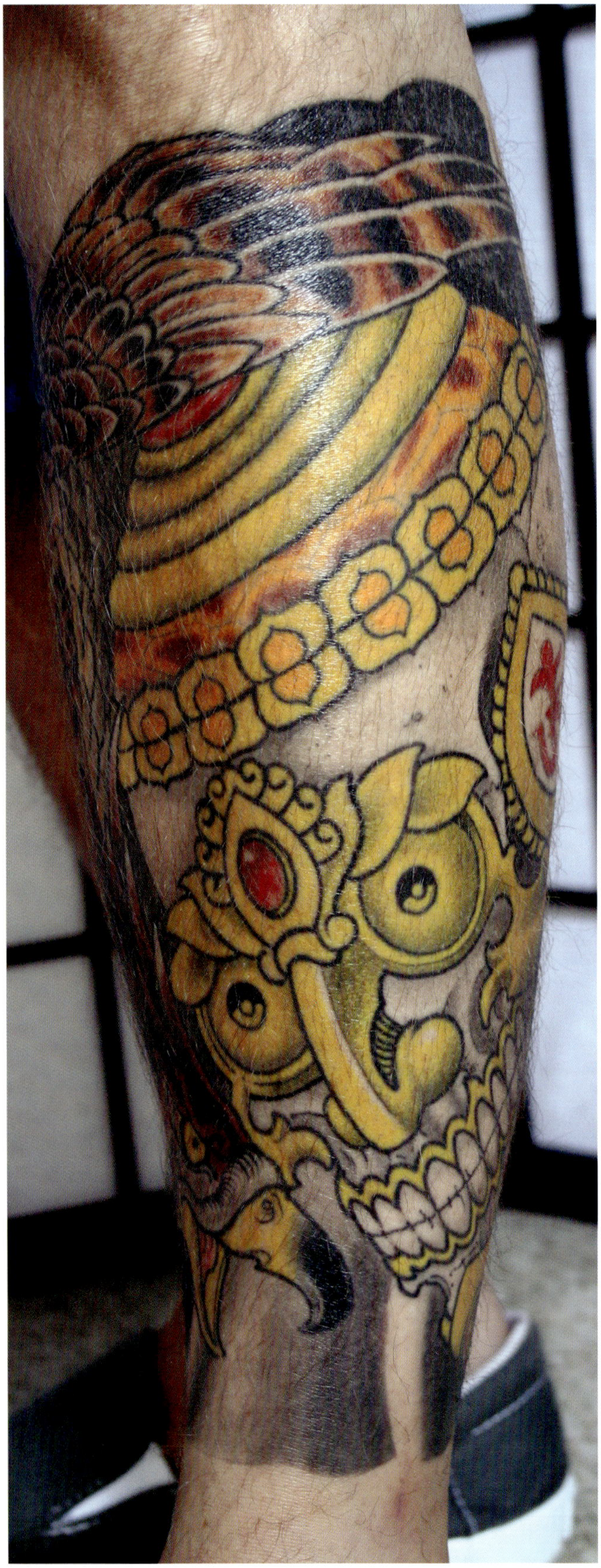

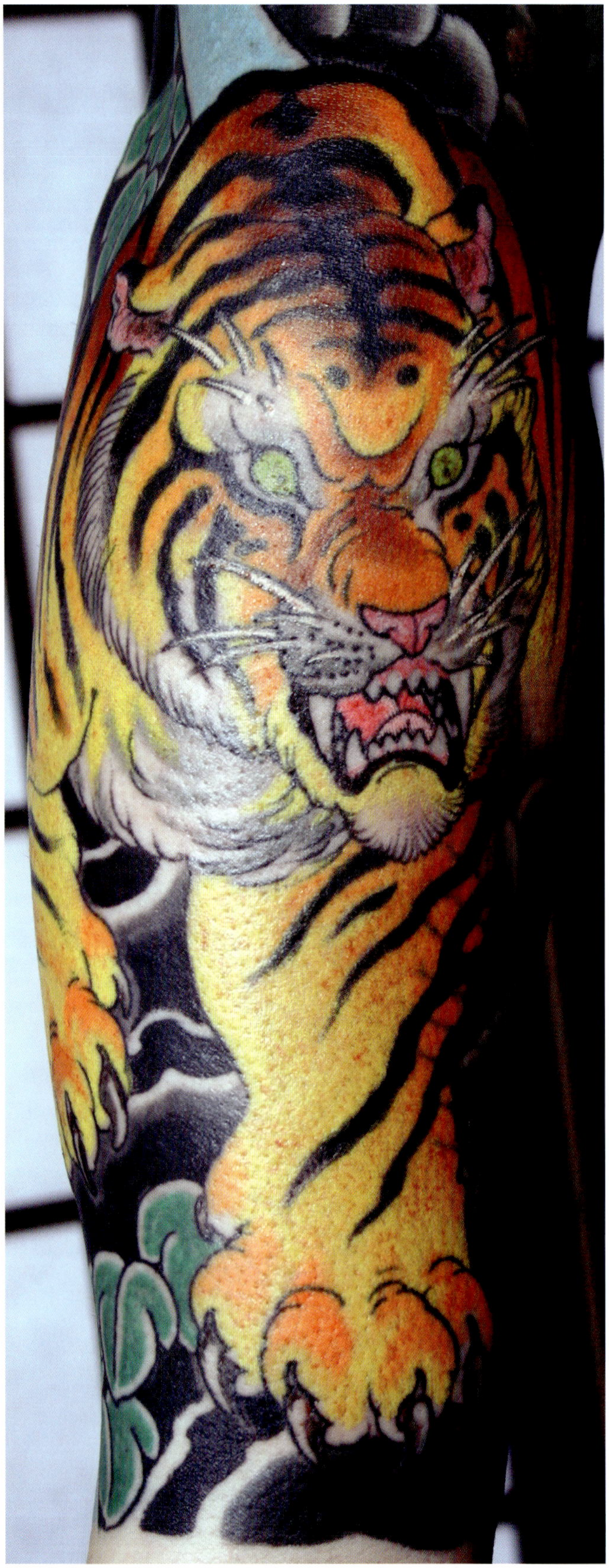

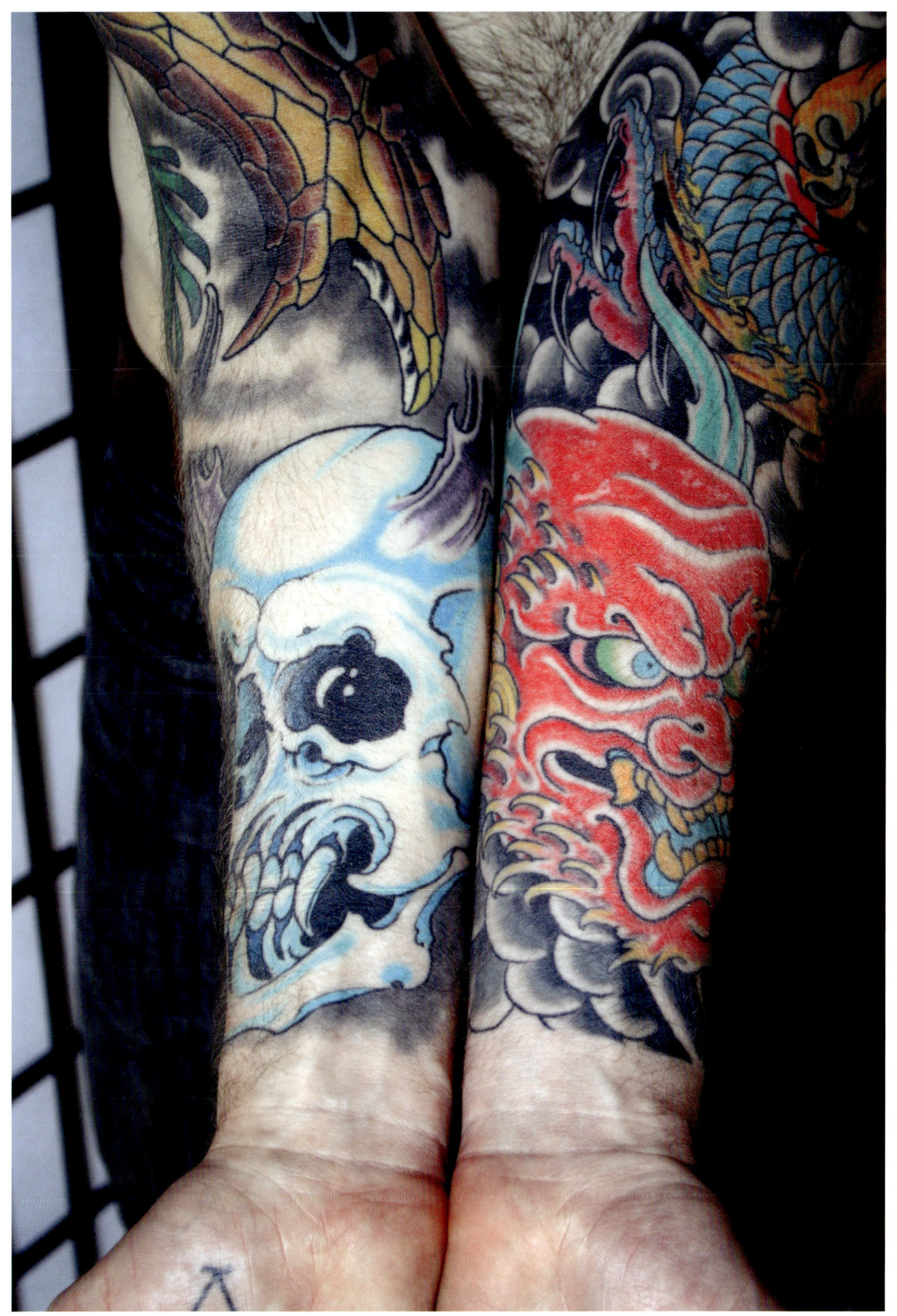

Paulie

When you're first starting out, giving your friends tattoos of Jesus from some self-fashioned basement studio, it's easy to think that's all there is. But then one thing leads to another, and you're in a shop and your work is getting better. Suddenly, you've got your own shop, and your work has become something you can be proud of. People start to notice you, you pick up a following, and you think you're really the man.

Then you see someone's work that kicks the shit out of yours. And you're mentally kicked back to the basement. And it's good for you.

This whole thing has been about learning for me. My work only gets better through the challenge of my peers' work. So bring it on.

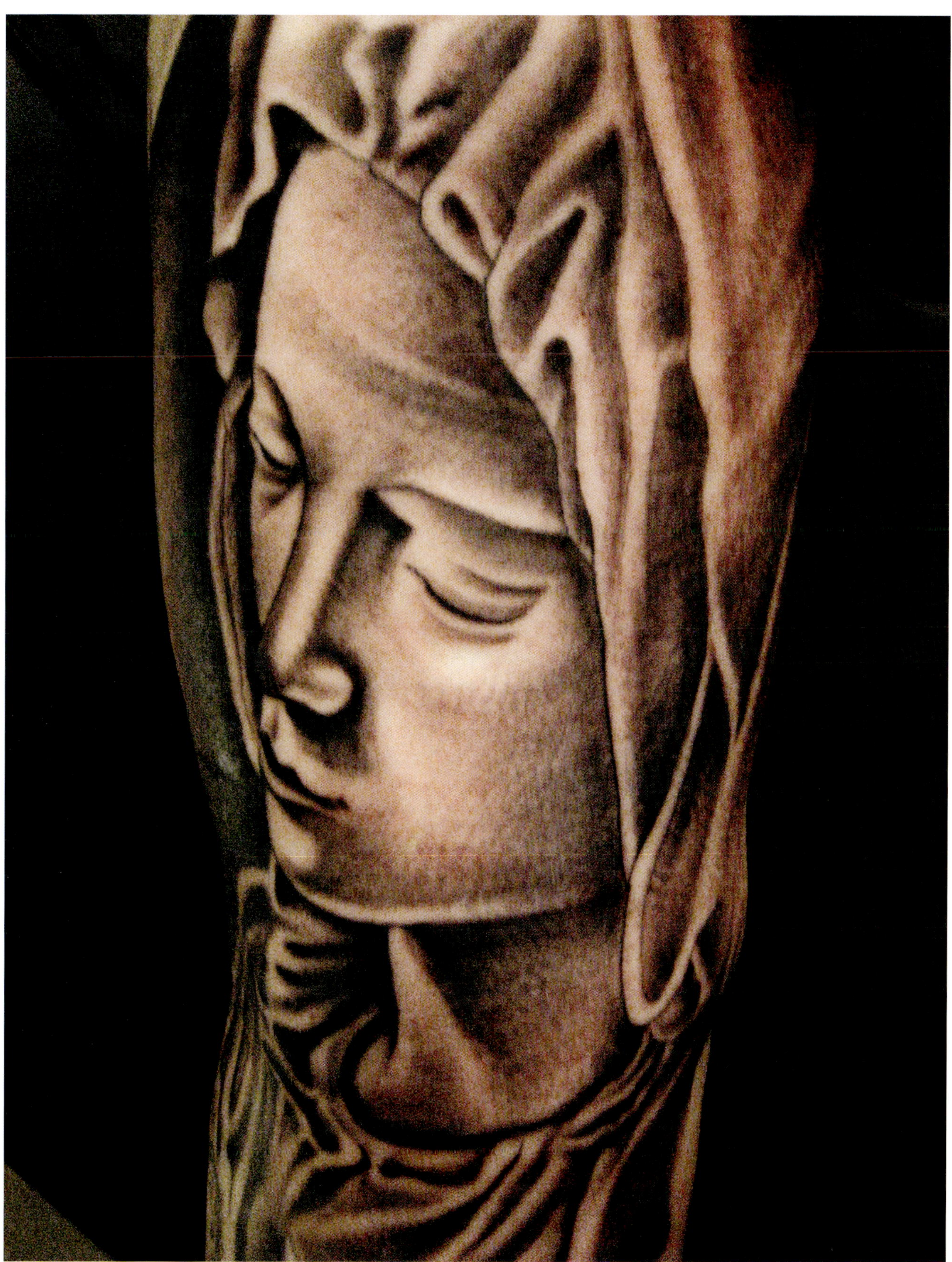

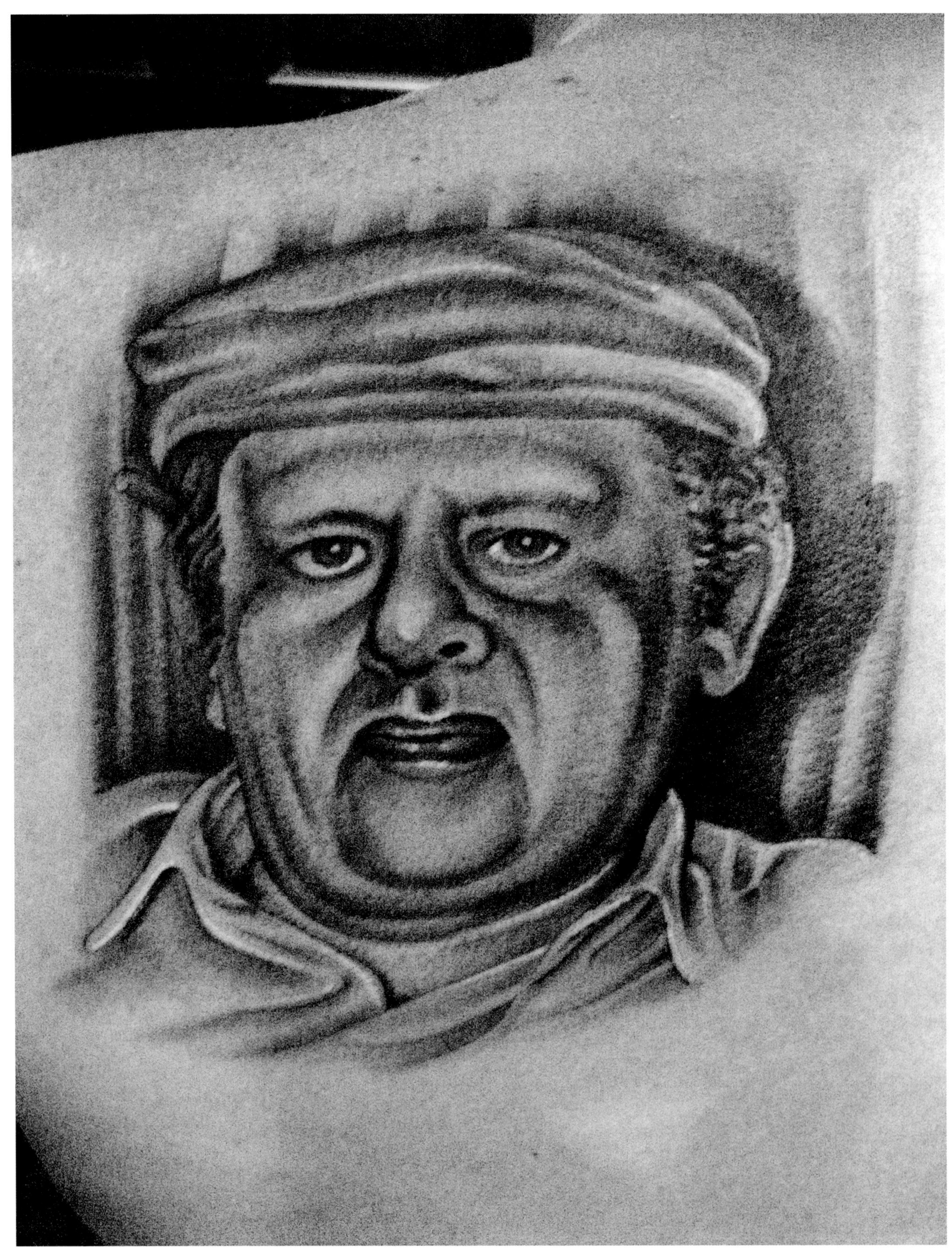

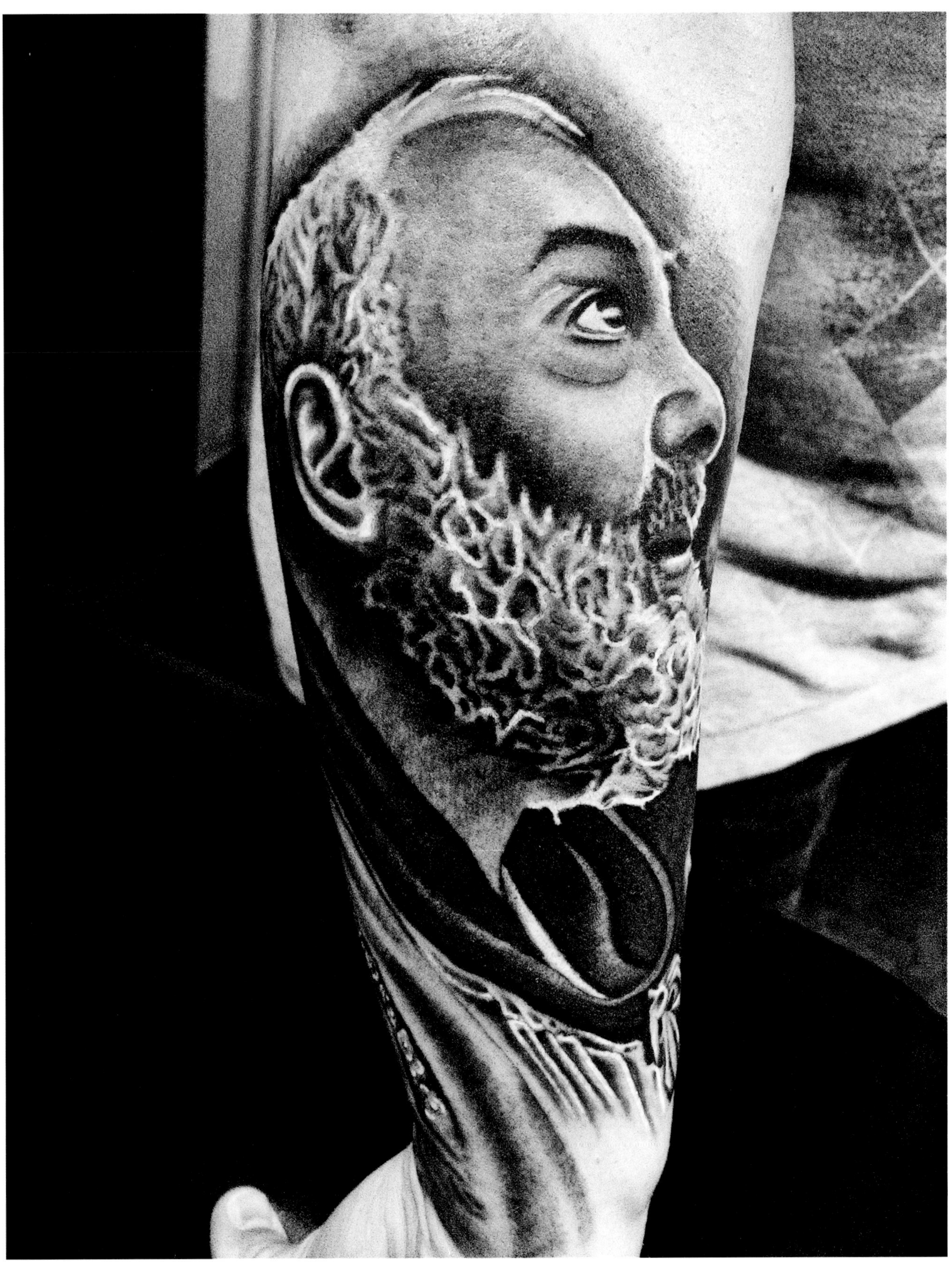

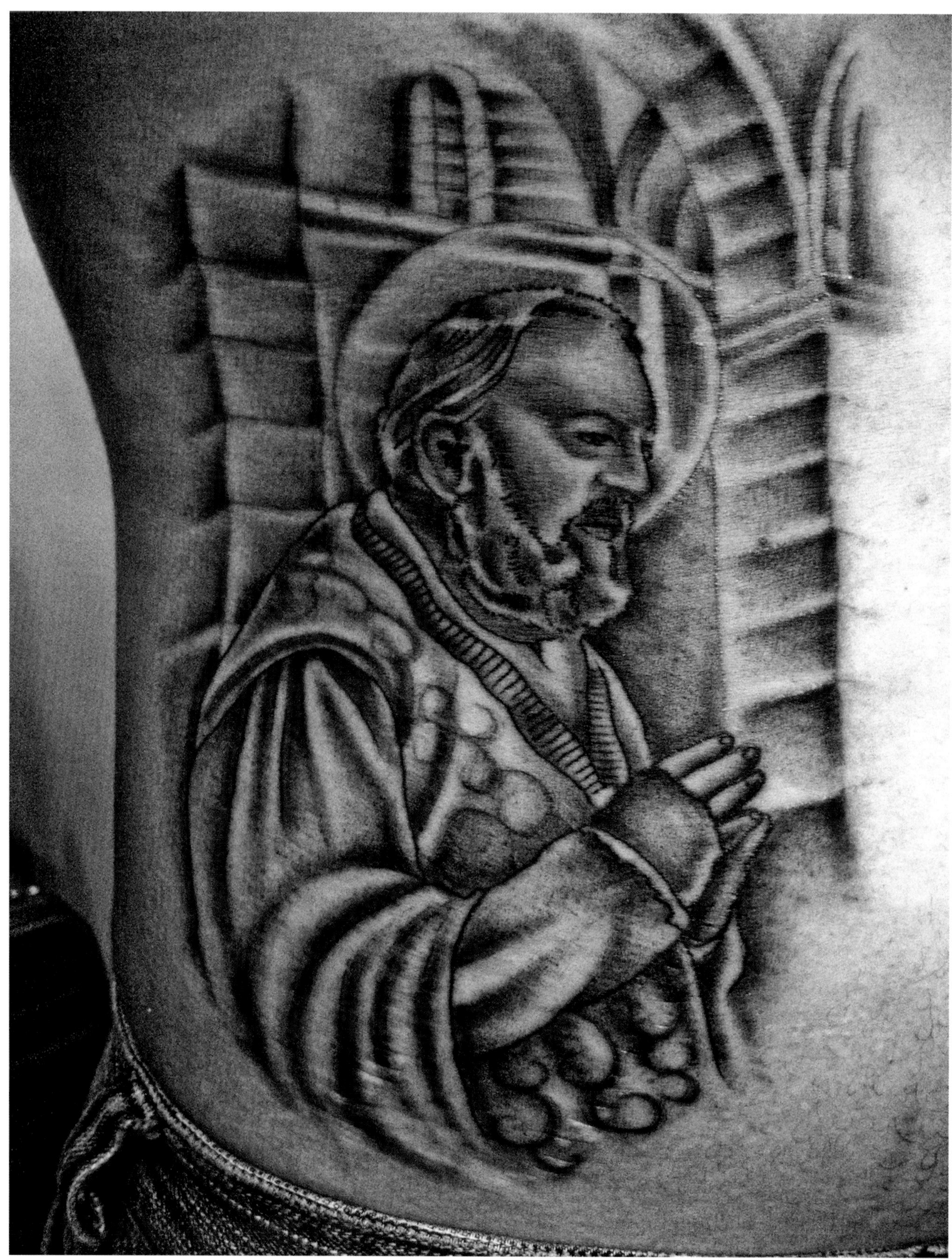

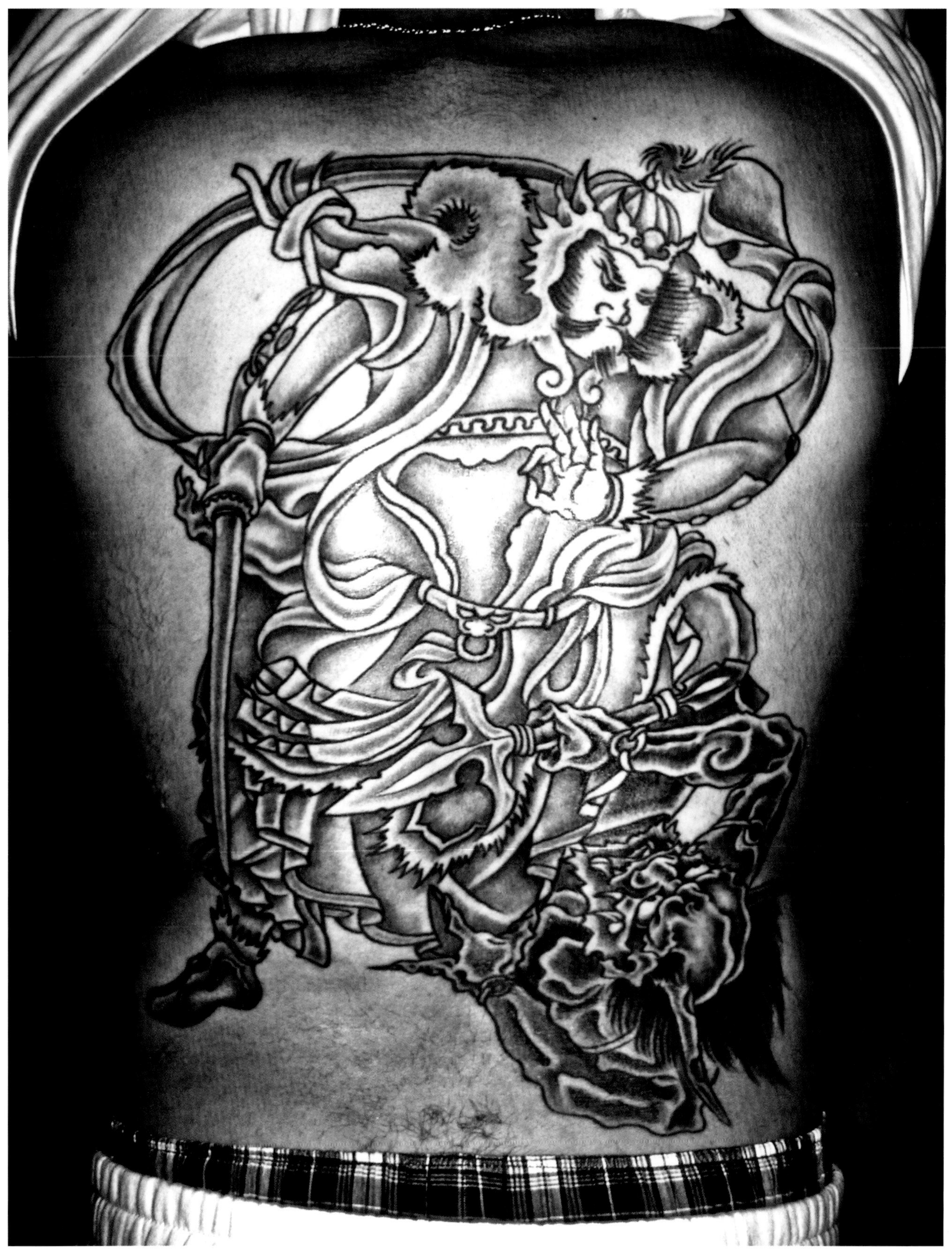

Colin Stevens

Not every tattoo will have some deep personal meaning for the wearer, but when I tattoo, the artwork must fit the wearer. Photographs of tattoos are not complete representations of the artwork. To see a tattoo you must see it on the wearer. The artwork carries some of the person's personality with it. The way the tattoo fits on the wearer's body, the way that wearer carries the tattoo every day, and the overall composition are together a full representation of the final work.

I was raised in Japan and quickly submerged myself in the folklore of traditional Japanese artwork. A single block print may carry a story for thousands of years. When I create a tattoo, deep within the design there is always a story connected with the wearer's personality. I try very hard to find the best fit for each person I tattoo, to make it fit on their body and show a greater strength in the wearer.

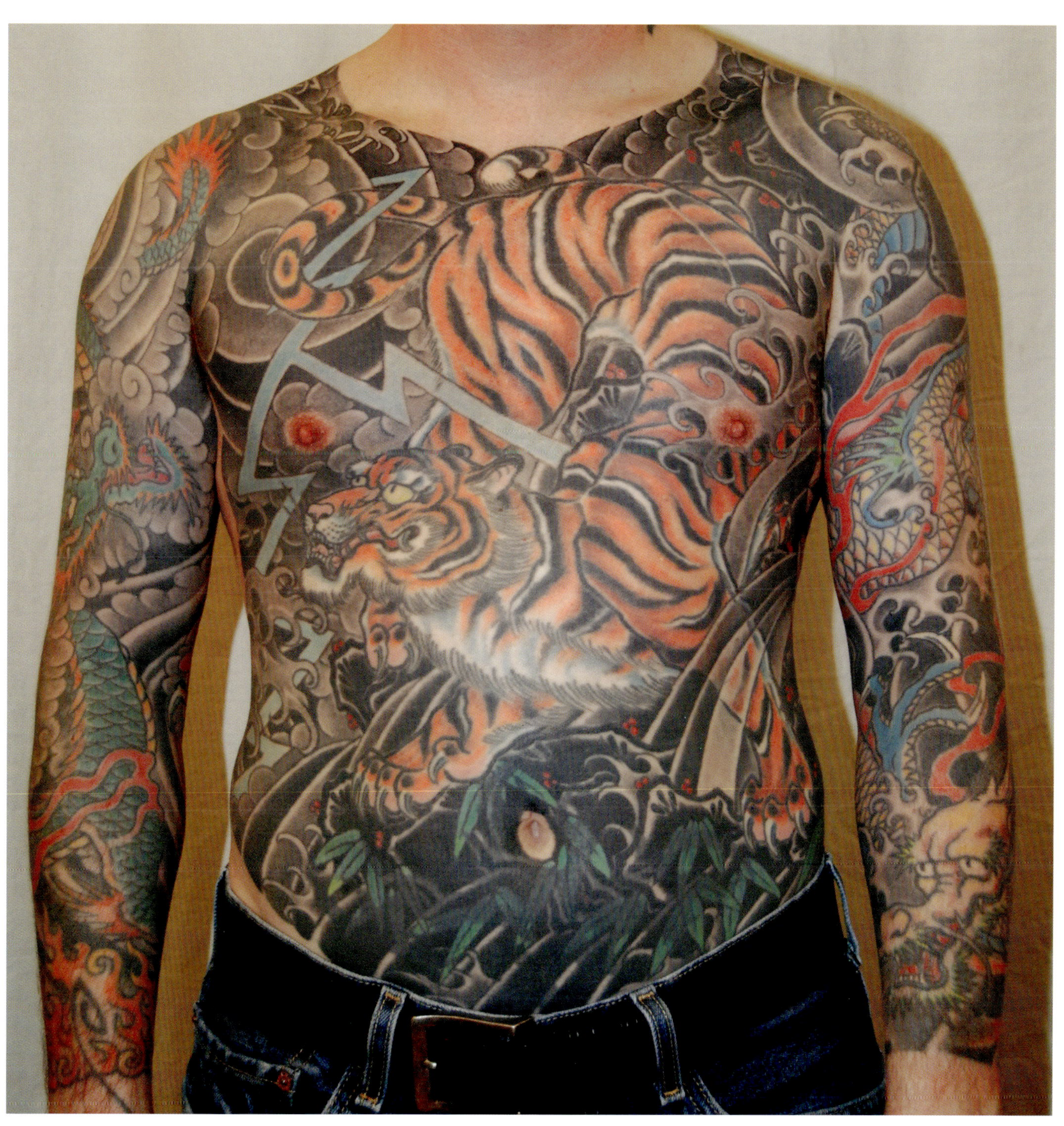

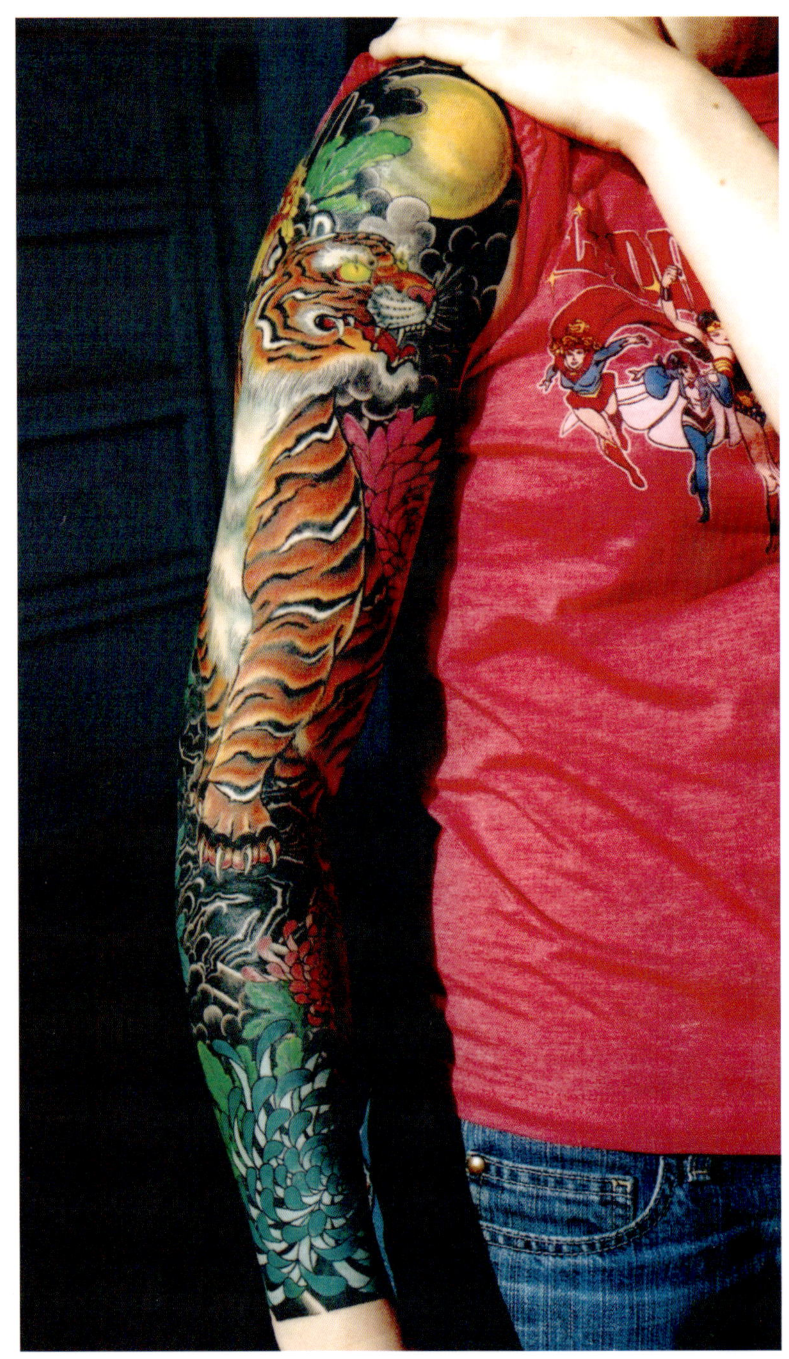

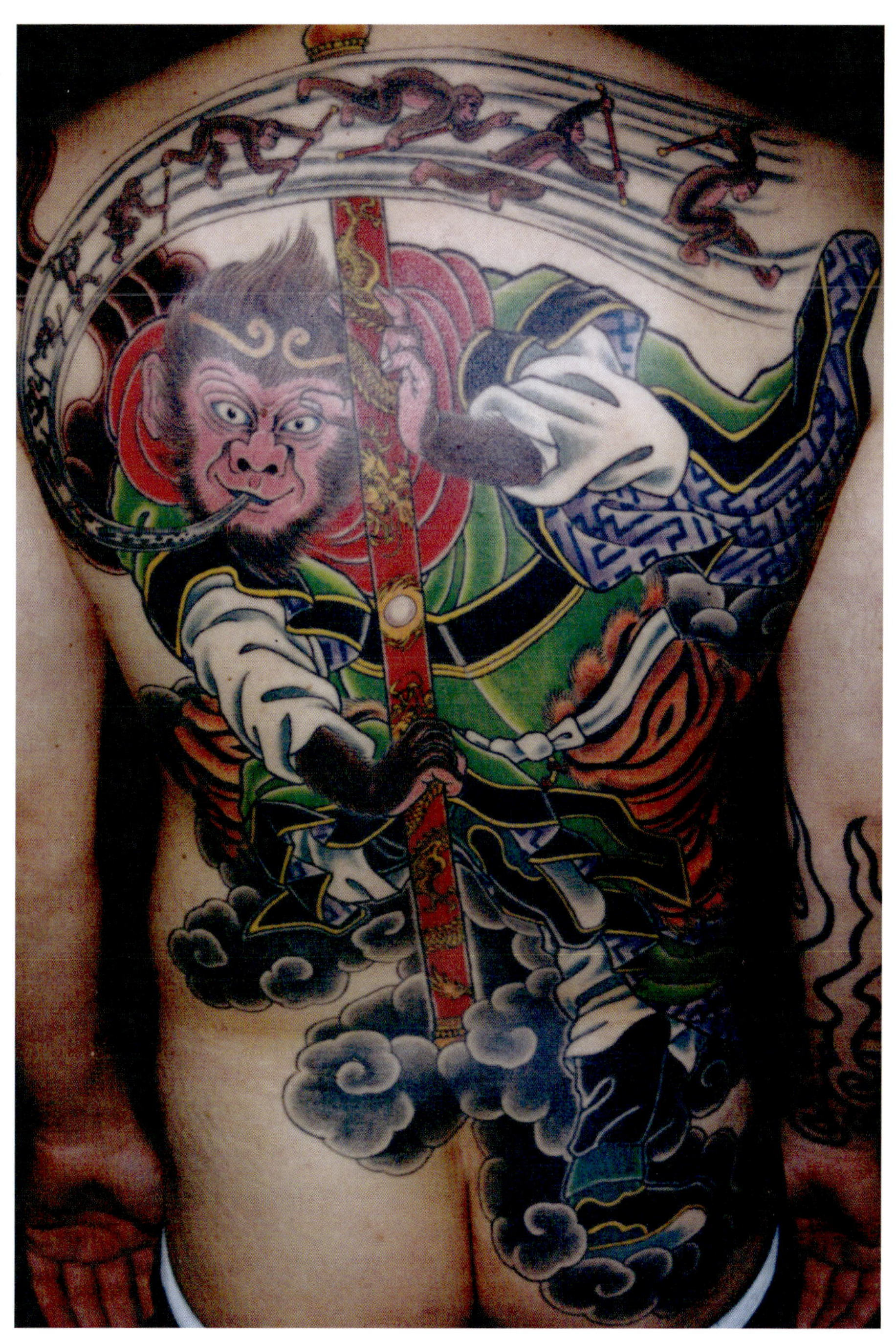

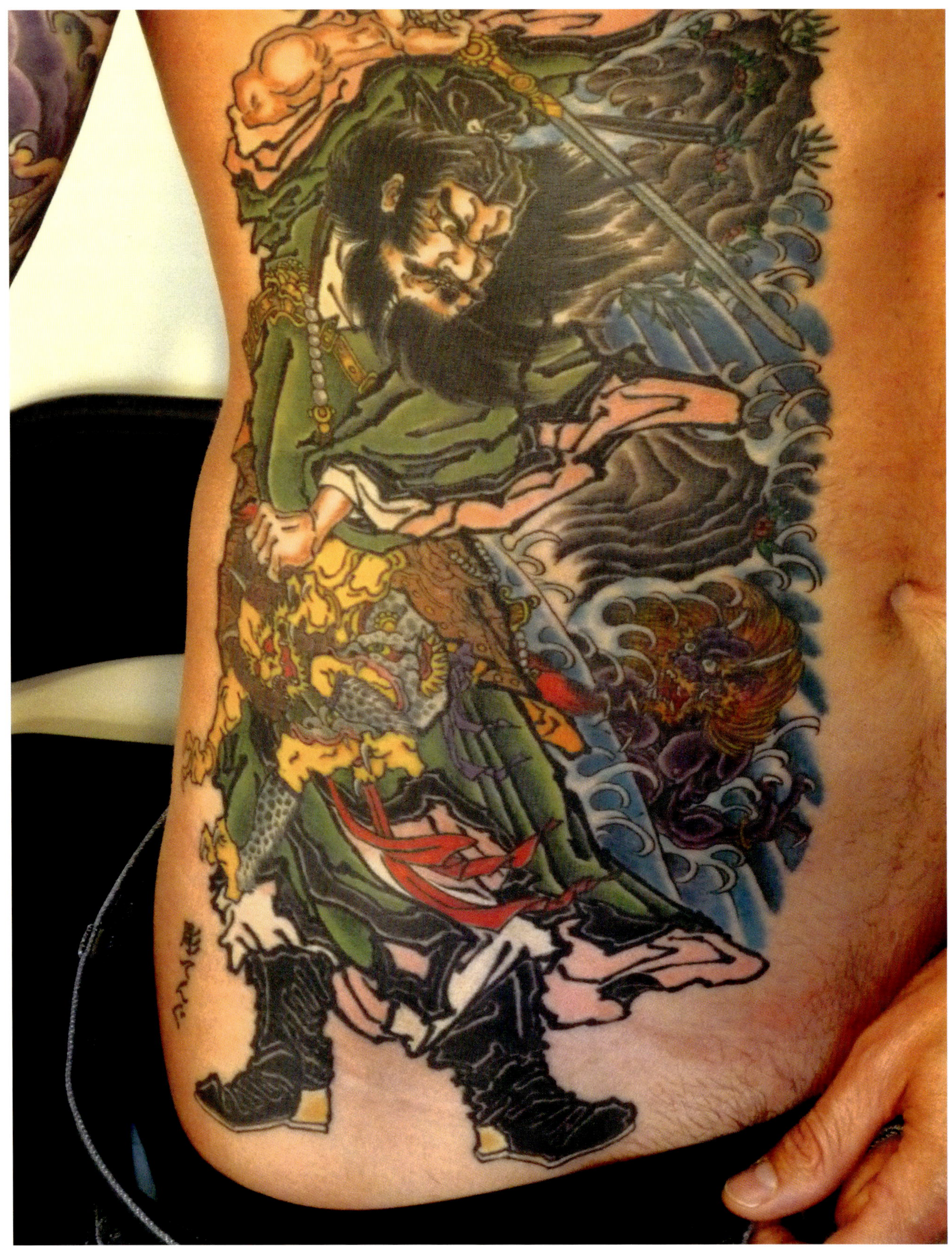

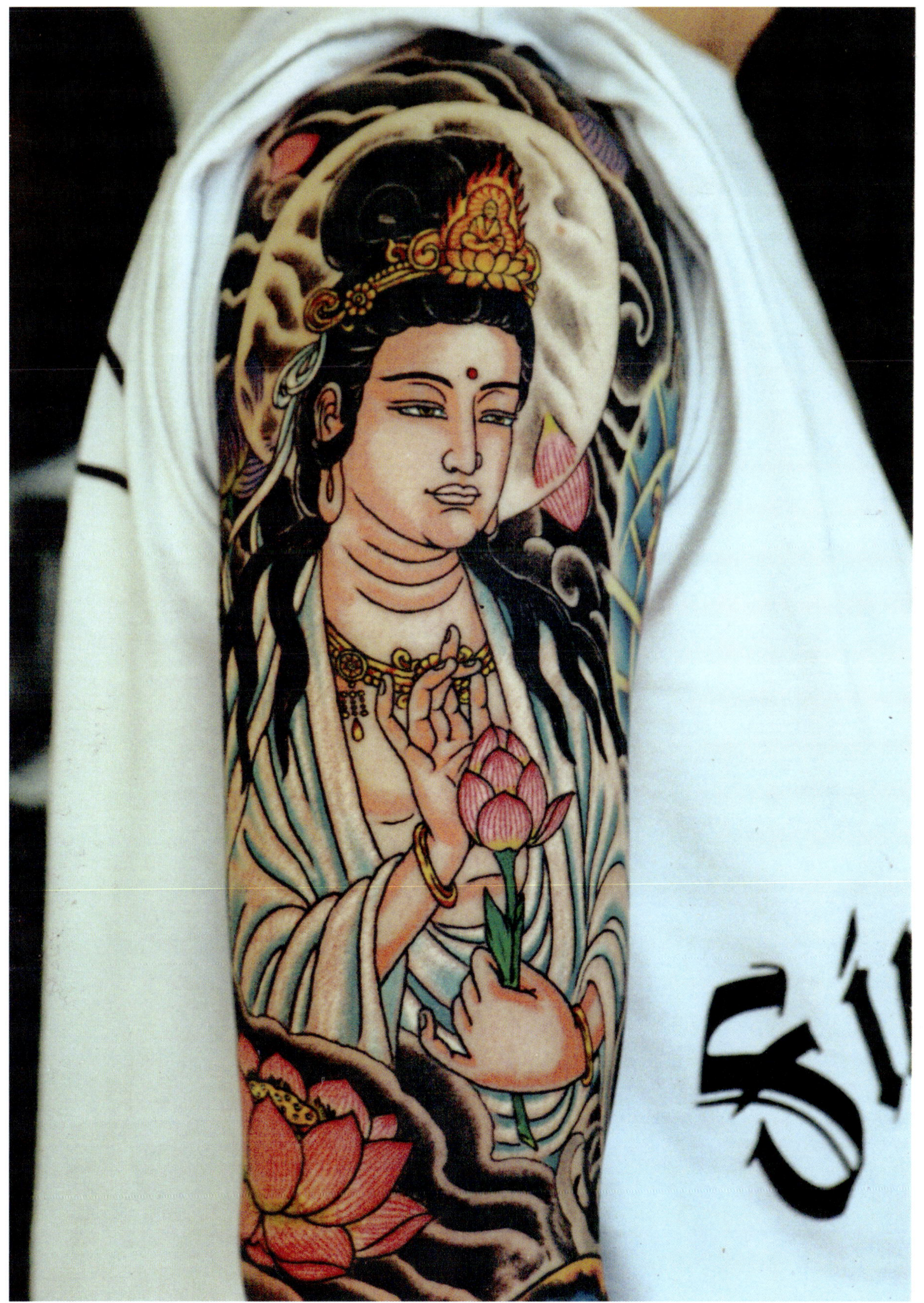

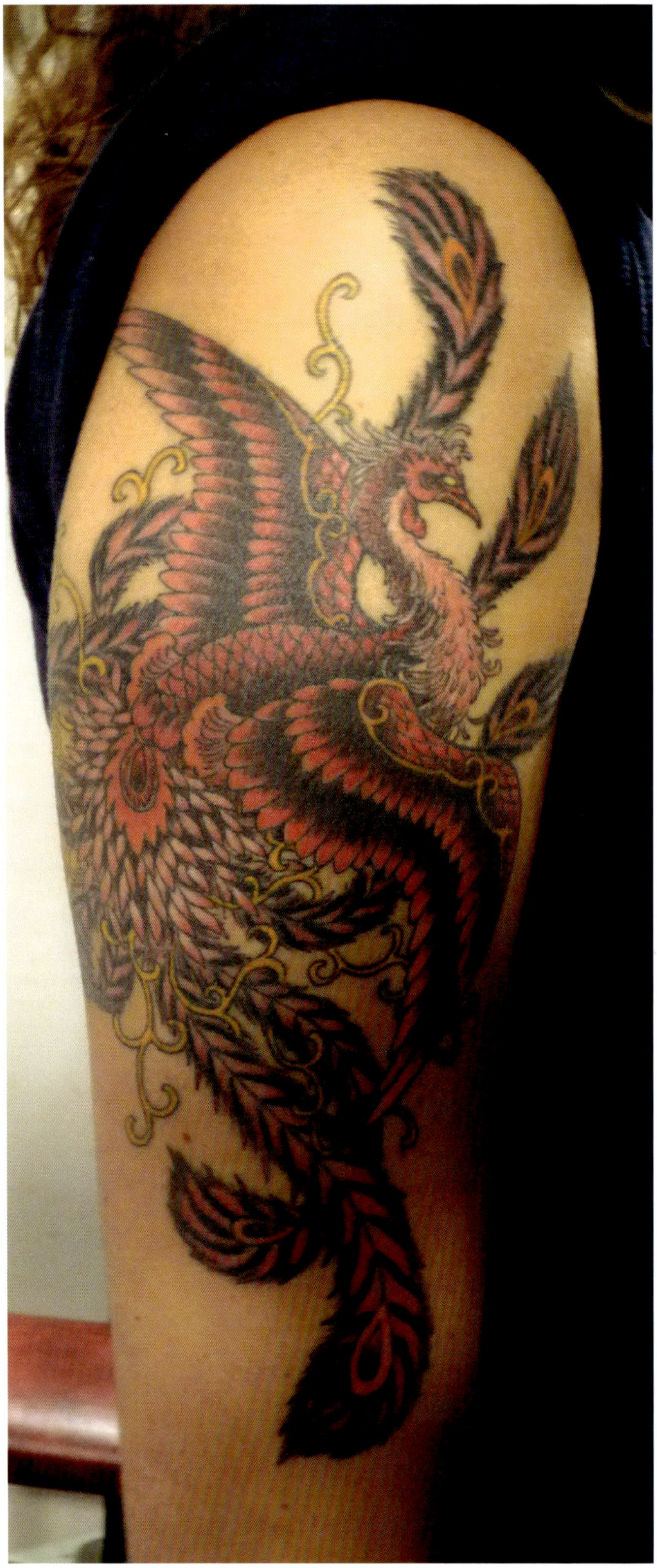

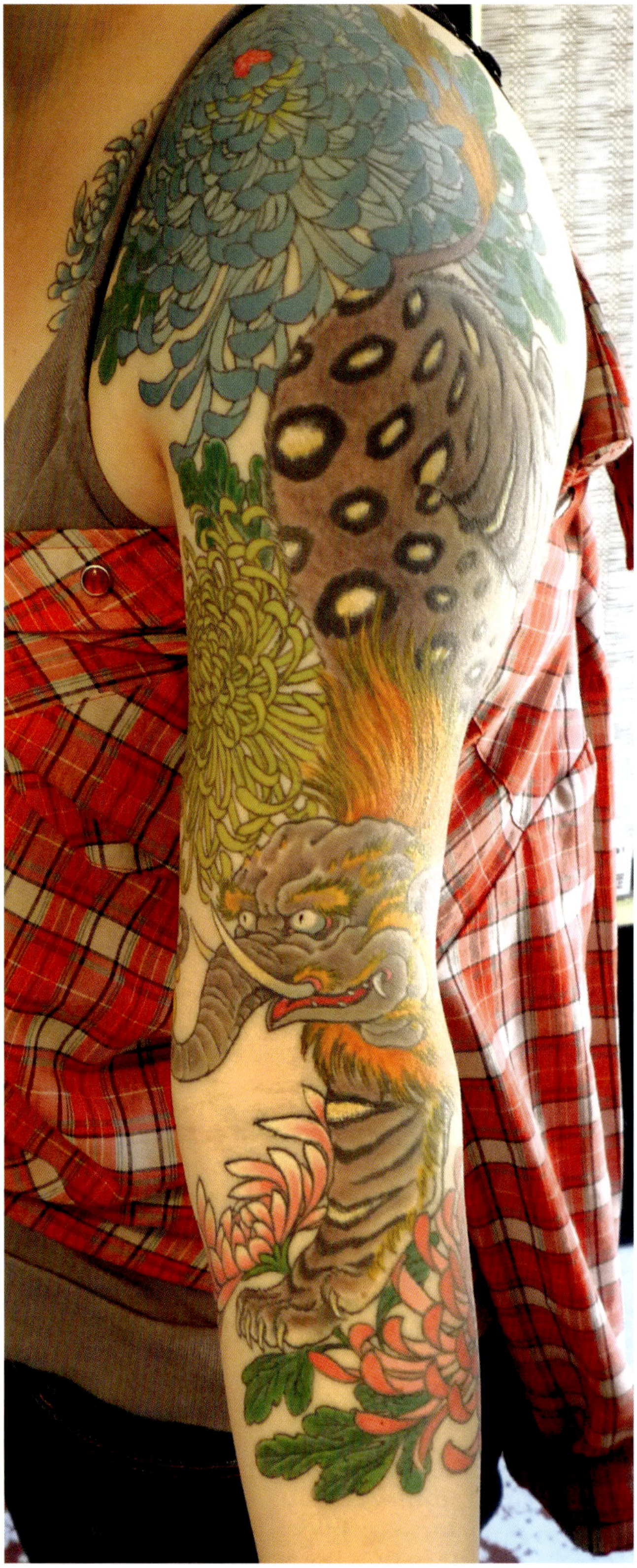

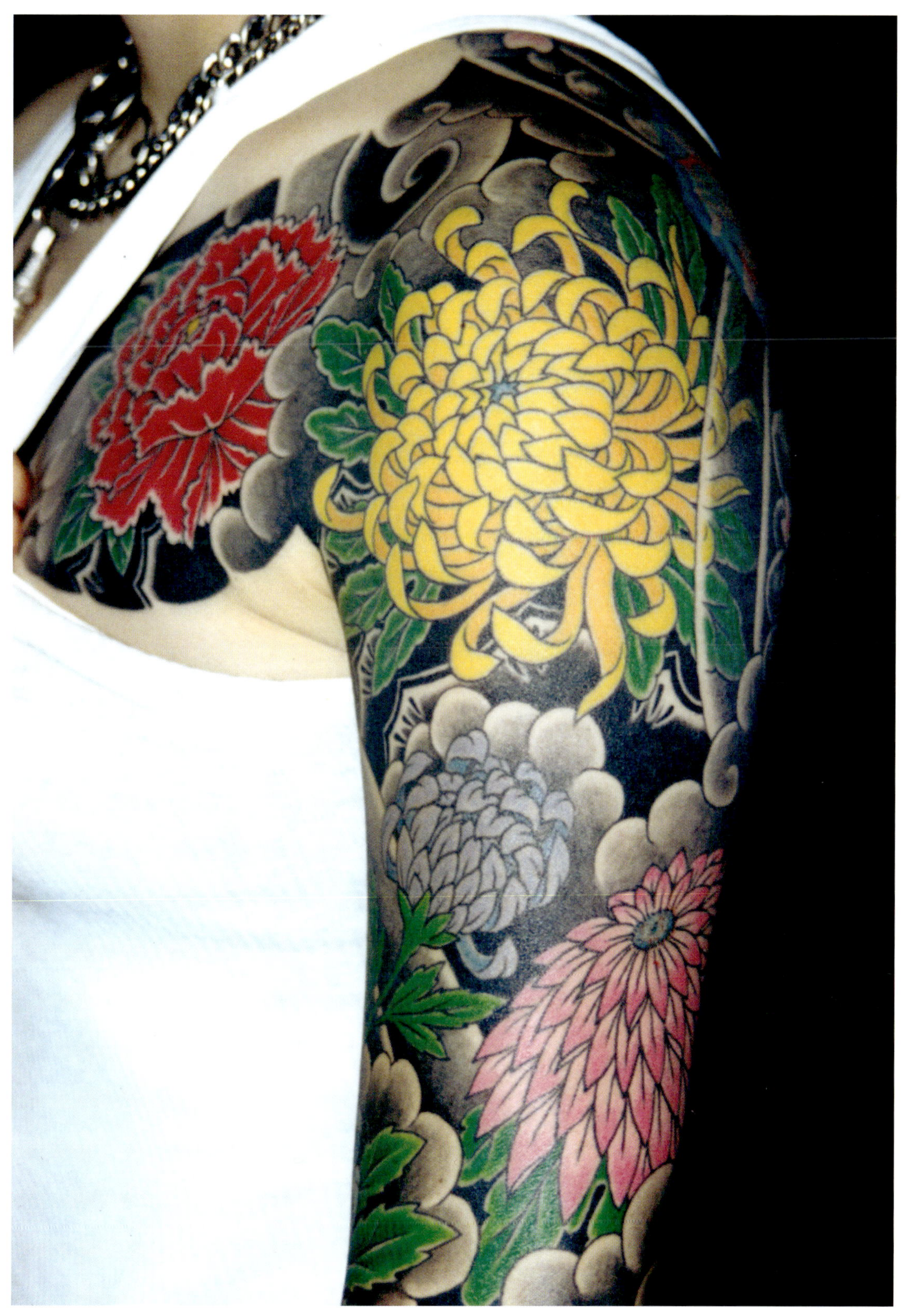

Stephanie Tamez

I have always been attracted to ancient civilizations, science fiction, symbolism of spiritual ideas and myths. I recently moved into a new apartment and had 55 boxes of books — thank the gods for the movers. I think this quote from C. G. Jung says it all:

"... There is a thinking in primordial images, in symbols which are older than the historical man, which are inborn in him from the earliest times, and, eternally living, outlasting all generations, still make up the groundwork of the human psyche. It is only possible to live the fullest life when we are in harmony with these symbols; wisdom is a return to them."

Tattooing has been kind to me and I thank all the people I have had the good fortune to share with in this experience.

Stephanie Tamez
— Brooklyn Adorned, New York City - 2010

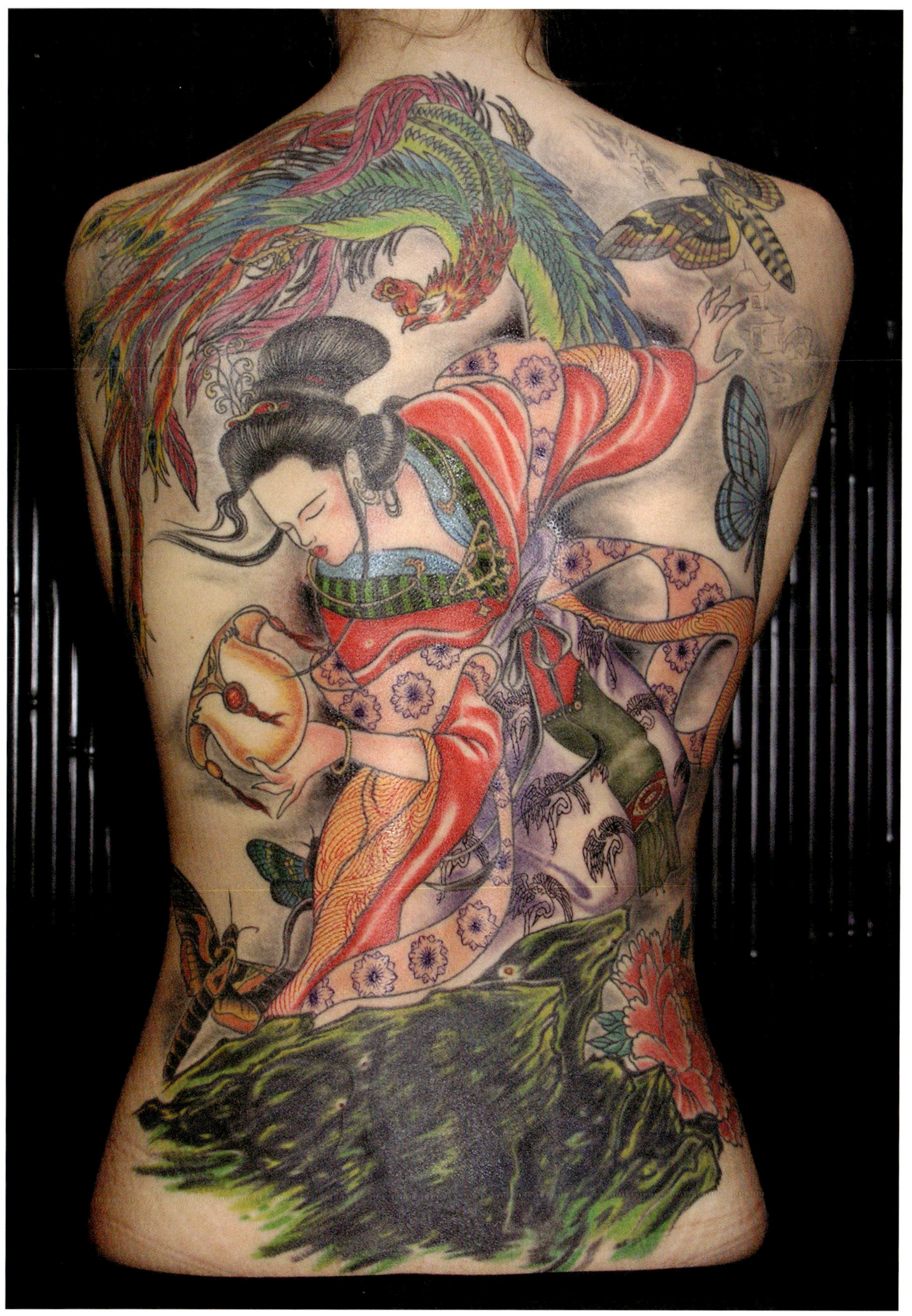

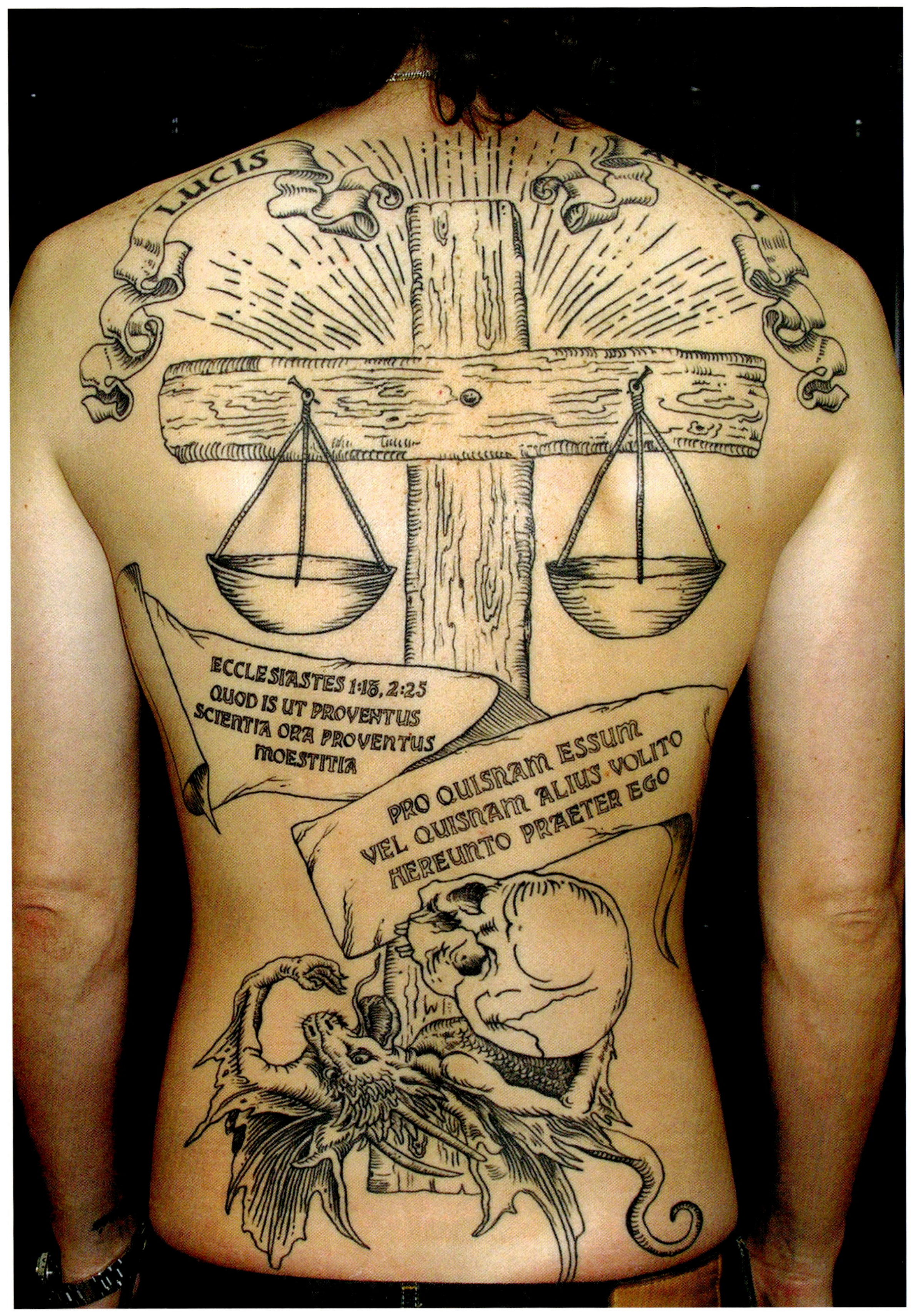
LUCIS
ECCLESIASTES 1:18, 2:25
QUOD IS UT PROVENTUS
SCIENTIA ORA PROVENTUS
MOESTITIA
PRO QUISNAM ESSUM
VEL QUISNAM ALIUS VOLITO
HEREUNTO PRAETER EGO

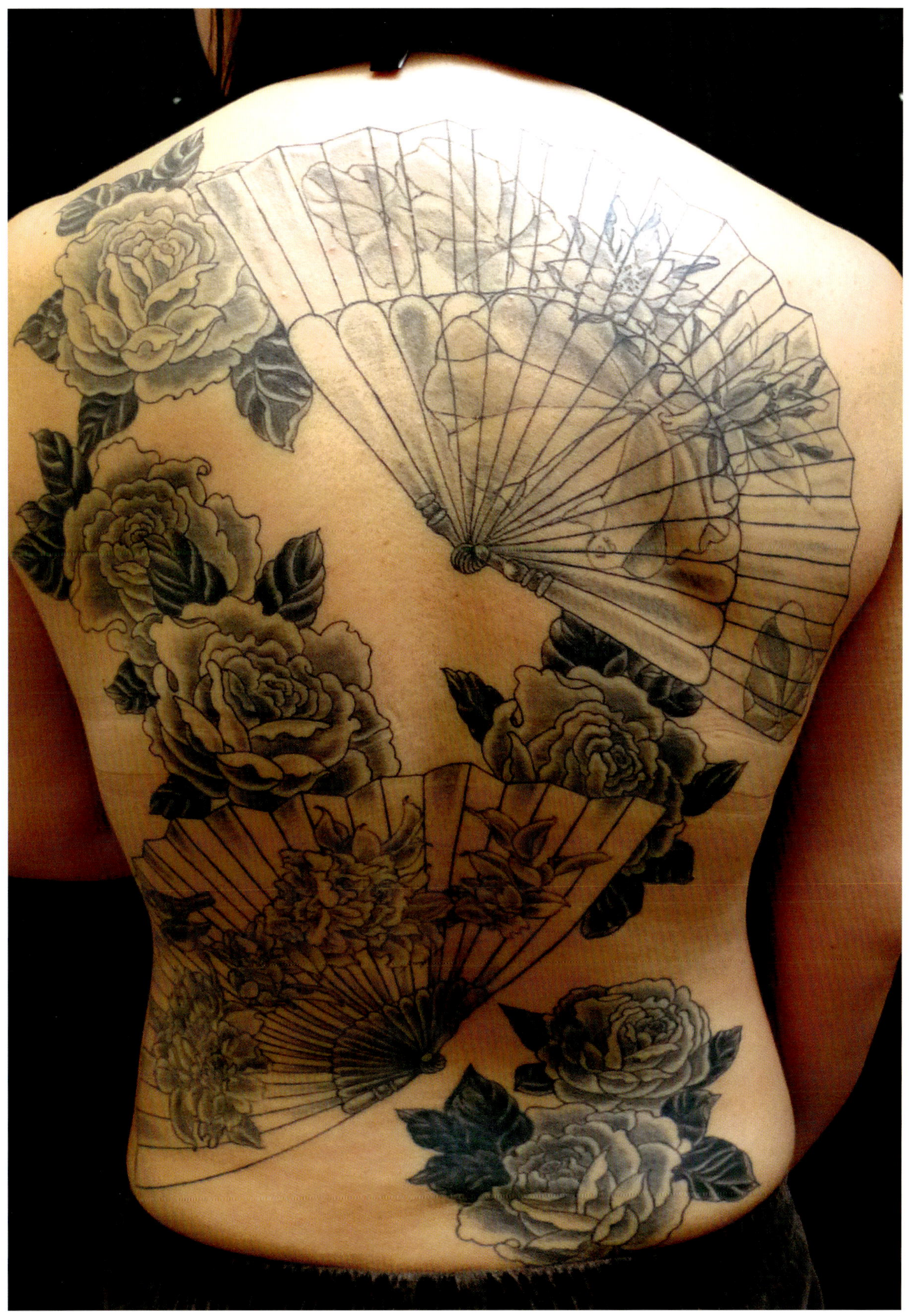

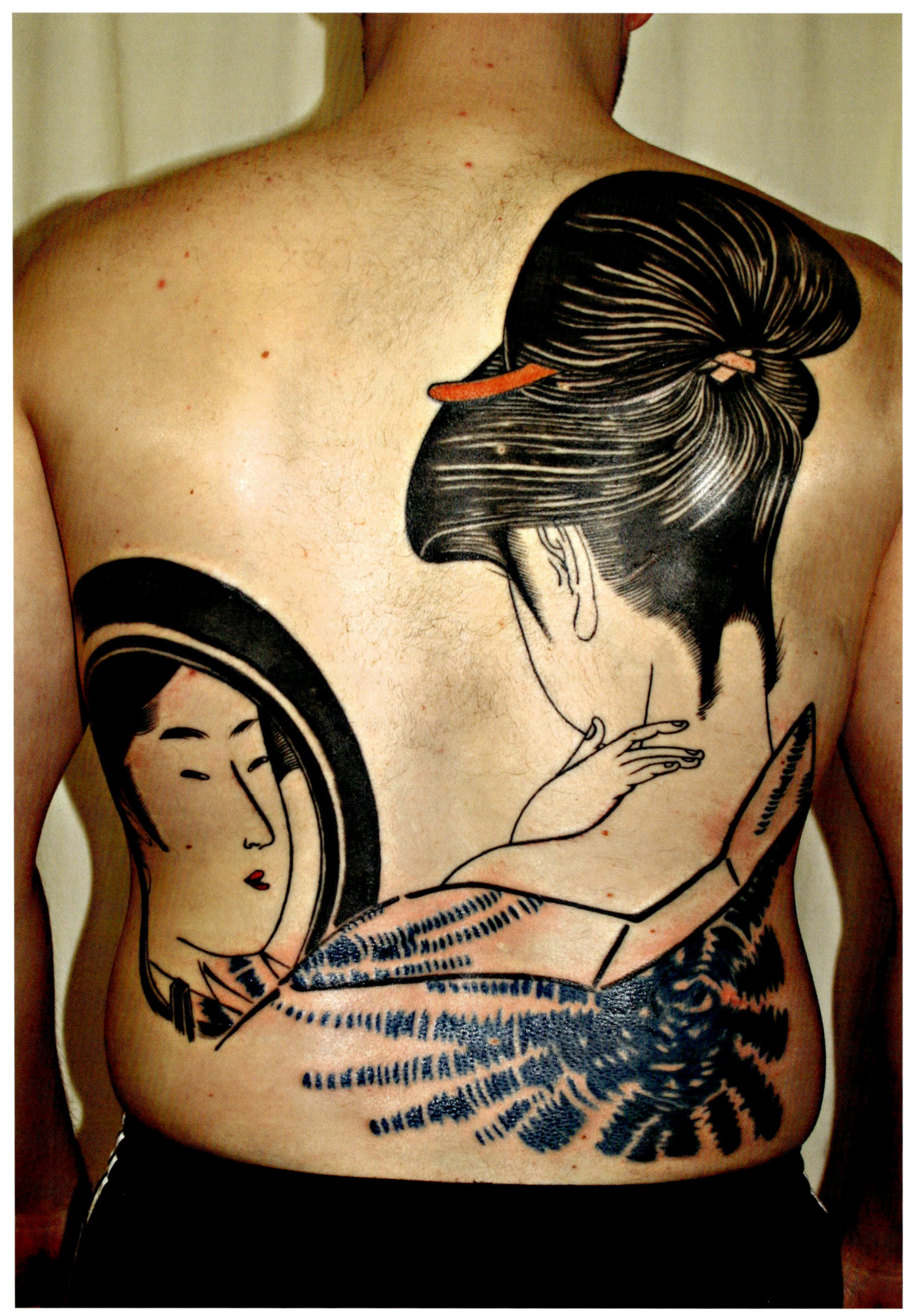

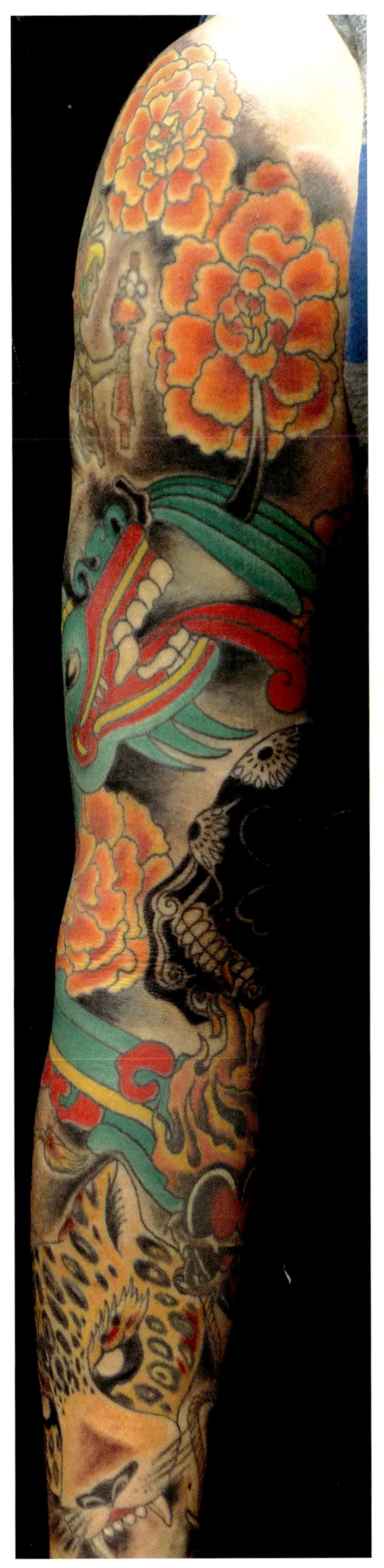

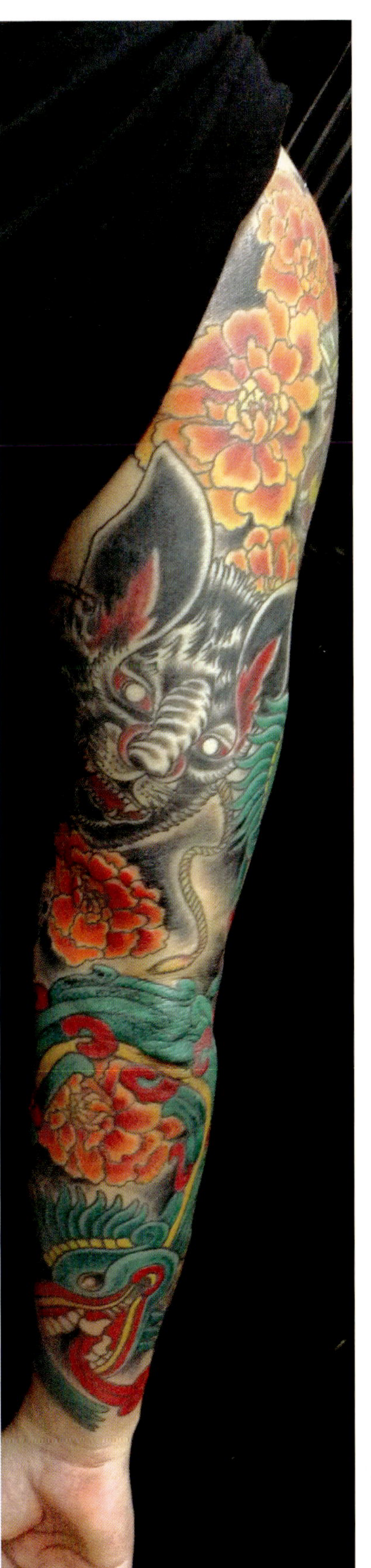

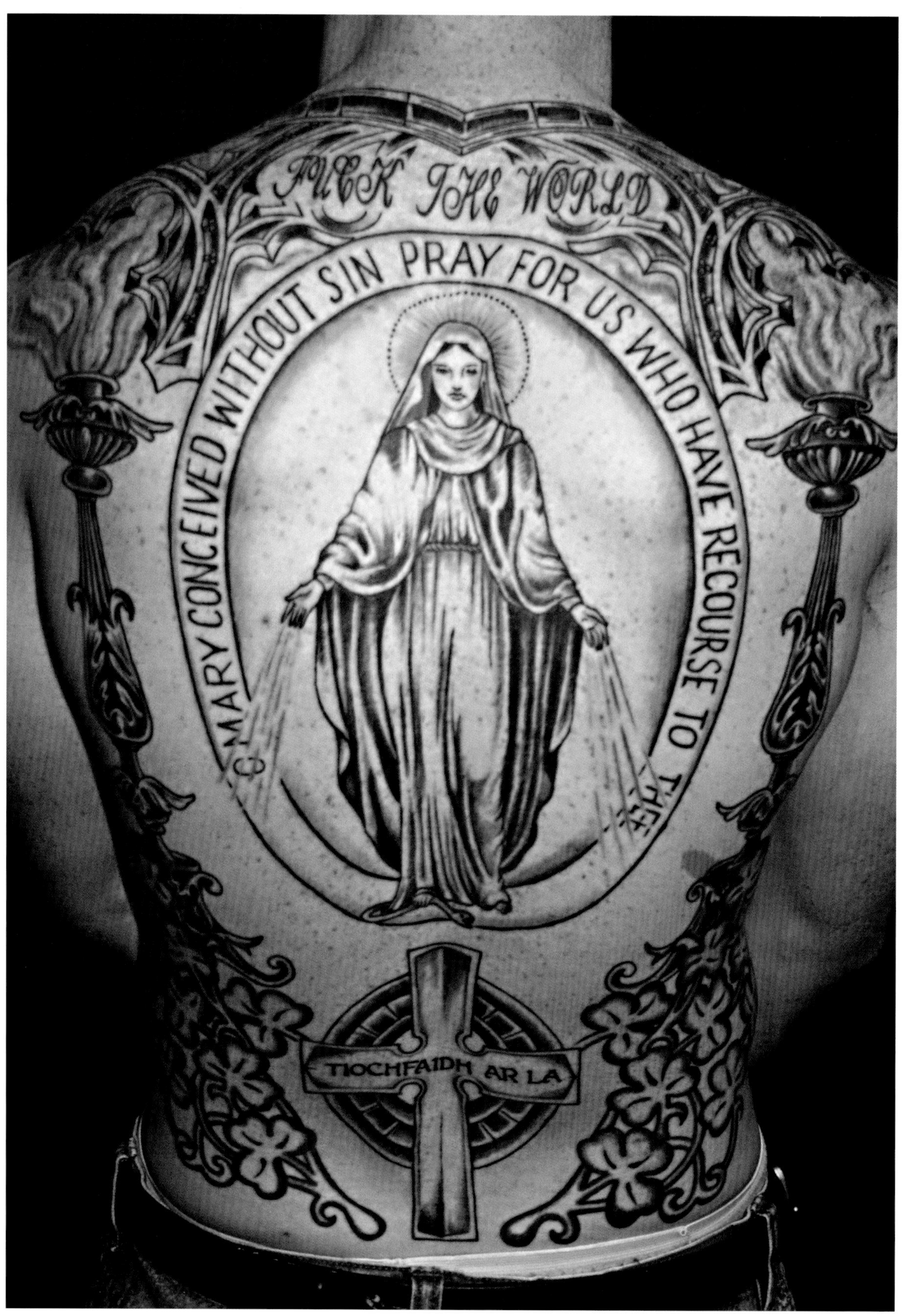
FUCK THE WORLD
O MARY CONCEIVED WITHOUT SIN PRAY FOR US WHO HAVE RECOURSE TO THEE
TIOCHFAIDH AR LA

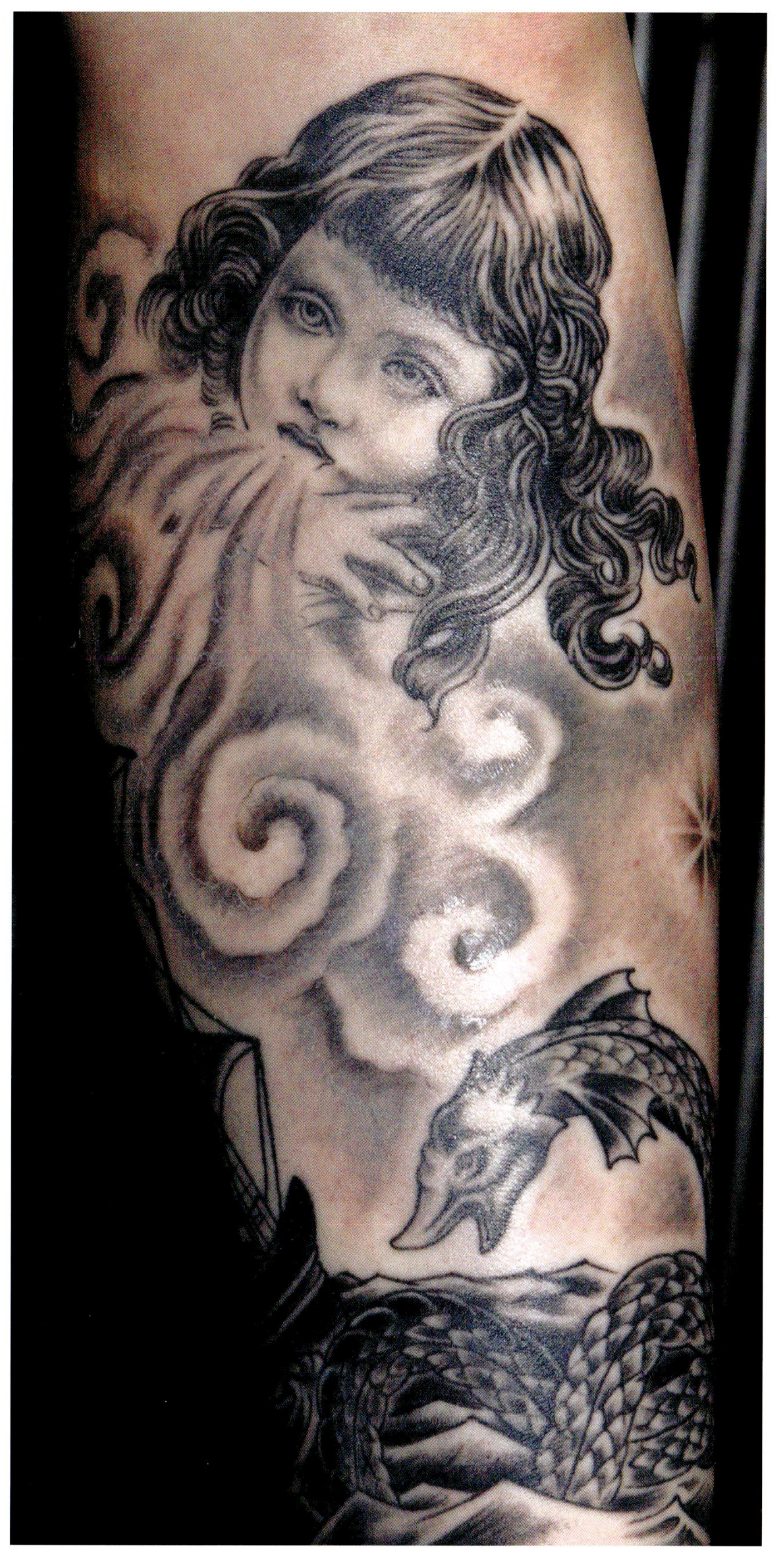

Clae Welch

While helping my mom clean out her storage unit a few months ago, I came across all kinds of objects from our lives: photo albums, broken skateboards & terrible paintings. One thing I happened upon was an old report card from the third grade. As I looked down through the list of below average grades, there was a note and in the comments it said, "Clae seems to have a problem focusing, he would do better in his lessons if he would just stop his favorite pastime: drawing."

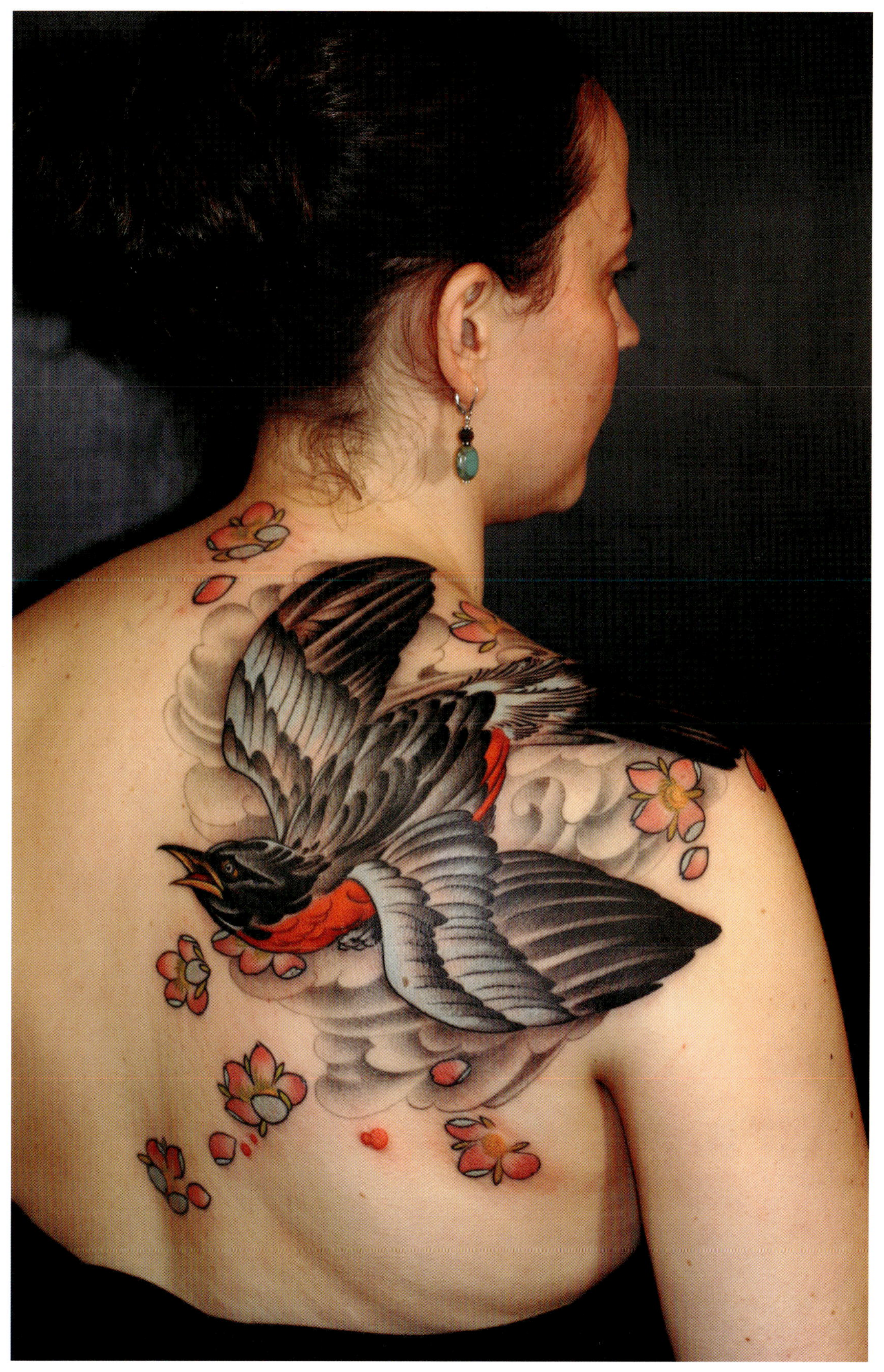

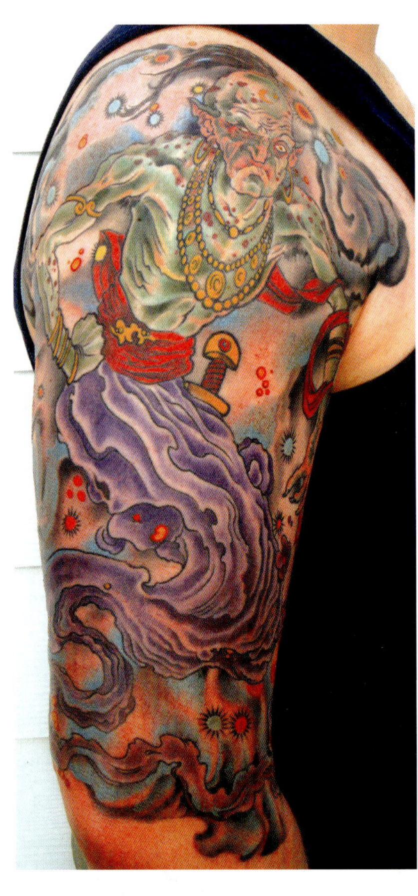

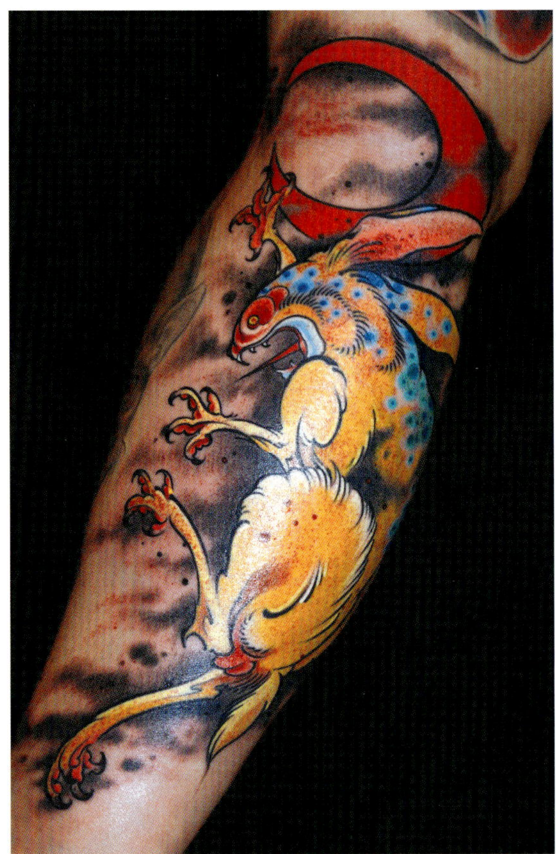

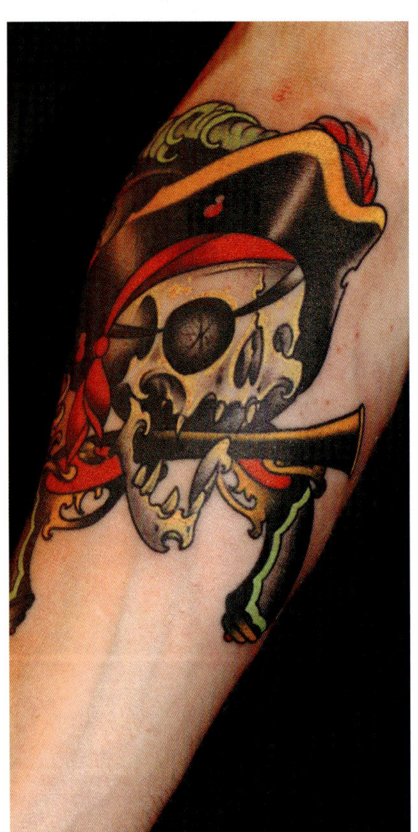

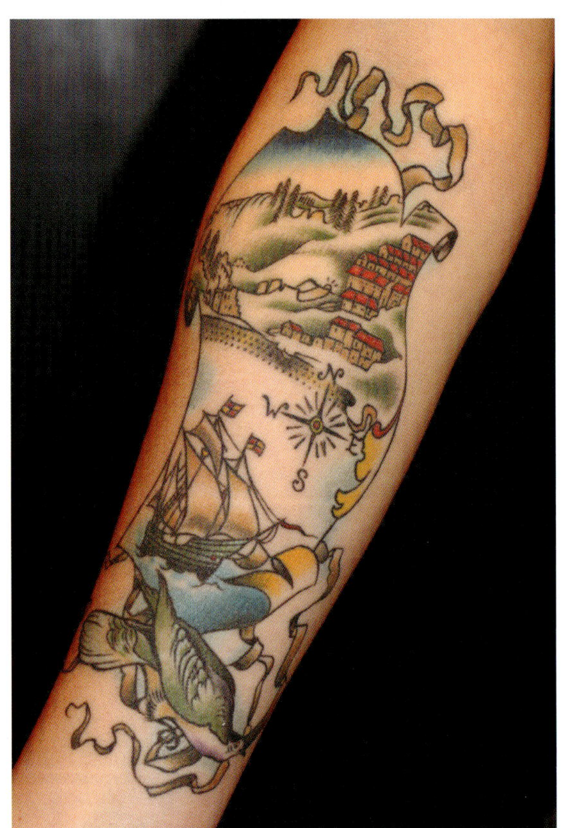

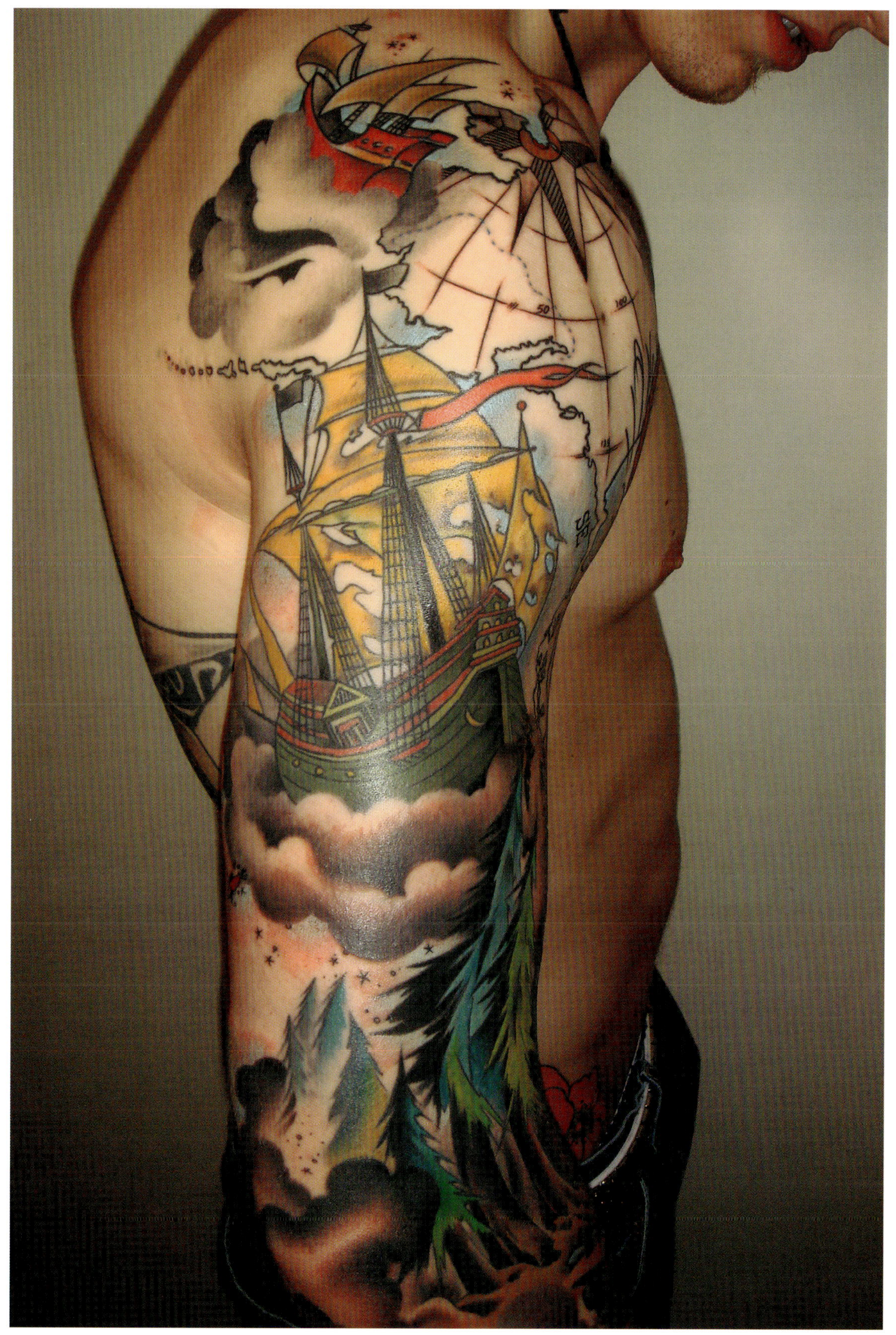

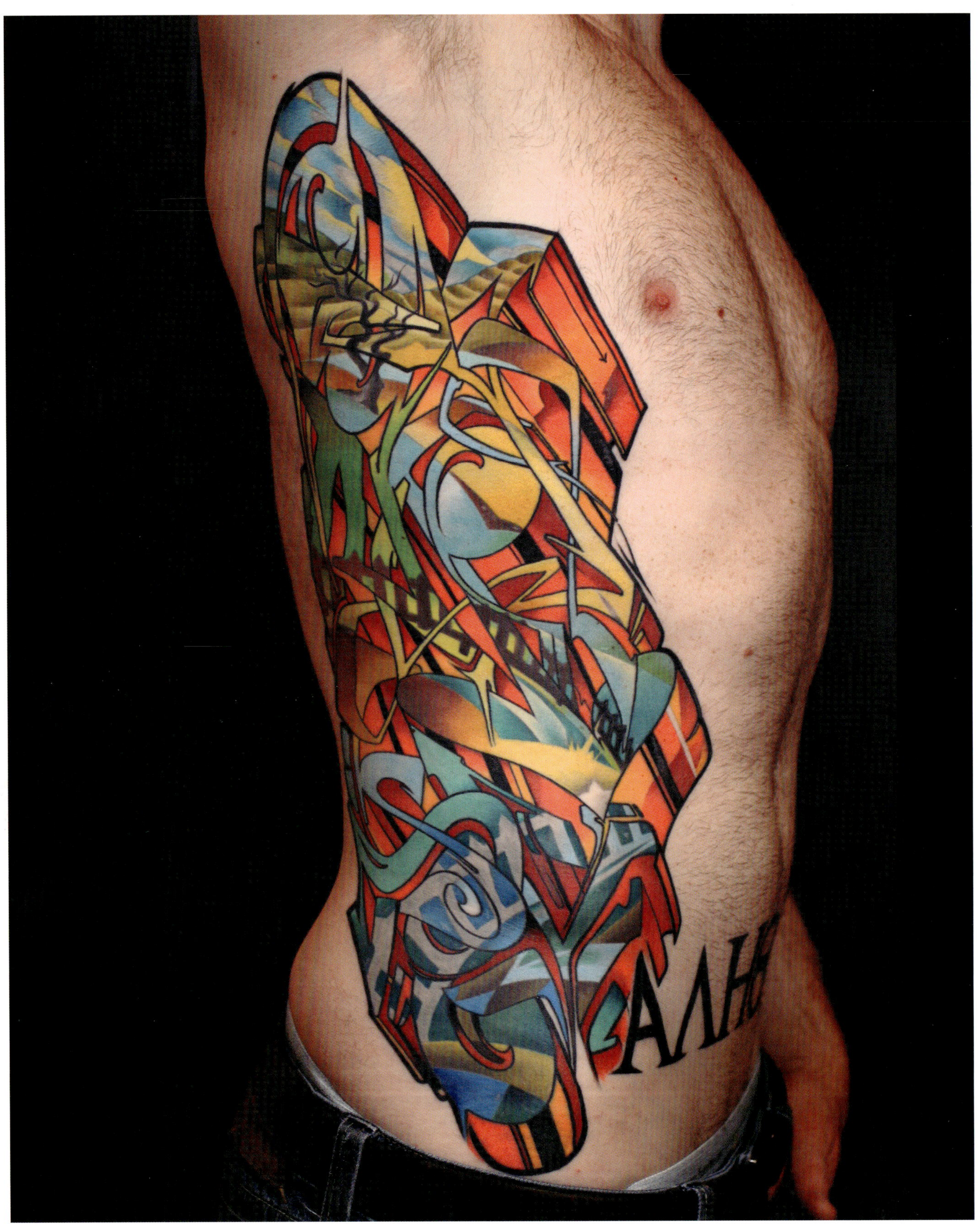

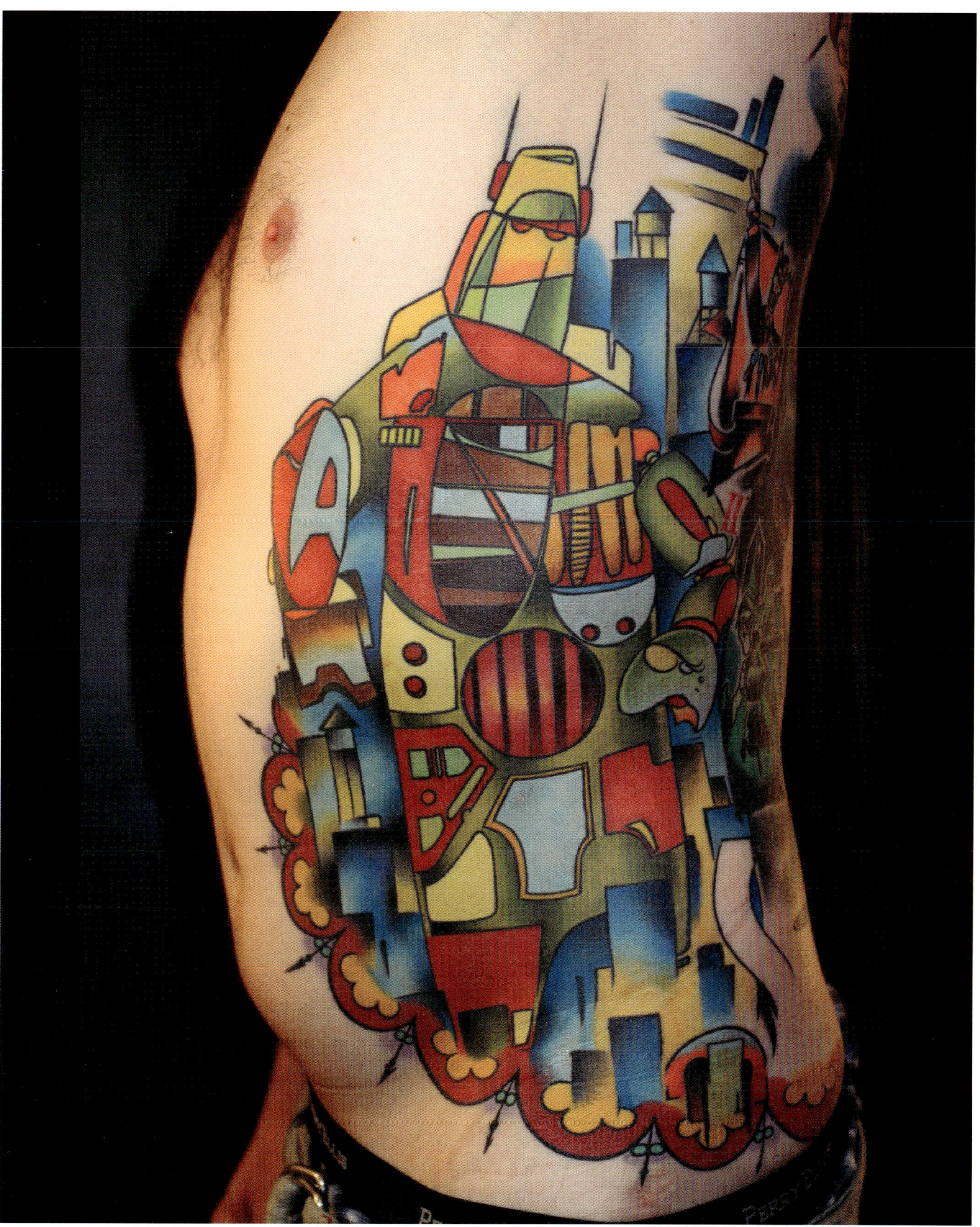

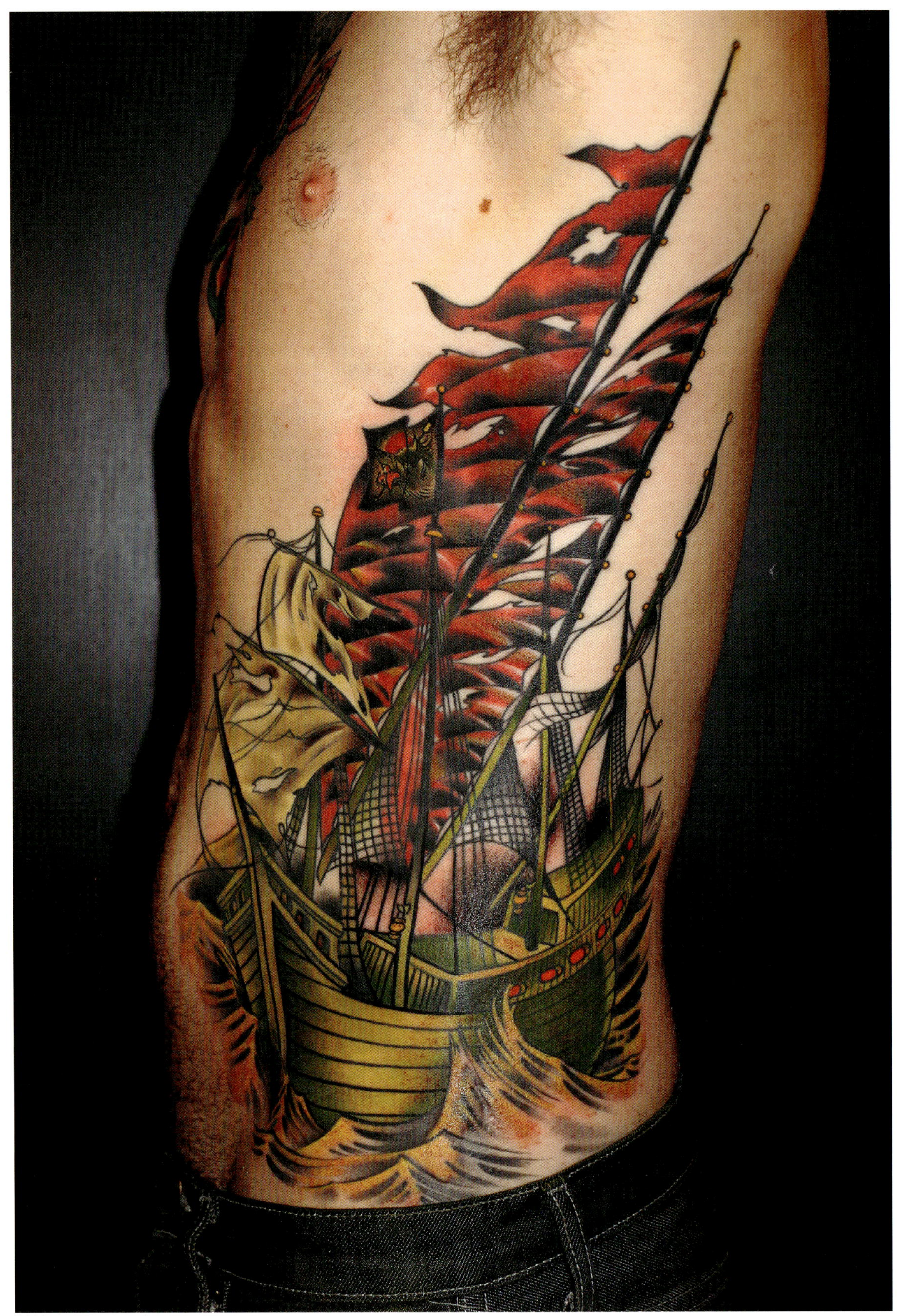

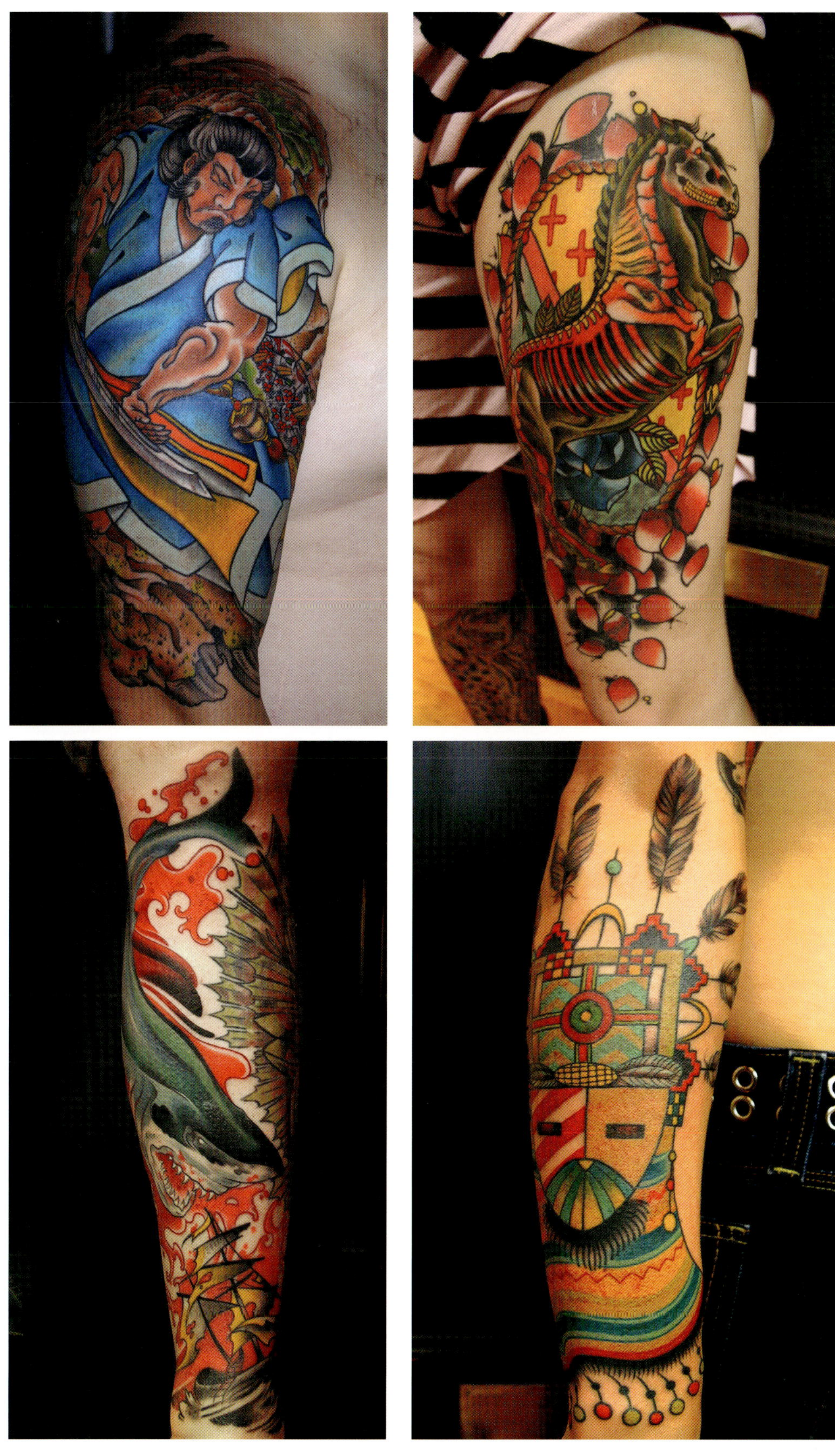

Yoni Zilber

Yoni Zilber began tattooing in Tel Aviv in 1998. Currently he works at New York Adorned. In 2007, good fortune brought with it a Master of Tibetan art: Pema Rinzin, an accomplished Tibetan Tangka painter and contemporary artist whose work adorns walls in the Dalai Lama's temple in India as well as the Rubin Museum. He agreed to take Yoni on as his apprentice. Though Yoni enjoys and excels in a range of artistic genres, he has increasingly been focused on translating the Tibetan style into tattoo art. Although tattoo is not part of the Tibetan culture, he strives to be respectful of the ancient tradition upon which he draws.

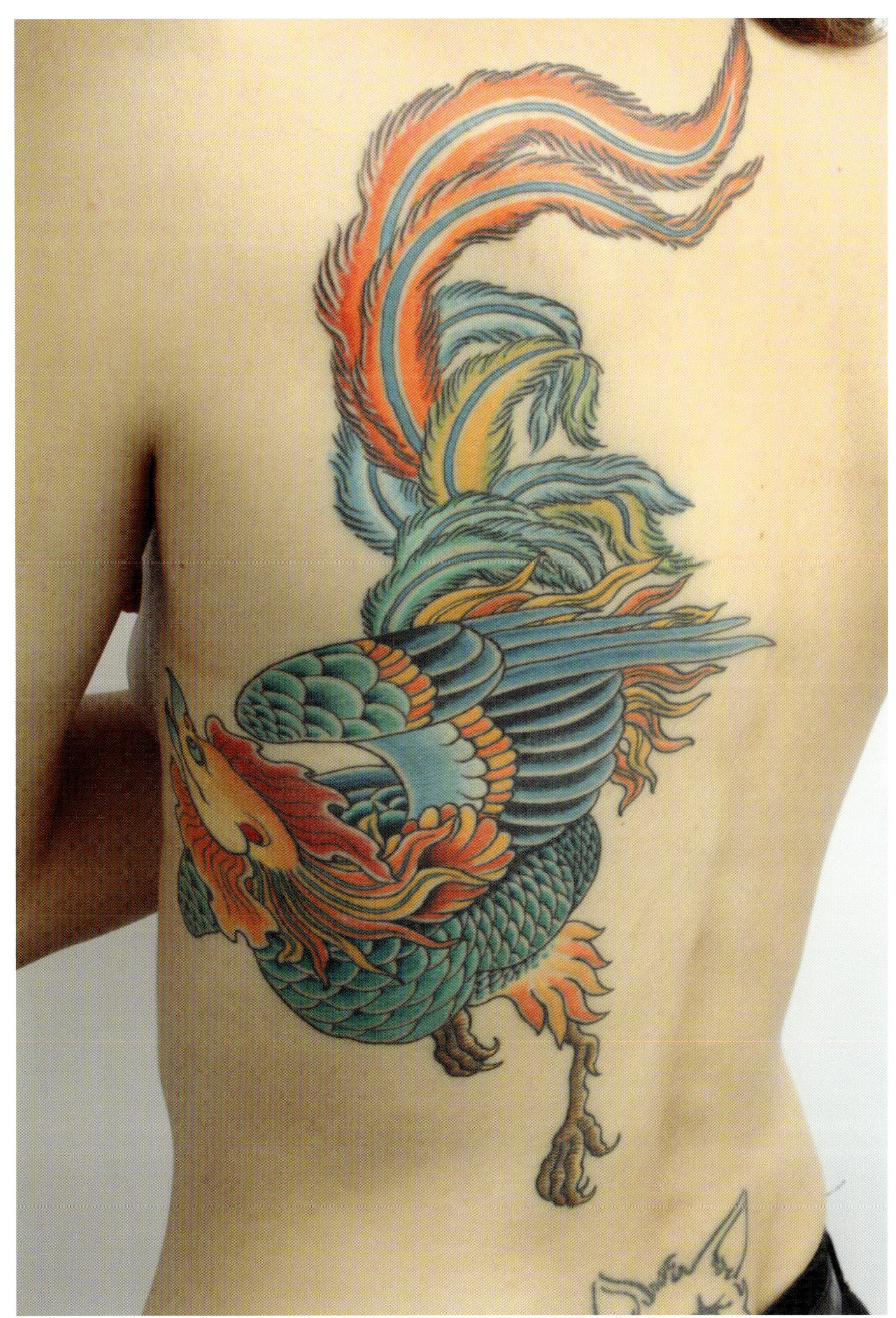

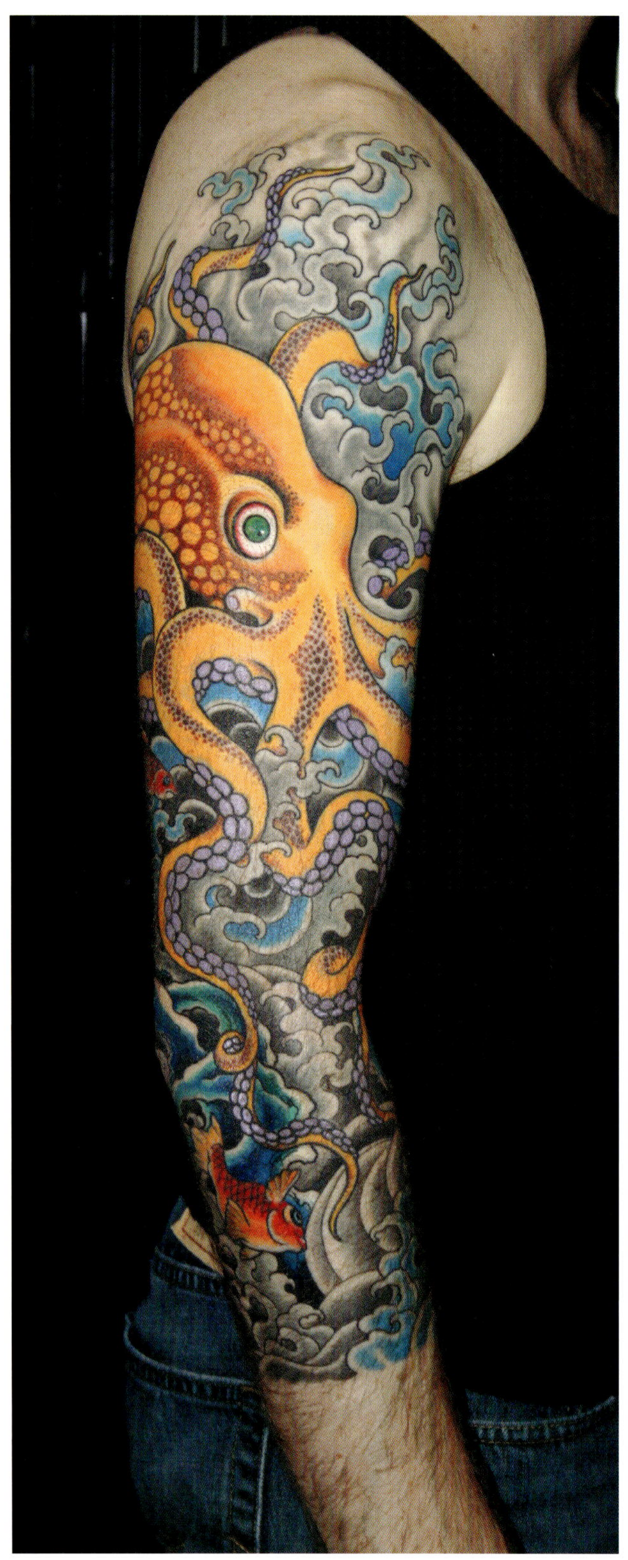

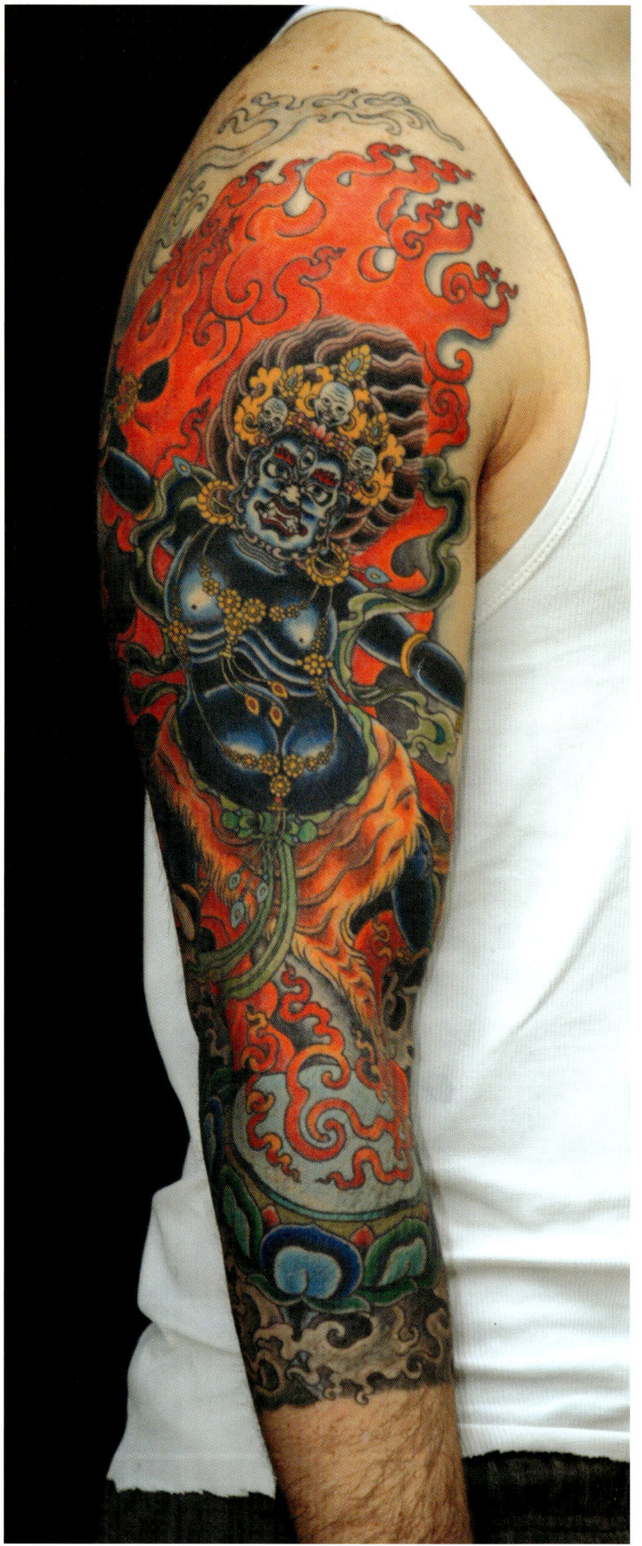

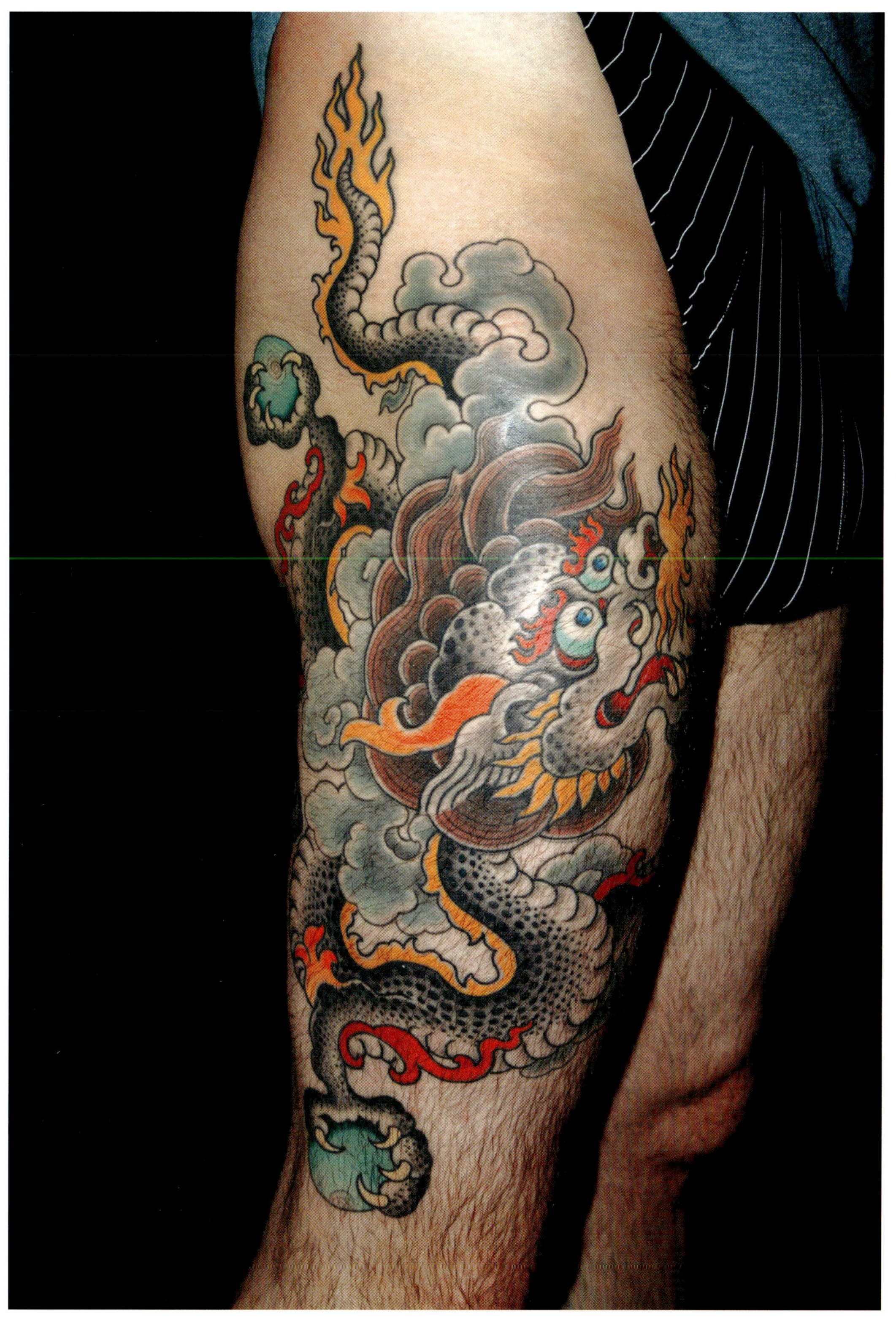

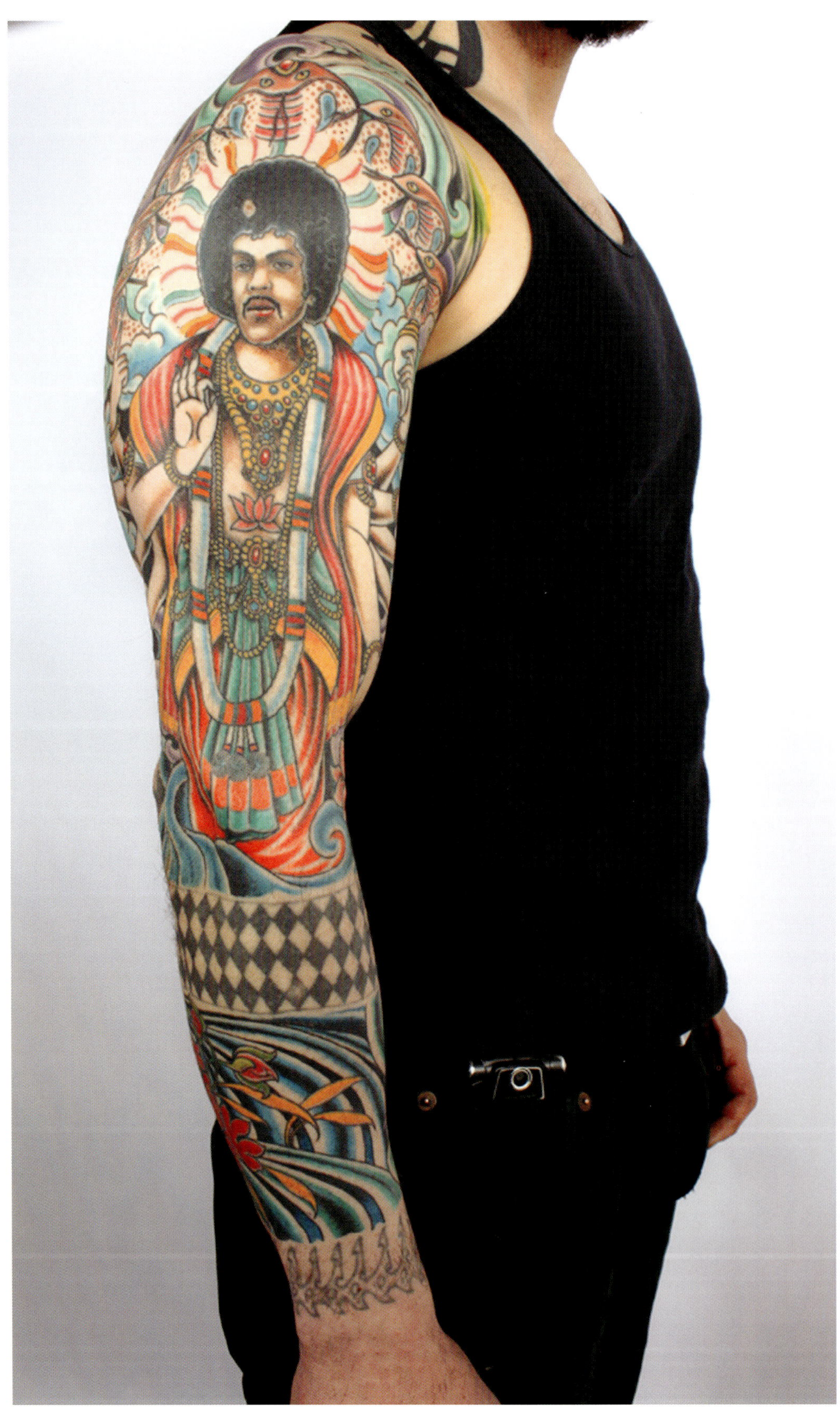

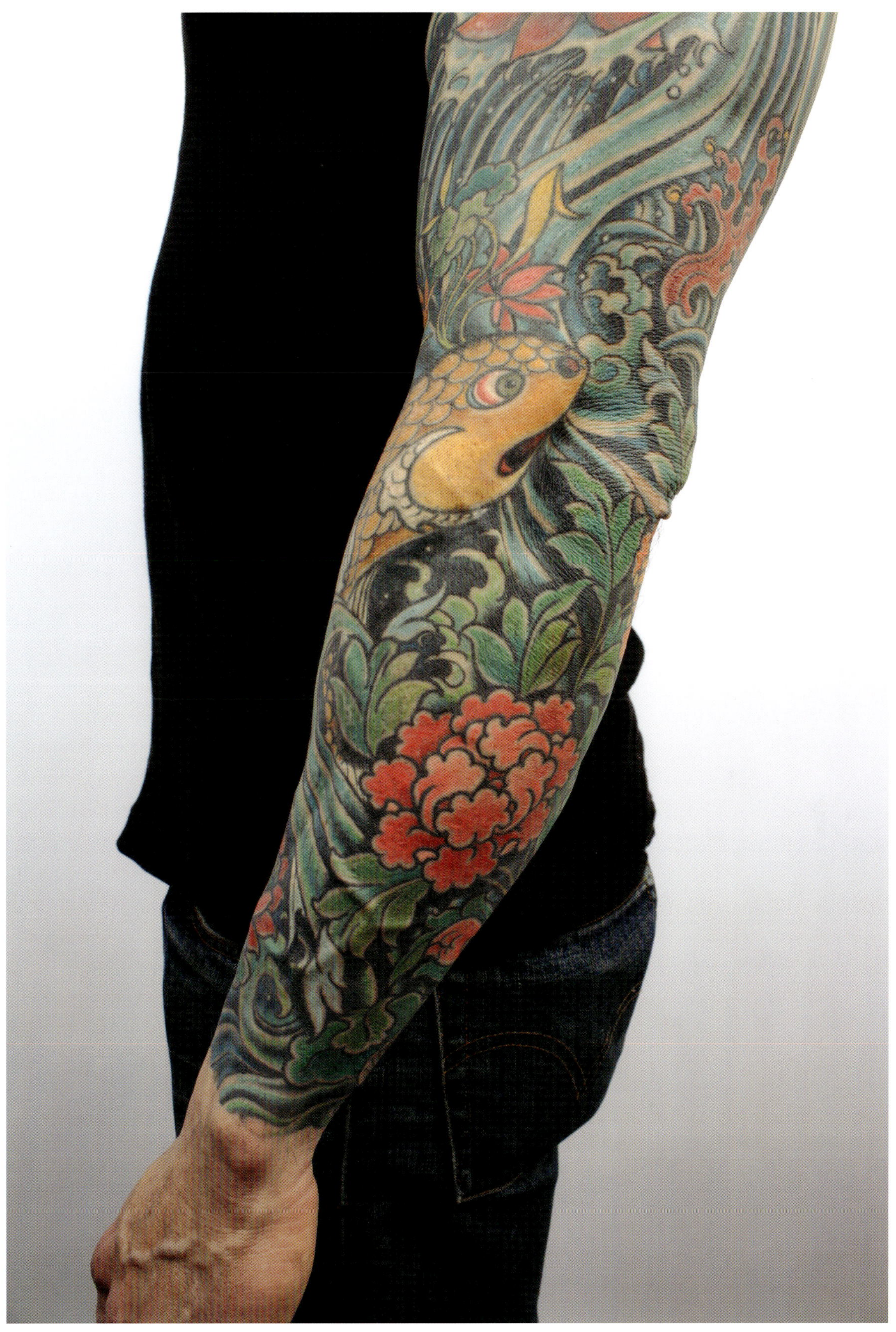

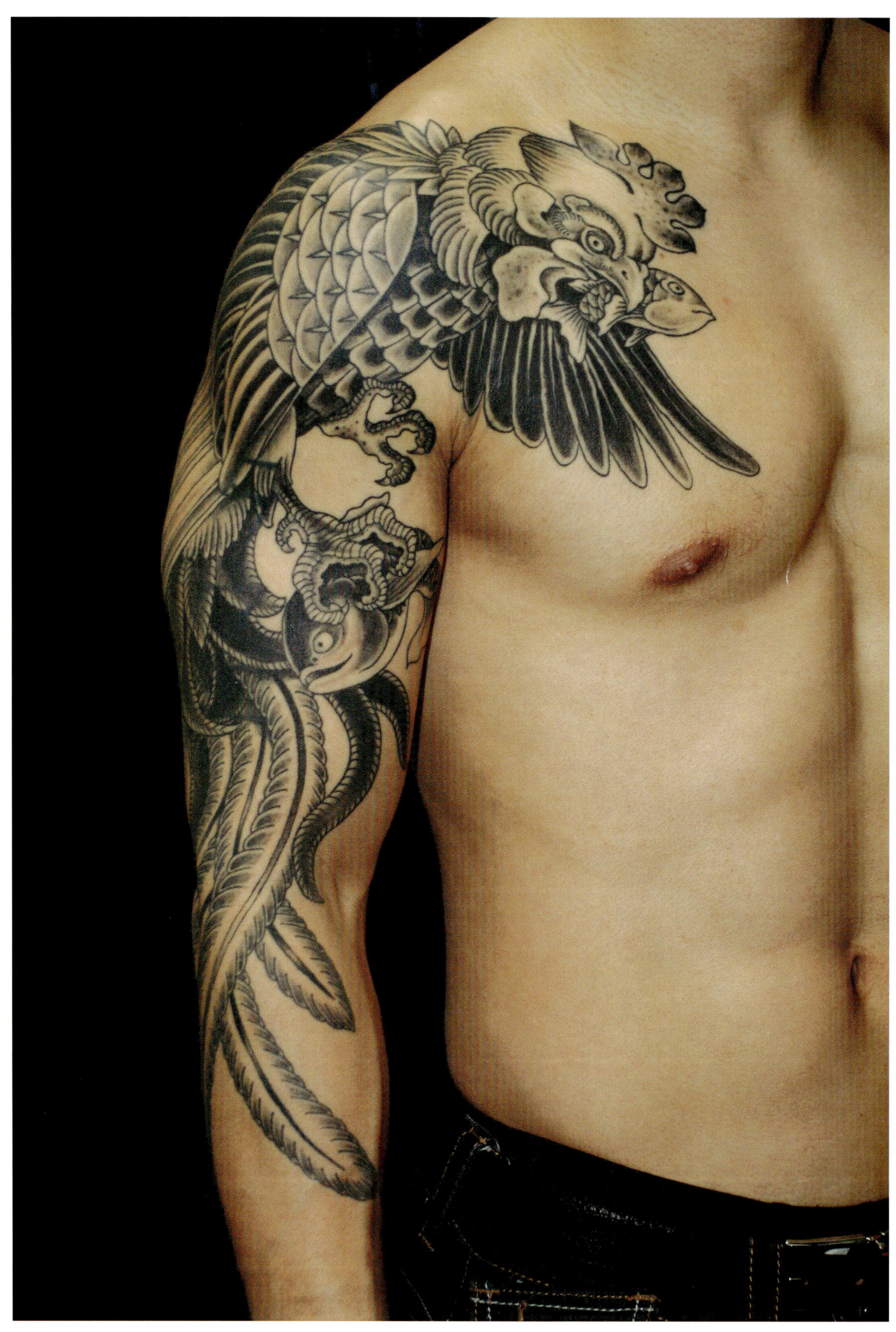

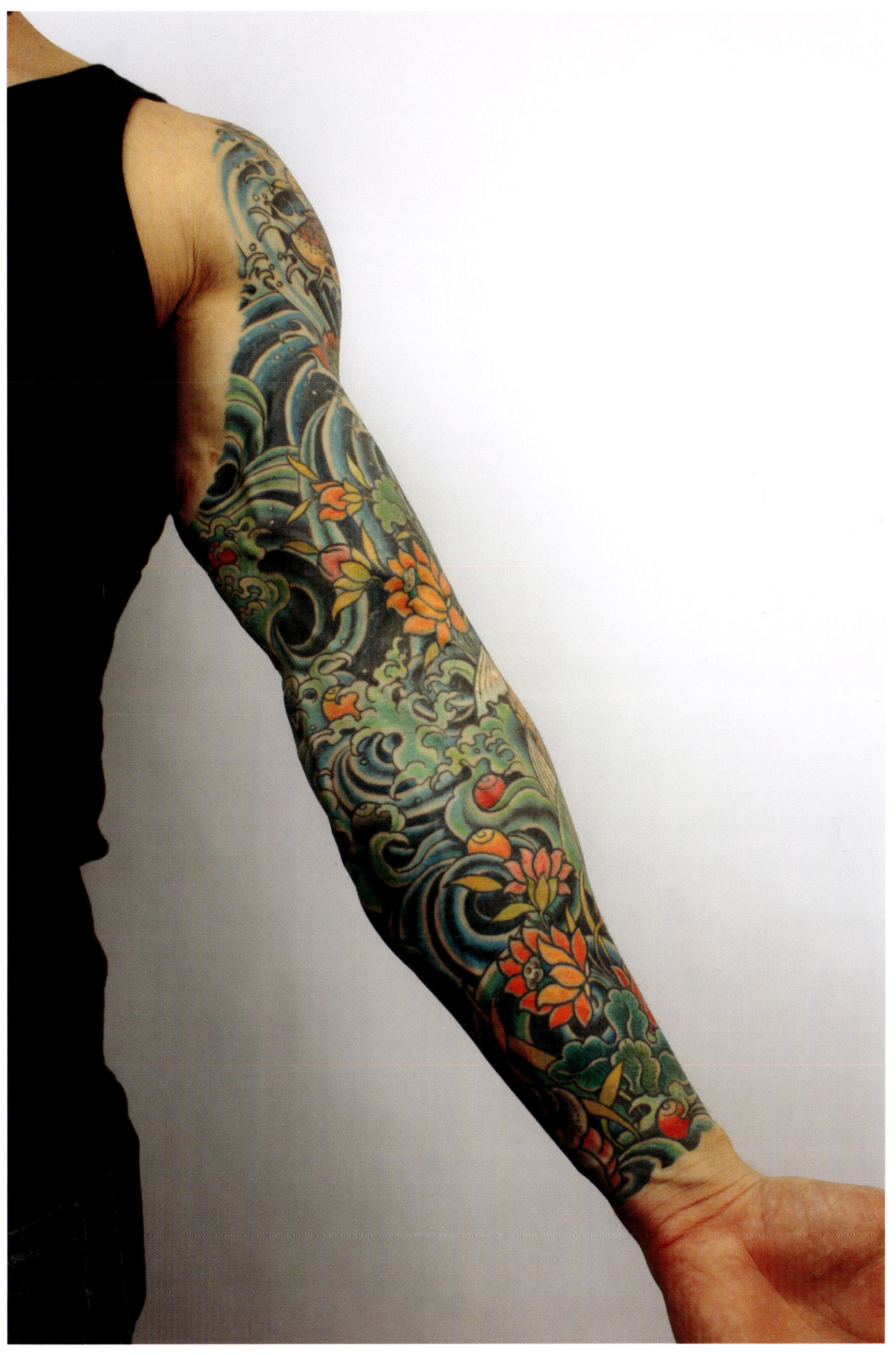

ARTIST INDEX

SHAWN BARBER
www.sdbarber.com; www.memoirtattoo.com

ANDY BARRETT
www.horseshoesandhandgrenadestattoo.com

MARIO BARTH
www.mariobarthtattoo.com

MARK BODE
www.markbode.com

SUNNY BUICK
www.sunnybuick.com

STEVE BYRNE
www.rockofagestattoo.com

JUN CHA
www.juncha.net

VIRGINIA ELWOOD
www.virginiaelwoodtattoo.com

LIZ GRUESOME
www.sgtattoo.com

MARK HEGGIE
www.markheggie.com

ANGELIQUE HOUTKAMP
www.salonserpent.com

EVA HUBER
www.myspace.com/evajean

NATHAN KOSTECHKO
www.nathankostechko.com

MIKE LEDGER

JIME LITWALK
www.jimelitwalk.com

JOSE LOPEZ
www.lowridertattoostudios.com

JON MIRRO
www.handofdoomtattoo.com

PAULIE
www.paulietattoo.com

COLIN STEVENS
www.bodym.com

STEPHANIE TAMEZ
www.stephanietamez.com

CLAE WELCH
www.claewelch.com

YONI ZILBER
www.nyadorned.com

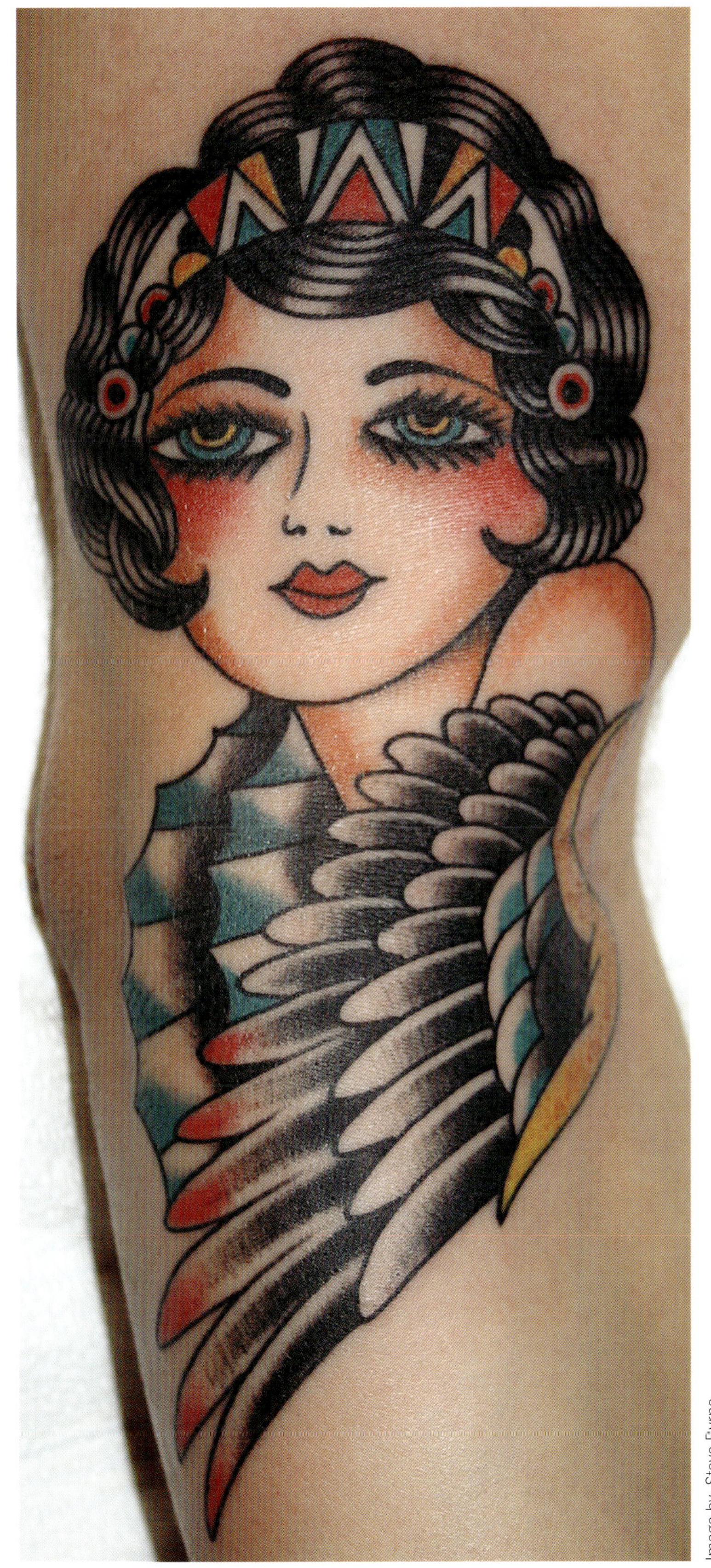

Image by: Steve Byrne

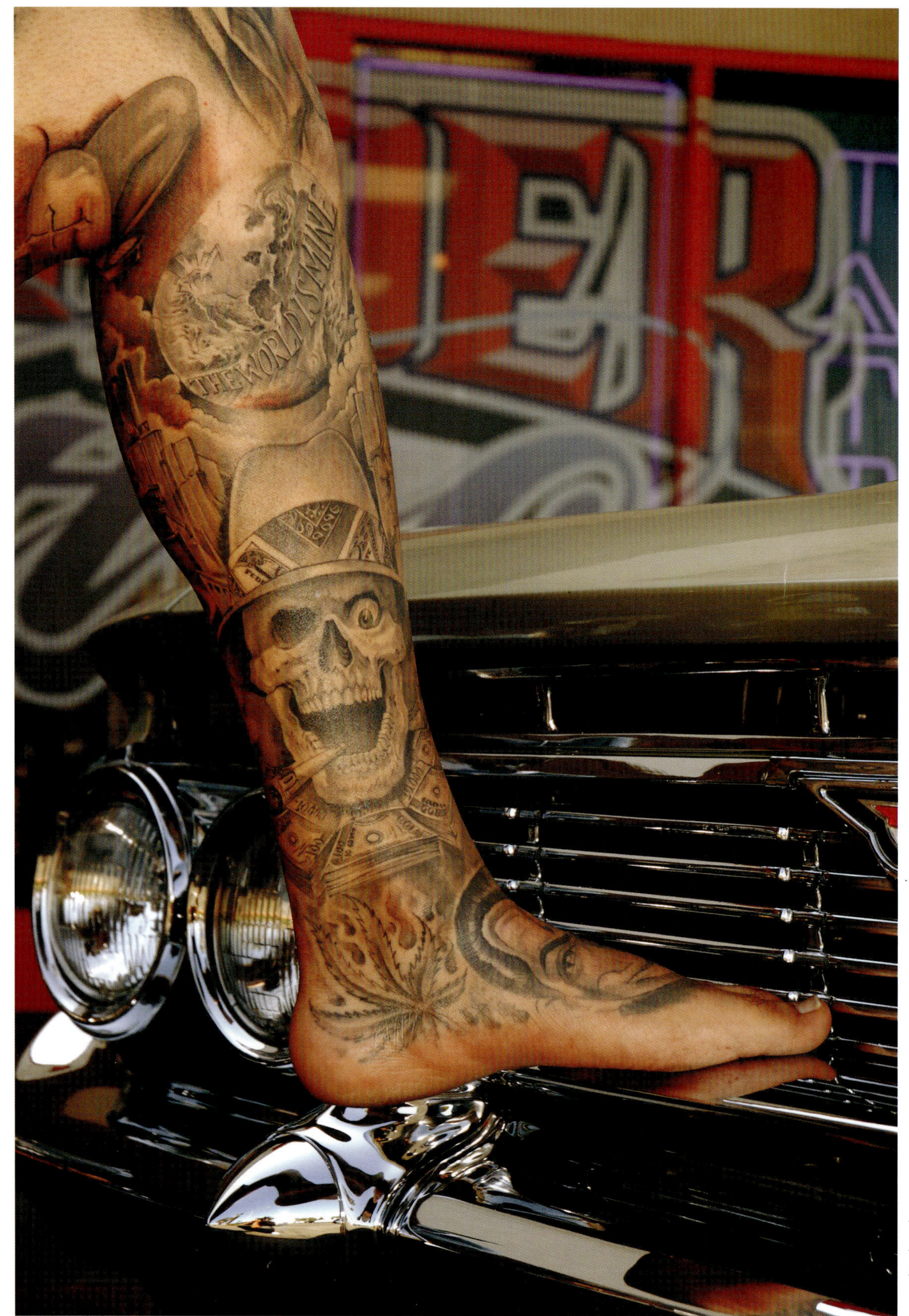

Image by: Jose Lopez